D0048450

THE EARLY CHILDHOOD YEARS

THE 2- TO 6-YEAR-OLD

The Princeton Center for Infancy
and Early Childhood

THERESA and
FRANK CAPLAN, authors

Includes a Minicourse in Early Childhood
Development with Growth Charts and
Over 120 Photographs and a Chapter with
14 Special Parenting Topics

BANTAM BOOKS
NEW YORK • TORONTO • LONDON • SYDNEY • AUCKLAND

This edition contains the complete text
of the original hardcover edition.
NOT ONE WORD HAS BEEN OMITTED.

THE EARLY CHILDHOOD YEARS:
THE 2- TO 6-YEAR-OLD

A Bantam Book / published in association with
GD/PERIGEE BOOKS

PUBLISHING HISTORY

GD/PERIGEE Books edition published November 1983
Bantam edition/November 1984

ISBN 0-553-26967-4

Published simultaneously in the United States and Canada

Bantam Books are published by Bantam Books, a division of Bantam
Doubleday Dell Publishing Group, Inc. Its trademark, consisting of the
words "Bantam Books" and the portrayal of a rooster, is Registered in U.S.
Patent and Trademark Office and in other countries. Marca Registrada.
Bantam Books, 1540 Broadway, New York, New York 10036.

PRINTED IN THE UNITED STATES OF AMERICA

OPM   16 15 14 13 12

Thanks are due to the following for permission to reprint copyright material:

Simon & Schuster, Inc., for material from *Oneness and Separateness: from Infant to Individual* by Louise J. Kaplan. Copyright © 1978 by Louise J. Kaplan. St. Martin's Press, Inc., for material from *Child's Eye View: A New Way of Understanding the Development and Behavior of Children* by Dr. Carol Tomlinson-Keasey. Copyright © 1980 by Carol Tomlinson-Keasey. Bank Street College of Education for the excerpt from *Life and Ways of the Two-Year-Old* by Louise Phinney Woodcock. Pantheon Books, a Division of Random House, Inc., for the excerpt from *The Learning Child* by Dorothy H. Cohen. Copyright © 1972 by Dorothy H. Cohen. Escondido Union School District for "Steps to Reading" by Kaye Foremaster. Copyright © 1977 by Escondido Union School District, Escondido, California. Charles E. Merrill Publishing Company for the excerpt from *Teaching the Child Under Six* by James L. Hymes, Jr. Copyright © 1974 by Charles E. Merrill Publishing Company. Marion Wilson, Director of Early Education Programs, for use of material from the Saturday School programs of Ferguson-Florissant Schools, Ferguson, Missouri. We are indebted to Mrs. Myrna D. Jenkins, Director of the Crossroads Nursery School; Mrs. Elaine Toscano, teacher of the kindergarten in the Community Park School; and Ms. Joanne Lupica of the YWCA Toddler Play Center, all of Princeton, New Jersey, for their full cooperation and permission to photograph their children at play and at work. We also thank Mark Czajkowski of The Princeton Packet for permitting us to use his photographs of children on the first day of kindergarten in a school in Princeton, New Jersey. Harper & Row for material from *Partners in Play* by Dorothy G. Singer and Jerome L. Singer. Copyright © 1977 by Dorothy G. Singer and Jerome L. Singer. E. P. Dutton for material from *Thinking Is Child's Play* by Evelyn Sharp. Copyright © 1969 by Evelyn Sharp. Macmillan and Company for material from *Perceptual and Motor Development in Infants and Young Children* by Bryant J. Cratty. Copyright © 1970 by Bryant J. Cratty. John H. Meier, Ph.D., for material from his self-published book *System for Open Learning, Book I.* Copyright © 1970, 1973 by John H. Meier, Ph.D. Harper & Row for data from *The Mental Health of Children: Services, Research and Manpower* by The Joint Commission on Mental Health of Children. Copyright © 1973 by The Joint Commission on Mental Health of Children, Inc. Harper & Row for material from *Infant and Child in the Culture of Today: The Guidance of Development in Home and Nursery School, Revised Edition* by Arnold Gesell, Frances L. Ilg, Louise Bates Ames in collaboration with Janet Learned Rodell. Copyright © 1974 by Gesell Institute of Child Development. Harper & Row for material from *The Child from Five to Ten, Revised Edition*, by Arnold Gesell, Frances L. Ilg, Louise Bates Ames in collaboration with Glenne E. Bulls. Copyright 1946 by Arnold Gesell and Frances L. Ilg. Copyright renewed by Gerhard A. Gesell, Katherine Gesell Walden and Frances L. Ilg. Copyright © 1977 by Louise Bates Ames, Frances L. Ilg and Glenna E. Bullis. E. P. Dutton, Inc., for material from *Thinking Is Child's Play* by Evelyn Sharp. Copyright © 1969 by Evelyn Sharp.

Grateful acknowledgment is made for permission to reprint the following poems:

Charles Scribner's Sons for the stanza from "One, Two, Three!" by H. C. Bunner from *"Second Crop" Songs* by H. C. Brunner. Charles Scribner's Sons, 1892. E. P. Dutton, Inc., for "The End" from *Now We Are Six* by A. A. Milne. Copyright © 1927 by E. P. Dutton & Company; copyright renewed 1955. Doubleday & Company for "The Elephant's Child" from *Rudyard Kipling's Verse: Definitive Edition* by Rudyard Kipling. Copyright © 1940 by Doubleday & Company.

ACKNOWLEDGMENTS

We could not have written this third book in our series on early childhood growth and development if several medical, psychological, and educational researchers in this fascinating field had not already attempted to build a data bank of observations and anecdotal records of infant and early childhood behavior. They recognized years ago that there were no reliable testing or measuring instruments for evaluating growth, play, and development during the earliest years. Instead of "waiting it out," they listened in on children's conversations, observed and recorded their growth in all areas, and charted the beginnings of a "child's-eye view" of the world.

Cooperating early childhood teachers wrote brief narratives of behavioral incidents after the child left their nursery classrooms, but while the incidents were still fresh in their minds. Parent-teacher conferences were written up. The shared observations of these important witnesses became a sensitive instrument for gauging each child's state of being, thinking, and learning.

Among those who gathered vital records in the late 1930s and the 1940s were Drs. Arnold L. Gesell and the late Frances L. Ilg. With their collaborators, Louise Bates Ames, Ph.D., and Janet Learned, they reported the real-life behaviors and conversations of their subjects to describe the "ages and stages" of children's development. Their approach became a basis for child-rearing manuals right up to the present time.

The recorded observations of the late Dr. Jean Piaget, renowned Swiss biologist turned psychologist, have been used as a base for many of the learning, play, and behavior theories that influence today's methodology for the education of children from earliest childhood through the primary school years.

Louise Phinney Woodcock, a sensitive teacher in an experimental nursery school for two-year-olds, in the late 1930s and the 1940s, recorded short biographical incidents which became the core of her teacher education book, *Life and Ways of the Two-Year-Old.* Unfortunately, it is no longer in print.

Since the 1960s, pediatrician T. Berry Brazelton and other forward-looking pediatricians, child psychologists, and early childhood educators—appreciating the value of collecting descriptive material on the growth and behaviors of infants and young children in their own homes—have made their insightful findings available to first-time mothers and fathers and other caregivers.

We recommend that parents themselves augment this growing body of literature on child development by keeping careful observational and anecdotal records of their children from birth up to at least sixteen years of age.

We are deeply grateful to Grace Bechtold, executive editor of Bantam Books, for urging us to write this book.

Special thanks to Mary Kurtz for her meticulous copy editing of our manuscript, and to everyone at Perigee who helped steer our book to completion.

Finally, we will always value the friendship of Dorothy J. Naylor and her uncomplaining and steadfast typing and retyping of this manuscript. She has shared our writing trials and tribulations with patience and enthusiasm.

THERESA AND FRANK CAPLAN
The Princeton Center for Infancy and Early Childhood

To all caring parents

CONTENTS

CHAPTER ONE

A Minicourse in Child Development

In our earlier books we stressed that parenting books cannot *tell* parents how to rear their children; rather, such books can try to help them understand the ages and stages of childhood growth and development. We described how parents can sensitively intervene to correct a particular behavior, to enrich the learning environment, or to further a child's social interactions with agemates or adults other than the parents.

Knowledge and understanding of how a child grows and learns can help parents avoid many problems. Actually, you will discover that much of your child's behavior is normal. When you understand this, you will be able to modify your attitudes and your child-rearing techniques.

Child development encompasses the unfolding of behaviors from immature to mature; from patterns that are simple to those that are complex; and the evolution of a human being from dependency to autonomous adulthood.

In this book, our minicourse in child development includes (in chart format) the bits and pieces of child-rearing information found in our previous books as well as highlights of the major theories of leading professionals on early childhood growth and development. They and we are especially concerned with the formative early years of the life cycle—the first six years of life.

LANDMARKS IN PHYSICAL, PSYCHOLOGICAL, AND SOCIAL DEVELOPMENT

To comprehend childhood development, it is helpful to sort out and chart the physical, social, intellectual, and medical landmarks from birth to adolescence, as outlined in the chart that follows. As you draw an imaginary dotted line across the five vertical columns in any six-month time-life period, you can study factors that may affect child growth or may create behavior problems.

Knowing about children's growth, recognizing the various signals and milestones, and doing something about them can make child-rearing less frightening and more satisfying.

Developmental functioning can be divided into four categories: motor behavior, adaptive behavior, language behavior, and personal-social behavior. Motor behavior typical of the newborn to six-year-old involves the maturation of skills that permit the control of the body (pushing up his chest to rest on his arms; the ability to turn his head; eye-muscle coordination at six weeks that allows the baby to focus on and recognize distant objects and familiar faces).

Adaptive behavior implies adjusting to different environments—learning to overcome the limitations of the crib or carriage by pushing or peering out, for instance. Once the baby has mastered this, she may vocalize and establish social contact with a nearby person. A child's adaptive behavior is dependent upon large- and fine-muscle control as well as intellectual endowment and suitable stimulation. The child puts all these skills to use in solving the practical problems presented by her surroundings. From her early successes, she gains confidence in her ability to cope with the things and people around her, and she works diligently to practice her new skills.

Critical Periods

One of the prime reasons for observing human growth is in order to attain an awareness of critical periods. A critical period is that span of time during which new behaviors appear most easily or optimally with regard to the very young child's learning readiness. With the utmost energy expended by the child and the least amount by the parents, and minimal distraction from other learning processes, the child will more easily master the particular skills of that period. Teaching and learning are more difficult before or after each critical period. It appears, too, that the probability of change in most areas is smaller with each successive year.

Maturation

Maturation is the unfolding of inborn patterns of physical and other behaviors in ordered sequence. For example, walking and talking are innate capacities; they do not depend upon training. Of course, babies need opportunities for practice in these areas, but the seeds for these abilities are already there at birth. Developing any dexterity is dependent upon when a child's nervous system is biologically ready to perform a particular task. For this reason, it is important not to try to teach your child to do something if she is not ready because this will only frustrate her—and you.

There is some disagreement as to when parents should promote their child's exercise of his budding abilities. Child psychologist Myrtle McGraw thinks that a child can and should be encouraged at the first sign of any new capacity. Other child development authorities maintain that parents should permit each maturing process to unfold naturally without any intervention.

Maturation and the Environment

Although no one can force growth, since that comes from within each child, parents can provide a setting that is congenial to it. When a child is physically ready to walk, it is much easier if there is adequate space in which to walk. When he starts to talk, he will learn faster if he is spoken to. (In fact, he should be spoken to right at birth.) Opportunity, encouragement, and practice will determine whether a child will be good at something. Many psychologists believe that the environment determines which of the child's potentialities are developed or exaggerated.

For example, an aggressive tendency can be developed into an overaggressive personality. By the same token, a child who is innately aggressive may actually become a very timid

LANDMARKS IN PHYSICAL, PSYCHOLOGICAL,

PERIOD	CHRONO-LOGICAL AGE	PHYSICAL GROWTH	DEVELOPMENTAL LANDMARKS
INFANCY	Birth		Social smile (2 mos.) 180° visual pursuit (2 mos.)
	3 months	Rapid skeletal growth Muscle is 25% of body weight	
	6 months		Reach for objects (4 mos.) Roll over (5 mos.)
			Raking grasp (7 mos.)
TODDLERHOOD	9 months	Eruption of deciduous central incisors (5–10 mos.)	Crude purposeful release (9 mos.)
	12 months	Anterior fontanel of head closes (10–14 mos.)	Inferior pincer grasp (10 mos.) Walk unassisted (10–14 mos.)
	18 months	Eruption of deciduous first molars (11–18 mos.)	Words: three to four (13 mos.) Build tower of two cubes (15 mos.) Scribble with crayon (18 mos.) Words: ten (18 mos.)
	24 months	Increase in lymphoid tissue	Build tower of five or six cubes (21 mos.)
	30 months		Use three-word sentences (30 mos.) Name six body parts (30 mos.)
		Slower skeletal growth	Use personal pronouns "I," "you," "me" (30 mos.)
EARLY CHILDHOOD	36 months	Deciduous teeth calcified	Ride tricycle (36 mos.) Copy circle (36 mos.) Match four colors (36 mos.)
	42 months	Rapid skeletal growth	
	48 months		Talk of self and others (42 mos.) Take turn (42 mos.) Tandem walks (42 mos.) Copy cross (48 mos.) Throw ball overhand (48 mos.)
	60 months		Copy square (54 mos.) Copy triangle (60 mos.)
	72 months	Eruption of permanent first molars (5½–7 yrs.)	Tie knots in string (66 mos.)
SCHOOL AGE		Eruption of permanent central incisors (6–8 yrs.)	Print name (72 mos.) Tie shoelaces Ride two-wheel bike (72 mos.)
	7, 8, 9 years	Slowest skeletal growth Frontal sinuses develop Cranial sutures harden Uterus begins to grow in girls	Copy diamond (7 yrs.) Name days of the week (7 yrs.) Repeat five digits forward (8 yrs.)
ADOLESCENCE	10, 11, 12 years	Budding of nipples in girls Increased vascularity of penis and scrotum in boys Spurt in skeletal growth of girls (1½ yrs. ahead of boys)	Can define brave and nonsense Know seasons of the year (9 yrs.) Able to rhyme (9 yrs.) Understand pity, grief, surprise (10 yrs.) Can define nitrogen, microscope, shilling
	13, 14, 15 years	In boys, pubic hair appears; rapid growth of testes and penis; auxiliary hair starts (15 yrs.); voice changes (16 yrs.)	Can divide 72 by 4 without pencil and paper (12 yrs.) Know meaning of C.O.D. Can repeat six numerical digits forward

*Adapted from "Mental Health of Children: Services, Research, and Manpower" by Joint Commission on Mental Health of Children (New York: Harper & Row, Publishers, Inc., 1973).

AND SOCIAL DEVELOPMENT*

DEVELOPMENTAL STEPS	DEVELOPMENTAL PROBLEMS	RADIUS OF SIGNIFICANT SOCIAL RELATIONS
Normal autism (0–3 mos.) Anticipation of feeding	Birth defects Feeding disorders: colic, marasmus, feeding refusals, vomiting	Maternal person
Establishing "oneness" (symbiosis) with mother (4 to 18 mos.)	Early "infant autism"	
Separation anxiety (8–24 mos.) Begin process of separation; establishes a sense of self vs. others (12–28 mos.)	Extreme stranger anxiety Physiologic anorexia (lack of appetite) Sleep disturbances Resistance to overstimulation Extreme separation anxiety Bronchial asthma	
Self-feeding, messiness	Pica—unnatural food ingestion (lead) Teeth grinding	Parental persons
Oppositional behavior Exploratory behavior Parallel play (next to but not with peers) Pleasure in looking at and being looked at	Temper tantrums Negativism, pseudo-retardation Toilet learning disturbances: constipation, diarrhea	
Beginning of self-concept Orderliness Disgust Curiosity Masturbation Cooperative play Fantasy play	Bedtime and toilet rituals Speech disorders, delayed speech, elective mutism, stuttering Petit mal seizures Nightmares, night terrors Excessive thumb-sucking Phobias and fears Food rituals and fads	Basic family
Imaginary playmate Task completion	Sleepwalking School phobias	
Rivalry with parent of same sex Games with rules Problem-solving achievement	Lags and accelerations in cognitive functions Tics Psychoneuroses Bed-wetting, soiling, excessive masturbation Nail-biting	Neighborhood school
Voluntary hygiene Compete with partners Hobbies Ritualistic play Rational attitudes about foods Companionship	Learning problems Personality disorders and sexual deviations Dysmenorrhea Sexual promiscuity	Peer in-groups Peer out-groups
"Revolt" Loosen ties to family Cliques Responsible independence Work habits solidifying	Excessive masturbation Suicidal attempts	Adult models of leadership

person due to severe discipline imposed by the parents. The direction of one's proficiency is thus affected by one's environment. Indeed, many authorities believe that environmental influence is so strong that it may even modify hereditary factors.

A parent can manipulate the limbs of a newborn infant. Even though they are not initiated by the infant, if repeated sufficiently, these induced movements (head balancing, sitting up, grasping) will lead to that infant attaining these skills ahead of an infant who is not stimulated in this way.

A child's *temperament* results from the influence of her body on her mind; it is completely physiological. Crawling, walking, and talking depend upon physiological development. Thus, when the system for walking matures, the child will begin to walk; when the bladder matures, she will begin to learn to control it. Her body cannot perform these tasks before it is ready. This is why it is important not to force walking, talking, toilet learning, etc., until the child indicates that she is ready.

Growth and development impinge upon a foundation of a child's actual body movement, making sensory contact with the world of things and processes. It requires coordination of the child's muscular system with his sensory system and the general brain processes. Any bodily involvement brings about a patterning in the child's brain concerning that movement and all the sensory information related to it.

In *Magical Child: Rediscovering Nature's Plan for Our Children* (New York: E. P. Dutton, 1977), Joseph Chilton Pearce writes, "Intellectual growth is an increase in the ability to interact physically and mentally with the experience at hand . . . and with new phenomena. Intelligence can only grow by moving from that which is known into that which is not yet known . . . When the physical environment is unvaried . . . when there is no bodily contact with a stable caretaker (for example, verbal approval for each achievement), a child does not grow intellectually."

The first six years of life provide time for interaction physically, mentally, and verbally with a wide range of experiences, from each of which a child abstracts some aspect which eventually becomes a concept.

Growth

We are not merely concerned with physical exploits. Equally important are the infant's own sense of accomplishment and his interactions with the adults who understand him. When the two-year-old gains confidence in handling his body, it is reasonable to assume that his confidence will subsequently generalize to other areas. However, growth is not a straight onward and upward line of development. It is a jagged process of spurts forward and some regressions. "Older" is not necessarily more advanced. Behaviors need not occur at a specific month. Sometimes advancement in one area can interfere with growth in another.

Although all children grow and develop according to the same general pattern, there are normally great differences in the rate of their growth and development and in the age at which they are capable of doing certain things.

To be a sensitive communicator with very young children, parents need to be concerned not only with the attainment of an ability but also with signals of an emerging aptitude. As skills become manifest—walking, talking, socializing, playing—parents can provide enrichment materials that spark and enhance them. Aware of the child's desire to practice what he has just learned, the parent can supply the optimal stimulation and atmosphere for the use of these newfound powers. Since many of the young child's developing abilities are nonverbal, parents need to learn to recognize the various maturing skills and be prepared to offer suitable help. Of course, all this requires an understanding of what happens to a child as he is growing; how he changes in size and shape; how he uses his unfolding powers; and how he adapts to his environment at each age level. It also means exposing parents to the different child development theories and their impact on child-rearing practices; helping them arrive at their own child-rearing judgments in the light of these assumptions; and encouraging them to observe childhood development by studying their own children.

MAJOR THEORISTS

A number of outstanding pediatricians, educators, psychoanalysts, psychologists, and researchers have been of great help to parents and professionals alike by tracing child growth and development through the distinct ages and stages during which major changes occur. Each stage covers activities which the child concentrates on during that particular period.

Psychoanalysts, such as Erik Erikson, Margaret Mahler, Sigmund Freud, and others, have identified periods of great social, emotional, psychological, and personality change. The late Swiss psychologist and educator, Jean Piaget, researched and defined intellectual accomplishments and play by chronological age. Pediatricians such as Arnold Gesell and the late Frances Ilg recorded bodily growth, and carefully spelled out the ages and stages of physical growth and motor accomplishments. While these stages are not chronologically exact, they do indicate the general beginnings and endings of such periods. As a result, one can see the close relationships between patterns of behavior, motor accomplishments, and intellectual landmarks. In fact, a specific social behavior may be the result of reaching a particular physical milestone.

In the accompanying chart, we have presented only highlights from several carefully selected authorities who are most frequently mentioned in the professional literature dealing with early childhood. Since we are profoundly interested in these years, it is logical that we present in greater detail those authorities who believe that the most rapid and significant changes in growth and development occur during the early years.

In this book, we will be treating a particular segment of the lifeline—the span from the twenty-fifth month to the seventy-second month of life.

How to Use the Major Theorists Chart

As you follow the development of your child, you can mark off a one-year segment on the chart by a dotted line. As you read down the Gesell column and come to the section covering the two- to three-year age level, you will find that three of the most pronounced achievements in the normally developing two-year-old are the beginning of the ability to walk in an adult manner and even to start to run; beginning of control of bowel and urine elimination; and, assuming normal development and adequate language models (parents, caregivers, etc.), beginning to express thoughts in sentences.

Gesell's major contribution to growth and development theory was his accurate month-by-month reporting of the physical-motor development of babies and young children. His early research revealed how the newborn gains control over his body, and the fact that there is a predictable, orderly, head-to-toe sequence of physical development (influenced by the maturing sections of the brain during the first two years of life). The control of arm motion and muscles comes before leg control; finger control follows after arm control; grasping comes after head balance; standing follows sitting, etc.

With the maturation of physical and sensory powers, the infant gains control of her body and movement in space. She discovers objects by seeing, grasping, fingering. By interaction with her environment, she gains a feeling of mastery and of the power of self, which results in a sense of autonomy.

Erik Erikson addresses the intricacies of childhood growth from a psychosocial point of view. In his "Eight Stages of Man," he ascribes to the infancy period (newborn to twenty-four months) the time for building a *sense of trust,* thus laying the groundwork for a feeling of security throughout life. Affection and consistent caregiving provide infants with confidence that they will be fed, kept dry, and stimulated when bored. From this trust, they learn that the mother or other constant caregiver can be counted on to be there when called; that she is around even though she cannot be seen; that she will come back again and again.

During the early childhood years, Erikson continues, the child passes through the *period of autonomy* (twenty-four to thirty-six months), when he differentiates self from non-self; moves from dependence on parents and caregivers to separation and independence; experiences the power of bodily image and control that comes with the practice of walking, running, climbing, jumping; and discovers the power of communication and control that results from the acquisition of language. Self-esteem and ego are nourished and firmly established as part of the personality in this period.

The *period of initiative and imagination* (thirty-six to seventy-two months) follows, when the child explores the exciting range of people and things, reenacting the varied roles and activities in the here-and-now world. This is the critical period of play and learning in which parental encouragement can have considerable influence on drive and creativity. During this time span, a rudimentary conscience develops, regulating initiative and imagination. The child internalizes the dictates of his parents, spelling out what he may or may not do. When thoughts and wishes run counter to the commands of his conscience, he resorts to fantasy and his imagination to play out his guilt or shame.

Freud offered a psychosexual theory of child development, placing considerable emphasis on the child's (and caregiver's) early preoccupation with the mouth and love relations in feeding. Later on, in the second year of life, Erikson's period of "autonomy" is likened by Freud to the "anal" stage in psychoanalytic theory: the "opening and shutting off" inherent in early sphincter control of the bowels and bladder. Freud theorized that the pleasure and pain from these sensory actions influence a child's personality, making for self-confidence or uncertainty, generosity or stinginess, autonomy or inadequacy, courage or fearfulness, etc.

It was Margaret Mahler, renowned child psychoanalyst and educator, who first described the psychological states in a child's development leading to the acquisition of the sense of self. In her study of psychotic children (those suffering from tics, etc.), she uncovered a parallel set of conflicts in normal children as well as psychotic patients.

In the first three months of life, Mahler observed, normal children establish a sense of oneness with the mother, although they do not yet achieve the sense of self she terms "psychological birth." Psychotic children remain in a "twilight state of existence," where they do not seem to know where they begin and where "the other" leaves off. To portray the normal state of oneness of a child with her mother, Mahler borrowed the biology term "symbiosis," and used the term "symbiotic psychosis" for children who cannot establish oneness with their mothers.*

In Mahler's words, "Normally during the first five to eight months, an infant learns to use mother as a 'beacon of orientation.' The mother's presence is a fixed light which gives the child the security to move out safely to explore the world and then return safely to harbor." As the child separates from his

---

*See *The Psychological Birth of the Human Infant* by Margaret S. Mahler, Fred Pine, and Anni Bergman (New York: Basic Books, 1975).

mother, he continues to have an inner experience of a mothering presence which orients him in the world.

Inasmuch as normal children possess a reliable inner mother, they do not fear that being a separate self will cast them adrift in an alien world. The psychotic child, on the other hand, is not able to make effective use of her mother as a beacon of orientation, and those fragments of the mother that she carries within her are unreliable. Therefore, she is afraid to move ahead toward separate selfhood.

The symbiotic-psychotic child eventually comes to dread oneness as much as separateness. Rather than continue the struggle, he regresses in his development to the stage that precedes oneness—the autistic stage, in which he totally rejects human contact. His only relationship then is with an inanimate, nonhuman environment.

Mahler's research in child-rearing in the earliest months has led her to write in the aforementioned book, "When the process goes wrong, a human being will have difficulties loving others, nurturing the young, taming his own aggression, and caring about the welfare and destiny of the human species."

What Gesell did for the physically growing and developing baby, Freud for the affective domain, and Erikson and Mahler for the social domain, the Swiss psychologist Jean Piaget did for the intellectual, cognitive area of child development. It was Piaget who described in great detail the important period (the first eighteen months of life) when an infant practices the expanding sensory powers of seeing, hearing, touching, tasting, and smelling—relating one with another. The infant incorporates all his motor learning patterns into the data bank of memory in his brain. With these, he can deal more effectively with the world of people, things, self, language, and thought.

Piaget's careful studies of the day-by-day maturation of his own three children led him to develop a schema of how intellect unfolds and how cognition develops. He found that the child from two to three is still in the *sensorimotor* stage of development, acquiring information by acting on the environment, and laying the foundation for the evolution of the abstract thought processes of preadolescence. He documented the child's use of primitive labels and words (spoken and nonverbal) to identify ideas and objects in her environment and to define the relationships between these objects, thus gaining intellectual comprehension of complex thought processes in science, math, and in her play and fantasy life.

MAJOR THEORISTS: AGES AND STAGES

PERIOD	CHRONO-LOGICAL AGE	GESELL PHYSICAL DEVELOPMENT	ERIKSON PSYCHOSOCIAL DEVELOPMENT (Eight Stages of Man)	FREUD PSYCHOSEXUAL STAGES
INFANCY	Birth 3 months	*Infancy* Hearing control Head balance	*Trust vs. Mistrust* "Mom will return" Holding on and/or letting go ("I am what I am given")	*Oral* Sensory-kinesthetic Sensory-retentive
	6 months	Grasping Sit, creep, poke Stand, cruise Larynx—words		
	12 months			
TODDLERHOOD	18 months	Walk and talk	*Autonomy vs. Shame, Self-Doubt* ("I am what I will")	"Verbal diarrhea" *Anal-Urethral* Muscular, retentive, eliminative modes
	24 months		Discretion Paranoia	
	30 months	Sphincter control		Stingy, collector, "uptight" Messy: hangs loose
EARLY CHILDHOOD	36 months	Sentences	*Initiative & Imagination vs. Guilt* ("I am what I imagine I can be")	*Phallic* Locomotor
	42 months	Number and form	Superego Parental ideals	
	48 months	Kindergarten	Rivalry vs. success	Narcissistic Exhibitionistic
	60 months	*Childhood*	*Industry vs. Inferiority* Work is pleasure New ideas, new activities	Oedipus or Electra complex
SCHOOL AGE	72 months	Pre-puberty	Recognition from products	
	7, 8, 9 years		Preconceived incompetence ("I am what I learn")	*Latency* Homosexual
	10, 11, 12 years		*Identity vs. Role Diffusion* Friends (adult) Ego integrity Peer relations ("I know who I am")	Gang stage Castration anxiety
ADOLESCENCE		*Early Adolescence* Sexual potency and secondary characteristics		
	13, 14, 15 years			*Puberty* Heterosexual

*Adapted from John H. Meier, Ph.D., *SOL Facilitator's Handbook I, Foundations and Rationale: System for Open Learning* (Denver: 1970, 1973. Self-published).

OF CHILD DEVELOPMENT*

MAHLER	PIAGET	HAVIGHURST	GOODENOUGH
PSYCHOLOGICAL DEVELOPMENT	**INTELLECTUAL SCHEMATA**	**DEVELOPMENTAL TASKS** (Vocabulary)	**DRAW-A-MAN AND INTELLIGENCE TESTS** (Score)
Biological Birth Onset, practice of physical and sensory powers Love affair and oneness between mother and child (symbiosis)	**Sensory-Motor** Stage 1—Using innate reflexes Practice of sensory powers Stage 2—Intentional behavior Stages 3 and 4—Cause-and-effect actions	Dependence vs. independence Giving and receiving affection (3 words)	
Hatching Period Awareness of self and external environment Differentiates strangers from mother Separation from mother (reaching out— walking away) Shadowing and darting Love affair with world (upright baby)	Stage 5—Onset of experimentation Trial and error Stage 6—Beginning of mental pictures Organizes thought Uses symbols (precepts) Words for objects and actions Extracting concepts from experience	**Early Childhood** Relating to changing social groups (272 words)	Scribbling Some control Head
Psychological Independence (thinking baby)	Identifying a past, present, and future	Developing greater independence (1540 words)	Legs Arms (2)
	Pre-Operational Thought (pre-logical) Categorize, seriate Beginning to pretend Accurate perceptions Conserve quantity Weight and numbers	**Late Childhood** Learning (2072 words) Psychosocial Biological Sex role (2562 words)	Trunk Shoulders (6) Neck, eyes Nose, nostrils (10) Mouth, ears Clothing, hair
	Concrete Operational Thought Build a data bank on concrete, imaginary, and anticipatory operations	**Early Adolescence** Accepting and adjusting to changing body	Thumb, joints (18) Fingers (22) Proportions (26) Eye detail (30) Chin, forehead (34) Dimensions (38) Profile (42)
	Formal Operational Thought Operation with symbols and abstract ideas Comparisons and deductions made from information not concretely presented	Managing and learning motor patterns	

In addition to these theoreticians who have endeavored to explain childhood development and behavior, there are "test makers" who have attempted to quantify the degree to which a child is progressing in mastering selected developmental tasks that are considered important for competency at an adult level. They include Robert J. Havighurst, Alfred Binet, Lewis N. Terman, Raymond B. Cattell, Nancy Bayley, and Florence L. Goodenough. Some studied social development and human intellect; others measured a child's awareness of himself and his environment by evaluating his drawings of a person rather than assaying his verbal communication abilities.

Havighurst conceptualized and organized a series of developmental tasks that he believed to be most easily learned at certain "readiness" ages (or "teachable" moments), somewhat like the "critical periods" theory advanced by Myrtle McGraw and others. Havighurst considered the period beginning at two years as early childhood, and suggested that this is a crucial time for children to learn to interact with other individuals. Directly related to this in our highly verbal society is the ability of children to express themselves through spoken language.

"The ability to accumulate, understand, and use vocabulary to express ideas and perhaps to think about the real world is in part a function of the richness of the verbal environment, and is an index to the quality and quantity of language spoken by caretaking adults."*

The following growth facts form the basis for Havighurst's test to determine competency of two- to five-year-olds in the developmental tasks of early childhood:

- The child has developed freedom of locomotion in his environment.
- He has gained reasonable control over his larger muscles and to some extent over his smaller muscles.
- He has learned to communicate verbally with adults, although he often misunderstands the words they use.
- His increased freedom and control over himself and his environment lead to conflict and havoc in an adult-ordered world.
- His ability to classify and differentiate is improving.

*John H. Meier, Ph.D., *SOL Facilitator's Handbook I, Foundations and Rationale: System for Open Learning* (Denver: 1970, 1973. Self-published).

Havighurst sees further developmental tasks to be completed as follows:

• The child begins the process of learning to give as well as to receive affection.
• He develops rules of conduct and learns to meet adult expectations.
• He becomes more self-sufficient in dressing, eating, and play activities.
• He improves communication through the use of words and numbers.
• He explores various appropriate roles for gaining a place in the family and among playmates.
• He identifies with adults: parents, teachers, etc.

Failure to achieve those tasks may result in feelings of insecurity and frustration in the child, and the continuation of such negative behaviors as thumb-sucking and temper tantrums beyond the time these normally disappear; seeking adult help in doing things the child should be able to do for herself; withdrawal from the family or playmate group because of difficulty in working out an appropriate role to play; refusal to communicate or ineffective communication.

Florence Goodenough developed a technique for estimating a child's attention to and memory of detail, size, shape relationships, perspective, and related features of the human body as another way of gauging the child's ability to accurately perceive, retrieve, and express a given schema in two-dimensional representations. Although there is controversy as to the accuracy of her Draw-a-Man Test in measuring intelligence or learning with children three to four years of age (and older), some believe that as the child matures, and there are more items to be scored, this nonverbal estimate of awareness and intelligence might be useful.

In these days of startling electronic advances, much new information about how children develop has been forthcoming. Yet the plethora of books published in the last ten years covering every aspect of child-rearing has created a false notion about the possibility of bringing up children easily and smoothly. Parents soon discover that there is no royal road or right way to nurture children. All parents need to take into account factors beyond their control, including each child's inherited genes; the conflict between each child's needs and family and societal expectations and demands; the shortcomings of the well-intentioned parents themselves; and the reality of the generation gap. Writes Maria W. Piers in *Growing Up with Children* (Chicago: Quadrangle Books, 1966), "We ourselves were brought up with values and standards to fit the world of today, but our children have to be prepared for the world of tomorrow. And today and tomorrow differ much more widely than in all previous centuries."

PIONEERS IN EARLY CHILDHOOD EDUCATION*

Concern for the care and education of children under the age of six did not develop overnight. Actually it has evolved

*From *The Power of Play* by Frank and Theresa Caplan (Garden City, NY: Doubleday, 1973).

over the centuries. The premise that a child's beginning years are the most crucial has been expressed countless times in various ways in different cultures.

The ancient Greeks were the first advocates of play in education. Plato urged state legislation in regard to the games of children, and offered practical advice on play. He encouraged "those natural modes of amusement which children find out for themselves when they meet." In the following quotation from one of Plato's books, *The Laws,* he appears to have recommended the setting up of nursery schools: "At the stage reached by the age of three, and after the ages of four, five, and six, play will be necessary. There are games which nature herself suggests at that age. Children readily invent these for themselves when left in one another's company. All children of three to six should first be collected at the local sanctuary, all the children of each village thus assembled at the same place."

The teachings of Plato, Socrates, and Aristotle greatly influenced later educational theorists. Marcus Fabius Quintilian, outstanding teacher during the Christian era in Rome, had high regard for the inherent powers of children. He believed that children who could not learn were rare, and that children's play should be so arranged as to develop their intellects. Johann Amos Comenius, the last bishop of the Bohemian Brothers in Moravia in 1592, thought that all children should be taught in school. According to Comenius, first the senses, then memory, and finally understanding and judgment were to be developed. He considered playgrounds to be essential for children's schools, and established a system of educational institutions that included a preschool and went as far as an academy. The "maternal school" was under the mother's direction, and lasted through the first six years of the child's life. Comenius encouraged the play interests of children in his lower schools by using objects, pictures, and puzzles.

The writings of French philosopher Jean Jacques Rousseau greatly affected the world's thinking on freedom and progress. He believed that the ultimate objective of education is to teach one to live. While many eschewed his visionary ideas, one Swiss educator, Johann Heinrich Pestalozzi, was not only receptive to Rousseau's exhortations, but also articulated the educational principles associated with contemporary progressive education. Pestalozzi wrote, "The ultimate end of education is not perfection in the accomplishments of the school, but fitness for life; not the acquirement of blind obedience and prescribed diligence, but a preparation for independent action."

Pestalozzi tried to investigate the early history of the child who was to be taught, back to its very beginning, and was soon convinced that "the first hour of its teaching is the hour of birth. From the moment in which his mind can receive impressions from nature, nature teaches him."

He decided to put aside the first plague of youth, "the miserable letters" that were being taught at home and in schools for young children, and enlisted the services of the child's first teachers—the parents, the mothers—"the most powerful ally of our cause."

In 1803, Pestalozzi wrote a *Book for Mothers* and *How Gertrude Teaches Her Children*. In 1826, he published his autobiography in which he tried to express all his ideas on education. He sought to help the lower classes improve their way of life by having them use their minds; by having them learn about the life around them in the here-and-now. He was against rote memorization. Pestalozzi believed in the need to train the senses, in children's self-activity, and in their close contact with nature. Although all of his school enterprises failed (farm school, institute, etc.), he freed education from dogmatic limitations, and kindled in others an enthusiasm for universal education.

Friedrich Froebel, a student of Pestalozzi's, was the founder of the kindergarten movement. He was responsible for many of the advances in early childhood education. Froebel carried on Rousseau's theory of natural unfolding, emphasizing the importance of family and peer group companionship in play, work, and self-activity. He valued play very highly: "Play is the purest, most spiritual activity of man at this stage of childhood . . . It gives joy, freedom, and contentment . . . It holds the source of all that is good."

Froebel became a student of the relationship between mother and child, and in his zeal to share his insights, he wrote the following: "The destiny of nations lies far more in the hands of women—the mothers—than in the possession of power, or of those innovators who do not understand themselves. We must cultivate women, who are educators of the human race, else the new generation cannot accomplish its task." He also advocated comprehensive education for women.

Whereas many previous pioneers in educational theory

concentrated on interpreting their philosophy through books, Froebel accomplished his educational goals through practical teacher education programs and designing simple manipulative materials. In 1816, he founded a Universal Education Institute at Griesheim, Germany, to which teachers came to study his methods. Froebel asserted (like Pestalozzi before him) that children are attracted most by living things and by movable objects. These observations led him to create several playthings—which he called "gifts"—balls, cylinders, variously dissected cubes, quadrilateral and triangular tablets, sticks, and mats for weaving. According to Froebel, by playing with these, the child gained notions of color, shape, size, number, etc. He looked upon play as the cornerstone of his system, and planned his materials for the "self-employment" of little children. He believed that simple manipulative materials, games, stories, songs, group activities, and pleasant surroundings helped young children develop application and cooperation.

In 1826, Froebel wrote his most important book, *The Education of Man,* which was translated into English in 1885. It pointed the way to independent, productive, and creative activity in early childhood. He opened his first kindergarten in Bad Blankenburg in 1837. As originator of the kindergarten ("garden of children"), he aroused widespread interest in child play and learning. He fostered the development of vigorous gymnastics, language power through spirited conversation and song, and cultivated the social nature of the child without crushing individuality. In 1844, Froebel wrote *Mother Play,* which Susan Blow, an American, translated into English. In it he advocated self-activity on the part of the learner, and the principle of learning to do by doing.

Sometime after his death in 1852, his ideas began to spread throughout Europe and the United States. Froebel was also responsible for the eventual employment of female teachers in kindergartens and elementary schools. The original interest of Froebel and his followers in play, self-expression, and creativity as a basis for education was, however, forgotten until the 1890s by the reconstructive movement in kindergarten education in Europe, and especially in the U.S.

During that period, such philosophers and educators as William James, Susan Blow, John Dewey, and his colleague William Heard Kilpatrick lectured, taught, and translated and expanded on the ideas laid down by Pestalozzi and Froebel.

They also wrote many books. An interesting quotation from a work by William James reads as follows:

"Your pupils . . . are . . . little pieces of associating machinery. Their education consists in the organizing within them of determinate tendencies to associate one thing with another . . . The more copious the associative systems, the completer the individual's adaptations to the world . . . You may take a child to the schoolroom, but you cannot make him learn the new things you wish to impart, except by soliciting him in the first instance by something which natively makes him react. He must take the first step himself . . . During the first seven or eight years of childhood, the mind is most interested in the sensible properties of material things . . . The more different kinds of things a child gets to know by treating and handling them, the more confident grows his sense of kinship with the world in which he lives."

Dewey and Kilpatrick, his associate at Teacher's College, Columbia University, believed that children learn best when the material meets a recognized need, not by memorization of extraneous information; that children require contact with people, places, and things. Both educators maintained that traditional schooling allowed too little leeway to initiative. They believed that education must be interwoven with practical experience. The best known of Dewey's ideas is his "principle of learning by doing." Kilpatrick expanded it further by saying that "in the degree that a child lives (experiences) what he learns, so will he learn it."

Such innovative educators as Maria Montessori and Caroline Pratt furthered the cause of voluntarism in education by setting up model schools for young children. They designed their own programs, equipment, and play and learning materials. (See Chapter 3 for details about both of these outstanding early childhood educators.)

CHAPTER TWO

Overview
of the Early
Childhood
Years

In *The First Twelve Months of Life* and *The Second Twelve Months of Life,* we traced the phenomenal sequential growth of the newborn from an immature, crying, horizontal organism to the walking-running-talking twenty-four-month-old who can handle himself well, make decisions, and establish relationships with peers and elders.

Even during the period of complete dependency upon others for survival, the baby experiences and practices a measure of autonomy. At two, the toddler is ready and eager "to take on the world" of people and things.

The physical changes in the early months are dramatic, varied, and highly visible. Never again will the child grow so fast; nor will the parents have as many optimal opportunities for influencing development. The adaptations the newborn makes are biologically set (inborn). Numerous reflexes (the ability to breathe, suck, taste, turn over, and so on) spur the neonate's transition from a "water baby" to an airborne human being, making possible and enhancing his or her survival and growth. Various senses (hearing, touch, sight, etc.) foster adaptation to an environment of people, things, temperatures, and so on. Reflexes and senses set the stage for learning how

21

to live as a member of a family, and to cope with increasingly complicated social situations.

At the same time, the dependency of the newborn invokes the attention of parents and other caregivers which, in turn, lays the foundation for building loving and long-lasting relationships with people.

The number of external factors that affect and shape the personality as well as the intellectual and social competencies of a child is so great that it defies analysis. Although the newborn comes into the world equipped to handle himself physically by means of reflexes, his ongoing behavior and perceptual and intellectual abilities depend upon his brain development in the fetal period and during the first two-and-a-half years of life.

In the study of child development, there is a tendency to ignore the biologic growth of the brain. The brain—a hundred million nerve cells and two handfuls of "thick custard" in the storecase of our skulls—determines who we are, rules our behavior, the way we respond and adapt to our environment, the way we file and recall our experiences, and the way we play, think, and dream.

The brain is not an isolated body organ; rather, it is a controlling one. The retina of the eye is one of the brain's instruments for gathering information about the environment. The nerves in the fingers are the brain's way of learning what we are touching. The nerves in muscles are the brain's agents for enabling us to move about. There is both input—information delivered to the brain by light (sight), chemicals (taste and smell), and mechanical means (hearing and touch)—and output—one's reaction to the world and attempts to influence it. Between the two stand thought, memory, emotion, drive, and sexual identity.

In the past ten years, brain research has accelerated and grown in sophistication. Using computers, electronic equipment, and radioactive chemicals, scientists are measuring blood flow, brain waves, and energy consumption not only in incidences of brain disorders, but also in the performance of ordinary tasks.

One of the areas in which considerable animal and human research data have been amassed is that of nutrition and its effect on brain development. At least 80 percent of human brain development occurs after birth, and within the first two-and-a-half years of life. The consequences of malnutrition during the vulnerable periods, the last trimester of pregnancy and the first two-and-a-half years, are physical and behavioral damage. Animal studies reveal that as a result of malnutrition, brain size is reduced; the number of cells is also diminished; there is less lipid present, and enzyme levels are disturbed— all of which affect brain function. What is most upsetting is that this damage is not reparable by means of special feeding *after* the critical period of the first two-and-a-half years of life.

Inadequate and faulty nutrition causes impaired manual control, clumsiness, heightened excitability, and a lowered threshold to external stimuli. There is much evidence of impaired intellectual capacity in malnourished children, including their language acquisition, motor skills, and social interactions.

For the very young child, intellectual growth is also a biological process. From seeing, touching, hearing, mouthing and dropping objects, and continual interactions with people and things, certain schemata are indelibly imprinted as patterns in the brain. It appears that these primary sensory organizations and responses take precedence over all future learning. Advancement in the very young child's ability to interact results in ever-increasing rhythmic patterning in the brain and in corresponding muscular responses.

It is important to note that growth can be slowed to almost a standstill by subjecting young children to demands that are inappropriate to their particular stage of development; i.e., by trying to force them to deal with information suitable to a later developmental plateau, or by keeping them locked in an earlier stage. When children find that learning is difficult and not rewarding, the ego always suffers, and their learning falters.

Until quite recently, the study of the skin, the largest organ of the body, has also been neglected. The sense of touch is the earliest to develop in the human fetus, and its functioning depends upon the stimulation it receives at birth and thereafter. The skin protects inner organs from injury and invasion by foreign substances; regulates temperature; metabolizes and stores fat; removes salt by perspiration, etc.

However, of greatest significance to the infant and toddler, according to Ashley Montagu, noted author and educator, are the signals of comfort and love received through the skin. Montagu believes that "children who have been inadequately held and fondled will suffer as adolescents and hunger for such attention into adulthood."

In *Touching: The Human Significance of the Skin* (New York: Columbia University Press, 1971), he writes, "The skin itself does not think but its sensitivity is so great, its contributions to learning schemas via touch are so powerful, its tactile role in communicating an awareness of self is so important, that for versatility it must be ranked second in importance only to the brain. When the young child initiates in the beginning of the second year of life those exploratory behaviors which lead to separation of the self from mother, he is using those learnings which were acquired through touch experiences."

Montagu bemoans the fact that cultures in the Western world, and the United States in particular, are guilty of rigid nontouching attitudes. Long-standing sexual constraints dictate that touching is dangerous, even for children once they pass infancy. Fortunately, most of today's young parents are changing these rigid attitudes.

THE AGE OF TODDLERHOOD

Most professionals consider the ages of twelve months to twenty-four months the early toddler years; the period of twenty-four to thirty-six months the late toddler years. We prefer to label twelve- to twenty-four-month-olds as Toddler-Ones and twenty-four- through thirty-six-month-olds as Toddler-Twos. The British call both age groups the "runabout years."

The Toddler-One has been walking for several months, but somewhat off-balance, with hands up high and elbows close. She is so concerned about not falling that while walking she finds it difficult to use her hands for any other purpose than as balancers. Her steps are measured out. She rocks from foot to foot until she arrives at the position she seeks. If she has to get some place in a hurry, she still reverts to all fours (which she mastered in her creeping days). However, with each passing day, upright gait and speed improve.

In appearance, he still looks like a baby. His legs are short for his body, giving him a bottom-heavy look. This is further emphasized by bulky diapers and training pants. He is low to the ground, and his view of the adult world encompasses the undersides of tables, chairs, parents' legs, etc. It is hard to realize that by two he will reach nearly half his adult height.

When Toddler-Ones begin to get around on their own, they develop the ability to assert themselves. Just when their caregivers are getting used to attending to the needs of dependent infants, the youngsters suddenly shift gears from the age and stage of babyhood to that of early childhood. The Toddler-Two period is identified by Erikson as the *period of autonomy:* ". . . becoming aware of oneself as a person and wanting to do things by oneself."

The push for autonomy shows up in every moment of the Toddler-Two's day; in mastery of his body (walking, running, climbing, etc.); in controlling his sphincter muscles; in ruling over a world of objects (opening and emptying drawers, pushing oversized vehicles instead of sitting in them, removing his clothing, etc.); in demanding equal status with adults in their social relations (refusing parental commands or offers of help).

The Toddler-Two's attempts to take full control naturally run into conflict with her parents' concern for her safety as well as the disruption of daily routines. There is no way to make a Toddler-Two conform rigidly to the controls of the adult world without sacrificing some of her capacity for healthy and happy growth. Parents cannot fence Toddler-Twos in with playpens, cribs, stair gates, etc.; nor can they barrage them with continuous "No's" and still enable them to practice their need to move about, explore, and learn.

Parents may have to make adjustments in their lifestyles at this time; perhaps give up the larger bedroom for a play center for their Toddler-Two. By now they will have removed anything in the home environment that he could hurt himself with or that he could damage. Parents need to understand that the Toddler-Two's behavior is not malicious; rather, the child is an "eager beaver." Just try to accept the fact that at this period keeping a home neat and clean is difficult. Above all, prepare for "mock battles" as your child tries out his growing capacity to assert himself. You may expect whining, clumsiness, and increased demands for attention. This is the period of wide shifts in mood and annoyance about any change in routines. Try to be explicit about your expectations. If you can keep in mind that this behavior is a temporary phase of upgrowth, you may be less irritated and exhausted as you face each new and challenging day.

Toddler-Twos recognize that their mothers' wishes are not always identical with their own, and that their desires do not necessarily coincide with their parents'. Gradually young children learn to shift their emotional base from parents to their contemporaries. Toddler-Twos indicate a greater desire to imitate and identify with other children, and to have and do what other children have or do.

THE EARLY CHILDHOOD YEARS

Toddlerhood reaches a climax somewhere between twenty-eight and thirty-six months. The remaining months before a child's fifth birthday are usually designated the *preschool years.* Some professionals object to this terminology since it implies that further learning takes place only in school when the child is five (in kindergarten) or six (first grade). "The doctrine is dangerous," Dr. James L. Hymes, retired professor of education, warns in his book, *Teaching the Child Under Six* (Columbus, Ohio: Charles E. Merrill, 1968; second edition 1974). "Early childhood is a marked and definable stage in development with basic growth tasks that must be achieved at this time. No one knows for sure what is the price of stopping young children's play, of curbing their initiative and spontaneity, of deadening their energy, of blocking their social exploration. We are playing with fire when we skip the years two, three, four, and five, and hurry children into being age six."

We prefer to identify these important formative years as the *early childhood years.* There appears to be consensus among professionals that this early childhood period extends from two to seven years. The milestones of sitting, standing, crawling, and walking are easy to observe and record. Almost all authorities are in agreement that when infants begin to walk and talk, there is a marked spurt in the growth of personality, ego, social relations, and so forth. Erik Erikson identifies two years of age as the end of the period of building a bond of trust with caregivers, and the start of the formation of a sense of autonomy, initiative, and imagination. He considers the age of seven as the end of the "main concern with the sense of initiative." Jean Piaget assigns the first two years to building motor powers and the senses, and the period from two to seven as the time concentrated upon an expanding intellect. The North American six-year-old is required to commence the first grade of elementary school, and most cultures consider a child's seventh birthday as the time for preoccupation with the academic skills of reading, writing, and arithmetic.

There is a small but knowledgeable group of early childhood educators who would purposely delay academic work until the child's seventh birthday (the beginning of the second grade) because they have found from long experience that children can acquire these "tool" subjects much more efficiently when they have more physical and mental maturity than during their earlier years. And some researchers in the field of play have found that six-year-olds are still actively involved with play and fantasy, and are not prepared to abandon this medium of expression simply because school bells are ringing.

Throughout our presentation of the early childhood years, we sometimes go beyond the twenty-fifth to seventy-second months of life because there is no sharp break in the time a child gives up pure play and begins to concentrate on symbols. Moreover, *the age at which various achievements can be noted may vary considerably from one child to another.*

PHYSICAL AND BODY DEVELOPMENT

The period between a child's second and sixth birthdays is marked by many bodily changes. Within this brief span, the clumsy, bottom-heavy two-year-old will develop into a child with considerable mastery over his body. As a result of increased locomotion and stepped-up physical activity, he becomes more muscular and looks less like a baby. His body becomes large in proportion to his head size, and his arms become longer and stronger. Baby fat is gradually reduced by about 50 percent. As the ratio of head to body size changes, the child's physique approaches adult proportions. The child will change from a chubby infant in the first months of life to a slender child at five years.*

There are sex differences with respect to tissue and fat growth; for example, boys have more muscle and bone than girls. However, sex is not always the reason. Overfeeding, overeating, and poor nutrition may cause overweight. Recent research indicates that "feeding the fat cells" in the first two or three years of life makes for overweight adults (and that no amount of dieting will help in the adolescent and adult years).

Nutrition studies also indicate that malnutrition, especially before two-and-a-half years of age (as well as prenatally and postnatally), can permanently affect a child's growth. The effect can be reversed only if the contributing causes can be corrected as soon as they are apparent.

Growth data collected by the National Center for Health Statistics place the median height of three-year-old boys at 37.4 inches and median weight at 33 pounds. In the ensuing

two years, a further increase in height of 5 to 6 inches can be anticipated in both boys and girls, and a further gain in weight of about 8 to 10 pounds. A strong correlation exists between height in the early childhood period and adult height. A child who is taller than average at five years of age has a 70 percent chance of becoming a tall adult.*

How to Use Children's Growth Charts

Find your child's age in the column at the top of the page. Move down that age column until you find your child's weight in pounds. Circle that number. Follow the same procedure for height. Circle that number also.

Example: Girl, age 5 years, 39 lbs., 42" tall. Look to the left percentile column of the circled 39 lbs. This is the 50th percentile. Look to the left percentile column for 42". This is the 25th percentile. If your child's weight is in the 50th percentile, this means that at that particular weight and age, 50 percent of a large number of children will weigh less and 50 percent will weigh more. If height and weight do not fall in the same percentile, the chart will show if your child is slim for his age or overweight. If weight is at the 50th percentile and height at the 25th percentile, as in the example, find the weight in the 25th percentile to determine the ideal weight for this age and height. To find the ideal weight, move down the Age 5 column to the weight figure in the 25th percentile, which is 36 pounds. This indicates the child might be about 3 pounds overweight, depending upon her body build. If you feel your child is overweight, simply plot his or her weight on the chart to determine growth or weight six months from now, or a year from now. This will tell you whether your child should or should not gain any weight in the next year.

The important thing to remember is that *growth charts are only guides.* If you ever think there is a problem, consult your physician.

Children develop at different rates. However, despite normal variations, it is possible to pinpoint basic growth stages and their implications for future development.

On page 32 are average (50th percentile) weights and heights for the years two to six.

*Adapted from *Child Psychology* by Albert Angrilli and Lucile Helfat (New York: Harper & Row, 1981).

GROWTH CHART FOR GIRLS—AGES BIRTH TO 24 MONTHS

Percentile		Birth	1 Mo.	2	3	4	5	6	7	8	9	10	11	12	14	16	18	20	22	24
																				AGES IN MONTHS
95%	Wt.	9	11	13	15	17	18	19	21	22	22.5	23	24	25	26	27	28	29	30	31
	Ht.	21	23	24	25	26	27	28	28.5	29	29.5	30	30.5	31	32	33	34	35	35.5	36
75%	Wt.	8	10	11	13	15	16	17	18	19	20	21	22	23	24	25	25	26	27	28
	Ht.	21	22	23	24	25	26	27	27.5	28	28.5	29	29.5	30	31	32	33	33.5	34	35
50%	Wt.	7	9	10	12	13	15	16	17	18	19	20	20.5	21	22	23	24	25	25.5	26
	Ht.	20	21	22	23	24	25	26	26.5	27	27.5	28	28.5	29	30	31	32	32.5	33	34
25%	Wt.	6	8	9	11	12	13	15	16	17	17.5	18	18.5	19	20	21	22	23	24	25
	Ht.	19	21	22	23	24	24.5	25	26	26.5	27	27.5	28	28.5	29.5	30.5	31	31.5	32.5	33
10%	Wt.	6	7	8	10	11	12	13	14	15	16	17	17.5	18	19	19.5	20	21	22	23
	Ht.	18	20	21	22	23	24	25	25.5	26	26.5	27	27.5	28	28.5	29	30	31	32	32.5

GROWTH CHART FOR GIRLS—AGES 2 TO 15 YEARS

Percentile		2 Yrs.	2.5	3	3.5	4	4.5	5	5.5	6	6.5	7	7.5	8	8.5	9	9.5	10	10.5	11	11.5	12	12.5	13	13.5	14	14.5	15
		AGES IN YEARS																										
95%	Wt.	32	35	35	38	44	47	50	53	57	61	67	70	76	82	89	96	104	111	118	126	136	141	148	155	161	167	171
	Ht.	37	38	38	40	43	44	46	47	48	50	51	52	54	55	56	58	59	60	61	63	64	65	66	67	67	67	68
75%	Wt.	28	31	31	34	37	39	41	43	45	48	53	57	61	66	71	76	82	88	94	100	106	111	116	121	126	130	133
	Ht.	35	37	37	38	40	41	43	44	45	47	49	50	52	53	54	55	56	58	59	60	61	63	64	65	65	65	66
50%	Wt.	26	29	29	31	33	35	37	39	43	45	48	51	55	58	62	67	71	76	81	86	91	96	101	106	111	115	118
	Ht.	34	36	36	37	39	40	42	43	45	47	48	49	50	51	52	53	55	56	57	59	61	61	62	63	63	64	64
25%	Wt.	24	27	29	31	32	34	36	38	39	41	44	46	48	52	56	59	63	67	71	75	80	85	89	94	98	102	105
	Ht.	33	34	36	37	38	40	42	43	44	46	47	48	49	50	51	52	53	54	55	57	57	59	61	61	61	62	62
10%	Wt.	23	25	27	29	30	32	34	35	37	38	40	42	45	48	50	53	56	60	64	68	71	76	80	84	88	92	96
	Ht.	32	33	35	37	38	39	40	41	42	44	45	46	47	48	49	50	51	52	53.5	55	56	57	58	59	59	60	60

GROWTH CHART FOR BOYS—AGES BIRTH TO 24 MONTHS

Percentile		Birth	1 Mo.	2	3	4	5	6	7	8	9	10	11	12	14	16	18	20	22	24
95%	Wt.	9.5	12	14	16	18	19	21	22	23	24	25	26	27	28	29	30	31	32	33
	Ht.	22	23	25	26	27	28	28.5	29	30	30.5	31	31.5	32	33	34	35	35.5	36	37
75%	Wt.	8.5	10	12	14	16	17	19	20	21	22	23	23.5	24	25	26	27	28	29	30
	Ht.	21	22	24	25	26	27	27.5	28	28.5	29	29.5	30	31	32	32.5	33	34	35	35.5
50%	Wt.	7.5	9	11	13	15	16	17.5	18.5	19.5	20	21	22	22.5	23.5	24.5	25	26	27	28
	Ht.	20	22	23	24	25	26	27	27.5	28	28.5	29	29.5	30	31	32	32.5	33	34	34.5
25%	Wt.	7	8	10	12	13	15	16	17	18	19	19.5	20.5	21	22	23	23.5	24	25	26
	Ht.	19.5	21	22	23	24	25	25	27	27.5	28	28.5	29	29.5	30	31	32	32.5	33	34
10%	Wt.	6	7	9	10	12	13	15	16	17	18	18.5	19	20	20.5	21	22	22.5	23	24
	Ht.	19	20	21.5	23	24	24.5	25.5	26	26.5	27	28	28.5	29	29.5	30.5	31	31.5	32.5	33

GROWTH CHART FOR BOYS—AGES 2 TO 15 YEARS

Percentile		2 Yrs.	2.5	3	3.5	4	4.5	5	5.5	6	6.5	7	7.5	8	8.5	9	9.5	10	10.5	11	11.5	12	12.5	13	13.5	14	14.5	15
95%	Wt.	35	37	40	42	45	48	51	55	58	62	66	71	76	81	87	93	100	107	113	120	128	136	143	150	160	167	175
	Ht.	37	38.5	40	42	43.5	45	46	47.5	48.5	50	51	52	53.5	54.5	56	57	58.5	59.5	61	62.5	64	65.5	67	68.5	69.5	71	72
75%	Wt.	30	32	35	38	40	42	45	47	50	52	55	58	61	65	69	74	78	84	89	94	100	107	114	121	128	136	143
	Ht.	35	36.5	38.5	40	41.5	43	44.5	46	47	48	49	50.5	51.5	52.5	53.5	54.5	56	57	58	59.5	61	62	63.5	65	66.5	67.5	68.5
50%	Wt.	28	30	32	35	37	39	41	43	46	48	50	53	56	59	62	66	70	73	76	80	88	93	99	105	112	118	125
	Ht.	34	35.5	37.5	39	41	42	43.5	44.5	46	47	48	49	50	51	52	53	54	55	56.5	57.5	59	60.5	61.5	63	64.5	65.5	66.5
25%	Wt.	26	28	30	32	34	36	38	40	42	44	46	49	51	53	56	59	62	65	69	73	77	82	87	93	99	106	112
	Ht.	33.5	35	36.5	38	39.5	41	42	43	44.5	45.5	46.5	47.5	48.5	49.5	50.5	51.5	52.5	53.5	54.5	55.5	57	58	59	60.5	62	63.5	64.5
10%	Wt.	25	26	28	30	32	33	35	37	39	41	43	45	47	49	52	54	56	59	62	66	69	74	78	84	90	96	102
	Ht.	33	34	35.5	37	38.5	39.5	40.5	42	43	43	45	45.5	46.5	48	49.5	50.5	51.5	52	53	54	55	56.5	57.5	58.5	60	61	62.5

Age	BOYS Average Weight	GIRLS Average Weight	BOYS Average Height	GIRLS Average Height
2 yrs.	28 lbs.	26 lbs.	34"	34"
3 yrs.	32 lbs.	31 lbs.	37.5"	37"
4 yrs.	37 lbs.	35 lbs.	41"	40"
5 yrs.	41 lbs.	39 lbs.	43.5"	43"
6 yrs.	46 lbs.	43 lbs.	46"	45"

By two years, the average child increases his birth height by 75 percent; and he is one-fifth as heavy as he will be at eighteen years. By four years, the average child will double his birth height.

Graphing your child's height and weight in these early years will give you some indication of things to come in his adulthood.

CHARACTERISTICS OF THE EARLY CHILDHOOD YEARS

The years from two to six are very special. Children under six are in the process of taking great developmental strides. They are moving into independence; from clumsy coordination to more refined skills; from body talk to verbal communication; from strong reliance on outer controls to developing inner controls; from personal awareness to growing social concern; from the here-and-now to wider intellectual awareness and curiosity; from acquiring isolated facts to conceptualizing and developing a deepening interest in symbols.

The early childhood years are critical years for venturing, exploring, playing, and creating without fear of failing; for testing ideas; for learning to learn; for problem solving; for widening trust in adults; for building relationships with agemates. During these early years the attention span enlarges, and children expand their store of knowledge.

What makes two- to six-year-olds different from other children? The obvious answer is that they are young and have their own style of operating. At this stage in their development they are extremely active, always on the go; they are not good at keeping quiet or sitting still. They are full of boundless en-

ergy. The world about them is inviting, waiting to be discovered and mastered.

The activity that counts most to them is making noise. They say what comes to their mind, and they have a great need to talk to their friends. The sounds of their friends working with their blocks or making music do not bother them.

Of course, some of the special qualities of being very young can be hard for adults to take. The willingness and capacity of parents and teachers to live with these conditions make for the difference between the good classroom for the early childhood years and one that does not accommodate this age group. Calm, understanding parents and teachers accept the natural clamor and exuberance of very young children at play.

Two- to six-year-olds are by nature very shy, with an uncomfortable sense of their own littleness. They love people and have a great need to form friendships with their peers. However, they "love people best in small doses." They are just beginning to make the transition from a private world of their closest adult relatives to a larger world of strangers. They need small nooks where they can be by themselves with a book or a puzzle, or at play with a few agemates.

MOTOR AND PERCEPTUAL DEVELOPMENT IN EARLY CHILDHOOD

Because motor development in the first two years is dramatic and clear-cut, parents tend to view the next four to five years as being routine with few milestones. Actually the transition from toddlerhood to early childhood entails a tremendous degree of neuromuscular development. During these years, the child's balance and stability improve considerably, enabling him to climb stairs in a vertical position, to jump, turn somersaults, hop and skip, walk a straight line. He moves and manipulates more like an adult. He masters the complexities of riding a kiddy car and a tricycle. Spinning around, sitting in a chair, and climbing are no longer studied motions; they are spontaneous, smooth actions.

According to Gesell's early studies in motor behavior, improved perception and finer muscular control enable the three- and four-year-old to hold a crayon; and to copy a triangle, button his clothes, and unlace his shoes by age five. Having worked through the developmental tasks of holding a glass, pouring from a pitcher, etc., he can feed himself neatly, and even carry on a conversation at mealtime without trying too hard.*

Hand and Foot Preference†

By two years, preference for using one arm, hand, or foot over the other (known as laterality) is not well established. Hand preference does not become firmly fixed until the fourth to sixth years of life. In the United States, by the end of the fifth year, nine out of ten children are right-handed. Inasmuch as heredity may play a role in handedness, it is wise to respect a child's preference for left-handedness when there are signs of such dominance. However, some authorities believe that handedness is a learned skill and a laissez-faire approach may create a problem.

---

*Adapted from *The First Years of Life* by Arnold Gesell et al. (New York: Harper & Row, 1940).
†Parts of pages 34-36 adapted from *Perceptual and Motor Development in Infants and Young Children* by Bryant J. Cratty (New York: Macmillan Company, 1970).

Left-handedness is usually noticeable when a child throws a ball, draws with a crayon or pencil, or uses utensils at mealtimes. Eating with fingers indicates the least preference. Most studies show a greater incidence of left-handedness and ambidexterity in boys than in girls. This may be due to social conditioning, since girls engage in more hand play and are amenable to training.

There is some feeling among psychologists that stuttering and handedness may be associated. Stuttering tends to occur at three or four years when hand preference is being established. When handedness is firmed up, stuttering tends to disappear.

Eye dominance also seems to be an inherited trait. Research studies reveal little meaningful relationship between hand and eye preference.

Leg preference is not as sharply delineated as hand use. It is more likely to correlate with hand choice than eye predilection. Research indicates that children will engage in learned motor skills with one foot; kicking a ball, for example. However, when asked to hop or stand on one foot, they may respond by using the other foot.

In fact, hand, eye, and foot preferences are extremely complex. Apparently they emerge relatively early in the life of a child.

During the early childhood years children undergo great progress and change in their ability to master movement skills. During this period the mystery of large-muscle movement becomes evident. Numerous ways are learned to throw a ball and to handle other objects, including bean bags, bats, and balls. Locomotion skills also improve, including walking in different directions, on various surfaces, at different speeds, and with variations that the children invent themselves.

Sex differences also emerge, especially in the manner in which the total body is employed by boys when throwing as opposed to the more limited movements of girls. Differences in body build obviously determine the movement capacities of children in this age range. Obese children are certainly less inclined to active use of their bodies than wiry, thin children.

By five years of age, most children can jump about two feet in the air, catch a large ball, broad-jump three feet, and balance on a line, walking beam, fence, etc. Five-year-olds are starting to throw effectively. They can run and climb in a well-coordinated manner. Their neuromotor system is nearing completion, and their physical maturity grows increasingly obvious.

The Importance of Movement to Young Children

"Movement is, for the young child, an important factor in self-discovery. Through manipulation he discovers one nose, two eyes, two ears, two nostrils, and the texture of his hair. Through locomotion he discovers independence and achieves a repertoire of body skills that generate self-pride. He gets to know how it feels to move and the feedback from each movement provides cues that are used to develop more and more intricate patterns of self-propulsion . . .

"The toddler finds that her world is extended by her own mobility. In the enlarged environment, new objects are discovered, examined, and named. Her vocabulary increases, for she must have new names for her latest discoveries.

"Movement assists the young child in achieving and maintaining his orientation in space. It is an important factor in his development of concepts of time, space, and direction."*

"Parents often report that a child who has been struggling to pedal the trike, ride a two-wheeler, climb to the top of some structure, swim or dive, and has finally mastered the skill, shows how wonderful he feels not only by outward display of pleasure, but also by a more active attack on other problems he has been avoiding. Often a feeling of fresh self-confidence enables a person of any age to try something he has thought he couldn't do. This component of the self-concept is rooted in early motor development; how it develops is influenced to an important extent by the way in which the environment supports autonomy in motor areas. The toddler who is always picked up bodily instead of helped up after a tumble, who is lifted down instead of helped to climb down . . . does not feel much confidence in himself."†

*From "The Young Child—What Movement Means to Him," an address by Keturah E. Whitehurst of Virginia State College at a 1971 Conference on the Significance of the Young Child's Motor Development, held in Washington, D.C.

†From "The Young Child: We Know So Much—We Know So Little," an address by Eveline B. Omwake of Connecticut College at a 1971 Conference on the Significance of the Young Child's Motor Development, held in Washington, D.C.

"Children's tempo, posture, movement of limbs and gestures, tilt of their heads, the thrust of their chests, their eyes, brows, mouths, voices—all give clues to the quality of what they feel and mean. In their walk one can see pride, caution, timidity, abandon, self-effacement or strength. Their bodily selves are their real selves and if we learn to read body language, we will be reading children."*

What can parents do to encourage their child's body mastery and other physical skills? Marguerite Kelly and Elia Parsons suggest in their book *The Mother's Almanac* that parents offer to their children constant challenge and opportunities to practice their emerging skills. They need to create an environment that lets their children have "a thousand small victories" each day.

Two-year-olds need opportunities to climb indoors as well as outdoors. It is worth even a long walk to get to a suitable playground. Two- and three-year-olds need to walk every day as much for exercise as for the enrichment. "Nothing makes a mid-two feel more like a daredevil than a chance to balance along a low brick wall."

Most Fours master a tricycle, a scooter, a rope ladder, a punching bag. Fives can pump a swing, run, skip, and jump.

If you are lucky enough to have a private or community pool nearby that offers swimming lessons for very young children, take advantage of it. Above all, include in each day a different physical challenge—enjoyable activities that help children build good posture, coordination, balance, and self-confidence.

LANGUAGE DEVELOPMENT

After an infant finds his legs, he then normally finds his tongue. Early communication between mother and child is practically nonverbal. However, the walking child needs language in order to communicate with adults and peers who are not members of his family. This calls for the acquisition of words. Every toddler knows instinctively that the time has come for him to learn words, and he gives his full attention to

*From "The Young Child—Learning to Observe, Observing to Learn," an address by Dorothy H. Cohen of the Bank Street College of Education at the same conference.

anyone who is willing to label his actions and the things in his world. For example, when he touches a rug, the mother or other adult can reinforce the process with the labels *soft, fur,* or *rug.* When he picks up a ball, the mother can give him the words *ball, round,* and *smooth.* On a trip through the park there are *birds, squirrels, leaves, carriage, little boy, little girl,* etc. He learns to meet a *dog* without fear. He loves to play with *water.* Repeating each word and associating it with an action mark the beginning of a labeling process that starts earnestly at about twenty-two months and goes on throughout life.

When a child learns that a particular set of sounds refers to or represents an object, event, or feeling, she has found the single most valuable tool for understanding and predicting what is happening in her environment—language. Language serves two functions: It is a means by which one expresses thoughts and feelings, and also a major tool with which one interprets, organizes, and relates material perceived through the senses. Language does not unfold of its own accord; it must be learned and practiced. Nothing will incite the beginning talker more than encouragement, and the response and praise of adults who care. During the initial phase of language learning, the child's time is taken up with learning verbs and acquiring the names of objects. The child will see that many objects have similar attributes. *Ball* becomes the name of a whole class of things; *hot* applies to the stove, toaster, the sun, etc. Thus the child not only labels, but also sorts out the various elements in her world. First she needs to handle the ball as her mother names it. Later on she will be able to visualize the ball without its being present. As this facility develops, the child can use language to free herself from things that are not actually present, and this expands her ability to deal with the world. Now she can begin thinking about things that are not visible to her at the moment, which is the beginning of abstract thinking. When labeling is rewarded or tied up with agreeable experiences, language ability accelerates.

Government research at the National Institute of Mental Health indicates that when adults intervene at the walking-talking stage, the greatest advance in language learning ensues, and IQ can be increased about twenty points. At no other age and stage can such a decisive change in oral language learning take place. A child listens and learns when he hears: "Please pick up the ball." "Now say ball." "Say doll."

"Give me the ball, dear." "Bring me your dolly, please." "Would you like to hear a story now?"

Every child needs to be encouraged to listen, to make sound discriminations, to mimic sounds, to use sounds correctly, to name objects and actions, and arrange words in meaningful sequence. Language-teaching tools should be the kind of materials that appeal equally to child and parent. Each activity should be a game parent and child can mutually enjoy. Food, drink, eating utensils, body parts, articles of clothing, similarities and differences, relative position and placement—all these comprise only a small segment of the hundreds of words needed for simple verbal communication.

Acquisition of Language

One of the most amazing feats during the early childhood years is the acquisition and mastery of language, especially during the period from twenty-four months to sixty months. Children not impaired by vocal problems, brain damage, or psychic disorders begin to babble at five or six months; utter first words at ten to twelve months; combine words at eighteen to twenty-four months; and acquire grammar and syntax almost completely at forty-eight to sixty months. When children discover that everything has a name, somewhere between eighteen and twenty-four months, vocabulary increases from twenty to twenty-two words at eighteen months to almost three hundred words at twenty-four months. Then, over six hundred words are added annually for the next two years, with the rate of vocabulary growth slowing down thereafter.

VOCABULARY ACQUISITION DURING EARLY CHILDHOOD

Age	Average number of words
12 mos.	3
18 mos.	22
24 mos.	272
36 mos.	896
48 mos.	1,540
60 mos.	2,072
72 mos.	2,562

There are various opinions among linguists as to how small children acquire language. The views with the greatest support are those of Noam Chomsky of Harvard, and especially of the widely quoted expert, the late Eric H. Lenneberg of Cornell University. Dr. Lenneberg believed that the child is not taught language; rather, the role of parents is simply "to provide him with the opportunity to teach himself, to pull himself up by his own bootstraps. If the child is talked to, if he is surrounded with language, if he hears people talking to one another, he will naturally go without any teaching from stage to stage in his own language development."

This development cannot be pushed by anxious parents. A simple and harmless experiment with nursery school children of thirty to thirty-six months of age provides a demonstration of the appropriate way to foster language. If your child is at the stage where he is beginning to string words together to make little sentences, try having him repeat after you sentences such as: "Johnny doesn't like dogs." "The cat is chased by the dog." "You like cookies and so do I."

You will find that your child will not repeat such sentences verbatim; instead she will restructure them into her own language system—for instance, "Johnny no like dogs." The reason the child cannot repeat the sentences exactly is that their structure is too advanced for her current skill. Children "constantly reformulate what they hear according to their particular stage of development."

Of course, this is not to say that the language environment is of no importance. As a general rule, the more verbal, vocal home will provide the more verbal child, at least initially. Experiments with deaf children, children living in institutions for the retarded, and so on, have shown that if a child has the capacity for language acquisition, "a remarkably limited exposure to language will be sufficient for the child to develop normal language himself." In short, parents do not *teach* children to talk. Optimally, they provide their children with an environment in which they can acquire language at their own pace and by their own strategies.

Perhaps the most important thing for parents to remember about language development is that there is a wide range of individual variation. In a study by Dr. Lenneberg of the language acquisition of three-year-olds, it was found that 10 percent may be said to be slow language developers. If by his third birthday a child has not yet begun to string sentences together, if he is not understanding what is said to him, parents are right to be concerned, and the pediatrician should be consulted. Most three-year-olds who are slow speakers are slow for entirely benign reasons, and will outgrow their problems within a year. Some have language delays due to more serious problems: learning defects or a retarding disease. Even such children will sooner or later acquire language, but they may need special help from a speech therapist.

Many young children can learn two different languages simultaneously. To avoid confusion, it helps if one parent speaks his or her native tongue to the child and the other parent speaks the other language. If the parents are bilingual and use both languages interchangeably, the child will be apt to confuse the two.

What amazes most parents and professionals is how young children master the complex grammar of their native language without outside help. Peter Farb, in his excellent book *Word Play* (New York: Alfred A. Knopf, 1974), puts it this way: "The child hears a small number of utterances, most of which are grammatically incorrect or misunderstood, and yet on the basis of scarcity and flawed information and without instruction, he discovers for himself the complex grammatical rules of his speech community."

The Development of Linguistic Skills

Children learn to speak without any of the deliberate instruction needed to read or write, and much of the speech of very young children has its own rules and contains forms which are not found in adult speech.

Research in this area reinforces the theory that children do not acquire grammar through imitation, practice, or reinforcement (reward), as is commonly supposed by adults. The experts claim that children learn by imitating those structures that appear in their own freewheeling speech. If asked to repeat something, they will drop portions of the original sentence to make it adhere to their own rules of grammar; for instance, "It doesn't fit" becomes "Not fit." This conforms to their idea of a negative sentence. Although parents correctly give the past tense of run as *ran,* children will add "ed" to it, saying *runned. Go* becomes *goed.*

The research literature does not indicate that parental reinforcement has any effect in changing the child's grammar. It is as if the child has developed her own game plan, and every phrase must conform to her own notion of the rules of grammar.

Some researchers, Noam Chomsky for one, even propose that "evolution has built in a readiness on the part of the human organism to acquire language—a kind of innate device specially attuned to organizing speech heard in particular ways." There are other theories about how toddlers develop linguistic strategies and even learning abilities during this critical period when they have a great desire and need to communicate. One theory that unfortunately gets little attention is that language acquisition takes place at a time when children discover the power of play and they treat language play as they do block play, fantasizing and practicing language combinations and grammatical structures without fear of failure or criticism. It is during this period that children who are introduced to the rhythms of singing and the rhyming of poetry carry over this special sensitivity to their adult life.

All phases of language—sounds, grammar, rhythm, and rhymes—lend themselves to play. It is only natural for the two-to six-year-old to discover these play potentials in their emerging language. The outstanding Russian writer of verses and stories for children, Kornei Chukovsky, wrote an excellent book, *From Two to Five* (Berkeley and Los Angeles: University of California Press, 1965), dealing with this verbal creativity. He delighted in the young child's unfettered acquisition of language: " . . . this newcomer to the world of linguistic sounds and symbols brings a fresh eye to the marvels of language."

A child can learn by rote to count from one to ten forward and backward, but if he gets six cookies and is asked how many he has, he will not necessarily know. With language, the child can connect both words and thoughts, that is, think in words. Piaget distinguished two functions of language: the social and the egocentric. The first is directed to the listener and enables us to communicate with others; the latter is self-directed, an important tool of self-expression.

At early ages, especially between three to five years, the egocentric function is more important than the social one. The child talks and does not bother to know to whom he is speaking or whether he is being listened to. We see this sort of speech mostly in children's play and in the dark of night before

they go to sleep; they simply talk to themselves. Such "inner" speech or imaginary dialogues with toys are addressed to no person in particular.

In *Thought and Language* (Cambridge, MA: M.I.T. Press, 1962), Dr. Lev Semenovich Vygotsky defines inner speech as a "dynamic, shifting, unstable thing, fluttering between word and thought, the two more or less stable, more or less firmly delineated components of verbal thought." Vygotsky believes that inner speech later becomes the basis for overt talking. At seven to eight years, the child's desire to work with others increases, and social talk takes on greater importance. The child uses his speech to put order in his world and plan his actions. One of the reasons why egocentric speech disappears at school age is because it becomes inner speech. Now the child can talk to himself soundlessly; he has learned to think.

Naming and Labeling

Naming objects and labeling processes represent the one-year-old's realization that through countless repetitions in various circumstances a word brings about a desired response. The word and the object are one; for example, "Mama" brings mother. From twelve to sixteen months, the association becomes more stable for two reasons: the child's repeated experience of hearing the word spoken by others and her own repeated use of the word as well as the possible reinforcement she receives for using it. The feedback of one's own sounds may be one of the most important reinforcements of the early

The young toddler attempts to represent everything with single words. The first words spoken by the one-year-old usually are simple labels for persons, objects, or acts. Single words may represent entire sentences. "Shoe" may mean "Take off my shoe." "Eat" may mean "Is baby going to eat now?" "Truck" may label an entire play sequence with toys.

Mothers usually know instinctively that depending upon the intonation, "Mama" can be a mere statement ("Here's Mama"), a demand ("I want Mama!"), or a question ("Is that Mama?"). In fact, intonation patterns at this age are the first bits of language mastery. At sixteen months, the toddler uses single words predominantly.

Frequently a toddler's words are enmeshed in streams of what adults consider meaningless gibberish. This jargon generally disappears by twenty-four months of age, probably because it does not receive feedback. It has the rhythm and fluency of adult conversation, uses various sounds, and often accompanies an activity. The occasional real words used may suggest what the child is trying to convey, while the nonsense sentences accompanying them are backdrops for words.

Language learning helps define the boundaries of the self, and makes the toddler aware of the individuality of others. The child names himself (*me*) and other people (*Mommy*) and also things around him (*car*). Perceiving differences in things allows him to act on them more efficiently, to plan, and to make better use of them.

Sentence Formation and Grammar

It takes awhile for a child to talk in real sentences. At first, each word represents a complete thought: "Ma" may mean "Mommy, come here." As she adds more words, the child can communicate more needs and feelings. When the toddler begins to put together two words to make a sentence ("Get ball." "Give cookie."), she is well on her way to piecing together a grammar that will grow more complicated and parallel her increasingly complex thought processes.

Chomsky believes that children are born with a blueprint for language that they use to analyze utterances heard in their speech community and to build a grammar system. Linguist

Peter Farb shows a fine example of this when he refers to the constant use of "hisself" instead of "himself" until the child is four years old. Why is it constructed by children who hear "himself" and never hear "hisself"? "Hisself" is a reflexive pronoun, like *myself, herself, yourself,* formed by putting together *me, her,* and *your* with *self.* Therefore, a child reasons, *his* and *self* should rightly produce "hisself." Children insisting on "hisself" rather than "himself" show that they have mastered a grammar system long before speaking; the inconsistency of the English language has not yet been accepted by them!

At the same time that the toddler is mastering grammatical rules, she is also learning the correct use of language from speech situations in her home and the community. By two, children can use speech to get what they want and to influence the social behavior of others. Although most children acquire the grammar system, appropriate use of speech and the growth of vocabulary depend upon parents, siblings, and peer groups. If this "speech community" provides opportunities to use language, as in structured play experiences or interactions with a verbal mother or other consistent caregiver, the child will readily gain the vocabulary she needs.

Reading and Writing

Research evidence indicates a high degree of interrelatedness among the communication skills of oral language, reading, and writing. In *Language Arts in the Elementary School* (New York: Ronald Press, 1970), Gertrude B. Corcoran writes that the child's ability to comprehend written material through reading and to express himself through writing appear to be directly related to his listening and speaking skills. Let us look now at each of the language arts and their relationship to one another.

In reading, as in the other language arts, the parent is the pacesetter. If you read a lot, you are saying to your child that reading is important and enjoyable to you. However, it is your reading aloud to your child that is vital to her future development. Even the one-year-old enjoys having a parent read to her. Although she does not understand most of what is being said, she will respond to the rhythm of the words, variations in vocal expression, parental attention, and the sense that you are doing something interesting. At first, content is of little

import, but as the child begins to master some words, content takes on added significance. Discussion of the story is important as your child's comprehension improves because this provides an excellent opportunity to enhance your child's verbal facility.

There is an important distinction between speaking and

reading. To speak, the child learns a vocal symbol for a concept. When the child is ready to read, he must associate a visual symbol with his previously learned vocal symbol. Reading instruction should be given *only* when the child indicates real interest and is able to hear and speak the language with success. Then the child may be encouraged to move on to the visual symbols of language.

Brandon Sparkman and Ann Carmichael, authors of *Blueprint for a Brighter Child* (New York: McGraw-Hill, 1973), state that there are three basic ingredients to reading readiness. The first, *interest,* is developed by regular reading to the child. The second is *visual discrimination,* the capacity to differentiate between shapes, colors, sizes, etc. The third essential is *auditory discrimination,* the ability to distinguish between different sounds. Oral communication, then, lays the groundwork for two of the three basic essentials of reading readiness.

Impression precedes expression; intake precedes outflow in all aspects of language learning. A baby listens to and responds to words long before he says those words aloud. Similarly, a child looks at and absorbs the written word before he does any real writing. It is only after the child is able to recognize the symbols for sounds that he is ready to learn to copy them.

Language takes two directions—receiving and transmitting. We receive when we listen and read; we transmit when we speak and write. A child needs to grasp the idea that writing is talk put on paper. To forward this thought, let your child tell you a story, write it down in large letters, and then read it back to her. Let her dictate to you a letter for Grandma, and let her mail it. Suggest that Grandma send back a letter addressed to your child.

Although listening, speaking, reading, and writing occur in this order, they also overlap. Children continue to develop new skills in listening after they are speaking. Effective oral communication continues after a child is able to read and write. Children learn to write while their reading skill is in its early stages.

Stuttering or Stammering

Stuttering or stammering is a disorder of speech that makes its appearance in a small proportion of children (estimates range from 1 to 5 percent), usually at about age two to four years. It has been defined as a disturbance in fluency of speech typified by occasional blocking, a convulsive repetition or prolonging of sounds, syllables, words, and phrases.

A child may say "I want to, I want to have that" or "I go, go downstairs" or "I g-g-go in here." Parents often become uneasy when they hear their child stutter, choke on a rush of words, or produce garbled sentences. Dr. Joseph Church writes, "This is simply the way young children talk and there is nothing to be done about it, except to be patient."

Stuttering is quite common at three or four. Generally it indicates that a child is in a hurry and cannot keep pace with his thoughts. Or his vocabulary is still inadequate to do so. It is not to be misconstrued as a major elocution or emotional problem. Dr. Benjamin Spock thinks that children who are urged to talk, recite, and otherwise "show off" are especially prone to stuttering.

In most cases, stuttering lasts a number of months with ups and downs. Do not expect it to go right away. Try to be content with gradual progress, and the less said about the condition the better.

Dr. Neil C. Henderson says that persistent stuttering may be due to tension or a new environment. Speech specialists believe a child's emotional state has a lot to do with stuttering. Most cases occur in somewhat tense children. Mothers report that their children's stuttering is definitely worse when they (the mothers) are tense. Also, stuttering may start when a father decides to be a stricter disciplinarian.

Trying to change a left-handed child into a right-handed one sometimes triggers stuttering. The part of the brain that controls speech is closely connected to the part that controls the hand a person naturally prefers. If you *force* a child to use her "wrong" hand, it seems to confuse her talking apparatus.

What You Can Do to Promote Language Development

Let your child talk! Between three and five, your budding talker will probably become a chatterbox, discovering the fun of communication through words, wanting to attract attention and to tell you things. Make sure he also has children and adults outside your family to talk to.

Do your child and yourself a real service—leave her speech

alone! Of course, it is good sense to suggest phrasings to her when she is having trouble making herself understood, but it is harmful to worry about her lack of fluency. You can help her articulate her ideas, but do leave her transient stammering alone. If she is tense, try to discover what is bothering her and see what you can do to remove the causes.

When your child speaks to you, listen attentively. Encourage him by indicating your interest and understanding. Show your delight in subtle ways at any obvious verbal achievement. Above all, do not make the mistake of calling attention to stuttering in front of others or permitting others to mention it in front of your child. Do not compare your child unfavorably with a more articulate older sibling. Avoid interrupting him when he is talking or otherwise showing impatience (this will only create more tension). Never punish a child for stuttering—or promise a reward if it stops. Refrain from offering such suggestions as "Take a deep breath" or "You must speak more slowly." Do not permit brothers or sisters to tease the stutterer.

Offensive Language

At about this time your child may begin to pick up swear words and unpleasant expressions from other children. If you act shocked and surprised at hearing such words, your child will be delighted with his power over you. Threats to your child demanding that he immediately stop using these words is the same thing as "handing him a full-size cannon and telling him 'For goodness sake, don't set it off,'" says Dr. Spock. It is best just to ignore this language. On the other hand, if it persists, you may have to tell him firmly that you do not like that kind of language and you do not want him to use it.

INTELLECTUAL GROWTH IN EARLY CHILDHOOD

Piaget saw intellectual development as taking place in four major age-related stages. He called the first, from birth to two years, the *sensorimotor stage.* During this stage, the infant is continuously learning how to direct the movements of his body, and endlessly practices his newly found sensory powers (seeing, hearing, touching, smelling, etc.). The baby takes in information through all his senses and learns how to use this information; for example, if a spoon is dangled over his head, he learns by trial and error how far to reach for it. He also learns what direction to look in to find out where a sound is coming from.

Psychologists have theorized that in the first few weeks of life an infant's world must be made up of successions of visual images, sounds, and feelings. The infant makes no distinction between herself and what is outside of herself. Gradually she acquires a view of her surroundings as including objects and people that are different from herself, and that exist even when they are out of her sight. She will be able to tell when a ball is really rolling or when it only appears to be because she herself is moving. She will learn some notion of cause and effect.

Somewhere toward the end of his second year, the child enters what Piaget called the *preoperational stage,* usually from two to seven years. The first part of this period, which ends at about age four, is called the *preconceptual period.* It is during this time span—more so than in any other—that the child develops the ability to deal with symbols. He can understand the relationship between an object and the symbol or word for that object. Despite these giant forward steps in his development, the child still does not see the world as the adult does. For instance, if upon taking a walk he sees six fire hydrants, he does not know if he is seeing a series of different hydrants or whether the same one keeps turning up again and again. In any case, it makes little difference to his thinking, as all of them are simply "fire hydrants." Piaget called this a "preconcept"—meaning that it is somewhere between the *idea* of an object and the *concept* of a class of objects.

At about age four, the child enters the second phase of the preoperational stage: the *intuitive period.* Intuitive thought can be illustrated by one of Piaget's best-known experiments, in which the child is shown two identical drinking glasses filled with equal amounts of juice. The child is asked whether each glass holds the same amount. When she agrees that this is so, the juice from one glass is poured into a taller, thinner glass so that the juice reaches a greater height. Now when the child is asked whether each glass holds the same amount of juice, she says that the tall thin glass holds more. She is also unable to realize that if the juice is poured back into the original short glass it will once again appear equal to its twin. In another experiment devised by Piaget, it was shown that a child at this stage of development will believe that a belt arranged in a circle is shorter than an identical one laid out in a straight line.

Piaget's third stage, which he called *concrete operational,* spans about age seven to eleven. During this time the child develops the ability to do in his head what he previously would have had to do through physical action. He can make estimates and is able to understand the concepts of relative length, amount, etc. His ways of thinking are becoming increasingly like those of an adult.

The fourth stage, the *stage of formal operations* (from about twelve years on), signifies the child's ability to think abstractly, and thus hypothetical reasoning becomes possible for the first time.

How Do Children Learn?

"Piaget's study of children led to insights into certain universalities of childhood thinking and learning. The first of these discoveries is the existence of a developmental sequence in each important area of understanding, a sequence through which all children pass; i.e., certain kinds of concepts cannot be understood by children before some degree of experiencing and maturing has taken place, *no matter how much we try to teach them.* On the other hand, the exact time at which the stages or sequences begin and end varies with individual children."*

Raymond S. Moore and Dorothy N. Moore believe that learning moves forward rapidly during the years from four to six and then from nine to eleven. Actually the potential for learning rather than learning per se is acquired during earliest childhood. The Moores believe that early academic instruction is questionable since there is no evidence of lasting effects of preschool academic training. In *School Can Wait* (Provo, UT: Brigham Young University Press, 1979), they write, "Time provides for the maturation of physical and mental abilities and also permits the accumulation of life experiences on which a child can build. He can then find meaning in academic tasks that he can learn after age seven or eight with much greater efficiency and far less frustration and stress."

In *Your Child Learns Naturally* (Garden City, NY: Doubleday, 1976), Silas L. Warner and Edward B. Rosenberg suggest that it is not important for parents to teach their very young children facts. Instead parents need to recognize and encourage their offsprings' curiosity and creativity. A major contribution parents can make is to help their children develop self-confidence so that they will be able to tackle new experiences gradually without any fear of frustration or failure.

---

*From *The Learning Child: Guidelines for Parents and Teachers* by Dorothy H. Cohen (New York: Pantheon Books, 1972).

Acquiring the Potential for Learning

Several years ago, Professor Benjamin S. Bloom of the University of Chicago showed by intensive study of the research literature that the development of intelligence accelerated most rapidly in the early years. Bloom stated that in terms of intelligence measured at age seventeen, an individual produces 50 percent of his mature intelligence from birth to age four.

This led to much confusion in the field of early childhood education. Many began to interpret it to mean that 50 percent of a person's actual adult intelligence developed by age four. Therefore, they started to introduce early reading, writing, and formal arithmetic—a conclusion many prominent researchers considered "unwarranted." These researchers showed that formal education before the age of six does not produce lasting effects on the IQ of children.

They indicated, too, that intelligence is more than rote symbol or word learning; that concept learning (as defined by Piaget and others) requires extensive firsthand experiences. Many educators believe that the maturation of various skills (visual and auditory perception, sorting out reality from fantasy, etc.) comes as children move out of the early childhood years and begin to attain control of their learning behaviors. This coincides with Piaget's period of concrete operations, when children are able to perform new mental operations with the concepts and symbols they have been accumulating through their play and learning experiences. The ability to reason, to think consistently, to perceive relationships, and to make logical choices appears to be a function of more advanced development.

Sorting and Classification

Children from three to six learn better if they work with ideas concretely, that is, if they manipulate familiar objects. Through such experiences they lay a basis for arriving at various ideas (relating to size, shape, color, sequence, texture, etc.) in math, science, art, and other areas. When adults make such manipulating activities possible, they are helping the child to think for herself, to experiment with ideas, and to build her self-confidence.

Concepts do not come easily. They require all kinds of experiments before insight comes. The concepts of *soft* and *hard* come from handling, dropping, squeezing, rolling, chewing, etc. Some things break when contact is made with hard surfaces; some bounce. From accumulated experiences the young child clarifies his thought process and adds to his memory bank. Soon the experiences are labeled with words, which turn out to be easier to play with than objects. If parents are supportive, if they both answer questions and ask the child challenging questions, they satisfy their child's curiosity and improve his feeling of self-worth.

Take, for instance, the topic of size discrimination. The child's first mental images revolve about her ability to discriminate an object or figure from its surroundings. She sees the object with her eyes, but it is given more meaning *after* she touches it and feels whether it is round or square, smooth or rough, etc. Her initial reaction is that the object is an extension of herself. In time she learns that it is a thing apart from herself and other objects. This is the beginning of the acquisition of spatial concepts.

Learning spatial relationships is necessary before a child can differentiate size. He must first experiment in reaching out to grasp an object in order to estimate distance. His concept of space gives him a sense of relationship to the objects around him. The very young child learns to measure space by muscular movements (squeezing into a small box, for example). In time, he learns that his eyes can give him a broader picture of his world.

A child cannot differentiate *biggest, middle size,* and *littlest* until she is three years of age or older. Her most difficult concept is that of middle size, but biggest is also hard for her to grasp. One of the reasons that size discrimination is so confusing to a young child is that she must take perspective into account. Of course, objects look smaller when we are far away from them. Studies reveal that children often have trouble making accurate judgments as the distance between them and an object increases.

The Role of Parent and Home in the Learning Process

Parents have a special concern for their own children. Early childhood educators believe this universal involvement can be put to work in the best interests of growing children.

In *All Our Children Learning* (New York: McGraw-Hill, 1981), Benjamin S. Bloom writes, "If the parents wish to improve the learning of their children, the home environment is the only place where they are likely to have some degree of control.

"Research findings indicate that an index of the home environment is far more predictive of school achievement than the best intelligence or aptitude test. The results suggest that the home has greatest influence on the language development of a child and his general ability to learn. It has least influence on specific skills taught primarily in the school . . .

"Children in many middle-class homes are given help in dealing with the world in which they live, in using language to fix aspects of this world in their memory . . . They are read to, spoken to, and subjected to stimulating experiences . . . and come to view the world as something they can master through a relatively enjoyable type of activity—learning."

THE GROWTH OF SOCIAL AWARENESS

The human infant is a "social organism" as soon as he is born. Actually even before birth, he affects everyone who is concerned about him. While his role in social relationships is fairly passive in the beginning of his life, his responses grow increasingly active. Thrust abruptly into the complicated world with its myriad social institutions, values, ideas, and language, he continually struggles to find his place. For many years his immaturity keeps him within the confines and protection of his family. Then, as he becomes increasingly self-sufficient, he begins to advance beyond the limits of his home into the realm of the larger society.

Although the family remains a fundamental human institution, many of its controls seem to be waning. Nonetheless, the values and attitudes in the home and the quality of interactions within the family help shape each child's social (and other) behaviors. Intentionally and otherwise, parents provide their children with awareness of social attitudes and contribute importantly to their offsprings' social precepts.

Even though a child's evaluation of herself and her capabilities is formed largely by parental attitudes toward her, her experiences in the company of other children sharply color her unfolding image of herself. There is little doubt that a child's first notions of social values are formed from the ways in which she is treated, and the behaviors of other children and adults. In brief, her interpersonal experiences are vital aspects of her early living. Fortunate indeed are children whose parents are loving, relaxed, responsive, and understanding.

Throughout the first year of life, it is usually the mother who is paramount in instilling a sense of well-being and security in her charge. However, good mothering becomes even more challenging when the mother needs to cease hovering. Children who remain bound to their mothers are rarely able to build self-reliance and comfortable sociality. A child has to learn to depend upon himself if he is to become an autonomous and contributing social being.

Fathers Do Count!

In *Infants Without Families* (New York: International Universities Press, 1944, 5th printing 1970), Anna Freud and Dorothy Burlingham wrote, "The infant's emotional relationship to the father begins later in life than to the mother, but certainly from the second year onward it is an integral part of his or her emotional life . . .

"The infant's earliest emotions directed toward the father are bound up with feelings of admiration for his superior strength and power, but there are two points where disturbances cannot fail to enter into this otherwise satisfying relationship. It is the father's role, even more than the mother's, to impersonate for the growing infant the restrictive demands inherent in the code of every civilized society. To become a social member of the human community the child has to curb and transform his or her sexual and aggressive wishes. What the mother does in this respect is day-to-day criticizing, praising, and guiding. The father normally reinforces by his very presence . . ."

No Child Can Flourish in an Unresponsive Environment

Healthy ego development requires stability, affection, and reliability in early family life. Friendliness and spontaneity are linked with a warm family atmosphere. Dependent behavior is heightened where a family lacks unity and parental discord or rejection is present. Every normal child has great drive for social competency unless she has been injured psychologically during the course of her upbringing. Throughout childhood, a child's expenditure of energy for growing and learning

is controlled by the emotional responses she experiences along the way from all the people who touch her life.

Communicating with others besides parents and siblings is a hard task for the toddler. Heretofore his nonverbalized needs usually were properly interpreted by family members, who perceived from his face or sounds what he desired. When he is able to walk, he suddenly needs usable language in order to get along with others. Now he is ready for vocabulary building as never before. Especially during this period, a child's command of language grows or retards, frustrations ease or become complicated, ego grows or deflates, depending upon the play settings and toys that are provided for verbal interchanges.

The Normal Toddler Is Egocentric

Not yet experienced enough to be aware of the feelings of others, the toddler is interested in other children or adults chiefly as objects to touch, explore, hug, and sometimes to hit or bite. If another child were to be in the way of a toddler pushing a carriage, the toddler would move forward as if the other child were an inanimate object. Should the other child fall over or cry, the toddler would continue along his self-centered way. At this stage, a teddy bear or other stuffed toy is a perfect playmate because one can do anything one wishes to it.

Infant-Toddler Playgroups

Some mothers form infant-toddler playgroups, which usually include five or six little ones who meet regularly in each other's homes to play, with each mother taking turns to supervise activities. Each play session usually lasts about two hours. Such playgroups are not baby-sitting arrangements; rather, they are cooperative undertakings. The participating mothers plan the play sessions and provide suitable play materials and activities. Even though the toddlers do not actually play together, it may be that their individual play takes on more meaning when they are in a group.

Even if very young children do not need or benefit from a playgroup, some psychologists say that it may be that their mothers do. Most new mothers, especially of firstborns, learn a great deal from watching the behavior and play of all the children in the playgroup, and many grow more relaxed. Even though very young children seem to learn more from older children and adults, the playgroup can help each cooperating mother to understand and enjoy her own child more. In addition, the organized play setting permits the children to select from a broader variety of well-chosen playthings and activities than they may have available in their own homes.

The Three-Year-Old Is More Outgoing

In *The Nursery Years* (New York: Schocken Books, 1968), Susan Isaacs writes, "Storms of open defiance are very common towards the end of the second year of growth and for a year or two later, even in children who have been placid babies. They seem to be largely an early form of self-assertion that passes away as the child comes to greater skill and social ease. They are trying enough at the time, but an atmosphere of calm and firm patience and steady affection helps them to disperse."

The behavior of the three-year-old toward his peers indicates that he is now better able to identify with others. He displays increasing interest in playing with other children, and is beginning dimly to understand what it means to wait his turn, although he usually does not relish this. Sometimes he will even share his toys. The playgroups of three-year-olds are in a constant state of flux. The children may play together for half an hour or so, but when the common objective has been achieved, the group falls apart, and each child usually goes his own way.

Early childhood education pioneers developed in the nursery school a planned environment in which social interactions are a natural outcome. The playroom is usually divided by screens into separate areas for homemaking play, block building, music making, arts and crafts activities, quiet play, and a daily rest period. In each section, the playthings and equipment are arranged so the children can play together at times and by themselves at other times. In all instances they can test and practice their relations with their peers. The child-sized wood stove, kitchen cupboard, sink, table and chairs, and utensils permit a few children at a time to "cook food for a dinner party" and to set the table with appropriate dishes and cutlery. The child-sized doll bed and dresser and assorted dolls also permit several children to play together. Very young girls and boys eagerly join forces to play at family living. Dress-up and theater arts activities as well as doll play thoroughly engage four-year-olds in imaginative role-playing. They like also to play simple picture lotto and domino games. Nursery school children rejoice in making music with their agemates and respond with enthusiasm to rhythmic activities.

Nursery school playground equipment was also designed to further social interplay between little children. Large packing crates require three or four children if they are to be moved about and played with. Eight-foot bouncing or seesaw boards need at least two children for their use. Building with hollow blocks invites group participation. Wagons need a puller and a rider. The ladder-box permits group adventuring, as do a jungle gym and a horizontal ladder-box. Unfortunately, the tendency of many of today's nursery schools to eliminate the "packing-crate philosophy" and substitute cheaper, light-weight items curtails social-physical interplay.

The nursery school can empower young children to handle and express their feelings of aggression by helping them learn how to cope with them in socially acceptable ways. Puppets, punching bags, giant push 'em balls, and other such toys make it possible for young children to release their tensions by bringing their pent-up emotions to the fore.

During the pre-grade school years children move from being relatively self-absorbed to becoming increasingly social. There are expansions in the size of playgroups, in the duration of cooperative activity, and in each child's ability to follow the rules of very simple games. Play with other children, more than any other activity, helps forward a child's social competence.

Social development can be measured in terms of a child's communication ability, self-care, self-directed activity, and social behavior. The competent six-year-old, for instance, is able to attend to his toilet needs, wash his hands and face, dress and feed himself, talk in complete sentences, ride a bicycle and scooter, use skates, get along with his agemates, wait his turn, and obey simple rules. The closer he comes to this level of maturity, the more he is ready to take his place in the larger world. Becoming proficient in all areas of living requires a background of years of maturing, experimenting, and playing out social situations.

Consideration for Others Is a Learned Social Skill

How well children relate to other children and adults depends upon their ability to get to know and accept other people. If children are to attain their optimal development, they must have suitable playthings and playmates and full opportunity for play. Children, if left alone, will seek out play situations and playmates as if their lives depended upon it—and perhaps they do!

PERSONALITY AND EMOTIONAL DEVELOPMENT

"Personality is one of the most difficult human qualities to define because it refers to the central core of a person— his or her uniqueness.

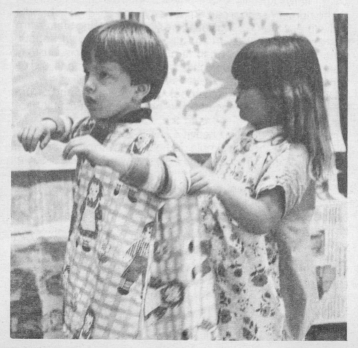

"Personality deals with how a child sees herself and how she responds to other people. It is concerned with her anxieties, fears, and fantasies; her ways of approaching problems; her likes and dislikes; and how she handles anger and hostility. Personality also deals with an individual's constructive behavior; how she acts on the environment to exert control, to master it, and to have an impact on it . . .

"Personality develops through the child interacting with the environment . . . We know much more about the effects of the development of grossly depriving or traumatic experiences than we know about the effects of subtle variations within the normal range of experience."*

The early childhood years are especially important for personality development. It is during this time that the child commences to test her autonomy. She starts to form the concept of "self" and "ego" and to establish her sexual identification. Increasing physical powers and motor coordination contribute to her feelings of being an individual who can make decisions and succeed at whatever she undertakes.

At the same time, the toddler is beginning to use his newly acquired language skills to further his separation from mother. He begins to say "No." He is asserting his individuality. Although a trying time for many parents, this period is also a challenge to their patience and ingenuity. Hopefully, they can keep in perspective what is going on with their child and recognize that it is a move toward self-sufficiency.

The Emotional Life of Children

The early childhood years are fraught with frustrations and fears, hostility and aggression, jealousy and rivalry. The toddler is entering the overpowering adult world in which people drive, build houses, manage supermarkets, run households. He is beginning to interact with people other than his caregivers. He comes upon objects that are hard to resist—another child's toys, mother's and father's clothing and prized possessions, fragile bric-a-brac, etc. He is becoming part of a family, a culture with rules, restrictions, and codes of behavior. Limited by inexperience and incomplete knowledge of the

*From an article by Robert J. Harmon, M.D., and Leon Yarrow, Ph.D., appearing in *The Parenting Advisor,* Frank Caplan, editor (Garden City, NY: Anchor Press/Doubleday, 1977).

world, he may express his primitive feelings in inappropriate ways. The Toddler-Two has to begin to learn to understand and control his emotions, and behave in ways that are approved by his family and the larger society.

Growth implies a move toward independence and assumes that parents understand and respect the child's right to become self-sufficient. Yet many parents find it hard to recognize such a right. What a very young child means when she says "Help me" is "Help me to help myself." Doing this properly and well is one of the most delicate and important jobs all parents have.

The behavior, emotions, character, and conscience of a child evolve gradually and undergo changes with experience and age. From three to six years, some of the "voice of society" becomes an integral part of each child's makeup. Morals and ethical standards are established by the rewarding feedback of affectionate, consistent parents and other adults and institutions in their lives (nursery school, Sunday school, etc.). Parents "teach" some of the patterns of behavior that constitute character by showing pleasure in their children's adherence to rules; "good" means to follow the rules and "bad" means not to follow them.

Helping Children Deal with Fear

All of us have times of fearfulness and/or anxiety. Since a child's understanding is limited and his imagination vivid, he distorts and magnifies things. Therefore, he has more fears than adults.

Parents need to teach their children that some fears are real and understandable.

In *Understanding Your Child from Birth to Three: A Guide to Your Child's Psychological Development* (New York: Random House, 1973), Joseph Church writes, "The long-range goal is to bring up a child who is neither fearless to the point of foolhardiness, nor so fearful as to be emotionally crippled. Parents are in a position to offer loving assurance and sometimes to encourage the child to explore a feared object, and find out that it is harmless. Isolated fears in a child who generally enjoys life are not anything to be concerned about. All children develop some fears."

Negative Methods That Increase Fears

1. *Fear as a method of discipline.* We are acquainted with the following threats: "If you don't take your medicine, the doctor will have to give you a shot." "If you don't behave, the police officer will come and get you." With such threats, the parents cause the child unnatural dread of persons, things, or occurrences.

2. *Severe punishments.* When parents use harsh punishments and threats as a regular part of their discipline, their child tends to harbor intense anger and a wish for revenge. These feelings trigger fear because they conflict with the child's need to depend upon the parents and to be loved by them.

3. *Excessive expectations.* A child may develop fear of failure when he knows his parents expect too much from him. He may refuse to learn to ride a bicycle or climb to the top of a

jungle gym because he fears his accomplishments will not come up to the standards set by his parents.

4. *Overprotectiveness.* If a child is kept overly dependent upon parents who come to her "rescue" every time and panic whenever she cries, she will lose important opportunities to develop confidence in her own capacities and to overcome any fears she may have.

5. *Overpermissiveness.* Very young children have powerful wishes and desires that they cannot yet control. Sometimes parents make little or no effort to limit the behavior of their children. They give up their position as authorities "to keep the peace" and that causes their offspring to feel out of control, which increases their fears.

Negative Ways of Dealing with Existent Fears

1. *Forcing the child into the feared situation.* When this is done before the child is mature enough to understand the situation and to handle it, it merely increases his fear. We often hear of a father urging his son to fight back when bullied by a neighborhood playmate or forcing him to approach a barking dog. Both are negative approaches.

2. *Ridiculing or punishing a child for being afraid.* Parents may see their child's fear as a sign of weakness and say "A big boy like you shouldn't be afraid of the dark. Even little Mary isn't afraid." Parents may even become angry with their child, which will cause him to deny his fears, but will not help him overcome them.

3. *Constantly ignoring fears.* When parents remain unaware of their child's fears or are indifferent to them, the fears tend to pile up because the child has not received the reassurance she may require to help her understand new things.

What Can Parents Do?

When parents seek to help their child cope with fears, they need above all to have an accepting attitude that enables them to watch, listen, and wait. There is no point in saying "There is nothing to be afraid of" without knowing what is behind the fear. Parents can help their child by:

1. *Explaining the situation.* You can tell your child what is

happening, answer his objections, and give him a clear idea of the events. Children seem to know that things are all right when their parents think so. Parents need to be realistic in explaining every situation. They can say that there is no need to be afraid of the puppy, but it will be difficult to convince the child that "dogs don't do any harm" because this is not always true.

2. *Setting an example of calmness.* For example, you can look at lightning and wait with a smile for the thunder that follows it, thus reassuring your child of the foreseen and natural event.

3. *Encouraging talk about your child's feelings.* You can tell your child that fears are natural and that everyone is afraid of something at some time. You can help your child distinguish between what is real and what is imagined. If a three-year-old thinks there is a bear in the closet, she needs to be shown that there is no bear instead of being told that the parent is going to drive the bear out.

4. *Trying to effect "positive reconditioning" by replacing the feared stimulus with an attractive one.* For instance, you can give your child a cookie or pet his head when he is looking at a dog, gradually bringing him closer to it.

5. *Limiting exposure that can cause fear or threaten danger.* A firm hand on the television switch is needed when a program depicts violence of any sort.

Dealing with Specific Fears

1. *Fear of animals.* Growing up with a pet will help a child come to understand that there is nothing to be afraid of. Watching animals, explaining to him how they live, what they eat, going to the zoo—all these can be of help.

2. *Fears about the body.* You can assume that the doctor's periodic checkups of your child's development will help keep her in good health. Do not be overconcerned about her health and do not be too anxious when she feels a little under par.

3. *Anxiety due to separation.* Always help and encourage your child to do those things that he can and should do by himself. You should tell your child when you have to go out and let him know when you expect to return. Although parents should not surrender to their child's dependence, they need to respect his need for reassurance.

4. *Nightmares.* If nightmares occur frequently, it may mean that the child is wrestling with upsetting feelings. These may stem from her developmental stage or from outside events, such as moving to another house or the birth of a new baby. Usually turning on the light to let your child see that she is in a familiar place is enough to calm her. A night light should prove helpful. You can talk with your child a little to help her forget the frightening dream. If nightmares persist for a long time, your pediatrician's advice can also be useful.

5. *Fear of death.* The very young child's first exposure to death may be seeing some dead insects or a deceased animal. His reaction is calm and casual.

In answer to the question of how parents can cope with their child's fear of death, Dr. Church believes that "The only honest thing you can say is that everybody dies sooner or later, but that the parents have no expectation of dying in the near future . . . and that there is no reason a healthy child like yours shouldn't live a long time."

Building a Healthy Personality

Psychologists generally agree that for children to reach adolescence with healthy personalities they must be taught values and attitudes that will help them grow and be happy in a society.

Bravery

Bravery is a desirable personal and social trait. True bravery, according to Dr. William E. Homan in *Child Sense* (New York: Basic Books, 1969), involves a sense of security at times when one is afraid. A two-year-old cannot understand that the pain she has just experienced from a needle in the doctor's office will go away shortly because she has no sense of time. She knows only that her arm hurts. To belittle the child by saying "Be brave" is to ignore how she feels. What she needs at that moment is comfort and the freedom to cry.

Bravery is the ability to face up to defeat (or success) knowing that others believe in you. A child who has understanding and sympathy will achieve courage by feeling free to venture forth, to explore, and to make mistakes while maintaining self-esteem and social approval.

Sportsmanship and Athletic Prowess

To be a "good sport" is another concept society values. Only after a child learns that he can lose a game and not lose his self-esteem will he want to try again. In our society, the loser is expected to "put on a happy face," to "grin and bear it," to render a "You deserve to win, you played a great game." Becoming a good athlete is another story. Parents often confuse sportsmanship with brilliant athletics. Those who set themselves up as experts in an athletic field only frighten their children, who often feel defeated before they start. If athletics are for fun, then children should be free to play. The emphasis on perfecting an athletic skill is very damaging to the child who prefers other interests or who cannot live up to parental expectations. Psychologists say that many personalities are warped in childhood through failure on the playing field.

Generosity

Observe a group of parents and two-year-olds at a playground. Inevitably you will hear the parental command to "Share your toys!" It is a popular attempt to instill generosity in very young children. Although Toddler-Twos are self-willed and subject to tantrums if they do not have their way, they are also at the imitative stage. Hence, the playground is important as a social setting. By observing other children at play, and playing near them, two-year-olds begin to learn that giving results in receiving. By sharing their toys, they reap praise from their parents and get the loan of someone else's toys. They learn that this is the acceptable way to behave.

A study of generosity in nursery school boys by Eldred Rutherford and Paul Mussen (*Child Development* magazine, September 1968, Vol. 39, No. 3) reveals the power of parental nurturance by sex-typing: a boy's perception of his father and a girl's perception of her mother. Through actual tests of generosity involving the sharing of candy and the acting out of family situations, two hypotheses emerged: (1) generosity is related to identification with the parent who is warm and affectionate. Fathers of generous boys are also perceived as sympathetic and comforting. They are models of altruism and compassion, too. The child interprets these qualities as expressions of generosity; (2) high levels of generosity are related to a strong sense of independence and maturity and an identification with adult behavior. Thus, generosity is part of a pattern of traits that children acquire through imitation of their respective parents.

Self-confidence

Another important trait for survival and happiness in society is self-confidence. Very young children first develop this trait from their parents' evaluation of them. If parents encourage each success, more successes will follow. A pat on the back for a job well done builds self-esteem. As for overconfidence, Dr. Homan says there can be none. The child who appears as a braggart may actually be trying to hide his poor self-image.

DEVELOPMENT OF SELF AND EGO

Three to six is an ideal period for the germination of self and ego, when parents are in the best position to augment their children's sense of self-worth. Children who attain positive self-feelings are better equipped to function comfortably in the larger world than those who do not. It has been found that when children have positive internalized standards, they are less vulnerable to peer pressures.

The concept of oneself includes several different but interdependent facets: body image encompasses the real or imagined image of one's physical self. It also relates to one's perception of one's size and build: "I am too small." "I am too big." "I am too fat." "I am too skinny." Physical performance is another criterion: "I can run fast." "I am strong." "Look at me jump!" Children who have negative feelings about their bodies most often have negative feelings about themselves.

One's social self is determined to a great degree by one's racial, ethnic, and cultural heritage. First parents, then agemates and teachers transmit their standards and expectations that color one's social self. Children who have undergone good physical and social experiences generally have positive feelings about their bodies and their interpersonal relationships.

Yet some children may not develop confidence in their cognitive abilities when they enter school, which may be due either to inadequate stimulation or expectation in the home or preconceived teacher attitudes. (Sometimes a teacher may

have low expectations for minority or less-privileged children.)

The following are some suggestions for building ego and a sense of self-worth in young children:

- Provide consistent, warm, responsive care.
- Exert firm but reasonable discipline.
- Establish schedules that include regularity in eating, napping, and sleeping times to enhance physical and mental health.

- Allow your child to explore in a planned, safe environment.
- Refrain from hovering needlessly over your child.
- Encourage him to learn to be happy by himself.
- Welcome your toddler's participation in household duties.
- Make it possible for your child to do things for herself.
- Allow your toddler to make feasible choices (i.e., select clothing, etc.).
- Respect her desire to carry out her ideas by herself, and to succeed.
- Serve as a model for your child to follow.
- Never discuss strengths or weaknesses in your child's presence.
- Know what to expect—this gives children feelings of security and confidence.

Discipline

The aims of discipline certainly are not to form children into automatons responding mechanically to commands. Rather, discipline should be regarded as a procedure that will enable young children to learn to internalize controls gradually while feeling free to express themselves. A child whose discipline is too strict will feel inhibited in her attempts to express herself for fear of reprisal. At the same time, a child who has had no reasonable limits set may feel anxious about her own omnipotence and may express her need for controls by escalating her negative behavior in attempts to have limits set for her.

During normal development, there are many personality crises that concern parents, most of which usually are transient and seem to resolve themselves in time. Food jags, thumb-sucking, toileting lapses are but a few that are part of normal development. Others, hyperactivity for one, do not seem to pass away with time. Some may require guidance from a pediatrician or other professional to lessen the likelihood of later serious problems.

One of the most widely discussed topics in the field of child behavior covers discipline techniques. Many years of research and study have gone into most professional opinions. Gradually, trial-and-error child-rearing is being replaced by more developmental and humanistic approaches. Especially reassuring is the fact that the experts are in agreement in many important areas concerning the nurturing of good mental health and a sense of responsibility in children. They view discipline as guidance that corrects, molds, strengthens, or perfects. It encompasses the child's ongoing learning of socially useful behavior. Discipline is something you do *for* and *with* your child, not *to* him.

All child-rearing authorities agree that only under the most extraordinary circumstances should a parent spank a child before the age of two-and-a-half. Some recommend no spanking at all. A parent saying "I told you *not* to hit" while administering blows to her child's bottom is incongruous. (However, with older children and in certain situations, other experts believe a good swat on the posterior may be just what is called for.)

A more effective alternative to spanking is to reinforce positive behavior, i.e., to reward appropriate conduct, and to ignore or discourage unsuitable behavior. Praise your child when she does something you approve of or something you have asked her to do. Within this framework, parents need to establish reasonable and clearly defined limits that are understood by their child. Children should not be allowed to harm themselves, hurt other people or pets, or destroy property. Adult language has to be broken down for the very young to simple directives: "Use the crayons only on the paper." "Friends are to play with, not hit."

Controlling the child's environment is another helpful way to promote acceptable behavior. Common examples of this are changing seating arrangements, removing a toy from the table, etc. In addition, some rooms in the house may be made "off limits" to children in consideration of the particular needs of the parents.

THE IMPORTANCE OF PLAY IN EARLY CHILDHOOD*

We believe the power of play to be extraordinary and supremely serious. Play is a child's way of life practically from infancy to his eighth year. The young child plays from early morning until he goes to sleep at night. It is the most natural way for a child to use his capacities, to grow, and to learn many skills. What is it that gives play its exceptional power?

Playtime aids growth. It takes time to grow! A child needs sufficient time to find her place in the culture. In time, she

*Parts of pages 73-78 adapted from *The Power of Play* by Frank and Theresa Caplan (Garden City, NY: Doubleday, 1977).

learns the rudiments of control and responsibility and forms useful habits. Our society is tender with the young child and gives her the playtime to imitate, to explore, to find herself, and to test her ideas.

An important by-product of play is the feeling of power it gives a child, offering soothing relief from the sense of inadequacy and frustration that many children experience as junior members of a well ordered adult society. In play, the child is free from environmental threats. Play reduces the stress of anticipating success or failure.

Play aids learning. We believe, as have many other educators past and present, that an enormous amount of learning takes place during the first six to eight years of a child's life. Learning appears to level off dramatically in the ensuing years. Is this a phenomenon that nature has ordained or is there something in our educational procedures and institutions that has determined it? We think it is the latter. Let us now look at how learning takes place during those formative six to eight years.

The infant lives essentially in a play environment. Little is expected of her except that she thrive and learn to amuse herself. By and large, she accomplishes this by responding well to her nurture and by choosing her own way to play with the people and objects at hand. The infant selects those activities she can manipulate and control to her own satisfaction. Hers is a "self-choice" environment, and her play is voluntary, self-directed, and intensely personal. Therefore it has a high degree of motivation. Because of the self-choice, she builds confidence in her own powers.

Young children usually choose to play in an unstructured situation since it offers them the greatest freedom to explore and enjoy. There is no "right way" to use blocks, paint, or clay, for example, and there is no "right way" to draw. Children select those activities in which they are most likely to succeed, and the likelihood of accomplishment is reinforced by the fact that at an early age, and in a play situation, parents are unlikely to criticize their young children. Few parents would say to a very young child, "Johnny, that's not the way to draw a cat." More likely they would say, "Johnny, what a lovely picture!"

Play is investigative. Because the very young child lacks sufficient imagery to clarify his thoughts, he must constantly seek and find out. He engages in countless "doing" ac-

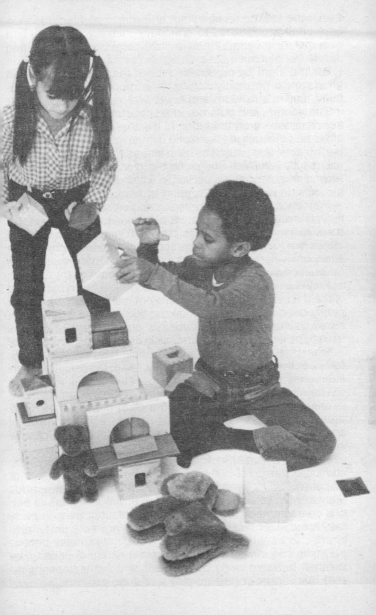

tivities—handling, classifying, ordering, matching, measuring—all of which serve to enrich his thinking.

In the early years of play a child learns by trial and error, which is one of the most exciting and satisfying ways to learn. Often the "right" approach is revealed through the child's own efforts and is not rigidly dictated by someone else. Early childhood play is a random and rewarding learning process.

The young child puts her imagination to work for her and superimposes it on the fabric of the real world. She tries out ideas and rearranges her world by manipulating fantasy people, objects, and situations. She shares her ideas with others; she is fully involved. She is the decision maker; the inventor. Play is an autonomous pursuit in which the child assimilates the outside world to the support of her ego.

Play encourages deep interest and close attention. A normal child can play for hours. He becomes totally involved. He tears himself away from his play with great effort. No one forces him to play; rather, he responds to free interactions with a responsive environment. It is this intensity that prepares him for the concentration that is basic to all learning.

Play is a voluntary activity. In her play world, the young child is the decision-maker and the play-master. There are no superimposed directions to follow, no rigid rules to which to adhere. Ultimately, in the academic environment, a child is usually called upon to perform according to set patterns. The teacher does the directing, and the child has no choice but to follow. In the play world, on the other hand, the sensitive adult intervenes tactfully, if at all.

The more thoughtfully and flexibly organized the play environment, the more confident the child becomes. His outgrowth of drive and self-esteem is the result of years of engrossing, satisfying play. Like nothing else, play develops a child's ego as it builds his will power.

Play offers a child freedom of action. In her play world, the child can carry on trial-and-error activities without fear of ridicule or failing. Free from well-meaning but restrictive adult interference, she can pretend and role-play any adult or animal character, any real or imaginary situation. Play and fantasy are a vital need of childhood. Every normal child likes to pretend to be a giant, a lion, or a train. In her make-believe play, she can inspire terror and gain a sense of power. The contrast between her make-believe and earnestness is so fluid that a child considers play a real-life experience.

Play provides an imaginary world a child can master. Every child is born with a desire to affect his environment. In a well-planned play world in which the real world has been brought down to manageable size via suitable playthings, the child can manipulate it to suit his own whims. Play gives a child the feeling of his own worth. In the ideal play setting a child can initiate an action or oppose it. He can be the subject or the object. There is freedom of choice and action, an absence of boundaries and restrictions that he cannot be granted in the adult world.

Play provides a base for language building. The very early years are nonverbal years. Words come only from a foundation of play experiences, from encounters with people, objects, and events that comprise the world.

Play has unique power for building interpersonal relations. It provides contacts with others without demanding inappropriate adjustments. Play fosters group life since it often requires more than one child to reenact home and community life situations. Through such play, a child practices interpersonal relationships with her equals and learns consideration as well as techniques of leadership.

Spontaneous dramatization, role-playing, doll play, and disguises enable a child to work out interpersonal relations, personality difficulties, and emotional disturbances. It takes years of play with his varied interpersonal relationships to help a child become a social human being.

Play offers opportunities for mastery of the physical self. Young children relish play that gives them facility in locomotion and permits the maximum use of energy. They learn bodily control: running, jumping, skipping, pushing, pulling, hopping, climbing, balancing, throwing, and keeping up with one's own age group. The discovery of spatial relations, the many patterns in space made by a moving body, is a fundamental concept. Laterality and directionality—left and right, up and down, behind and in front—are relationships incorporated in every physical play program.

Play is a way of learning adult roles. In early imitative play children recreate the behavior, attitudes, and language of the important adults in their lives. Play may be considered a rehearsal for eventual participation in adult life.

Play is vitalizing. The act of play has important neurophysiological effects on children as well as adults. Play is a diversion from routines, from cultural demands and pursuits.

For a period of time, play permits one to reverse one's behavior and do the opposite of what one has been doing. It is an "upside-downing of behavior," as Professor Edward Norbeck of Rice University terms it, "during which the social hierarchy is inverted and customary rules of conduct are suspended." These rites of reversal turn out to be important safety valves for the release of feelings of aggression, disapproval of authority, and resolving other conflicts.

Play enables children to learn and polish physical, mental, social, and emotional skills. Through imaginative play young children come to terms with many of the fears and hurts to which they are vulnerable. They appear to heal themselves of emotional upsets through their play. If children did not play, they could not thrive.

If play has such positive power, why is it not valued in today's life schema? We have been conditioned to think of "play" and "work" as completely antithetical. Due to the puritan ethic of North American adults, play is placed at one end of the value scale and learning and work at the other. Educators relegate all play to the preschool period and all work to the primary and secondary school years. A sharp line is drawn between kindergarten and first grade. The demands of formal academic training (reading, writing, and arithmetic) remove all semblance of free choice, self-direction, exploration, and self-discovery that are inherent in a free-play environment in the home, nursery school, and kindergarten. The school replaces the environment of early childhood play with a setting the child can no longer control. Soon the child loses interest, and ceases to be responsive to academic learning.

Many childhood educators believe that by eight years of age, the end of the most intense period of play, a child's personality, creativity, and academic motivation are 80 percent accomplished; that the subsequent years enlarge the information base, but do little to increase personal commitment or interest in learning. In short, the early childhood years are most important ones for intellectual growth even though many people erroneously consider them a time of *waiting for education to begin.*

Parents' and Teachers' Roles in Pretend Play

Parents and teachers generally encourage the fantasy play of young children. They build playhouses or buy heavy cardboard models. They make available the paraphernalia that encourages make-believe play, including jewelry, all kinds of hats, ribbons, ties, scarves, adult shoes, handbags, whistles, keys, assorted costumes, and dress-up accessories.

Fantasy play is further enhanced by adult stimulation: playing at the seashore; exploring a forest; riding in a bus, car, train, or airplane; visiting the community post office, bank, bread factory, shoe repair shop. Children's interviews with community workers (the police officer, firefighter, boat captain, garbage collector) also provide invaluable experiences.

"Can Make-Believe Be Dangerous to Mental Health?"

In *Partners in Play* (New York: Harper & Row, 1977), Dorothy G. Singer and Jerome L. Singer write, "Some parents may worry that make-believe will confuse their children's ability to distinguish between reality and fantasy, or encourage them to withdraw emotionally. We have very little evidence that this ever occurs. However, there are a few dramatic cases described in the psychiatric literature that involve children who have spent an excessive amount of time playing fantasy games or developing imaginary kingdoms . . .

"We must, therefore, avoid any circumstances in which a child who learns imaginative play will find it so appealing as to discourage real encounters with other children. Fortunately, excessive withdrawal into fantasy is extremely rare . . .

"For the parent or teacher who is concerned about how much fantasy life is too much, the answer is relatively simple. If a child has withdrawn so completely into the world of make-believe that the learning of simple skills suffers drastically, there is no companionship at all with other children . . . then there is obvious reason for concern. . . . But the risk of such developments is far slighter than the much greater risk to children who fail to make sufficient use of their capacity for imagination."

Maria W. Piers and Genevieve M. Landau, in *The Gift of*

Play and Why Young Children Cannot Thrive Without It (New York: Walker and Co., 1980), write that "Fantasy play includes more than making up situations and roles to act out, or playing with an imaginary friend. It also includes skits and games based on stories that have been read to the child or those he or she makes up . . . The stories chosen and the roles children assign to themselves tell us a great deal about the concerns of the youngsters at play—and about the times we live in."

Ages and Stages in Play

Children at each age have to cope with changing and maturing sensory, motor, social, mental, and emotional powers. As they develop, they have a driving desire and need to practice their skills in an ameliorating milieu of play and challenge. Piaget divided play into three ages and stages:

• Sensorimotor play that takes place during the first two years when a child is busy acquiring control over his bodily

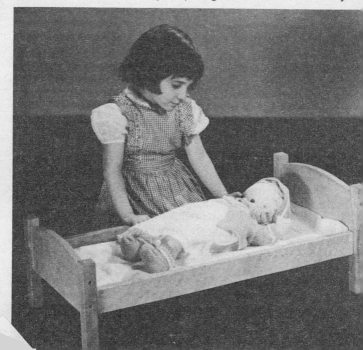

movements, learning to coordinate actions with perceptions of their effects ("When I pull this string, I make the feet and arms of a jumping jack move"). Play at this stage consists of repeating and varying physical movements. The baby derives pleasure from mastering motor skills and experimenting with touch, sight, sound, etc. He delights in causing events to happen. He is actively learning "cause and effect."

• Pretend or symbolic play occurring between two and six years when the child uses pretend play, symbols, or objects to represent reality. Wooden cylinders are made to represent soldiers or other people; she moves them about to make them march or climb up to the roof of one of her block constructions. Dolls are fed, washed, "disciplined," and put to bed. Sand is made into pies to be "eaten." This is the type of imaginative sociodramatic play that one finds in the nursery school and kindergarten.

• Play involving games with rules that encompass both competition and teamwork. This type of play starts in elementary school beyond the eighth year (the third and fourth grades) when children are greatly involved with their peers.

Group Games

Usually when children reach about seven years of age, they begin to participate in a form of peer group play that entails child-determined organization, rules, leadership, and boundaries.

Games that require some physical dexterity include marbles, darts, ring toss, jackstraws, tiddlywinks, and pick-up sticks. All are good social games because two or more children are needed to play and enjoy them. Temporary defeat is an acceptable part of the games because otherwise the players could not continue to take turns, and each game would bog down. (As children approach their teens, they want to engage in highly organized team play. At this time, most are better able to think of the good of the group and not merely their own desires. So it is that children "graduate" from their early unorganized, rough-and-tumble physical games to such rigidly organized sports activities as baseball, hockey, basketball, football, volleyball, soccer, and team swimming.)

The young child plays group games with complete disregard of the rules. In fact, there is a constant "stretching" and rearrangement of the rules of a game to suit the whims or the lack of skill of most young players. With older children, however, disregarding the rules is frowned upon and even considered cheating. Of course, children differ broadly in the degree of their interest in group sports, and some who lack experience and practice in motor skills often become onlookers instead of active participants.

Children are usually most cooperative when engaged in satisfying play together. They can turn rivalries into make-believe play instead of open conflicts. Social learning takes place in relation to the resolution of conflicts as well as in cooperative play. While adult behavior, criticism, and sugges-tions serve as part of the basis for the learning of sociality in the young child, the subtleties of sharing, playing, or working together, tolerance of diverse personalities, and agreeable participation in group life come from a long period of early practice in which all kinds of social encounters and obstacles are met and resolved. No period offers more opportunities for practice in social living than the first ten years of life.

Children become increasingly able to take the perspective of other persons (pretend play) and interpret their actions in different situations (role-playing). They move gradually from being "loners" in their play to interacting with others.

Sociodramatic play is often carried on alone. In this play children build a fantasy world for themselves and pretend to be other people or other things. In taking the part of another character, the child tries to speak, move, think, and perhaps even dress as he thinks the character does. Children learn about other people, things, and happenings during the course of this type of play. When they recreate a situation in their dramatic play, they seem to be paying closer attention to what they see than they would otherwise.

Young children often have misconceptions which they re-veal in the course of their dramatic play. Parents and teachers can then offer corrections that sharpen the children's observa-tions and thinking.

Social Play

During the early childhood years, children show interest in each other and enjoy playing near one another. Parents claim that one of the reasons they send their children to nursery school is that "they need playmates." Generally, two-year-olds merely watch others, and although they occasionally cooperate, for the most part they carry on *parallel play*—that is, they engage in the same activity as another child, but in a solitary fashion. They get satisfaction in just being near each other.

Although two-year-olds are not gentle with each other, they really do not wish to hurt their agemates. Actually, they desire to learn more about their characteristics. ("How do they sound when they talk?" "Will they cry if I pull their hair?")

Because a two-year-old is still clumsy and egocentric, he may unintentionally walk into the play construction of a neighbor and upset him. This behavior is termed "egocentric" because children this age cannot recognize people and things as "others" or outside of themselves. With more experience, more encounters, and more language ability, three-year-olds learn how to play together, talk about what they are building with their blocks, or why they are putting their dolls to bed. Soon they are able to recruit a "mother" and a "baby" to play out a scenario that is in their minds. Groups of two and three children playing together are typical of three- to six-year-olds.

During the beginning period of group play, younger children move in and out of the group without changing the theme of the play. However, as they reach four to six years, the play group is more stable, and its size may expand to five or six children. Fighting over toys decreases as children learn to take turns. Give and take is practiced. Leadership is shared, but usually the child who has good play ideas and knows how to get things going is the leader. Friendships are formed. Although quarreling, aggression, and hostility may grow, this behavior is due to the fact that the social play becomes more complex. Most children learn how to settle their quarrels by themselves.

Selecting Play Materials for the Early Childhood Years

The selection of play materials should never be haphazard or casual. A good toy leaves room for the free exercise of a child's imagination and can be used in many different ways. It is handsome in shape and color, is good to touch, beautiful in line, and interesting in texture. It is sturdy and will take heavy use. A good toy can fit into varied play settings as dictated by a child's fancies. It quickens curiosity and invention as it lets the child find things out for herself. A balanced assortment of good playthings and play equipment should be chosen for the sensory experiences they can offer for manipulative and constructive purposes—unstructured materials for creative expression, equipment for homemaking play, dramatic play, and outdoor physical activity.

Toddler-Twos live dangerously in their press for bigness. Therefore, parents and toy manufacturers need to guard against providing them with playground equipment they cannot reasonably manage. Slides should not be too high because great heights do not deter the toddler and he will even slide down head first! Playground equipment must be well designed, well constructed, and suitably scaled to the abilities and limitations of their users. Some concerned toy manufacturers are now producing sturdy, safe, toddler versions of large outdoor equipment in the form of a rocky boat, climb-around, jungle gym, low slide, etc. These items look so much like the older children's models that two- and three-year-olds conceive of them as being equal to what the "big boys" and "big girls" use. The rocky boat, a long-time nursery school favorite, provides rocking motion to enthrall one to four small children when turned on one of its sides; turned on its other side, a small child can run up the stairs to a raised platform and then scamper down.

As soon as he is able to climb stairs, a child enjoys sliding down a stairway slide. The toddler's gym has steps, a slide, and a hiding area under its platform. Toddlers express their burgeoning expansiveness by driving large ride 'em trucks, trains, oversized furry animals, and carriages on free-wheeling casters. Casters are most successful because toddlers can make their vehicles go where they want them to. As they scoot about on these, foot and leg muscles are being exercised and strengthened. Two- to four-year-olds adore the kiddy car and later the tricycle. Seeing how fast he can go, how sharply he can turn, how to bring his trike to an abrupt halt— these are some of the exciting physical experiences every child wants and should have.

Mechanical toys should be avoided for young children because they are destructive of play: the toy does everything while the child sits passively by. Also, all too often, fragile wind-up toys break in a youngster's hands. This is not only frustrating; it fills her with feelings of wrongdoing and guilt.

We especially like the way Joseph Lee put it in his book *Play in Education* (New York: Macmillan, 1919): "Toys, not fiz-jigs; it is the child's own achievement, not that of the clever man who made the toy, that counts. A toy with very small children is chiefly a peg to hang imagination on. It is the child's alter ego, to which he assigns the parts that he cannot conveniently assume himself. Literal resemblance to their originals is the last thing he requires in his subordinates. An oblong block will be successively a cow, a sofa, a railway train, and will discharge each part with perfect satisfaction to its impresario. Too much realism is indeed a disadvantage."

The very young child's patterns of action come from a host of play activities that are stimulated by materials in the outdoor and indoor environment. Indoors, they can be the aluminum or pliant plastic measuring cups, spoons, and nesting bowls found in the average kitchen. However, the home kitchen does not boast enough safe, manipulative objects that will permit a young child to follow the dictates of his curiosity. Young children require manifold experiences in putting things in order of size, and classifying objects by shape, texture, and sound.

Likewise, they need to learn to apprehend perspective, scale, weight, quantity relations, space, cause-and-effect actions, sound discrimination, and so on. It is because many of these ideas can be structured into playful experiences that modern designers have been creating toys that incorporate such concepts.

Criteria for the Choice of Toys

"Toys should appeal to sensorimotor and intellectual needs. They should catch and hold the child's attention, provide repetition, and stimulate new kinds of exploration. They should have strong primary and secondary colors so that the child can learn their names, and come in a variety of sizes so the child can learn the meaning of *big, little, medium-sized*—and even *tiny, huge, larger, smallest.* There should be many shapes among them: squares, circles, triangles, oblongs.

"There should be opportunities for sorting parts by many kinds of classifications: color, size, shape, by what they can do. The toys should be explored for the kinds of sounds they make, and for how they feel. The child's attempts to devise unconventional ways of playing with a particular toy should be encouraged."*

Block Play

We cannot overemphasize that building blocks are the finest home and school play material for children from two up to seven years and even beyond. Hardwood unit building blocks are sturdy and stable. They offer a great variety of play possibilities and values. Children who have been made fearful by parents who want them to be too careful with things are not afraid to play with blocks. Block play helps children believe in themselves. It bolsters their self-image because they can control the structures they create.

At first, Toddler-Twos carry blocks. Then they stack them or lay them out on the floor. Later they enjoy knocking down their simple piling of blocks. Experienced three- and four-year-old block builders erect detailed structures. Fives start reproducing the world and bring their constructions to life with such

*From *Play: Its Role in Development and Evolution,* edited by Jerome S. Bruner, Alison Jolly, and Kathy Sylra (New York: Basic Books, 1976).

supplementary materials as cars, boats, trains, planes, toy people, and play animals in appropriate scale. Sixes and Sevens build even more complicated layouts. They use their building as a background for the information they garner about community living. Inasmuch as blocks can be used in countless ways, the child's interest usually remains keen and active over a long period of time.

In an article entitled "Play Boys and Girls," originally published in the magazine *Two to Six* in 1949 (and reissued in 1965 as a leaflet by the Bank Street College of Education in New York City), nursery school educator Jessie Stanton wrote, "It is easy to expect block play to bring finished results too soon. A two-and-a-half-year-old with his limited knowledge of the world, his awkward use of his hands, his ignorance of the law of gravity does not have much to show from his block play. By the time he is four or so he will know the relationship between store and goods, fire engine and fire house, boat and dock. Then when he has learned to use his hands cleverly by handling, playing, eating, and dressing, he may spend as much as an hour in concentrated block play and come up with something pretty fine!"

Homemaking Play

Child-size equipment is especially needed in the homemaking play corner where children enthusiastically imitate real home-life situations. Housekeeping is a natural play activity that both little boys and girls enjoy. They take turns being the mother or father, the baby, nurse, or visitor. They cook food and care for their babies. They clean the house and wash and iron the doll clothes. Domestic play activity provides children with socially accepted outlets for expressing their aggressive feelings, for "letting off steam." A child in a housekeeping game can punish other children in a manner that would not be tolerated outside the play setting.

Manipulative toys promote manual dexterity while reinforcing self-image. The nursery school child has fairly good control of her large muscles. As she learns how to control her small muscles, she likes to test her developing dexterity with large Masonite sewing cards, wood and metal nut-and-bolt construction sets, a lacing boot, postal station, large colored beads to string, a landscape pegboard, color cone, parquetry blocks, Tinkertoys, snap blocks, jigsaw puzzles, and a woodworking bench with good tools. Manipulation, experimentation, and functional construction are the stages through which

children pass as they handle wood and nails. Imaginative ideas as well as paper, cloth, wood, and metal collage materials motivate creative construction projects. Besides a finished product, each participating child's feeling of personal worth is strengthened by the use of such play material.

Water play has irresistible fascination for young children. Water is one of the few natural substances still available for exploration by city children. It permits a great variety of activities and experimentation: immersing objects, pouring, blowing bubbles, splashing to produce movement, etc. The home, the nursery school, and the kindergarten should make greater and more frequent provision for free play with water.

Sand is another basic material all children (and especially the emotionally disturbed) deeply enjoy. Cups and spoons of various sizes, sieves and sifters, and molds of all kinds heighten the play and pleasure. A child at the beach will play contentedly for hours. Why? Because sand and water are natural, unstructured substances with which a child can do anything his imagination and desire dictate. Most children are completely at ease in a sand-and-water milieu. Child psychologists make use of both to soothe disturbed children during play therapy sessions.

Doll play sparks role-playing and promotes understanding of others. Doll play goes back to the beginning of recorded history. An eighteen-month-old may grab a doll by one leg, drag it along the floor, hug it, and then summarily drop it on the floor and leave it there. The Toddler-Two will pick up a doll with more care. He may put the doll in a doll bed and cover it to keep it warm. The three-year-old may dress and undress the doll and even talk to it. The four-year-old begins playing with the doll dramatically—calling a doctor to the bedside, taking the doll's temperature. The five-year-old's doll play can be an involved project that is carried over imaginatively from one day to the next.

According to Piaget, doll play not only shows the maternal attitudes of the child, it also serves as an opportunity for the child to relive her own life symbolically in order to more easily assimilate its various aspects, to resolve conflicts, and to try to realize her unsatisfied desires vicariously. Happy or unpleasant events in a child's life are often exposed in her doll play, as well as her homemaking and dramatic activities.

Little boys and girls enjoy pushing a doll carriage in the nursery school. Caring for a baby doll satisfies the need to act

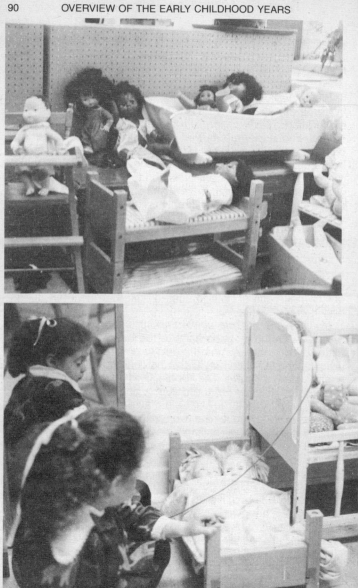

out the mother and father roles. For this primeval and imaginative play there are all kinds of sturdy and appealing dolls, doll carriages, high chairs, rockers, cradles, and beds.

All children need assorted art materials so they may express themselves freely. Painting is a prime medium whereby a child's imagination is permitted full sway. The years between two and four, when a child's painting is least representational, and most directly reflects his playful responses to the raw art materials, are especially appropriate for painting as a purely expressive medium. Painting appears to have its greatest significance for supporting self-image when the child's products seem to have their least apparent meaning. The child should always paint for the fun of it rather than to please others.

In the very beginning, it is much more important for the

young child to enjoy painting than to learn its techniques or to have to adhere rigidly to rules about cleanliness and order. The mother and then the teacher need to value his efforts and show their sincere appreciation for his finished paintings.

Young children use paints and crayons to communicate the experiences and preoccupations they are unable to express in words. When a child first attempts to draw, she goes through an exploratory stage. As she acquires some manual control, she attempts to make designs. At about three-and-a-half to four, she begins to make representational drawings. The younger the child, the more spontaneous and direct is her art work. It is as natural for children to paint and draw as it is for them to walk and talk. Nonverbal children especially express their innermost feelings in their drawings and paintings— which are more elemental than spoken or written words because they are more immediate and straightforward.

An adjustable easel, good poster paints, assorted long-handled, flat bristle brushes, large sheets of paper, a smock, finger paint materials, paste, scissors, construction paper, and large crayons are a child's surest passport to the fascinating world of free art expression. A wall board on which his finished drawings and paintings can be displayed enables parents to tell their child concretely that his efforts and products are appreciated. Nevertheless, at all times parents need to steer clear of prizing a child's talents over the child himself!

Clay is another unstructured material that lends itself to creativity and ego building. The very young child regards clay only as a means for immediate sensory investigation and fun. Gradually it becomes a raw material out of which she finds she can make something else. Nursery schools and kindergartens provide moist clay because children can work it easily. After a piece dries out thoroughly, if she so desires, the child can decorate it with poster paint.

HEALTH, SELF-HELP, AND ROUTINES IN THE EARLY CHILDHOOD YEARS

The twenty-fifth to seventy-second months are all-important for establishing good health, self-help, and eating patterns because habits formed during this time are apt to persist. A regular schedule needs to be set up for washing, toileting, eating, sleeping, playtime, etc. Accustomed regularity encourages children to accept routines without too much dawdling or unhappy encounters. Parents and early childhood educators need to understand the tempo of young children, and provide unpressured regularity for managing their daily routines.

Feeding, Nutrition, and Eating Habits

The years between two and six are a prime period for establishing good eating habits and healthful standards of nutrition. Unfortunately, it appears to be the span of time when eating problems often begin. With body growth slowing down, appetites are reduced. Parents begin to worry when they see their child refusing or toying with food. Instead of being pleasant family affairs, mealtimes become disagreeable encounters during which the child practices his autonomy. The child becomes picky and choosy about what he will or will not eat. How parents handle this problem will affect the child's ego as well as his health.

Even though the child's eating capacity is reduced, her growth needs continue to be demanding. Therefore, parents should waste no time in establishing high nutritional standards and sensible eating habits. A three-meals-a-day routine, with casual morning and afternoon snacks that contain a balance of carbohydrates and proteins, minerals, and vitamins, and short on sugar and salt, should be followed. Junk foods with their empty calories must be avoided; also, foods prepared with preservatives, artificial flavors, and coloring. Young children can learn to enjoy raw vegetables and foods prepared with little or no salt and sugar content. Wholesome food can be attractive to look at and enjoyable to the palate.

Two, three, and four are the best years for developing food tastes and a zest for eating. Parents need to try not to overload the plates of their children. "The sight of too big a helping often seems to make children less eager to eat," writes Dr. Richard H. Granger in the 1974 edition of *Your Child From One to Six* (Washington, D.C.: H.E.W., Children's Bureau). "They do better if they are offered small portions and are allowed to ask for more if they want it. How much the child eats varies from day to day and week to week depending on a number of things like the child's health, activity, and even the weather."

Do not get frantic if your child goes on food jags and insists on the same food at every meal, every day—for example, peanut butter sandwiches.

Children are not addicted to sweets at birth. If started early enough, your child will like unsugared and unsalted foods, and prefer their natural goodness. Children develop a taste for sweets because adults teach them to do so. After all, most of the adults in their lives prefer their foods sweetened or salted. Sometimes parents use sweets as a bribe, which makes children regard sweets as something special. Of course, no food should ever be used as a reward or a punishment.

Mealtime should be a time for bringing the family together for nourishment and providing children with opportunities for exploring new food tastes and textures, for socializing, for learning to use tableware, and practicing manners.

Of course, the parents of very young children have to live through a period of messy eaters, but children who are encouraged to improve their eating skills will learn to feed themselves earlier.

Many pediatricians believe that the idea of food allergies has been greatly overstated; that most children can eat almost all foods without trouble. It seems that even such serious problems as asthma and eczema are rarely related to food allergies. If possible, encourage your children to take a tiny taste of everything you prepare. However, if he is violently opposed to a given food, do not make an issue of his rejection. After a reasonable period of time, remove the food. You can try to present it at a later time.

According to Dr. Myron Winick, director of the Institute of Human Nutrition at Columbia-Presbyterian Medical Center in New York City, infant obesity is much worse than obesity in later life. Dr. Winick is one of the leading experts in childhood nutrition who maintains that the years from two to six are critical ones for parents to set patterns of nutritious eating that will permanently affect the lives of their children. This probably is the last stretch of time during which parents have some control over what their children eat. Dr. Winick cautions that parents cannot expect their children to develop good eating habits unless the eating habits of the whole family are good.

Of course, a good diet will guarantee sufficient calories to insure a normal rate of growth and to supply the energy the body needs. Too few calories result in malnutrition; too many lead to excess fat storage and obesity. In *Growing Up Healthy: A Parent's Guide to Good Nutrition* (New York: William Morrow and Co., 1982), Dr. Winick writes, "There are no absolute rules for the exact number of calories required, as needs vary with age, sex, body build, activity, and with individual metabolism. . . . Any table of average caloric requirements should be viewed as an approximation and then fine-tuned for each individual."

The average one- through three-year-old requires 1300 kilocalories; the average four- through six-year-old requires 1700 kilocalories. (A kilocalorie is the amount of heat required to raise one kilogram of water one degree.) The amount of kilocalories must be apportioned into proper amounts of carbohydrates, proteins, and fats. Federal government and other nutrition experts agree that most North Americans consume too much fat and too little carbohydrates. They recommend a decrease in the amount of total fat and saturated fat consumed and an increase in the consumption of complex carbohydrates in the form of grains and grain products. This means eating less meat, fewer eggs, and smaller quantities of dairy products. More poultry, fish, and other sources of protein should be consumed.

Dr. Winick recommends that parents use the needs of their growing Toddler-Twos to change the whole family's eating habits. He urges moderation: replacing butter with margarine; eating an egg or two no more than two or three times a week; using lean cuts of meat (limiting the consumption of pork, beef, and other fatty meats); choosing rice or a baked potato instead of french fries. Even snacks can be changed to meet proper nutritional goals: fresh fruit instead of cake or cookies; raisins instead of candy, etc. (An ice cream cone contains 175 calories, a banana or pear 100, and an apple only 80 calories.)

If you did not curtail the amount of salt and sugar in your infant's diet, now is the time to begin. Too much salt is harmful to children and adults alike. Salt should not be added to foods at the table. Pickled foods should be avoided (except for a rare treat). High salt intake can contribute to the development of hypertension (high blood pressure), which is one of the major killer diseases in the Western world.

Sugar is overabundant in our food supply: baked goods, desserts, many processed foods, salad dressings, even canned soups contain it. Sugar can add up in calories without your being aware of it. Curtailing sugar in your family's diet will require more careful planning of meals; controlling consumption of "empty" calories by making your own desserts; encouraging your family to try new foods that you prepare with limited sugar content.

Proper nutrition for the whole family can be ensured with a wide variety of nourishing foods, in many different combinations, if a few basic principles of meal planning and preparation are kept in mind. Eating a variety of foods is especially important in ensuring an adequate supply of vitamins and minerals.

Childhood Obesity

Dr. Winick believes that "Overfeeding during infancy or childhood will result in the production of *too many* fat cells. By contrast, the adult who overeats develops obesity characterized by a normal number of fat cells that are *too large.* Since the total number of fat cells is determined during childhood, a child with too many fat cells will become an adult with too many fat cells. When an adult loses weight, it is the size of the fat cells that is reduced, not the number . . . It is much easier to *prevent* a child from becoming obese than it is to treat the already obese child."

Sleeping Needs

Sleep is a protective function which permits the repair and recovery of tissues after activity. Living and learning are more positive when one has sufficient sleep and rest. Adequate sleep and regular rest periods are essential for active two- to six-year-olds. (A short midmorning and/or afternoon nap are still a good idea for this age group.) This age level sleeps an average of eleven out of twenty-four hours. It is difficult to judge how much sleep is enough. Most parents make their own decisions by how cheerful their children are, whether they can get up easily in the morning, how actively they play, their posture, skin color, etc. It has been found that a specified bedtime and a regular, pleasant ritual for going to sleep help considerably.

Children who are engaged in a full day of exciting physical activity sometimes find it difficult to accept the notion of going to sleep. They resist bedtime by making demands: a drink of water, another hug, "I go to the bathroom." When parents realize that such requests are delaying tactics, they can shorten and simplify the bedtime ritual by anticipating as many of the demands as possible: have the favorite stuffed toy in bed, provide the final drink of water, suggest that she go to the toilet before being tucked in, etc. After a good-night kiss and a firm "Good-night," a child may call out a few more times, but getting no response, she is likely to give up and go to sleep.

Rituals are part and parcel of the life of three- and four-year-olds. What you need to do is to establish in your child's mind that going to bed is as inevitable as the "setting of the sun."

Masturbation and thumb-sucking are sometimes present during sleep periods. Such behaviors are temporary and normal, and should be regarded as such.

Control of the Sphincter Muscles

Voluntary control of the sphincter muscles that govern elimination of feces and urine does not take place until about the eighteenth month, and more often not until well into the twenty-fourth to twenty-eighth month. Making demands before muscles and nerves are fully developed places undue stress on the child. Freud and other psychoanalysts claim that punishment and other guilt-inducing behavior may lead to eventual personality problems for the child.

We prefer to use the term "toilet learning" to "toilet training" to describe the period during which a child gains control of certain bodily functions in a way that is comfortable and makes sense to the child. Toileting is not and should not be treated as a disciplinary process, nor become a struggle between parent and child. We think that the expression "toilet training" implies that the training is something done *to* a child. In reality, achieving elimination control should be something a child is permitted to learn herself, without any coercion, but with some helpful direction from the parents.

No one can set forth the exact time when *your* child will be ready for toilet learning. However, there are certain maturation points that will indicate he has acquired the necessary readiness to achieve the complicated bowel and bladder control without undue stress. Watch for the following indicators:

• *Muscle control.* There are special muscles, like small valves, that control the opening and closing of the outlets of the bladder and the bowels. Children must be able to operate these muscles in unison with the larger abdominal muscles to eliminate properly. Children do not have such control until they are well into their second year of life, usually several months after they are walking.

• *Communication.* Your child must be able to tell you either with gestures or words, or some other way, that he wants to go to the bathroom. Obviously, he needs your help in undressing and getting up on the toilet seat.

• *Desire.* The Toddler-Two must *want* to learn to function in the toilet. Whereas parents may want to rid themselves of messy diapers, toddlers find nothing offensive in their use. Children must show an overpowering desire to imitate family members in using the toilet or readiness for a playgroup or nursery school, at which being dry is often a prerequisite for admission.

Some parents want to start the toilet learning process long before their child is ready. Starting too early can be a waste of time and create needless tension and wrangling. Some parents can "read" their child's need to go, and get their child on the toilet seat at just the right moment. However, such luck is not consistent or reliable—and in any case reflects the parents' and not the child's controlling impulse.

Getting the right equipment that both child and parent are

comfortable with is an important part of the learning process. Some prefer a potty chair that sits on the floor; others like a child's seat that fits over the regular toilet. Each has its drawbacks and good points. A child can use the potty chair without adult help and does not have to worry about falling. However, it must be emptied and cleaned after each use. The toilet seat may be more convenient, but a child needs help getting onto it. Many parents prefer a child's toilet seat that has arm supports and a footrest.

Of course, when your child seems ready, you will have to explain the procedure in simple terms, and express confidence in your child's ability to use the potty or child-sized toilet seat. You need to assure your toddler that you are available to help, not to force him. Many experts think that most parents show too much anxiety about toilet learning and that children normally learn to use the toilet without any effort on their parents' part. Most two-and-a-half to three-year-old toddlers become uncomfortable when wet or soiled, and want to be changed. They prefer wearing training pants to the diapers of their babyhood.

Patience and self-control on the part of parents are requirements for any toilet learning procedure. Forcing the child to sit on the toilet seat and perform before her sphincter muscles are in control can only create a warlike atmosphere. (Remember, too, that physical illness can cause relapses.)

Most pediatricians think it is best to begin toilet learning at around twenty-four months. By that age, children are aware of a bowel movement coming, or of a full bladder. Many know how to hold back if necessary. Toddler-Twos begin to want to be well groomed and wear neat, clean clothes, which appear to be additional signals of readiness for toilet learning.

Dr. T. Berry Brazelton, Boston pediatrician and author, in a study of 1,170 of his own patients (small children who started "training" at 24 to 30 months), reported that the average age for complete daytime control was 28.5 months; average age for nighttime control was 33.3 months. Girls gained nighttime control almost 2½ months sooner than boys.

Unfortunately, some mothers feel they cannot wait this long and so place their child on the toilet seat at anywhere from 8 to 15 months. Many very young children in the United States would be better off if their parents were less concerned about this normal functioning.

Enuresis

Persistent bed-wetting beyond the age when most children have learned control is called *enuresis.* It can refer either to bed-wetting which has never ceased or to bed-wetting that occurs after the child has achieved control. This may be due to a physical or psychological reason. Hence, a checkup by a doctor is often advisable.

When uncontrolled bowel movements or daytime or nocturnal wetting are a problem (especially in the handling of four- or five-year-olds), try to be casual and optimistic. Tell your child that you know he will do better someday. Do not scold your child. What your child needs most from you at this time is assurance of your faith in his ultimate control.

Illness and Accidents

Promoting health and keeping the home clean and safe are demanding jobs for the parents of young children. The twenty-fifth to seventy-second months of life are the peak period for childhood illnesses. In addition, accidents (via motor vehicles, drowning, falls, burning, firearms, and poisons) kill more young children than any individual disease.

When young children begin to get around, they come in contact with many poisons. According to a Metropolitan Life

Insurance study, about 25 percent of the annual deaths from accidental poisoning in the United States were deaths of children between one and four years of age. Cautioning a child verbally is not enough; poisons must be removed from all areas to which the child has access.

Very young children are susceptible to many contagious diseases because of their contact with agemates in playgroups, day-care centers, or nursery schools. Colds, gastrointestinal infections, and respiratory illnesses are rampant. Fortunately, most of the serious communicable diseases are preventable through immunization and good home hygiene.

Parents need to be prepared to care for the sick child at home. They can provide comfort and sympathy at home or in the hospital. Despite improvements in hospital care, much still needs to be done about the psychological care of sick youngsters.

Abusive Parents

Child abuse has received little public attention until quite recently because no one likes to admit that parents can be so outrageously angry as to physically or psychologically harm their small children. Of course, all parents who abuse their children require immediate psychiatric help. (For a more thorough discussion of this topic, see the section on child abuse in Chapter 9.)

CHAPTER THREE

The 25th Through 30th Month of Life

The period of toddlerhood is considered by most professionals to cover the twelfth to thirty-sixth month of life. Within this time, there are two ages and stages of development: Toddler-Ones (twelfth through twenty-fourth month) are the beginning walkers with parents hovering close by; Toddler-Twos (twenty-fifth through thirty-sixth month) are the beginning runners and talkers whose physical, linguistic, and mental powers are the most active of a child's entire life.

In this chapter, we shall review the growth, development, and behavior of Toddler-Twos from the twenty-fifth through thirtieth month. (See Chapter 4 for the stage of Toddler-Two development from the thirty-first to thirty-sixth month, the "Terrible Twos.")

PROFILE OF TWO- TO TWO-AND-A-HALF-YEAR-OLDS

The Toddler-Two is an energetic "super-snooper," who climbs, searches, and checks everything within his dominion, as any good scientist would. He requires parental supervision much of the time so that serious scrapes can be avoided. For instance, he loves to take things apart, but cannot yet always put them together again. Whereas last year he was content to look at books in the company of a parent, now he is apt to "test" the binding and tear out pictures. He is likely to put nails and hairpins into the uncovered holes in light sockets in the wall unless they are child-proofed.

In their social relations, Toddler-Twos sometimes embarrass their parents by pulling back from the children and adults they already know. Toddler-Twos not only declare their independence, they actively try to prove it by disobeying, being negative, and doing what they feel like doing. However, they still like to have parents play with them, chase them, play hide-and-seek, and read and sing to them.

Toddler-Twos soon discover that independence and freedom are possible only when they observe family rules; that if they disobey these regulations, there is a force outside themselves that helps them to refrain from upsetting the freedoms the family would like them to enjoy. There is also an inner force (known as self-discipline) which parents strive to establish in their children until they are voluntarily able to live by the mores of the family.

Analysis of the growth and development of two-year-olds as against eighteen-month-olds discloses minimal differences. On the surface, the former is physically an advanced model of the latter, but dig a little deeper and you will discover many developmental differences and advances. The striking increase in language acquisition also indicates progress in mental capabilities. Two-year-olds indicate that they are becoming thinking animals. They ask many questions and talk in short sentences. The tremendous increase in vocabulary enables them to get their needs fulfilled.

The two-year-old sleeps some thirteen hours, and has a nap of between one and two hours, usually in the afternoon. Her legs are still short and her head is oversized, but her improved running and climbing are changing her former "Neanderthal features." Surer on her feet, she loves to wander, run, chase, and be pursued. She continues to rise and bend awkwardly and still falls a lot. She throws things— sometimes her toys.*

The two-year-old needs to be told that he is "good"; that his

*Adapted from The First Five Years of Life by Arnold Gesell et al. (New York: Harper & Row, 1940).

parents are proud of him. He needs to be held when hurt or frightened; to have help when angered; and to be told simply but firmly what he can and cannot do.

To the average adult who has never had a child, the two-year-old appears to be an unpredictable, miniature whirling dervish whose drive and direction are uncertain, and whose satisfactions come from efforts and accomplishments hardly worth the energy invested in them. The Toddler-Two is constantly on the move, eager to affect his environment, interacting with every object in his path and trying to make it do his bidding. However, his attention span is very short.

The Toddler-Two does not separate people from things, and freely mixes inanimate and animate objects in his spoken responses. He will tell a cloud or wagon to "go away," and will say "hello" to pebbles, trees, or flowers. He uses a single word, "mommy," to identify all the women he sees.*

Toddler-Twos are obsessed with spatial exploring (wandering, climbing, balancing on low fences), with picking flowers, throwing pebbles into a pond, etc. In a supermarket or department store, they can't resist hiding behind counters or clothes racks or grabbing candy or toys off counters. Of course, such behavior upsets parents and shop managers who are not always enthralled by typical Toddler-Two behavior. Whatever attracts Toddler-Twos, they will try to touch. They will poke, twist, and drop anything within reach.

The social contacts of the Toddler-Two are brief and transitory, due in large measure to his short attention span. This "touch-and-go" relationship with everyone in his environment extends also to things. A beloved dolly or stuffed panda will be dropped unceremoniously the minute a novel object catches the child's eye.

Another way of thinking of the two-year-old is in terms of her narrow field of understanding and the immaturity of her association of one experience to another. A two-year-old will struggle to close a door without finding the block at floor level that is the obstacle. Her ability to "interconnect," "to see" more than one thing at a time is minimal.†

Yet the twenty-five- through thirty-month-old is a fairly calm and collected runabout. Over a period of two years, he has solidified his bond of trust with his primary caregiver. This

*From Life and Ways of the Two-Year-Old by Louise Phinney Woodcock.
†From Life and Ways of the Two-Year-Old by Louise Phinney Woodcock.

enables him to start moving forward in the direction of ultimate autonomy. He now has sufficient control of his bodily powers to have a degree of confidence in his efforts to master his physical world.

As the child approaches her third birthday, there is greater interest in activities outside of the home as well as a lessening of dependence upon the mother and other family members. She is now genuinely interested in forming relationships with her agemates and seeks interaction with them. She appears to be somewhat better at controlling her emotions, and no longer falls completely apart when frustrated.

The toddler continues to spend much time exploring and practicing simple skills on objects in his environment. However, according to research by Dr. Burton L. White, the time devoted to this is decreasing—from 18 percent at eighteen to twenty-one months to 14 percent at thirty months.

Language development is startling at this age. A great deal of looking, listening, and attending is taking place at all times. The use of two- or three-word sentences and simple conversations enable the Toddler-Two to enter into the self-speech of fantasy play with himself as well as with his peers. With his burgeoning command of speech, he moves from problem solving *with actions* (using his hands and eyes on a trial-and-error basis) to the increasing use of ideas in his mind, *thinking* things out.

GROSS-MOTOR DEVELOPMENT

Young Toddler-Twos are busy acquiring the important skills of running, jumping, turning around, kicking a ball, climbing a stairway, and throwing and retrieving all kinds of small or large objects. With these abilities, she can get about without adult help. Her world naturally enlarges from a closeness to mother to a larger world of strange people doing fascinating things: driving a car, pedaling a bicycle, operating a train, digging a trench, building a house. Stimulated and challenged by a world in motion, she attempts to recreate some of her new learnings with her building blocks, toy cars, or play people. She is not averse to including parents in her play or imitating them as they perform their household duties.

Two-year-olds are motor driven. They have made some advances in their postural control and body balance and can now hasten their steps without losing their balance. Nevertheless, the two-year-old usually monitors his walk and the placement of his feet so that he will be able to deal with obstacles in his way by circumventing them. By the age of three, he will walk without the need for close inspection of his moving feet. Running and climbing are especially intriguing. These toddlers can walk up and down stairs and jump down the first tread without help. They are able to walk up to a ball and kick it. Young Twos toss balls and other objects haphazardly. They prefer throwing and trying to catch large balls. Older Twos are more coordinated and can focus on a target.

Toddler-Twos are somewhat like clowns in a circus; they delight in rough-and-tumble play. However, fathers need to curb their own exuberance when they toss their small acrobats into the air. Sometimes the squealing of their little ones can signify fright more than delight. Two-year-olds accompany all their bodily activities with dancing, screeching, and laughter. They like to talk even if they have nothing to say.

Toddler-Twos show lack of muscular coordination and awareness when a parent struggles to dress them; for example, they will curl their fingers when a parent is trying to straighten them out in their respective glove slots; step on mother's feet as she is trying to button up the child's coat; and even walk off with the job unfinished when the impulse takes them.*

Playgroup or nursery school children show complete disregard for their safety when swarming over each other in a sandbox or climbing over a packing crate. They will set off in small groups on journeys of exploration, stopping here and there to practice a stepping-up skill, to open or close a door, or to pick up a shovel and dig for a few minutes. Playyard settings encourage them to try their hands at a physical skill; for example, the steps or the rungs of a ladder invite them to climb; inclines inspire them to use their feet. They will use their hands and feet to master heights. Holes in a tunnel prompt back and forth exploration. They are attracted especially to objects that roll: a ball, a keg, a wagon, a push truck, etc. Toddler-Twos are intent on practicing their new muscular skills and enjoying their "bigness."*

It is important for parents or other caregivers of Toddler-Twos to keep in mind that children grow and develop differently, and that their rates of growing and developmental progress differ at different ages.

Having left crib and carriage not too long ago, and bursting to make her way on her own power at home and in the community, she discovers that she has much to learn in dealing with the dynamic properties of objects. She clutches an object for support, but unexpectedly it moves and lets her fall. While she can manage a slide, she is not ready to cope with the bulk of one of her playmates hurtling down and knocking her off her feet.

The properties and behaviors of materials around her and the ways she can control them form a major portion of her daily learning. Her inability to see more than the simplest spatial relationship makes her vulnerable to accidents and frustrations.

The Toddler-Two is so observant of where things are kept in the home and meticulous about daily routines that he gives a misleading appearance of easy participation in the life of his family. In fact, few opportunities for trial-and-error exist because his uncertain and/or potentially dangerous tryouts are nipped in the bud.

In a playgroup or nursery school, the Toddler-Two's prob-

*From *Life and Ways of the Two-Year-Old* by Louise Phinney Woodcock.

lems are real and physical—she has difficulty setting up a circle of chairs, or bringing a chair close to the dining table. In a playground, young Toddler-Twos have trouble synthesizing the motions necessary to mastering a tricycle's pedals and steering mechanism, or pumping and not falling off a swing. It requires parental supervision and help to push the swing until the child feels totally secure with the heights and motions of swinging.*

This period calls for the sensitive intervention of parents to reinforce a child in his achievements; to name actions and objects so he can expand his language ability; to create a safe environment that is manageable and not too frustrating. Toddler-Twos want to be independent. They want to be recognized as worthy individuals in the adult world. Although this is a difficult time for parents, if managed properly, it will result in competent children who will be able to take leadership in a competitive world.

FINE-MOTOR CONTROL

Manual control has also advanced. Toddler-Twos now turn the pages of a book, one page at a time, with improved release. They are able to build a tower of six blocks. They can

*From *Life and Ways of the Two-Year-Old* by Louise Phinney Woodcock.

use small scissors; string beads with a large needle or lace; hold a glass of milk or juice securely (often with one hand); handle a spoon with thumb and radial finger and hold it palm up (or by overhand grasp). A twist of the wrist, and they can turn a knob. They can grasp an object without danger of its dropping.

These improved bodily powers indicate their readiness to handle themselves at the family dining table.

ADAPTIVE BEHAVIOR

The memory span of Toddler-Twos has lengthened somewhat. They look for missing toys. Their imitative and perceptual behaviors show finer discrimination. They can put a square block edgewise into the rectangular hole of a shape-sorting box. They sense *oneness* versus *many.*

There is an interdependence of motor and mental development; for example, they think with their body and muscles when enacting a fairy tale about an elephant. They are not yet ready to move their hands in different directions and they have trouble folding and creasing a piece of paper.

The two-year-old's eyes no longer show an unfocused stare or wandering glance; now she attends to the scene about her.

LANGUAGE ACQUISITION

There is great variability in the language skills of Toddler-Twos. Some use few words and some talk volubly most of the time. Speech is erupting rapidly at this stage. The average two-year-old North American toddler has about three hundred words in his vocabulary, although not all are of practical use. Some provide interesting sounds; others are actively used in forming two- and three-word sentences. Words that name things, persons, and actions are dominant; adverbs, adjectives, and prepositions appear less important. In the unique telegraphic-type speech of the two-year-old, "flowery" words are nonessential. Pronouns such as *mine, me, you,* and *I* are being used more often, probably because the child's sense of self is maturing. However, this age group prefers using personal names; for example, "*John* slides down" rather than "*I* slide down" or "*You* slide down."

During this period of active speech, words become imprinted on the brain because they are practiced and elaborated upon. A Toddler-Two will play with the potentials of salient parts; for instance, "*slide down*" will become "Mary *slide down*." It becomes a sing-song chant and poetry long before it becomes a grammatically correct sentence. Pronouns and transitive verbs are added and, before you know it, the child will articulate a grammatically correct five-word sentence: "I saw John slide down."

There is an overwhelming parade of verbs with reversible subjects and objects, past and present tenses, plurals, prepositions, etc., that a child must master to satisfy adult standards of English. Given a year of free play with words and words spoken to him by his siblings and adults, most children will master all of the complexities of their native tongue. Some children master two languages at the same time if parents follow the rules rigidly, that is, one speaks English all the time while another member of the household (Grandpa or a caregiver) communicates in the foreign language *all the time.*

The two-year-old has been practicing making sounds and vocalizing for many months. Early on she babbled, squealed, and shouted unintelligible sounds for her own satisfaction without any communication purpose. Just as she enjoyed exercising her powers of bodily movement, so she gained pleasure in using her vocal cords for the rhythmic patterns she could make them produce.

The Toddler-Two derives great satisfaction from combining his expanding motoric and vocal skills. He accompanies each action with appropriate telegraphic language: "Shut door." "Sit down." Riding his kiddy car, he chants a rhythmic "la-la-la." On a swing he sings, "Me go up, me go down."

Rhythmic language is not limited to physical activity; it can arise out of experimentation with a word the child likes: "Pokey-pokey-poke." Sometimes the vocalizations take the form of alliteration: "Susie's galoshes make splishes and sploshes" or poetry: "Remember the gold fish? Has no hands, has no feet, goes round and round."

Linguists tell us that no one has to teach a child to talk; that this comes naturally. In *Life and Ways of the Two-Year-Old,* Louise Phinney Woodcock wrote that there is a "sudden bursting forth of language after a long period when learning and practice must have been internal. It seems that the child learned to talk overnight. Some children over a period echo almost every phrase they hear."

A few question words occur in the early vocabulary of Toddler-Twos. The commonest ones are "what," "where," and "why." One word that arrives late in the vocabulary of Toddler-Twos is the word "Yes," perhaps because it is difficult to pronounce at this age. Some children use the negative "No" for a short period to express the affirmative. Adults need to look behind the spoken word of little children to find what meaning has been obscured by the inadequacy of language.

Fostering Mental Development Through Language

"Mental development is largely dependent upon language development. When the baby reaches the stage in his development that he can react to gestures and words, he can also recall and remember. As soon as he can use even a few words himself, while understanding the meaning of many more, he is better able to control his world . . . The child whose parents help him to recognize many words and expressions in relation to his experiences is able, when only two or three years old, to remember, to compare, and to reason what will happen in certain circumstances."*

Social Development Through Language

"One of the values of the nursery school is that it provides children with many experiences and encourages them to verbalize their activities . . . The child becomes a human being through his language contacts . . . The need to communicate with other human beings is one of the strongest motivating forces for learning language."

Some Theories about Language, Thought, and Communication

The theories concerning the development of speech present varying points of view about the relationship between language and thought. The learning theory approach claims that the child listens to his parents, siblings, neighbors, and

*From *The Three R's in the Elementary School.* Prepared by a Committee of the Association for Supervision and Curriculum Development (Washington, DC: National Education Association, n.d.).

imitates them. We can teach him by saying a word and giving him some reward (attention, smiles, or the object he names) when he is able to repeat it.

Reinforcement theorists suggest that the world's 1500 languages give testimony to their approach; that is, every child learns to speak the language she hears in her surroundings. Children who do not hear much language or do not get sufficient rewards for saying words learn very little language.

Many linguists reject the "parrot view" of language acquisition. They believe that it cannot explain the child's ability to understand and produce complicated grammatical patterns

and sentences. They point to the role of internal processes and maturation. These theorists emphasize the developmental unfolding nature of language acquisition.

Other theorists maintain that the acquisition of language aids and abets the growth of thought. This view is based on the fact that humans have language and the most developed thought patterns of all animals. Dr. Jerome S. Bruner, formerly of Harvard University, now Watts Professor of Psychology at the University of Oxford, believes that through language we are able to play with ideas and share experiences with others. We can speak or write about an object without the necessity of having the object present. Language frees children from the necessity of manipulating the environment. By using symbols or words, they can select, store, and code complex concepts and then communicate them.

In the second year of their lives, children's memories increase—for things, people, places, and ideas. Not only do they recognize the familiar, now they begin to demonstrate the ability to recall and reproduce recent memories of words, actions, and events. In solving new problems, children rely on their old experiences. Toddler-Twos try out different known modes of action in each new situation, and toward the end of the year, they begin to develop new procedures by combining or changing old ones. They begin to have representations of real things in their heads (memories of pictures, sounds, feelings, etc.) that help them think about something without its being physically present—an important milestone.

Unlike many theorists, Piaget had a somewhat different point of view. He thought that the roots of logic are in actions, not words. He found that infants begin to act in intelligent ways from the day of their birth and that they practice their actions; in other words, infants "think with their actions." They soon learn that some things can be grasped, some cannot; some things move when they are pushed, some do not. Such insights are independent of language.

Piaget indicated that thought precedes language; that it derives from the child's interaction with the environment. Even without language, the child is capable of developing a logical symbolic system by ordering his environment—grouping objects, solving problems, imitating adult behavior patterns, and so forth. During every stage of their development, very young children are able to carry out activities that demand a good deal of intelligence without using language. Hence, language alone often is a misleading indicator of the level of a child's intelligence or understanding.

When a child learns language, she already has developed thought. Piaget distinguished two functions of language—the social one and the egocentric one. The first is directed to the listener and enables communication with others; the latter is self-directed and is a tool of self-expression.

During the early years, especially between three to five, the "egocentric" function is more important than the social one. The child talks and does not bother to know to whom he is speaking, or whether he is being listened to. We hear this sort of speech mostly in children's play and in the dark of night before they go to sleep; they simply talk to themselves.

In addition to being a means of communication, speech is a tool for expressing our thoughts. This does not imply, however, that all our thinking is done with the help of words. Many studies have shown that the child can understand many things before she has acquired and used speech. Many aspects of thought are nonverbal—imagination, creativity, art, etc.—and we should not undervalue them.

Encourage your child's curiosity. He has to have many experiences with different objects and situations. For example, in order to fully understand the word "dog," a child needs to see many kinds of dogs, to touch a dog, to hear one barking, to know what it eats, and even what smell it has. Real understanding of a thing comes only after a young child has seen and experienced it from many angles.

Stuttering

At about three years of age, children often develop fluency problems because of their lack of sufficient words to express their thoughts. Stuttering may be triggered if parents evince impatience, anxiety, or displeasure while their child is searching for words. Patience and gentle suggestion to the child at such times may help further his speech development.

If you are relaxed with your child and accept her as she is at this stage of her growth, and her stuttering persists for some time, you might discuss your child's lack of fluency with her pediatrician. However, if the stuttering continues to be severe, the help of a competent speech therapist may ameliorate the condition.

Some Good Books for Older Twos and Threes

Inasmuch as children differ greatly, it is up to you to discover which books will be best for your child.

Aliki. *Hush, Little Baby* (Prentice-Hall, 1968)

Berenstain, Stanley and Janice. *Inside, Outside, Upside Down* (Random House, 1968)

Brown, Margaret Wise. *A Child's Goodnight Book* (Addison-Wesley, 1950)

————. *Goodnight Moon* (Harper & Row, 1947)

Browner, Richard. *Everyone Has a Name* (Walck, 1961)

Bruna, Dick. *Animal Book* (Methuen, 1976)

————. *The Fish* (Methuen, 1975)

D'Aulaire, Ingri and Edgar Parin. *Animals Everywhere* (Doubleday, 1954)

Flack, Marjorie. *Angus and the Cat* (Doubleday, 1931)

Francis, Sally R. *Scat, Scat* (Platt & Munk, 1940)

Fujikawa, Gyo. *Babies* (Grosset & Dunlap, 1963)

————. *Mother Goose* (Grosset & Dunlap, 1968)

Gág, Wanda. *ABC Bunny* (Coward-McCann, 1933)

Green, Mary McBurney. *Everybody Eats and Everybody Has a House* (Addison-Wesley, 1961)

Hoban, Tana. *Big Ones, Little Ones* (Greenwillow, 1976)

————. *Where Is It?* (Macmillan, 1974)

Kessler, Ethel and Leonard. *Do Baby Bears Sit on Chairs?* (Doubleday, 1961)

Kunhardt, Dorothy. *Pat the Bunny* (Golden Press, 1962)

Lenski, Lois. *Debbie Herself* (Walck, 1969)

————. *The Little Auto* (Walck, 1934)

————. *The Little Family* (Doubleday, 1932)

Matthiesen, Thomas. *Things to See: A Child's World of Familiar Objects* (Platt & Munk, 1966)

Mayer, Mercer. *Frog on His Own* (Dial Press, 1973)

Miles, Betty. *A House for Everyone* (Alfred A. Knopf, 1958)

Ogle, Lucille and Tina Thobur. *I Spy with My Little Eye* (American Heritage Press, 1970)

Puner, Helen W. *Daddies, What They Do All Day* (Lothrop, Lee & Shepard, 1946)

Rey, H.A. *Anybody at Home?* (Houghton Mifflin, 1942)

————. *Feed the Animals* (Houghton Mifflin, 1944)

————. *Where's My Baby?* (Houghton Mifflin, 1943)

Rojankovsky, Feodor. *Animals in the Zoo* (Alfred A. Knopf, 1962)

————. *Animals on the Farm* (Alfred A. Knopf, 1967)

————. *The Tall Book of Mother Goose* (Harper & Row, 1942)

Scarry, Richard. *Busy, Busy World* (Western Publishing, 1972)

————. *The Great Big Car and Truck Book* (Western Publishing, 1951)

————. *What Animals Do* (Western Publishing, 1968)

Skaar, Grace. *Nothing But Cats and All About Dogs* (Addison-Wesley, 1947)

———— and Louise Woodcock. *The Very Little Dog and the Smart Little Kitty* (Addison-Wesley, 1947)

Steiner, Charlotte. *My Slippers Are Red* (Alfred A. Knopf, 1973)

Wildsmith, Brian. *Brian Wildsmith's ABC* (Franklin Watts, 1963)

————. *Mother Goose* (Franklin Watts, 1964)

Williams, Garth. *Baby Animals* (Western Publishing, 1956)

————. *Baby Farm Animals* (Western Publishing, 1959)

Witte, Pat and Eve. *Who Lives Here?* (Western Publishing, 1961)

Wolde, Gunilla. *Betsy's Baby Brother* (Random House, 1975)

————. *This Is Betsy* (Random House, 1975)

Zolotow, Charlotte. *Sleepy Book* (Lothrop, Lee & Shepard, 1958)

SENSORY POWERS/LEARNING

Virtually all professionals agree that the early childhood years are of prime importance for sensorimotor learning. All the senses (seeing, hearing, touching, tasting, smelling) are brought into play in discerning the world. The kind of universe we perceive and the kind we make for ourselves are largely dependent upon the manner in which our senses have been trained to function.

Each normal infant is born with all her senses marked "Go!" She is ready to take on everything her environment has to offer and needs as much early stimulation as she can get. Stimulation of all the senses will set a learning pattern that will

be decisive for the child's ongoing learning and coping capabilities.

In his fascinating book, *Touching* (mentioned earlier), Ashley Montagu writes, "It has been said that adults are deteriorated children . . . In the Western world as the individual grows he tends to become progressively desensitized. His senses and sensitivities tend to become blunted. Aware of this, prepared parents will provide their children with all those sources of stimulation (without overstimulation) for the growth and development of the senses."

Most middle-class parents are intuitive about the needs of their toddlers for sensory experiences, and they surround them with manipulative materials and playthings to develop their sensory and perceptual acuity. In their homes or playschools you will find pegs and pegboards, color cones, nesting cups, form boards and shape-sorting boxes, depth cylinders, puzzle boards, and other manipulative materials to help the learner discover certain concepts about the physical world and the properties of objects through play.

As children put together, take apart, stack, match, nest, group, and rearrange, they not only observe but participate in their environment.

Most middle-class children are surrounded by words and experiences, and as they grow they sort their experiences and come up with workable concepts. There are parents, teachers, and researchers who consider such learning to be the result of the gradual maturation of a child's physical and learning powers, and believe it happens "naturally" without planning or stimulation. We, however, think that children who do not have a variety of enriching experiences are deprived.

Learning and teaching in the earliest years are subtle; they are not obvious either to the child or the caregiver. For example, the nine-month-old interacts with the animate and inanimate objects in his environment; he sees them, touches them, and tries to mouth them. He learns something about special features, textures, and behaviors. If an object seems important to him, he *notes* it and then *distinguishes* it from other objects; he *relates* it to other objects in his environment, and even *locates* it (points to it) if asked to identify it. However, the learning about these objects appears to be minimal.

As your child becomes more verbal, she is able to *name* the object as you point it out. By changing the rules, you are making the learning task much more difficult. It is more complicated for the child to name an object than it is to point to one when you give her the name for it.

In *Give Your Child a Superior Mind* (New York: Simon & Schuster, 1966), Siegfried and Therese Engelmann outline a procedure for teaching a child the naming of an object:

"Can you find a flower? . . . Good. Can you find another one?"

"Soller."

"Yes, flower. Good boy."

"The child will not burst into language. His development will be gradual before two years, and then rather fast (averaging better than four new words a day). The two-year-old will have a tendency to overgeneralize words . . . He might want to call all brightly colored things flowers . . . Be careful how you treat overgeneralizations . . . 'Yes, it does look like a flower, but we call it a *scarf.*'"

By the time your child is two years old, she should be able to locate most of the parts of the body. At this time, the emphasis changes from locating to naming. Do not get too technical. It is important that you have fun with your child. If naming gets boring, forget about it for a day or two. You can make use of bathing and dressing to teach your child about body parts.

After twenty-six months, you can put more emphasis on the identification of objects never seen before—household objects, animals, etc. The same technique applies to all objects. There are names for the colors of objects; links between objects (over, under, between); action words (ball *rolls*, Mommy *jumps*). There are names for actions associated with senses.

Sight—"See the red ball." Hearing—music on a record player or radio. Touch—Daddy's beard. Smell—a flower, vinegar, etc.

You can draw geometric shapes on a board or piece of paper, and ask your child to find their position (in, on, behind, under, over, next to); and to learn the use of comparative words (bigger, hotter, faster, taller, shorter than).

CONCEPT FORMATION AND TOTAL DEVELOPMENT

From the moment a baby is born he is bombarded by many different kinds of stimuli. These impressions are unconnected to the infant; they have no sequence and no meaning. To make a predictable world out of all these impressions, he must learn to assign meanings to the events that involve him. In this way, he begins to form concepts.

To fully understand what a concept is and how it develops, one must try to see the world as the infant does. For example, at first the baby experiences the mother as the feeder and cuddler. After many months, he develops a concept of "mother." The infant will probably identify all women, if they are reasonably similar to his own mother, as a mother. A concept, therefore, is a classification of stimuli that have common characteristics. The concept is formed when the classification is carried beyond one event, as when the child identifies other women as "mother" after repeatedly seeing and processing female images placed before him.

There is evidence that the development of concepts is closely tied to the child's total development. As the infant gains control over more of his own body, he is able to come into contact with more things. Accompanying this increased contact is the process of assigning meanings to events and things. Meanings are related to certain feelings; for instance, comfort or tension. A baby will smile when he sees his mother coming with a bottle or cry when the nurse approaches with a hypodermic needle. While this does not indicate a high level of thought, it does demonstrate the beginnings of concept formation.

Perhaps one of the most important ways baby learns about herself and her environment is by her sense of touch. When the baby sucks her thumb, the mouth feels the thumb and the thumb feels the mouth. This is called *self-sentience*. It is from such beginnings that the baby learns about herself and forms the concept of "me." Once the baby knows that she is separate from her surroundings, she has opened the door to forming concepts about those things that are part of her environment.

Since the baby is constantly forming and expanding his concept of himself, the way he experiences his world will affect the way he thinks about himself. He needs a safe world in order to develop a sense of adequacy. One way in which he does this is by relating to certain people, referred to as "significant others." These normally include the parents and other people the baby sees frequently. Through contact with these people, he will develop a basic trust in people that he will carry later on beyond the small circle of this significant group. Of course, the process is a slow one. Many parents are dismayed when grandmother comes to visit and the baby cries when she tries to pick him up. The problem is that the baby has not had time to develop meanings about that person, and therefore has not yet formed a concept of what "grandmother" means to him.

Concepts are formed and then changed to fit each new experience. Children develop new concepts by building on ones previously acquired.

Number Concepts

One aspect of intelligence on which our society has placed great emphasis is mathematical proficiency. Approximately one-half of the time children spend in elementary school is devoted to the study of numbers. All North American children are expected to acquire a competence in mathematics far greater than that of the most intelligent Greeks of the sixth century B.C. Because adults use many sophisticated mathematical processes in their daily lives and take them for granted, there has been very little study about how and when these mathematical processes become possible for the child.

Piaget, however, did extensive studies on how children develop an appreciation of quantitative relationships. The results of his experiments show a slowly unfolding system of awareness of relationships between things, their number or quantity, weight, shape, and size. Piaget believed that before the age of twenty-four months, the child's concepts of number relationship are undifferentiated; for example, a two-year-old would decide a piece of popcorn weighed more after it was popped because it looked bigger.

During the period from twenty-five to twenty-eight months, dawning number concepts include *ordination* (counting objects in sequence—one apple, two apples) and the process of *classification* (a dog is an animal, etc.). Maria Montessori's colored rods (developed long before the Cuisenaire rods that are used in today's schools) are one example of material that can help teach a child number relationships. Ten differently colored and sized rods are used to symbolize the numbers 1 to 10. Since the ordination process can be improved with practice, the mother who works with her toddler is providing necessary training and feedback.

By two-and-a-half, the child begins counting and classifying objects. He can tell you, "I am a boy," "Daddy is bigger than I am," and "I have two cookies." Every few months, parents can see increasing sophistication in their child's dealings with quantity.

An excellent time to help teach your child concepts about more and less, full and empty, and the like is when you are measuring the ingredients of a recipe. Only frequent exposure will enable your child to learn these things; once learned, they will become permanent concepts. Counting objects in sequence is something that can be done any time. As you go up the stairs, count your steps out loud and soon your child will be joining you. Count the people in your family, the fingers on your child's hands, and the things you buy at the supermarket.

By the time your child is ten or eleven years old, the "why" of these concepts will be explained in school, but for now your child is struggling to understand complex mathematical relationships and perceptions on a more rudimentary level. Anything done in the spirit of play for ten or fifteen minutes a day that employs the principles of ordination and natural numbers will help your child make additional sense out of her environment.

Parent-Child Activities for Learning Natural Numbers and Ordination

• Take advantage of the counting potential in a child's play. If she is playing with pegboards, nesting cups, counting cubes, bead counters, or large beads, or if she is working with clay

making cookies, balls, or snakes, count each item as it is finished. "Mary has made one cookie; now she is finishing the second one. One, two, three." "How many beads can fit into this box?" "Let's count them together."

• When your child has learned to build a nesting cup tower ask, "How many nesting cups are in the tower you made?" Using a bead counter, show your child how to move one bead at a time across the bar. Then let him push the beads while you count. Learning the order of number series helps a child to count.

• Some commercial houses sell "number pegs," numerals cut out of wood or Masonite with holes punched through so that a child can insert pegs on either side. After several days of playing with these, you can count the pegs in each of the numerals: "One, two, three pegs . . . and this is the numeral 3."

Learning About Time

Time is a complex concept that is especially difficult for toddlers to master. Time is complicated because we cannot see, hear, touch, or taste it. There are two distinct kinds of time: conventional abstract time with a measurement system to be learned (hours, minutes, seconds), and our own personal temporal time (the time at which we eat, go to school, etc.). Most parents teach temporal time informally. The child is told, "Not now, wait a minute, Daddy will be home soon." Some time learning develops as a result of interaction with the environment: parents point out night, day, seasons of the year, and so on.

Dr. Louise Bates Ames of the Gesell Institute conducted a study of time concepts in children from the ages of eighteen months to eight years. A short compilation was made of verbal expressions about time over a two-year period during direct conversations. It was found that a child first responds to a time word, then uses it in spontaneous conversation, and finally is able to answer questions dealing with the concept. For example, at eighteen months the child responds to *soon;* at twenty-four months he uses the word *soon;* and at forty-two months he can answer a question about the notion of *soon.* Words referring to the present were used first, at twenty-four months; words referring to the future were used second, at thirty months; and words referring to the past were used third, at thirty-six months.

In *Your Two-Year-Old: Terrible or Tender* (New York: Delacorte Press, 1976), Ames and her colleague Frances Ilg write that Toddler-Twos have only a dim notion of time. When they want something *now,* *later* has no meaning for them. Most Toddler-Twos understand *in a minute, today,* and *pretty soon.* However, although they possess some idea of the meaning of *today, tomorrow, morning,* and *afternoon,* an understanding of *yesterday* is not within their ken.

What can parents do to aid their children in developing a concept of time? Call attention to the one-thing-follows-another scheme of time learning; for example, "It is noon now and time to eat lunch." "Today is Monday and it's the day we wash our clothes." It is helpful to emphasize what is going on now, what has already happened, and what will happen next. Through your daily conversations with your child, you can use such expressions as "That's something for after nap time" or "In a little while it will be time to go outside to play." Since children understand time concepts based on a sequence of events before they understand those based on intervals, the use of such words as *before, after, first, next, last, soon,* and *later* will enable them to further their ideas of temporal order.

Give your Toddler-Two practice in remembering several things in order: a toy, a doll, a fork, etc. Then take them away, and ask her which came first, which is next . . . and last. Talk with your child about past events: a visit to Grandma last week, to the zoo yesterday, etc. Show your child photographs of how he looked when he was a year old or two years, and tell him how much bigger he is now. Despite the fact that Toddler-Twos use such words as *big* and *little,* they are still not able to tell which of two things is bigger!

Since counting is the basis of our system of measuring time, you might teach your child how to count. Although Toddler-Twos are able to distinguish two cookies, most are not able to count beyond two unless given special training. Later the counting can be related to groups of objects.

Teach your child the meaning of time-related words, such as *new* and *old, fast* and *slow.*

Let your child play with an egg timer. A cuckoo clock, which has different sounds for quarter, half, and hour intervals, is another good learning tool. Include in your playroom a large, attractive calendar with spelled-out days of the week, and give each day its own "personality"—"Sunday is our family day," "Tuesdays we go shopping," etc. "When does the garbage man come?" "No, it isn't Thursday, it's Monday."

Exploring Scientific Concepts

The young child is an avid explorer. He comes equipped with an insatiable interest that can be fostered and encouraged by the parent. As a child touches, smells, and looks at the world around him, he questions, looks for cause and effect, and tests his conclusions, *playing all the while.*

The name given to this questioning pattern is "the scientific method." There are five steps to this approach: state the problem, form the hypothesis, observe and experiment, interpret data, and state conclusions. A child will naturally follow this pattern even though there may be large time lapses between

each step, and she will not always verbalize her questions and conclusions.

Walks in a park, a city setting, or the country can be inspiring if the parent will point out leaves, birds, the height of trees, shadows, the feel of the air, the way the rain dries on the skin, the differences and similarities of things in the environment, etc. The child may wish to touch an object or see how it feels in his hands. This should be encouraged when possible. An excellent toy to stimulate curiosity at this stage is a large magnifying glass.

An important way parents can encourage their child in the first step of the scientific method is by helping her with her vocabulary. Even Toddler-Twos will profit from learning that *water* or *wet* applies equally to the hot and cold liquid that comes from the faucet, to what's left when the ice melts, and to rain.

After a child forms a basic concept of water, he will begin to have certain expectations about it; for instance, he may expect it to pour from a hole. This expectation is his hypothesis. Other expectations may be that a candle will go out when he blows it, or that his blocks will fall if he piles them too high or crookedly. The expectation may or may not be clearly stated. After it is formed, however, the child will proceed to test his hypothesis.

This step will probably take the most time. It is the most easily observed by parents. Parents who witness their child's curiosity can help focus it on one aspect. For example, the child who is playing with ice cubes (letting them melt, feeling their wetness, etc.) might enjoy having the water refrozen in the ice cube tray, and then letting them melt again.

SOCIAL DEVELOPMENT

Toddler-Twos are physically and psychologically ready for social experiences. At the same time, the combination of dependence-anxiety (fear of being left by the mother) and independence (insisting on doing everything one's own way) can place tremendous stress on the patience and understanding of parents. Some Toddler-Twos refuse to be separated from their mothers, while others are no longer completely dependent upon their caregivers for company. The more mature children can play alone; some even enjoy companionship with their agemates, but only for limited periods of time.

However, for most Toddler-Twos adjusting to agemates individually or in a play group is socially very awkward. Some children feel friendly enough, but are not yet able to express themselves. A Toddler-Two will hug another child roughly or even knock the companion down because of her strong feelings. Of course, she will be shocked when she receives similar treatment. Hitting and biting are prevalent in the beginning stages of social learning.

Toddler-Twos need to learn how to defend themselves quite as often as they need to be restrained from fighting. They are still consolidating their sense of self by obtaining and hoarding possessions. At three they no longer seem to surround themselves with possessions. At three-and-a-half they establish themselves with other children and treat them as individuals. Their play has ceased to be egocentric; now they prefer cooperative play.

Peer Relationships During Early Childhood

Friendships are fundamental to the lives of most children from about age three through adolescence. They provide their greatest pleasures and deepest hurts. Peer social relations furnish the participants with the gratifying feeling of belonging. They contribute, too, to the acquisition of the social skills of coping with conflict, engaging others in activities, taking turns, and so on. By the time children are three and four years old, most are more likely to prefer others of their own sex as companions, possibly because they like to do the same things.

There are times when children need adult help in forming alliances with their agemates. There also are occasions when parents need to intervene and remove a child from a harmful friendship. Friendships end in various ways, sometimes against a child's will; for example, when one child moves to another city or when one or the other decides that the friendship is no longer desirable. The end of a friendship can be very stressful. Sensitive parents can help their child make new friends if need be. In this regard, you might want to read *Children's Friendships* by Zick Rubin (Cambridge, MA: Harvard University Press, 1980).

Let Your Toddler-Two Help You

Toddler-Twos insist on being mother's helper, assisting in everyday housekeeping chores. Try to be appreciative even if your child's efforts get in your way or things are spilled on the floor. Never let your child see you do again a task he thinks he has completed for you because this can arouse resentment in him. If you feel it is quicker always to do things yourself, you will rob your child of the opportunity to learn family cooperation. When he reaches the preteen and teenage years, *you* will be resentful that he is so unwilling to share some of the household chores you now justifiably feel he should be able to manage on his own.

If you are inconvenienced by your toddler's taking over your household equipment, you can provide her with her own sturdy child-size broom, dust pan and hand brush, unbreakable cups and saucers, etc. (Check your local kindergarten or school supply house or educational toy shop for the above.)

Very Young Children Are Self-Oriented

Up until about the age of two, a child sees and experiences the world mostly in terms of what it has done and is doing to her.

The social techniques of Toddler-Twos are very crude. Healthy children this age will ceaselessly explore and manipulate the inanimate objects that are available to them. In their examination of the adults and children they are exposed to, they extend pretty much the same treatment as they bestow on things. They accord to everything the salutations and even the friendly reproofs they have learned thus far.*

Ethical standards of conduct have no meaning for Toddler-Twos. It appears that in their social behavior, feelings of affection and tenderness can get mixed up quixotically with shoves and punches.

Relationships with Siblings

Although parents are the most important people in the life of very young children (and older ones, too), brothers and sisters also play a major role. By living in the same house, sharing the

*From *Life and Ways of the Two-Year-Old* by Louise Phinney Woodcock.

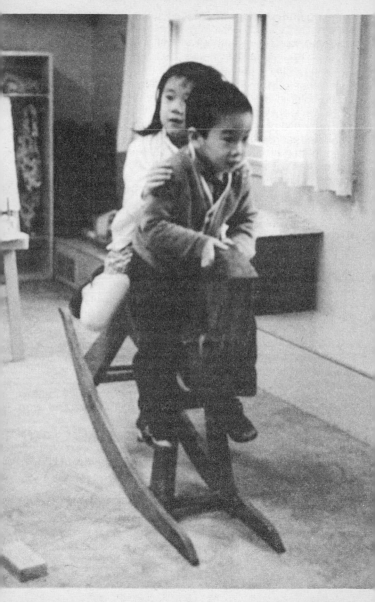

same parents, the same food, and so on, siblings form a vital segment in the world and daily life of Toddler-Twos. All children in a family compete with each other for a share of the parents' affection and attention.

Their common interests enable the children in a family to unite and support each other at times of loss, loneliness, or other crises, as well as to share in family adventures, celebrations, etc. Nevertheless, siblings will be angry with each other at times, be jealous of each other, and will fight. This range of contradictory feelings and behavior is entirely natural.

In *Your Child from One to Six* (Washington, DC: DHEW Publication No. [OHDS] 77-30026, 1974 edition), Dr. Richard H. Granger writes that children who are allowed to resolve their spats by themselves usually do so better than when parents try to interfere. He suggests that "exceptions occur when there are big age differences and the younger child gets the worst of it, or when all the other children gang up on one child. If those things happen you may need to interfere to protect life and limb, but there is usually a reason for such events." He recommends that parents try to find out quietly why such flare-ups happen. "In most families where children feel good about themselves, and feel they have been treated fairly by their parents, such mistreatment of one child by another rarely happens."

In *Primer for Parents of Preschoolers* (New York: Parents' Magazine Press, 1972), Edith G. Neisser writes, "In the daily interchanges between children in the family, each is constantly learning from the others. Much as the skills and information they acquire in this way contribute toward their development, perhaps what they discover about the feelings of others and about their own feelings is even more valuable.

"They [learn] . . . that it is possible to be angry at those one loves and to recover from that anger. They discover, too, that . . . because moments of mutual affection come and go in others and within oneself, the part-time absence of affection does not mean a lack of basic regard for those others, nor does it weaken the potential for compatibility with them.

"These are among the lessons that are taught, without anybody putting them into words, as the children in a family grow up with both love and friction as their daily fare."

Alternative Child Care

Some years ago, professional opinion asserted flatly that only full-time mothers could insure the optimum psychological growth of their infants and toddlers. That opinion held sway when most mothers were homemakers. Today, with more than half of our nation's mothers in full-time employment, the need for alternative child care is a major concern.

Will today's young children be shortchanged by this sharing of caregiving? Dr. Henry Ricciuti of Cornell University evaluated the research on infant and toddler day care for the U.S. Department of Health, Education, and Welfare, and concluded that there is no evidence "that a prolonged experience in day care beginning as early as the first year of life has any adverse effects on the intellectual development if the *care period is of high quality.*"

Are children enrolled in day care less attached to their parents? Dr. Ricciuti's finding is that "no evidence supports the view that extended experience in day care beginning in the first two years of life has a disruptive influence on the affectional relationships between infant and parent." He believes that high-quality day care does not appear to harm very young children; in fact, if it enhances their home experiences, it may be intellectually beneficial.

According to Robert B. McCall in *Infants* (Cambridge, MA: Harvard University Press, 1979), "Most child-care professionals are in agreement that adequate physical facilities (safe play inside and out, adequate play equipment, etc.) are not sufficient. One caring, competent adult for every five two- or three-year-olds is also important. Recent research reveals that the size of the group is even more important than the number of caregivers."

CHOOSING AN EARLY CHILDHOOD CENTER AND SOCIAL PROGRAM

Young children depend upon loving adults to nurture them. However, from about two years or so onward, they are curious and eager to talk to and play near their peers. This is especially true when the toddler is an only child or lives a distance away from a population center.

With today's mobility, few of us truly live in friendly neighborhoods; for the most part we live among strangers. Many young children, especially those living in high-rise apartments, can go out to play only when someone is free to supervise them. The young child is cooped up at home and with her in practically every living room there is a TV set feeding her scenes of violence as well as encouraging her passivity. It is no easy task to provide the growth ingredients a child needs: suitable stimulation, space, companionship, patience, tolerance for the noise and mess of young children, raw materials for the expression of ideas, etc. Parents today are reaching out wherever they can to early childhood centers to supplement their own efforts to promote their children's well-being.

For over five million working mothers of children under six, an early childhood group is more than a desirable supplement to family life; it is an essential. Groups for young children are recognized as helping parents, too: The care of young children is confining, demanding, and exhausting; mothers need some time away from their youngsters to refresh and refuel themselves.

Most parents recognize that their Toddler-Twos require more than their homes can provide. Locating and evaluating the playgroup, child-care center, nursery school, or kindergarten that is most suited to the needs of your child is no simple task. The following is a guide to help you decide what alternative will best fit your needs and those of your child.

The Formal Playgroup

Parents carefully organize this type of playgroup. A supervisor is selected to coordinate activities and mediate problems should they occur. The supervisor handles problems of illness as well as special projects. All the parents discuss what activities should take place, in addition to matters of hygiene and safety, provision for snacks, toys and other materials, frequency of the playgroup meetings, and transportation arrangements. A formal playgroup attempts to provide an atmosphere similar to the one children would encounter in a standard nursery school.

The Informal Playgroup

The informal playgroup may have similarities to the formal playgroup except that its purpose is to provide as much free

play as possible. The informal playgroup may offer less structured activities (cooking, crafts, etc.), whereas the formal playgroup has teacher supervision as a regulatory factor most of
the time.

You can check the laws pertaining to playgroups in your
area by calling a local social services agency or a lawyer.
Often state licensing is required if you have more than five
children in your home at one time on a regular basis. Unlike
the nursery school that has many teachers and children, the
ideal number of children for a playgroup seems to be five or six
in one house under the supervision of one adult caregiver.

Parents who have participated in a playgroup feel that the
five children should be approximately of the same age so the
types of play and other activities made available can be enriching to all the children. They usually believe, too, that meeting twice a week for two or three hours per day is adequate.
How the playgroup is organized depends upon the people
involved, but generally speaking, if you agree to have the playgroup in your home for two days one week, you are free the
following four weeks.

In *How to Start Your Own Preschool Playgroup* (New York:
Universe Books, 1973), Harriet M. Watts presents useful ideas
about how to get started without making a lot of mistakes. She
discusses the activities appropriate for different age levels
and outlines the basic organization of one playgroup in which
she was active, as follows:

Transportation: Each parent would drive her or his child to
the destination, or a car pool could be formed. The parent in
whose home the group was meeting would drive the children
back.

Health: A sick child would not be allowed to attend the playgroup since very young children are highly susceptible to each
other's germs. The telephone number of each child's doctor
and where the parent could be reached would be available to
the person in charge in the event a child became ill while at the
playgroup.

Equipment: Before the playgroup began, a low table and
chairs where all five children could sit comfortably were set up,
as well as plenty of building blocks, transportation vehicles,
play people, crayons, paper, wooden puzzles, paints, blunt-
nosed (but sharp) scissors, picture books, soft clay, etc.

Discipline: This was discussed beforehand with all the parents. It was felt that a good rule to follow is "Scold and let

scold," each parent in her or his own way. This would provide the children with beneficial exposure to different methods of discipline.

Snacks: The supervisor would provide a light snack midway through the session or each child could bring his or her own. Any food allergies should be noted.

First Aid: A refresher first aid course for all the parents was highly recommended.

If overburdened or working parents accept the reality that each young child requires individual attention and daily routines they themselves cannot always supply, then quality day-care centers can contribute greatly to the strengthening of family life, fulfilling the wants of both the children and the family.

A day-care center is only as good as the caregivers who work there, who must earn the trust and affection of their little charges by being sensitive to their desires, feelings, and needs. The adults have to be conscious of how the children respond to what they do with them.

Early childhood specialists agree that in addition to complying with local safety regulations, a good day-care center should have a cheerful environment, suitable equipment, and well-trained, caring teachers as well as:

1. Forty to fifty square feet of indoor space per child.
2. One hundred square feet of enclosed outdoor space per child.
3. A nourishing lunch and no junk food snacks.
4. A place to nap with privacy, and a cot for each child.
5. Medical attention at the center as well as home care when the child is too sick to attend.
6. Diapers and changing tables.
7. Furniture and toilet facilities adapted to the child's height.
8. Two to three adults available to each group of eight to ten children.
9. Ample storage space for each child's clothes and toys.
10. Mandatory parent participation.

The last point cannot be stressed too strongly. Parental participation is fundamental to a successful operation. Parents and teachers need to exchange information on a regular basis about each child's behavior, likes and dislikes, health, strengths and weaknesses, etc.

Should a mother feel guilty about wanting to send her toddler to a day-care center? Is a day-care center as good as home care? Is day care only for working mothers?

Dr. Bruno Bettelheim, distinguished child psychiatrist, writes, "I feel that it is too narrow to think of day-care centers merely for mothers who have to work or as therapeutic centers for underprivileged children . . . There is no doubt that mother is the most important person for a child, but we are aware of too intense a mother-child attachment . . . We need to find a better balance between home care and day care . . . A child feels much better about himself and the world if he spends part of the day in a planned setting that exists only for him."

Syracuse University's Experimental Day-Care Center

In the 1960s, Syracuse University set up a day-care center for children beginning at six months of age. The center began as an experiment to show how culturally determined mental retardation could be prevented among children from disadvantaged areas. It deliberately tried to stimulate each child's intellectual development by offering highly individualized care. The experiment proved that the children thrived, and their IQ scores increased with time. The study also demonstrated that early day-care experience, with its attendant separation from the mother, does not lead to emotional insecurity.

Effects of Day Care on Children Under Three

Two child psychologists and a pediatrician set up a fascinating, controlled study in the 1970s of the effects of day care on infants from three-and-a-half to five-and-a-half months of age. Half the infants were Chinese and half Caucasian, of working- and middle-class parents. The babies were either firstborn or second-born, the products of full-term, normal pregnancies, without serious neurologic, physiologic, or genetic disorders. The families were intact and supportive of their offspring.

The experimental program was housed in an established infant center in a housing development in Boston's South End. The babies attended the day-care center five days a week, seven hours a day, until they were twenty-nine months old. They were matched with a control group of children of the

same age and sex, who stayed at home with their mothers. Eight times during the two-and-a-half-year period, all the children were tested and assessed.

Jerome Kagan, Richard B. Kearsley, and Philip B. Zelazo concluded from their study that "Attendance at a day-care center staffed by conscientious and nurturant adults during the first 2.5 years does not seem to sculpt a psychological profile very much different from the one created by home rearing." Another interesting finding was the overwhelming preference both the day-care and home-control children showed for their mothers when they were bored, tired, or afraid. Also, the day-care children were neither more nor less apprehensive in uncertain situations than the children reared at home.

Nursery Schools

In selecting a nursery school, parents are sometimes bewildered by the different programs that are available, as well as by the variations in methods, materials, and goals. Many nursery schools do not have "formal information sheets" that describe their educational philosophies, so astute parents need to visit the schools and observe the classes in session. Before making a final selection, you should discuss your child and the school's program in detail with the head teacher. Do not hesitate to ask questions. It is much better to ask such questions beforehand than to enroll your child in a program your child and you may be uncomfortable with.

No two early childhood programs will ever be exactly alike. The most important variable is the teacher. You should feel that she is genuinely enjoying her work with young children. You should see whether she acts as a "caretaker" or as a sensitive adult who knows when and how to enter into the play life of the group to enhance their learning. The second most important variable is the physical space and equipment.

Matching a Nursery School to Your Child

The philosophy of the nursery school you select for your child should not conflict greatly with your own brand of child-rearing. If you tend to be a permissive parent, you probably would not choose to enroll your child in a highly structured program. If you encourage independence, self-discipline, and responsibility, you probably would be unhappy to have your child in an "anything-is-okay" school. Of course, it is also essential that you consider your child's personality and innate tendencies.

Further, you need to take into account the number of children in the class, their ages, and the child-adult ratio. How much individual attention does your child need? Most nursery schools use chronological age grouping, whereas many Montessori schools use mixed-age grouping.

In evaluating any nursery school, you need to look carefully at its program. What is included in the content of the curriculum? Can you judge how much preplanning takes place? How many trips are taken? Are there special teachers to enrich the program (music, dancing, etc.)? What are the opportunities for group interaction and for social and dramatic play? Equally, are there opportunities for individual concentration and solitary play? How is snack time handled—as an established group social time when everyone eats together or individually at any time a child asks for food? How is rest time handled, and moving from one activity to the next?

How would you describe the atmosphere in the classroom? Is it chaotic, spontaneous, controlled, or stilted? Do the children seem happy? Do you feel their social, cognitive, and affective needs are being met? Do the children seem bored, restless, or overstimulated by the program? What values are stressed—sharing, cooperation, cleanliness, routines? Are the children encouraged to learn to do things for themselves? Finally, are fathers involved in the program in any way?

What kinds of behavior are encouraged, and what are the limits on a child's behavior? How is discipline handled? How effective does it appear? How much pressure is put on the child to join the group and learn to get along with the group? Does the teacher allow for a child's individuality? How are the children helped to grow?

The Staff

It is important that you feel some rapport with your child's potential teachers. You should feel comfortable with the way the teachers are handling the children and satisfied with their competency and warmth.

Do the teachers appear in any way to be overwhelmed by the classroom situation? How well do they handle disputes among the children? Do the teachers listen fully to the children when they are talking, or are they busy getting something ready for the next project? Do the teachers interact with the children as individuals, or is the majority of their time spent dealing with small groups? Are they friendly without "smothering" the children with affection? Are they genuine with the children? How do the children respond to the staff members?

Physical Equipment and Surroundings

Examine the physical surroundings carefully. Are they clean and inviting? Are the children learning to handle the equipment with care, or are they behaving destructively? Are the books and puzzles accessible and attractive? Are the children encouraged to clean up after themselves; to put their own toys, books, and materials back on the shelves? Is there enough of a *variety* of stimulating materials to meet the changing interests of the children? Are the materials varied during the school year?

What is the physical arrangement of the room? Are there activity areas—a doll corner, housekeeping corner, art area, a workbench, a comfortable book corner, and child-sized tables and chairs?

Is the outdoor equipment attractive, safe, supervised, and adequately spaced? Are the children able to move freely from indoors to out, or does the group as a whole have an indoor time and an outdoor time?

Indoors and outdoors, is there opportunity for sand play, water play, and other "messy" activities? Is there a variety of art materials available at all times or only during art time? Are the art projects appropriate for the preschool child? Is there enough physical space inside, and provision for indoor large-muscle exercise and play on rainy days?

Comparing Early Childhood Curriculums

An important point to keep in mind is that although nursery schools may share common goals and materials or even a common name (e.g., Montessori), they may have very different atmospheres. This results from the variety of the teachers and their individual methods and philosophies of education. There is no "typical" Montessori school or "typical" nursery school. It is essential, therefore, to visit the *specific* programs you are considering, spend some time observing the groups of children during a session, and discuss the program with the head teacher afterward.

Many prekindergarten curriculums share similar long-range objectives. For example, both Montessori and more traditional nursery schools are philosophically dedicated to the optimum development of the individual child.

The Montessori Method

Maria Montessori (1870–1952), the first woman to be awarded the Doctor of Medicine degree at the University of Rome, conducted her experiments in early childhood education while serving as the first director of the State School for Defective Children in the slums of Rome. Influenced by the educational work of Édouard Séguin, an early nineteenth-century French physician and educator, she undertook postgraduate work in education and psychiatry.

She developed a curriculum and "hardware" for mentally retarded children which enabled them to take the public examination for primary certificates and pass. Her success with teaching the mentally deficient resulted in her being invited in 1907 to organize a school for normal infants in the slum tenements of Rome—the Casa dei Bambini ("House of Children").

The main features of what came to be known as the Montessori method were the development of the child's initiative through freedom of action, improvement of the senses, and the cultivation of coordination through exercises and games. The low cupboards of the classrooms offered an amazing array of manipulative learning aids. To teach the children daily personal tasks, there were wooden dressing frames, each mounted with cloth or leather to be fastened and unfastened by means of buttons and buttonholes, hooks and eyes, lacings, etc. To train the tactile sense, there were boards covered with sandpaper, cloth, and fur. For weight learning, Dr. Montessori provided equal wooden rectangles of different thicknesses whose weight had to be matched. To teach size, there were cylinders with knobs that had to be fitted into corresponding holes. One set of cylinders had equal height but differing diameters. To teach the concept of length and elementary addition, there were ten four-sided colored rods in sizes from one to ten inches that were to be put together in step-up sequence with alternating colors of red and blue. There were metal insets for the perception of size, shape, and color. To sharpen color awareness, there were sixty-four color tablets with gradations of three colors. A series of whistles were used for training sound discrimination. Small boxes filled with different substances (sand, pebbles, etc.) were employed to sharpen sound and hearing acuity. To teach the letters of the alphabet, there were sandpaper letters for the children to handle.

Over two hundred different structured teaching materials were developed for the practice of sensory powers and for academic learning. Although Dr. Montessori veered away from spontaneous play, her materials communicated academic concepts that words alone could not. No one before or after her has developed so many ways of experiencing the full array of learning skills. Her influence on the toy business in Europe and the United States has been profound.

Shunned by American educators advocating "free" play during the early childhood years, the Montessori method and materials did not do well in the United States until the 1960s and 1970s, when a concerted effort was made to establish Montessori schools and to exhibit her materials and publish her books.

Pioneers of the traditional nursery school movement complained that Montessori's program and materials were too closely structured to academics; that the classroom environment was "too prepared" and lacking in flexibility; that the method was firmly anchored in reality and left little or no room for spontaneity, fantasy, and play. Dr. Montessori's concept of freedom, they claimed, was based on the Catholic ethic of freedom to do what is "right" and that the authority, in this case the teacher, always retains the power to decide what is "wrong." Many of the early nursery school educators disliked the "rosary-type" beads used to communicate the decimal system of units, tens, and hundreds in mathematics study. They believed, as do many educators and child psychologists today, that the mental powers of very young children are not mature enough to handle such complex activities as formal mathematics and learning to read.

Albeit an incomplete system for early childhood education, the Montessori Method represents the considered work of a gifted, competent, dedicated woman who sought greater involvement of very young children in their own learning.

Visitors to Montessori classrooms are often impressed with the ordered environment. Children are usually working very intently individually or in small groups. They are free to work with a material as long as they choose, after which they return the material to its assigned place. The role of the Montessori directress is not to teach per se, but carefully and scientifically to observe the child and introduce materials when he is ready for them. She serves thus as a resource person and a catalyst.

A significant aspect of Maria Montessori's pedagogical understanding and contribution to learning is her recognition of and respect for individual differences. In a Montessori classroom, each child is free to learn. The Montessori method seeks to develop an inner discipline that comes from interaction with a wide assortment of self-corrective learning materials and tasks that provide a physical manipulative base for grasping number concepts; mastering shape, form, and color; experimenting with musical tone bars and sound, etc. There are some parents who have mistakenly interpreted these materials as early academics instead of recognizing them as sensory challenges and experiences.

Other important aspects of the Montessori method include:

- Heterogeneous grouping by age
- Emphasis on reality (as opposed to fantasy)
- A respect for nature
- Emphasis on structure and order
- The coordination of motor and mental activity
- Clearly set limits against destructive and asocial actions
- Daily life exercises (physical care of the child and surroundings), sensorial exercises, and academic exercises
- Correlation between sensitive periods of learning and maturation of bodily skills

Traditional Nursery Schools

By comparison, free, imaginative, social play is usually the most important activity in the traditional nursery school. Social and emotional growth through play is its primary goal. Building a positive self-image comes from construction play with blocks; creativity from painting, clay work, collage, and dancing.

However, in response to criticism of a lack of cognitive stimulation and academic preparation, many nursery schools have redefined their goals and restructured their programs in an attempt to provide more learning stimulation. In addition to the now familiar activity areas (a housekeeping and doll corner, an art area with double easels, blocks, an outside play area with hollow blocks, a sandbox, jungle gym, tricycles, etc.), there may be a puzzle and game table and an inviting book corner. Some traditional nursery schools also have Montessori materials available.

Many nursery schools have planned curriculums that include learning about community workers, animals, the seasons, and nature. Still other nursery schools actually have become prekindergarten programs with reading readiness drills, workbooks, etc.

In general, traditional nursery schools offer:

- Chronological age grouping and an emphasis on maturational development (age norms)
- Emphasis on *process* (process of playing, process of experimenting with art materials, etc.)
- Physical space divided into activity centers or zones (doll corner, dress-up corner, etc.)
- Emphasis on unstructured dramatic play and self-expression
- Emphasis on socialization and affective growth
- Emphasis on peer group interaction
- Some teacher-directed activities (group singing and games, community trips, storytelling, etc.)
- Concern with large-muscle development

The major differences between the Montessori and traditional approaches are that the Montessori program puts less stress on play and more on structured sensory exercises and achievements, and that the Montessori method allows a child

to move into early reading at her own pace. Most nursery schools have reading readiness materials, but do not include formal reading activities in their curriculum.

(Another completely different approach to preschool education is that of Carl Bereiter and Siegfried Engelmann, as presented in their book, *Teaching Disadvantaged Children in the Preschool* (Englewood Cliffs, NJ: Prentice-Hall, 1966). Their emphasis is on improving language skills, and they employ a strict drill-and-rote approach. Although their program was originally designed for disadvantaged children, it has received attention in middle-class areas also.)

"School Can Wait"

There is one group of educators, led by Raymond S. and Dorothy N. Moore, who advocate that the home rather than the early childhood center should serve the needs of children under six. In *School Can Wait* (Provo, UT: Brigham Young University Press, 1979), the Moores discuss factors which they believe have a major influence on learning in early childhood:

- The significant people in a child's life
- The nature of the material environment
- The interaction of people and the environment to provide opportunities for experience and exploration
- Values and self-esteem developed within the family and cultural context
- Physical, neurophysiological, and cognitive development and maturation
- Human and environmental resources that help develop the potential of the whole child for learning and living

A child relates to people and to the world primarily through interaction with parents (or other constant caregivers). This attachment enables the child to define herself as a person, separate yet related to those around her. Premature interference with this tie can threaten a child's satisfactory performance of her role as a social being. The home still appears to be the best place for acquiring a sense of security. At present no substitute is known for the family in this regard. Frequent interaction with both parents enables the child to accept separation with the least problem. Nevertheless, most children cannot tolerate separation from their mothers before the age of five; and for insecure children, this may continue until age eight.

PERSONALITY DEVELOPMENT

Emotionally, walking and running abilities make the Toddler-Two more self-sufficient. He fights to be included in every family activity, to do things independently ("I do it myself!"), including dressing, eating, cleaning, and dusting. The average Toddler-Two is a hellion physically, testing his newly found skills on furniture, carrying pots filled with liquids, pulling on a tablecloth to get at some snack—all of which add to the consternation of his parents. It takes special ability and endless patience as well as good humor on the part of parents (and teachers) to cope with the ups and downs of this age bracket.

Negativism

Most children between the ages of two and three assert their independence by saying "No!" Psychologists label this odd behavior as "negativism."

In *The New Parents' Guide to Early Learning* (New York: New American Library, 1976), Sara Bonnett Stein writes that "Negativism is a normal and even essential part of development and, unless it is inflated into a major issue between parent and child, is soon assimilated to the more constructive aspects of growing more independent."

Often a Toddler-Two will protest just for the fun of finding out how it feels to say "No." If parents overreact to this transitory phase of disobedience or rebellion, they will reinforce rather than discourage the negativism that they find so disconcerting. The child saying "No" is actually declaring herself in a very positive manner. She is letting you know that she has ideas of her own, and that she is desirous of saying or doing some things on her own.

"Most of the time, the toddler cooperates cheerfully, but negativistic behavior, real and intense but short-lived, can erupt in the midst of conformity. When a real battle of wills emerges, the parent needs to carry through with complete authority, as when a child persists in trying to do something dangerous or destructive. In the aftermath, though, the adult has to be careful that the child does not suffer damaging loss of face—which is possible even at a very early age."

Fitzhugh Dodson, in *How to Parent* (New York: New American Library, 1973), describes negativism as a passing stage between babyhood and early childhood. He considers it to be a *positive* stage in a child's development because "without it he would remain stuck in the equilibrium of babyhood." And Sara D. Gilbert, in *Three Years to Grow* (New York: Parents' Magazine Press, 1972), writes, "We shared the baby's delight when he discovered his hands and feet, and his pride when he took his first step. 'No!' and 'Mine!' may be harder to take, but they are just as surely signs of progress toward independent selfhood."

Toddler-Twos are often defiant of their parents and very inflexible in what they will or will not do. They want everything immediately and insist that things be done in the same manner every time. They will attempt to dominate their parents and make unreasonable demands of them. Their moods will change frequently, and their emotions will be violent at times, as in a temper tantrum.

Children at this stage will even say "No" to those things they do want to do. For instance, a child may be exclaiming loudly, "No, I don't want to take a bath," while actually climbing into the tub. In *The Magic Years* (New York: Charles Scribner's Sons, 1959), Selma H. Fraiberg says, " . . . to do just the opposite of what mother wants strikes the child as being the very essence of his individuality."

Often when your Toddler-Two is saying "No," she does not expect to be taken seriously. On the other hand, there are many instances when she means exactly what she says. It is up to you to determine when a situation may become harmful.

There are some methods for avoiding an impasse with your child. You can ignore his "No" as much as possible. Lead your child rather than ask him what he wants to do. Try to divert his attention by making simple games out of what you want him to do. Avoid questions that can be answered with "No." It will help if you limit your commands to as few as possible. In short, although you should insist upon obedience when it is absolutely necessary for your child's well-being, you might let him have his way when no danger or havoc may ensue.

Happily for all concerned, toddlers do not spend all their time being negative. As aptly stated by Mrs. Fraiberg, negativistic behavior "is a kind of declaration of independence, but there is no intention to unseat the government." It has been found that toddlers will stage a full-scale rebellion only if they are subjected to too much pressure or forceful handling by their parents or other caretakers.

No one has yet figured out exactly why children from twenty-four to thirty (or so) months of age are so contrary and contradictory. Actually the main thrust of these toddlers is not negativistic: it is merely one aspect of their innate need to become self-sufficient and independent. All children go through this rather trying stage of growth, even those who are developing smoothly.

Toddler-Twos Have Difficulty Making Choices

It is easy to understand why psychologists advise parents that "solving the problems of a child this age usually calls for direct action rather than long parental lectures."

A mother learns that when a Toddler-Two races across a dangerous intersection, it is not the time to moan about his disobedience and to reason with him. Instead, she needs to race after him, swoop him up in her arms, and firmly return him to safety.

Parental supervision is especially imperative now because although Toddler-Twos have a very efficient system of locomotion, they possess neither the judgment nor the experience to go with it. Therefore, they wander into all kinds of danger: busy streets, abandoned refrigerators, irrigation ditches, etc. Toddler-Twos do not yet have enough sense to take care of themselves.

In *So You Want to Raise a Boy?* (Garden City, NY: Doubleday, 1962), Cleon W. Skousen writes, "Mealtime for a two-year-old can be wracked with difficulties making decisions. Mother prepares an excellent lunch and then after everyone is seated around the table, she suddenly discovers that her child is rejecting the entire menu and holding out for crisp bacon and coddled eggs. If he is offered strained beans, he may be hankering for yellow carrots. If she tries to reason with him, he is likely to respond by dumping the whole mess on the floor."

Temper Tantrums

There are times when no strategy works with a defiant Toddler-Two. Using her limited vocabulary of two hundred words or so, she will try to argue back. When she fails to make an impact, she feels abused and frustrated. Eventually she discovers a powerful method of arguing back—she throws herself on the floor, kicking and screaming so fiercely that the neighbors think her mother is "killing her." From previous experience, she must have learned that this shocking behavior will get a reaction from her trembling parents. They plead, beg, or bribe her to stop. This infantile blackmail is called a *temper tantrum.*

Let's face reality! The child from two onward is faced with all

kinds of family and community-imposed pressures to "fit in" and to "behave properly." The Toddler-Two is expected to share toys with his agemates, begin to learn better table manners, refrain from climbing on furniture and making a mess in the living room—on and on ad infinitum.

The very active child who possesses a volatile temperament can become difficult and defiant if continually curbed and corrected. When acutely frustrated, she is liable to extremes of rage as well as fear. Most two-year-olds will have tantrums once or twice a week; indeed, few children reach their third birthday without experiencing any. "Those who have a lot of tantrums are usually lively children—who know what they want to do—and they mind a great deal when someone or something prevents them," writes Penelope Leach in her book, *Your Baby and Child from Birth to Age Five* (New York: Alfred A. Knopf, 1980). "A tantrum is like an emotional blown fuse; it is not something which a toddler can prevent. The load of frustration builds up inside him until he is so full of tension that only an explosion can release it."

How to Handle a Temper Tantrum

Many authorities believe parents should neither argue with nor threaten their distressed child; that physical punishment will only increase the screaming. Rather, they suggest, pick your child up and take him to another room. It is helpful to leave him alone until he settles down. To prevent your child from hurting another child, it might be necessary for you to hold him gently but firmly on the floor until his outburst subsides. Eventually his screams will become sobs, and "the furious monster becomes a pathetic baby who has screamed himself sick and frightened himself silly."

If you are in a public place when an explosion erupts, do not let it embarrass you. If your child sees that her actions affect you in this way, she will stage tantrums more often, even for years to come. You might try to figure out what caused the thundering encounter in order to be able to avoid another one in the future.

What the child needs most during an emotional outburst is that the parent remain as tranquil and firm as possible. It is recommended that the child be removed as quickly as possible from a public situation to a quiet place. Young children must learn gradually to control this violent response to frustration. It may take time before the child's screams and kicking subside (never allow him to kick you). When he is quiet, he will need you to comfort him. Show him you love him, and gently bring him back to normalcy. Try to give your child a chance to get out of the episode in as face-saving a way as possible. You might suggest something quiet but interesting to do together.

Constant temper tantrums can signify overtiredness or some medical problem. More often, they indicate that a parent has not found the solution to some personality problem that is troubling the child. Are there too many restrictions in your child's life? Is he getting sufficient attention, approval, and affection under less trying circumstances? Did you choose the right moment to interfere with his play or make an unreasonable demand just before his outburst?

Establishing Limits

When the two-year-old begins to take first steps toward expressing her independence, the parents are placed in the delicate position of deciding how much freedom is to be tolerated and when to assert themselves. An atmosphere of complete permissiveness can encourage continual testing by the child to find out how far she can go. Research shows that children feel more secure in an environment where reasonable limits are set by the parents.

Some parents are uncertain about setting limits when their toddler is expressing his emerging selfhood. Of course, the two-year-old lacks sufficient nuances in language expression to comprehend the why and wherefore of every rule set down by a parent. At the same time, parents cannot expect to be able to reason well with a child so young.

Now is the time for you to say "No" and mean it, especially if it concerns your child's health or safety, or the well-being of others in the family. This is *not* the time to give your Toddler-Two too many alternatives; nor is it the time for getting into endless confrontations with her. "The moment parents have to bargain with a child," write Lee Salk and Rita Kramer in *How to Raise a Human Being* (New York: Random House, 1969), "you're in trouble."

Normal Fears

As babies grow older they become increasingly aware of their environment. They seem to have some appreciation of size and depth, and realize that their parents are big and they are little. They become more sensitive to new and strange objects and people and unanticipated changes in everyday occurrences. Infants startle at the loss of support and at sudden, loud noises; also at changes in temperature when they are bathed; and at sudden approaches by unfamiliar persons. Because mother has become someone very special, older babies may become unhappy if left with a stranger. These are normal fears, and almost all children experience at least some of them.

Without some fear, a child might injure herself. Fear of

heights is common, and serves a definite function. There are other fears that serve no useful purpose; i.e., fear of a vacuum cleaner, fear of the dark, fear of going to bed or going to sleep, fear of animals.

Toddler-Twos have a variety of fears that develop along with their expanding imaginations. Make-believe creatures such as ogres, giants, and monsters are especially prominent. These creatures represent in a concrete way a child's undefinable fears and anxieties. (Because fears are directed toward specific objects, they are relatively easy to deal with; anxieties—vague, fearful feelings unconnected to a particular source—are not.) Dr. Joseph Church notes that children this age are apt to develop fears about "intactness." Some children are afraid of or refuse to have anything to do with broken toys or broken cookies because they have a sympathetic reaction to such brokenness; that is, "If it happened to the cookie, it might happen to me."

How Children Cope with Fears and Fantasies

As perceived by a child, the world is full of magical possibilities, and as a result, the young child's thinking is not restricted to what is or is not possible. There could be something under her bed; she reasons that since her cat goes under there all the time, maybe other animals do, too. The obvious next step is to imagine something like a tiger under the bed. Children react differently to this imaginary fear. One child may stay awake all night to be ready for the tiger if he should come out; another might cling to mother or father and scream hysterically at bedtime. One Toddler-Two might stalk the imaginary tiger during the day; another might develop fear of all animals. Selma Fraiberg, in her fine book, *The Magic Years,* tells of two-year-old Jan, who created a playmate she named Laughing Tiger. By stalking and conquering her imaginary enemy under the dining room table, Jan worked through her fear.

Fear may lead a child to learn more about the frightening object or situation. As an example of a positive response to a fear of noise, there is the two-year-old child who disassembles the vacuum cleaner in his search for the source of the noise.

Young children develop a variety of defenses against fear. Some withdraw totally from threatening situations, an example being the nursery school child who stands in a corner with her coat on day after day to try to mitigate the effects of separation from mother. The child who cannot deal with his fears may claim that a frightening event never happened; for example, his pet did not die. Children who are afraid of admitting something "bad" about themselves may blame the "badness" on someone or something else. It is natural to use defenses like these, and sometimes they are helpful. However, their persistent use as a way of avoiding facing reality is a sign that the child is overly anxious.

Children have their own way of dealing with their fears, whether real or imagined, and it is up to the parents to reassure them that there is no need to be afraid.

Aggressive Behavior

In the course of maturing, a child learns to bring his aggressive tendencies more and more under control. Early on, he feels and shows affection for people and situations that make him feel pleasant, and anger and aggressiveness at those who frustrate him. Most young children engage in some fighting, biting, and hitting as they learn to get along with others. However, if a child constantly resorts to such actions in his everyday relationships, and persists in hurting other children over an extended period of time, then perhaps it is a sign that he may require special help. Usually, as with many other problems of childhood, this is a passing phase that can be handled by the child and observant parent.

From a practical point of view, a parent may ask, "How far should I permit my two-year-old to go?" "Should I let her hit, bite, and scratch other children?" The answer, of course, is no. She must learn how to get along with other people and to respect their feelings and rights. Parents need to help their children understand that hurting others cannot be allowed. It is also important for each child to know that there is someone who loves her, but will not permit her to hurt others. Discovering that there are limits beyond which she cannot go is very reassuring to Toddler-Twos as well as older children.

You can teach your child gradually that some things are socially acceptable and some are not; that when he does certain things, such as hurting others, people do not like it. Make sure, however, that you do not let him build up a fear that he is not loved, or that he will be loved *only* if he is a "good" boy.

If a child of two always seems to be a grabber, it does not necessarily mean that she is going to become a bully. Since she is still too young to have much feeling for others, you might let her grab sometimes. Should she do this constantly, it might help if you let her play occasionally with older children who will stand up for their rights and "put her in her place." If she seems to be intimidating a particular child, it might be better to keep them apart for a while. Sometimes just removing your child in a matter-of-fact way and getting her interested in something else can be very helpful.

Sara Gilbert maintains that even though parents need to be firm in dealing with Toddler-Twos, they should *never* resort to severe punishment. No one wants to completely crush a child's newly found ability to assert himself because some of this behavior will be useful later on in life. What is really called for is to help the child redirect his aggression into less harmful activities.

Studies of aggression indicate two major factors that contribute to the instigation and learning of "bullying" behavior:

• *Frustration, restrictiveness, and rejection.* The effects of punitive and restrictive child-rearing practices have been studied by many psychologists, who have found that the highest percentage of aggression is associated with high permissiveness and high punishment; the lowest with low permissiveness and low punishment. Parents who go to extremes by permitting destructive behavior or by instituting severe punishments appear to be fostering intense childhood aggression.

• *Modeling after aggressive figures in the environment.* The parents' use of punishment serves as a model for the learning of aggression. Ironically, its employment provides a living example of the use of aggression at the very moment parents are trying to teach the child not to be combative.

As you guide your Toddler-Two, keep in mind that you are the parent and that you must set the controls. It does not help your child if you deny your authority. The trend today is to set clear and consistent limits without forgetting love. As often as you can, establish reasonable limits without blowing up, and then live by your decisions.

The "Too-Obedient" Child

When a child always gives in meekly, it is time for the parents to investigate the cause. Often the too-obedient child has aggressive feelings, but is deeply afraid to express them. For motives that are not always clear, a child who has every reason to feel loved and secure may instead be uncertain, shy, and timid. Instead of being alarmed, parents should feel relieved when one day their child finally fights for his rights or answers back instead of giving up. Children who never rebel need encouragement to speak up for what they feel and want. At the same time, healthy self-assertion need not show itself as constant readiness to fight physically or speak loudly. Many gentle, soft-spoken people are very effective in protecting their rights and opinions.

Sexual Differences in Toddler-Twos

Considerable research has been undertaken in this field. It appears that one-year-old girls have already been influenced by parents and relatives and are distinctly feminine in their choices of toys to play with (manipulative toys and quiet play) as against active play for boys. This type of behavior may stem from children imitating their parents.

There also are studies showing that girls walk, talk, and learn to use the toilet earlier. Of course, there are differences in the way parents react to the behavior of boys as against girls. Boys are given freedom to assert themselves, to roughhouse, to explore. Playrooms also reflect adult attitudes: dolls and dollhouses for girls, cars and trucks for boys.

In *Your Two-Year-Old: Terrible or Tender* (New York: Delacorte, 1976), Louise Bates Ames and Frances Ilg write, "That [sex] differences do exist is generally admitted . . . In the past it was assumed that they were inherited. Today many feel that they are, at least in part, caused by society's expectations and stereotypes. Today in many families, these expectations are changing. Many parents take special pains to give their children . . . the feeling that it is all right for boys to behave in a soft or gentle way; for girls to be rough, tough, and vigorous."

PLAY AND PLAYTHINGS

The most uninhibited period in a child's life, when he can build his ego firmly, covers his second and third years. At this time, play may be his only real means of building self-image. The child *must* be the center of every play situation. He must play the mother, father, or the baby. He is not ready to allow dolls to play these roles. He becomes the baby, occupies the doll carriage, and often destroys it by his weight or its lack of sturdiness. In their search for bigness, Toddler-Twos imitate the important people in their lives: mother talking on the telephone, tackling father's tools, helping push the lawnmower, walking in big sister's high-heel shoes, etc.

Because of her smallness, the two-year-old is shut out from playing any role in the exciting real-life world of adults: driving a car, steering a boat, building a skyscraper. The two-year-old deliberately creates a make-believe world of roads with her blocks, cars, and play people, and makes all do her bidding. As more language develops, she uses words to fantasize and recreate many of the settings and events in the real world. As she maneuvers her play people and trucks in this imaginative play, she is fortifying her inner feelings about her own powers. In *Understanding Children's Play* (New York: Columbia University Press, 1952), Ruth E. Hartley, Lawrence K. Frank, and Robert M. Goldenson elaborate: "When they build airports, skyscrapers, they are not merely reproducing objects; they are, at least in fantasy, gaining control over things that ordinarily dwarf them."

Transportation toys, whether of the ride 'em type or miniatures, give Toddler-Twos and three-year-olds the feeling of being "in the driver's seat." They feel titanic as they cause harmless head-on collisions of their toy vehicles on their building-block roadways. When a child of two-and-a-half or three knocks down his block structure, he is merely asserting his right to destroy his own self-created product.

The play materials that most readily enable a child to affect her environment are the unpainted hardwood nursery school unit blocks (for indoor use) and hollow blocks and play boards (for indoor and outdoor use). With such large blocks a child can build a "big world" in a short time.

Structured versus Unstructured Toys and Play

Dr. Mary Ann Pulaski reports, in Jerome Singer's book *The Child's World of Make-Believe* (New York: Academic Press, 1973), that the structure of the toys available to a child has a profound effect upon the level of her make-believe play and creativity. One of the characteristics that distinguishes human from animal play in childhood is the capacity for make-believe. Dr. Pulaski is concerned that in today's society there are increasingly less opportunities for children to exercise their imagination. Through movies, television, and their toys, children are provided with the utmost in prefabricated play materials. "Dolls as well dressed and sophisticated as Vogue models, and war toys so realistic as often to be gruesome are rampant. Nothing is left to the imagination. Thus, it is conceivable that imagination and fantasy may decline in some groups for lack of practice."

What is the difference between structured and unstructured toys? Generally, structured playthings have more detail, lack multipurpose, and can be used for one situation only; they are less flexible in a play setting. For example, a milk truck designed with great detail can be used only for playing at milk delivery. However, a wooden block on wheels or a cab and trailer shape with no detail can be used in all kinds of floor play. Why pay for elaborate play settings (playhouse, farm, airport, hospital, marina, etc.) when one set of blocks and a few play people and animals can reproduce almost all of these at a fraction of the cost?

A child has more play choices with unstructured play materials in which the reward lies in the excitement of discovery and in the play activity itself. There are no preconceived goals engineered into unstructured playthings, no adult-imposed objectives. Most often, such toys are the *raw materials of play*, which include nursery school unit building blocks, clay, sand, finger paints, water, poster paints, brushes, paper, pegs and pegboards, design cubes, etc.—for all of which there are no restricting blueprints to follow.

Initially the child "fools around" with the material; i.e., she may arrange blocks in long roads or stand them up on end and topple them. She may try filling a large piece of paper with broad strokes of paint. All children gain pleasure and a real

sense of confidence in themselves each time they master the elements in their play world.

Caroline Pratt Playthings

Caroline Pratt, teacher of woodcraft and founder-principal of the City and Country School in New York City for three-to-thirteen-year-olds, was also a pioneer educational toymaker. She knew that the secret of good toys is multiple usage, freedom from frustrating details, and ease in manipulation.

She created wedge-shaped people, six-inch-high wooden cutouts of everyday community workers and family figures, wide at the bottom and thin at the top so that they could stand without toppling. She designed wooden trucks and cars and interlocking floor trains without wheels for easy maneuvering by the youngest girls and boys.

Miss Pratt set about providing young children with a climbing-carrying-pulling-pushing environment with limitless city and country building and dramatization possibilities. From the carpenter, she borrowed the sawhorse; from the painter, the ladder and walking board as well as wide paint brushes, pails, and rope. From the bricklayer, she adapted large wooden hollow blocks for building houses, stores, etc. From the cement worker, she took the single-wheel barrow and made it into a two-wheel barrow for greater stability. From the dock worker, she adapted the oversized wooden packing crate, barrel, and platform truck. Out of all these Miss Pratt created a mobile play environment that could start physical activity and imaginative play working overtime.

Lifting the heavy but portable hardwood hollow blocks activates the back muscles. Maneuvering a packing crate and building a house or a boat require the cooperation and strength of several children. The walking board exercises physical coordination and a sense of balance.

In play and work projects, Miss Pratt believed in teaching all children to "manage danger." For example, she removed guardrails on climbers, slides, and raised platforms.

We believe her finest accomplishment remains her unit building blocks. These floor play blocks consist of many matched units: the unit block, square or half unit, double unit, and the quadruple unit. Also included are curves, cylinders, ramps, triangles, pillars, etc. The smooth, accurately engi-

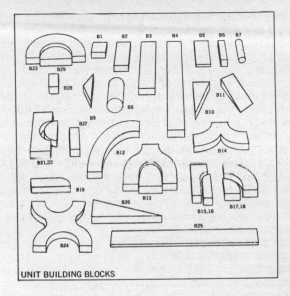

UNIT BUILDING BLOCKS

UNIT BUILDING BLOCKS BY THE PIECE

B 1	SQUARE.	1⅜″x2¾″x2¾″
B 2	OBLONG.	1⅜″x2¾″x5½″
B 3	DOUBLONG.	1⅜″x2¾″x11″
B 4	QUADLONG.	1⅜″x2¾″x22″
B 5	ROOF BOARD.	⅜″x2¾″x11″
B 6	PILLAR.	1⅜″x1⅜″x5½″
B 7	COLUMN.	1⅜″x5½″
B 8	LARGE COLUMN.	2¾″x5½″
B 9	DIAGONAL.	1⅜″x2¾″x2¾″
B10	TRIANGLE.	1⅜″x2¾″x5½″
B11	RAMP.	1⅜″x2¾″x5½″
B12	ELLIPTICAL CURVE.	1⅜″x8¼″x11″
B13	LARGE SWITCH & GOTHIC DOOR.	1⅜″x8¼″x11″
B14	Y-SWITCH.	1⅜″x5½″x8¼″
B15		
& 16	HALF ARCH & BUTTRESS.	1⅜″x2¾″x5½″
B17		
& 18	CIRCULAR CURVE & QUARTER CIRCLE.	1⅜″x2¾″x7¾″
B19	LARGE BUTTRESS.	1⅜″x2¾″x5½″
B21		
& 22	ROMAN ARCH & HALF CIRCLE.	1⅜″x5½″
B23	HALF CIRCULAR CURVE.	1⅜″x5½″x11″
B24	DOUBLE SWITCH CURVE.	1⅜″x11″x11″
B25	FLOOR BOARD.	⅜″x2¾″x22″
B26	DOUBLE UNIT TRIANGLE.	1⅜″x2¾″x11″
B27	HALF PILLAR.	1⅜″x2¾″x1⅜″
B28	QUARTER PILLAR.	1⅜″x1⅜″x1⅜″
B29	SOLID HALF CIRCLE.	1⅜″x5½″x2¾″

neered, natural-finish hardwood blocks are easily handled by children and can be put to an infinite variety of uses.

Miss Pratt thought that blocks were suited perfectly to children's play purposes because a simple geometric shape could become any number of things: a house, truck, plane, boat, railroad, car, barn, or skyscraper. Building with blocks starts out at about two years of age as a simple, individual play activity; cooperative block play begins at about four or five years of age, when plans and constructions grow increasingly complicated.

A child cannot build unless she has sufficient building blocks on hand; at least twenty or more units and twenty or more double units. If your department store or toy shop does not sell blocks by the piece, try the school supply house listed in your telephone Yellow Pages directory.

Here are our recommendations for age-graded block sets:

Starter Block Set for Two-Year-Olds
10 half units (2¾" × 2¾")
10 units (2¾" × 5½")
10 double units (2¾" × 11")
8 pillars (1⅜" × 5½")
8 small triangles (2¾" × 2¾")

Block Set for Three-Year-Olds
12 half units (2¾" × 2¾")
16 units (2¾" × 5½")
16 double units (2¾" × 11")
2 roof boards (2¾" × 11" × ¹¹⁄₃₂")
12 pillars (1⅜" × 5½")
2 small cylinders (1⅜" × 5½")
2 large cylinders (2¾" × 5½")
10 small triangles (2¾" × 2¾")
2 large triangles (2¾" × 5½")

Block Set for Four-Year-Olds
12 half units (2¾" × 2¾")
16–26 units (2¾" × 5½")
16–30 double units (2¾" × 11")
4 quadruple units (2¾" × 22")
12 pillars (1⅜" × 5½")
4 large cylinders (2¾" × 5½")
6 small triangles (2¾" × 2¾")

6 large triangles (2¾" × 5½")
2 ramps (2¾" × 5½")
2–4 elliptical curves (2¾" × 13½")
1 Y switch (8¼" × 11")
1 right-angle switch (5½" × 8")
2–4 circular curves (2¾" × 8")
1 Gothic arch and door

The thickness of all blocks, unless indicated otherwise, is 1⅜".

Keep adding to a starter set each month until your child has enough blocks to build a structure as tall as he is. Do not worry about their cost. After your children have used them daily for about eight years, you will be able to sell them as desirable "seconds" to schools or other parents. You will be amazed at the prices people pay for these hardwood block sets twenty years later. So beg, borrow, or budget the money; hardwood unit building blocks will be your best toy investment! (We recommend that you buy your building blocks from a reputable nursery school or kindergarten supplier. Blocks are hard to make at home because they require precise measuring and heavy-duty cutting tools.)

Bendable or wedge-shaped play people in proper scale (one inch to one foot), assorted animals, and cars and trucks expand the play possibilities of unit building blocks. Parents who watch a city or country scene unfold can accelerate learning by introducing signs to identify streets and buildings, ferries and barges for food and other waterway transport, etc. They can intervene with suitable stories and trips to local places of interest to keep curiosity perking.

Of course, intervention is a role that parents need to assume with great care. Children relish interchange of playfulness with adults, but only when it is not heavy-handed. There is real·imprinting on creativeness in later life if a child has enjoyed adult support for his or her early play fantasies and efforts. The right suggestion, the right word at the right time can deepen and enrich play experience.

. The following lists are designed to help you choose appropriate toys for twenty-four- to thirty-six-month-olds:

Quiet and Manipulative Play
dress-me dolls (zippers, snaps, buckles, etc.)
self-help cloth books
beads to string (and laces with long metal tips)

filling and emptying toys (pocketbooks, coffee cans of varying sizes)
junior lock box
shape-sorting box
hammer-and-peg toy
activity boards (locks and keys, doors that open, latches, sliding doors, telephone dials, etc.)
stacking and nesting plastic salad bowls
pegs and peg board (wood or rubber)
finger puppets

Housekeeping and Social Play
child-size kitchen (stove, refrigerator, sink)
pots and pans (child-size)
stationary ironing board and wooden iron
tea set (child-size)
empty plastic bottles
housecleaning set (school quality)
push broom

plastic play foods
large doll bed (heavy-duty)
sturdy child-size rocking chair
rag dolls, rubber dolls
animals (cloth, wood, rubber)
wooden telephone (or durable plastic)
table and two chairs (child-size)
jiffy playhouse
lunch box
dress-up clothes, handbags, grown-up shoes, etc.
eyeglass frames without glass inserts
large mirror, hand mirror

Transportation and Community Play
hardwood unit building blocks (nursery school type)
wooden trains on tracks (Skaneateles)
solid wood transportation toys (interlocking train, tug and
   barge)
family and community play people (wood or rubber)
farm and zoo rubber animals (1″ to 1′ scale)

Active Play
rocking boat
double-wheel kiddy car
bent plywood doll carriage
giant ride 'em toys (tractor and trailer, etc.)
rocking horse (child should be able to mount and dismount)
toddler gym
doorway gym

Matching and Sorting Play
picture lotto and number lotto games
giant dominoes, picture dominoes
jigsaw puzzles (2 to 5 pieces with identifiable parts: head,
   body, arms, legs)
inset boards
color cubes

Craft Materials
jumbo crayons
poster paints, unprinted newsprint paper (18″ × 24″)
long-handled brushes (1″ or ¾″ wide)

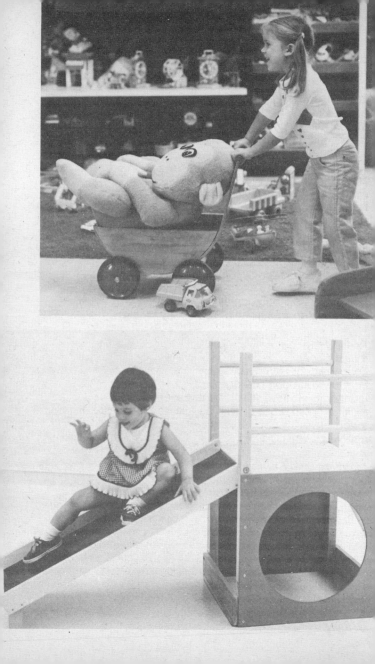

painting easel
moist clay or Play-Doh

Musical Toys
music boxes
sturdy wooden and metal xylophone
rhythm instruments: cymbals, triangle and striker, sturdy tambourine, rhythm sticks
record player

Play Yard Equipment
hollow blocks (5½" × 11" × 11"–5½" × 11" × 22") and
  playboards
sawhorses and teeter board
walking board
wooden ladder
rope ladder
packing crate (large and small)
large paint brush for water painting
wheelbarrow
containers to fill or empty
platform truck, porter's hand truck
steel or wood wagon
wooden barrels (white pine, 17" long × 10" diameter)
sandbox (shovels, sifter, pail, etc.)

(Also explore toys by Fisher-Price, Playskool, Childcraft,
Community Playthings, and local nursery school and kindergarten supply houses. Check the Yellow Pages of your telephone directory. You can ask the nursery school director for
recommendations and the loan of equipment catalogues.)

The Importance of Scribbling

In *Creative and Mental Growth* (New York: Macmillan, 5th
printing 1967), Viktor Lowenfeld and W. Lambert Brittain write
that "The first drawing attempts of a child can be extremely
important to the child . . . but also to the sensitive adult who
sees in these marks an individual's early efforts to express
himself.

"At some point, usually at about two years of age, the child
given a crayon will start to make marks on a piece of paper
(some children may start as early as eighteen months) . . . A

very young child will find a crayon more interesting to look at, feel, or taste. The first scribbles will be random marks . . . and out of this he gains great satisfaction . . .

"At some point a child will discover that there is a connection between his motions and the marks on the paper. This may occur about six months or so after the child has started to scribble . . . Now he experiences visually what he has done kinesthetically."

Inasmuch as motor coordination is a basic achievement of all children, they should be encouraged to scribble freely. Very young children delight in just moving their crayons across paper. There is no finished product at this juncture.

According to Lowenfeld and Brittain, color is of little import in the child's scribbling stage. Actually an assortment of colors can redirect a child from scribbling to playing with the colors. They recommend beginning with a black crayon on white paper. Using colors can come later on because it is more important in the scribbling stage for the child to create lines and shapes and to learn to control his eye-hand coordination.

Although most young children enjoy covering two or three sheets of paper with scribbles, very young children will not continue at this activity for more than a few minutes. The three-year-old may be involved for as long as fifteen minutes. If the four-year-old has reached the stage of naming her scribbling, she may keep at this activity for as many as thirty minutes.

Moist Clay or Play-Doh

Moist clay or Play-Doh is another fine material for this age level. Manipulating a pliant material enables a child to use his fingers in a different way. Pounding clay is a parallel stage to beginning scribbling. In time, a child may pick up a lump of clay, shape it a little bit, and call it a dog. This indicates that he has changed from kinesthetic to imaginative thinking. Clay should not be too hard to work with, or so thin that it sticks to the fingers. Moist clay can be stored in a plastic bag for an indefinite period of time.

Making Music

Children are musical beings. A newborn responds to his mother's voice and will turn his head to hear the household sounds. Five-month-old babies babble and coo (a first form of singing) for the sheer joy of trying out sounds. Six- to nine-month-old babies react positively to their mothers' songs and body games. Toddlers hum and sing as they go about their play. In essence, singing is a language that comes naturally to all children.

In *Guiding Your Child to a More Creative Life* (Garden City, NY: Doubleday, 1973), Fredelle Maynard urges parents to make singing a part of the family's daily activity. She points out that in many households the only singing occurs at Christmas. Singing at the table, after eating, is a happy thing to do. Singing in the car can also contribute to emotional well-being. Most adults know many songs whose rhythmical patterns and repeated melodies make them especially appealing to children. To make songs more meaningful, parents can personalize them by introducing the child's name into the songs.

Every home should have a collection of recorded folk, ethnic, and traditional songs, and an assortment of songbooks. Listening to records will extend musical enjoyment and knowledge. Since your child will want the same songs played repeatedly, you will find music time more enjoyable if you do not confine yourself to children's records. Broaden your child's musical taste. Try everything from classical guitar to Indian sitar. Better still, take your young child to a live concert where there is a folksinger.

You might purchase (or request as gifts from grandparents, etc.) some standard percussion instruments for accompanying familiar songs. Select a well-loved song, "Old McDonald," for instance, and let the children beat out its rhythm. Rhythm sticks can be used to beat out the underlying rhythm, and other instruments can provide the sound of animals: *Quack, quack* can be the rattle of maracas; *Oink, oink* a scraping of two sandblocks, and *Baa, baa* triangle tones. Another good game to play with a rhythm band set is imitating common sounds; for example, which instrument sounds like a *knock on the door?* (rhythm sticks and a drum); *a telephone ringing?* (wrist bells); *marching soldiers?* (a snare drum); *an alarm clock?* (a metal triangle).

In their infant studies, Gesell and Ilg attempted to set down the growth of music sensitivity as follows:

Twenty-four Months*
- Sings phrases of songs (most often not on pitch)
- Enjoys rocking and swinging equipment (rocking boat, rocking chair, swing); spontaneously sings songs while engaged in these activities
- Enjoys repetition of familiar tunes
- Responds to musical rhythms by swinging arms, swaying head, tapping feet

Thirty Months*
- Knows all or parts of several songs
- Enjoys band and marked rhythm music
- Runs, gallops, swings to music

Thirty-six Months*
- Sings whole songs
- Likes to experiment with simple rhythms
- Will listen to simple explanations about songs and musical instruments
- Some can carry tunes

*See *Infant and Child in the Culture Today* by Arnold Gesell and Frances Ilg, et al. (New York: Harper & Row, 1940, rev. ed. 1974).

Singing Enhances
Language Acquisition

Singing is closely connected to language as creative expression. It can be a pleasurable part of the daily life of all children. Especially enjoyed are action songs with repetitive patterns that generally are found in folk songs that children will repeat endlessly until they thoroughly master their words and absorb their rhythm and spirit. Cowboy songs, sea chanteys, ballads, and work songs have universal appeal. Children appear to relish such songs because of the quality of dramatic action in the words themselves.

Swinging and Singing

When little children are happy and busy, they usually sing. You can encourage singing by providing opportunities for such rhythmic activities as swinging, bouncing, pounding, etc. Most young children feel that swinging and singing go together.

When your child and you listen to a recording of a folk song, you can ask her, "Was the song loud or soft?" "Was it fast or slow?" "Was it the same all the way through?" Her responses will let you know how well she has been paying attention.

HEALTH, SELF-HELP,
AND ROUTINES

Keeping your child in safe and good health gets to be more difficult with each passing month. With increased locomotion, Toddler-Twos come in contact with more of their agemates. They are more active physically and socially and subject to more accidents and illnesses. Caring for a sick child passing through critical physical, verbal, social, and ego-building phases requires a balance between overprotection and considered negligence. Parents have to know and understand the hazards and become alert to "behind-the-scenes" protection of their children. They need also to have clear information on the growth and development of their children.

In a young child, the first sign of an incipient disease or handicap often is failure to grow and/or greatly lagging development. Early recognition of a developmental delay by parents and examination by a pediatrician can lead to helpful diagnosis, the correction of most abnormalities, as well as the prevention of illness and its potential complications.

Feeding and Nutrition

Proper nutrition remains an important parental consideration. Because growth rate and weight gain reach a plateau during this period, feeding schedules are harder to maintain. Definite food likes and dislikes appear. Exploring new foods and eating nutritionally become higher priorities. Two is probably the last time for establishing good eating habits.

Most professionals in the medical and nutritional fields agree that if good eating habits are not set in the first two to three years of life, by five to six years of age, children will lose the chance to grow up to be healthy adults. They must not eat the wrong foods ("junk" foods) and they must not be bribed with candy or cookies to eat everything on their plates—or even to behave. Another factor that leads to childhood obesity is the failure of children to exercise and thereby burn off enough calories.

Dr. Jean Mayer, Professor of Nutrition at Harvard University from 1950 to 1976, and presently President of Tufts University, has taken a firm stand against the use of sugar in the diet. In reviewing the evidence in an article that appeared in the June 20, 1976, edition of *The New York Times Sunday Magazine,* Dr. Mayer concluded that the habitual consumption of large amounts of sugar *is* a menace to health. *On sugar and dental caries:* 98 percent of North American children have some tooth decay, and by age fifty-five about half of our population has *no* teeth. A recent governmental study suggests that sugar consumption is related positively to tooth decay. *On sugar and overweight:* Current statistics indicate that 10 to 20 percent of all U.S. children and 35 to 50 percent of middle-aged Americans are overweight. Too much sugar in the diet in the form of "empty" calories (no nutrients) is a major factor. *On sugar and other diseases:* Overweight in general and too much sugar specifically have been found to be related to hypertension and the onset of diabetes in adults. Dr. Mayer urges parents to decrease sugar consumption. Never buy junk foods! Use other sources of carbohydrates: dry beans, unbleached flour, whole-grain cereals, and milk. Try to brush or rinse your teeth after eating and get your children to do the same, especially after consuming sugar-laden foods.

How Much Sleep Is Enough for Toddler-Twos?

Much has been written on the subject of how much sleep children need. In the second and third years of life, the range can vary anywhere from eight to seventeen hours. This time span indicates how different children are from each other. Certainly children who require only eight hours of sleep per night cannot be kept in bed for fifteen hours without distressing themselves and their parents.

Writes Richard H. Granger, M.D., in *Your Child from One to Six,* "Obviously it is essential to treat each child's sleep needs individually. How do you tell whether your child has enough sleep? One way is by setting regular bedtimes from the beginning, and noting when your child wants to get up. The child who gets up very early may be one of those short sleepers and may need to go to sleep a little later at night to keep peace in the family."

Another way of judging is to watch how your child behaves during the day. If she is alert and active, and eats and plays well, then she is getting enough sleep. If, however, your child is cranky and falls asleep in the wrong places, at the wrong times, then she may not be getting enough sleep at night. Of course, some days are more active and exciting, and sleep periods may be altered. When children are ill, schedules usually go haywire and do not readjust until life returns to normal. Most parents set a regular hour for bedtime for each child, which takes into account that child's age level and the adults' work and dining schedules. Once set, bedtimes should be followed except for special occasions, or when the need for sleep changes as children grow older.

Most two- and three-year-olds do not like to give up their play time for sleep time. To avoid doing it, they advise all kinds of rituals: requests for one last story, a drink of water, another trip to the bathroom, a special doll, stuffed animal, or favorite blanket to cuddle up with are common ploys. Parents need to be aware that if such security objects are destroyed or lost, a family crisis could ensue. Fortunately, children outgrow these attachments as they grow older.

Child-care specialists agree with Dr. Granger that whenever possible a child should sleep in her own bed, in her own room, with the door closed. If this is not feasible, she should sleep in her own bed in a room she shares with other children in the family. Preferably, children should not sleep in the same room or the same bed with their parents. It has been found that children sleep better and have fewer fears and fantasies if these procedures are followed from the beginning.

Some Other Sleep Questions

When should children give up a crib? Pediatricians and manufacturers are in accord that by their second birthdays, Toddler-Twos can climb out of a crib and should sleep in a youth bed or a regular low bed. (Some agile eighteen-month-olds can climb out of a crib!) The change from crib to bed should be made *before* a baby brother or sister is brought home to avoid emotional encounters about the toddler's being "replaced" by the new arrival.

Sleeping under a blanket or with a pillow? Young children do not stay under a blanket and are better off in pajamas with feet for cold weather. They all sleep better and more healthfully without pillows. Some parents purchase sleeping bags for their children to use when visiting relatives and friends. They are practical, too, when going on camping trips.

Night lights for young children? Most children sleep more comfortably in a completely dark room. Night lights can create scary shadows. However, if a child requests a night light, it is all right to use one. There are special plug-in night lights that employ bulbs of 4 watts or even lower wattage.

Nightmares and what to do about them. Very little is known about young children's nightmares. An overactive day or an upsetting event can trigger such a sleep disturbance. Calmly reassuring your child will usually quiet him and enable him to return to sleep. Because children up to age five have difficulty distinguishing reality from fantasy, a nightmare can be especially frightening. If they become frequent or severe, you should discuss the problem with your doctor.

What to do about children who wake up, cry, and won't stay in their own room or bed? This can be a serious problem, one that demands patience and firmness. Dr. Granger counsels parents to adhere firmly to the following procedure: Make sure your child doesn't seem sick, doesn't need diapers changed, and has had a drink of water. Then put your child back in his own bed and leave the room. Do not put your child in your bed. Do not lie down with your child in his bed. You may have to repeat the process twenty times or so the first night this occurs, but if you are firm, you will have to do it fewer times each night. Your child needs to know that you mean business; giving in even once can undo a week of patience. Usually, in a week or two, the child will go back to sleep without trouble and will stop waking at night altogether.

Routines and Rituals

Routines and rituals are of prime importance to the Toddler-Two. Among daytime rituals of the Toddler-Two are demanding a special bribe before coming to the table for dinner, being the one who always brings the newspaper in from outside, and so on.

The order of routines for ending the day also is important to Toddler-Twos. There is a bath routine, a going-to-bed routine, a good-night ritual (which may include kissing and a bedtime story), etc. If your Toddler-Two is having a temper tantrum over going to sleep, or experiencing insomnia, check out what routine or ritual you may have left out.

Remember, *any* change in routines and rituals must be gradual.

Dressing, Undressing, and Bathing

Toddler-Twos are gradually acquiring a positive attitude toward the daily routines of family living. They try to help dress and undress themselves. They find the armholes in their garments, and learn to pull off their pants and socks. Although they cannot handle shoelaces, they are beginning to take an interest in buttoning and unbuttoning. They can put on socks (but would rather take them off!), shoes, and hats.

Toddler-Twos will take twenty minutes to soak in the bathtub—a sign of growing independence. Try counting games to get your child to come out of the tub. All children like to wash their hands, but never their faces. Let your Toddler-Two splash water on his face by himself and then dry himself with a towel.

Marguerite Kelly and Elia Parsons, authors of *The Mother's Almanac* (Garden City, NY: Doubleday, 1975), have these recommendations for parents:

"If you keep your standards low, your praise high, he will be dressing himself quickly and completely by age three.

"Insist that your children wash, brush their teeth, dress and comb their hair before coming to the breakfast table, a routine established by Two and mastered by Six."

We suggest that parents choose easy, pull-on clothes for everyday wear so their children can attain self-help status in dressing in good time. Avoid small buttons, shirts or dresses that button in the back, sashes that must be tied, zippers that snag, tiny snappers, etc. Take time to help your child learn to dress herself and encourage her active participation. If you always dress your child because it is easier and faster, you are slowing down her building of independence and self-confidence.

Dawdling

Dawdling is a subdued form of negativism. You will find that your child will dawdle a great deal around the age of two or three. It will seem that he is taking forever to eat his dinner or take his bath. You might allow your child extra time for the tasks of trying to dress himself, washing, and eating. The aim is to get things done without creating too much commotion.

A parent's exasperation with a child's dawdling may also be shared by the child. Dr. Joseph Church explains that "the child's life is lived to the refrain of NOT NOW, SOON, LATER, or IN A LITTLE WHILE. These adult stallings and delays are probably well justified, but to the child they seem just like dawdling."

Grown-ups usually want to accomplish something by moving ahead in a straight line. However, Toddler-Twos will chart a zigzag course as they attend first to one thing and then to another; they are simply not geared to hurrying.

How can you handle dawdling? Drs. Gesell and Ilg suggest these approaches:

• Lead him away, if he is not resistant.
• Warn him in advance of a proposed transition: "Pretty soon we'll go to the bathroom, and then have juice."
• Pick him up bodily and carry him to the next situation.

Dr. Spock recommends the following:

- Start her bath early enough so she has time to dawdle and scrub the tub.
- If she is stalled in her eating, let her leave the table.
- Try to get things done without raising issues.

Band-Aid Stage

"The more conscious the child becomes of himself as a person, an 'I,'" writes Selma Fraiberg, "the more he values his body which encloses and contains his personality . . . This is the Band-Aid stage. If you want to establish longlasting friendship with a two-to-three-year-old, the gift of a box of Band-Aids will be long remembered."

Toddler-Twos love to apply Band-Aids on the tiniest scratches, or even on imaginary ones. They will feel immediately restored after a trifling hurt if a Band-Aid is pasted on.

Toilet Learning

Toilet learning takes time. Much of the distress and impatience parents experience is due to their doing things incorrectly. They try to "force-train" their child so that toileting becomes a battle of wills, which leads to mutual misery.

It is impossible to speed up physical maturation, and learning to use the toilet depends first of all upon the maturation of the anal and urethral sphincter muscles. Studies indicate that infants who are given early training and those who are not trained at all end by learning to use the toilet at about the same age—two-and-a-half years—because only at about that age is the body able to exercise complete control.

Dr. Hiag Akmakjian, author of *The Natural Way to Raise a Healthy Child* (New York: Praeger Publishers, 1975), writes, "Another advantage of postponing toilet learning until a more appropriate age is that communication becomes an aid. Then the child can better understand the parents' true intention with regard to toileting."

Dr. Akmakjian suggests that it might be best to use a child-sized seat placed over the adult seat rather than a potty. This eliminates the need to teach toileting on the potty chair first and the toilet seat later. If you tell your Toddler-Two that it might be fun to sit on the toilet seat when he feels the approach of a bowel movement, he might ask you to place him on the seat to try it out.

Children are willing to learn to have bowel movements in the toilet because it is their parents' way of doing things, and children want to be like their parents in every way. However, you can expect your Toddler-Two to continue to eliminate anywhere and at any time for several more months.

Maturation of the Bladder

The control of bladder function is an involuntary mechanism that is made voluntary by a slow process requiring physical and mental development that are attained only with the passage of sufficient time.

By two years of age, your child can usually hold his urine about one and a half to two hours. Between 5 P.M. and 8 P.M., there is often an increased frequency of urinating. However, he is more frequently dry than wet after napping.

When your Toddler-Two stays dry for as long as two hours, you can take her to the bathroom at two-hour intervals and before and after naps and meals. Even after remaining dry for two or three hours, she may still lack the muscular control to hold her urine even a second longer once her bladder is full.

Night dryness is quite variable, with girls achieving dryness considerably ahead of boys, but most Toddler-Twos are still wet upon waking in the morning. Sleep control over the bladder can be established only when two conditions have been met. First, the child must have learned through daytime control to respond to tension in his bladder by tightening his sphincter muscles. Second, he must keep his sphincters closed without waking up.

What should parents do to establish nighttime control? Nothing! The natural maturing of your child's bladder, plus the fact that he has learned from his daytime control that urine goes into the toilet, will sooner or later take care of the situation. *Remember to praise your child's successes and calmly accept his failures.*

Research concerning the causes of bed-wetting varies greatly. Dr. Marvin Gersh believes that enuresis is not usually caused by psychological problems; rather, it is the result of small bladder capacity. On the other hand, Dr. Neil Henderson and Rudolf Dreikurs maintain that bed-wetting due to physical abnormalities is rare; rather, they claim it usually is caused by tensions and emotional problems. However, everyone concurs that bed-wetting is not something a child wants to do.

Before four years of age, occasional night wetting is to be expected, although some children are dry at night even when they wet themselves during the day.

When a child who has been dry at night feels unsure about the way things are going (for example, when a new baby joins the family), wetting the bed may indicate his feelings of insecurity, jealousy, etc. *No child should be punished for wetting the bed.*

Care of the Teeth

The care of your child's teeth is an important responsibility. It is up to you to teach your child proper home care and to provide regular professional dental attention.

The American Dental Association recommends that you

start brushing your child's teeth after her first incisors (front teeth) have erupted and as soon as she will accept brushing. By the time she has most of her teeth, somewhere around the age of two, she will be able to do some of the brushing herself. Most children at this age readily try to copy the activities of their parents. Although they will certainly not be performing an efficient job at first, your encouragement and help will teach them to develop the necessary skill.

The best time for your child to brush his teeth is after meals. This cleansing will help to remove the food debris that can lead to tooth decay and irritation of the gums. Flossing needs to be done once a day, preferably before bedtime.

The toothbrush that you select for your child should be small enough to reach all areas of the mouth. The ADA recommends "a child-sized toothbrush with a small straight head containing soft bristles. The head of the brush should be small enough to reach every tooth." After each use, the brush should be cleaned and placed upright to dry.

The selection of a dentist for your child is an important decision. If you do not have a family dentist or if your dentist does not treat children, there are several ways to choose a competent dentist. You can contact your local dental society or the chief of dental service of an accredited hospital for the names of several qualified dentists who specialize in the care of children's teeth (a pedodontist). You can also ask your physician for a recommendation.

Your child's first visit to the dentist should be made when he is between two and three years of age, since a survey has shown that 50 percent of all two-year-olds in this country have one or more decayed teeth. The only indication for an earlier visit would be in the event of a dental accident, symptoms of pain, or if you notice some irregularities in your Toddler-Two's teeth.

At the first examination, the dentist will examine your child's mouth and teeth, and may also clean the teeth. Hopefully, the first visit will be a routine one so that the child's experience will be pleasant and friendly. This is important in influencing his feelings toward the dentist in the years to come.

Caring for the Sick Child at Home

"Let the child lead just as normal a life as is possible under the circumstances . . . and avoid worried talk, looks, and thoughts," is Dr. Spock's advice to parents taking care of a sick child at home. Of course, there will be changes in the normal routine as you follow medical instructions and try to make your child feel more comfortable as he gets better. Demands upon parents for care and comfort increase during an illness. Do not be afraid of "spoiling" your child with the extra attention that may be required. Keep in mind that 90 percent of children's illnesses are usually on the way to recovery within a few days after onset.

As your child begins to recover, his interest in his surroundings will return and excessive demands for attention should diminish. (Some authorities believe that a child can learn to enjoy being sick if it is made too attractive.) Therefore, it is best to resume normal relations with your convalescing child as soon as possible. Do not bargain with him when he is unreasonable. Have regular times when he can depend upon your company, and times when he knows you will be busy elsewhere.

Diet

When a child is sick, she usually is not hungry. Whole milk may upset her stomach. If your child has vomited, wait an hour or so to let her stomach settle and then offer her only one or two ounces of fluid at a time. A sick child's appetite is more quickly ruined by forcing than a well child's. Therefore, keep away from urging unless specified by your doctor. Your physician will recommend a suitable diet for your child during this special period.

Rest

Before you panic at the thought of "plenty of rest" for a child who rarely sits still, Dr. Virginia E. Pomeranz and Dodi Schultz, in *The First Five Years* (Garden City, NY: Doubleday, 1973), remind parents that "rest" does not necessarily mean bed rest. "Most common childhood ills do not require bed rest, although a good deal depends on how the child feels; if a youngster really feels pretty sick, he may choose to remain in bed for a couple of days, until he feels better." Ask your doctor to spell out the degree and length of rest that are necessary.

Activities

Once you know whether your child will require bed rest or a restricted activity regimen, you will be able to cope with your child and her illness. Assuredly a child who must remain in bed requires and should have more parental time than one who can be somewhat more active.

There are a variety of things for a sick child to watch. Birds can be attracted to the windowsill with feeders; goldfish also provide visual interest. Colorful streamers, balloons, and toy windmills can be fastened outside the window. Mobiles can be hung from the ceiling. If your child is able to hold a flashlight, he can have fun switching it on and off. A pair of binoculars and a magnifying glass will provide new perspectives on the most ordinary objects. A kaleidoscope also offers visual excitement.

A child who is less restricted can take part in her usual pastimes. You might try to offer her new play materials that are fun, but not overly challenging. A special "surprise and comfort bag" of toys and activities your child sees only when ill is suggested for a sick child in *What to Do When "There's Nothing to Do"* by The Boston Children's Medical Center and Elizabeth M. Gregg. To make one, just fill a shopping bag, old handbag, or plastic tote bag with an assortment of interesting "junk" and some basic materials: keys, jewelry, playing cards, walnut shells, big buttons, a new miniature stuffed animal or doll, etc.

Growth Chart—25th Through 30th Month

MOTOR DEVELOPMENT

Gross Motor

Walking pattern not smooth; foot and leg move as one.

Stand on right foot alone.

Monitor walk and placement of feet in order to deal with obstacles in path.

Like to walk unaided.

Dislike being carried or pushed in a stroller.

Walk up and down stairs alone, both feet on each step.

Walk backwards for 10 feet.

Walk a few steps on tiptoes.

Move around the house with ease; no longer bump into bric-a-brac.

Running still stiff and awkward.

Cannot turn sharp corners, or come to a quick stop.

Jump in place, both feet off floor simultaneously.

Climb with a purpose—to see better or reach for something.

Climb to top of gym; can't climb down again.

Delight in rough-and-tumble play with father and peers.

Throw and retrieve all kinds of objects.

Action toys (tricycle, swing, climber) used to work off boundless energy.

Difficulty mastering simple space relationships (getting in and out of chair, using tricycle pedals, etc.).

Vulnerable to frustrations and accidents.

Fine Motor

Can turn doorknob to enter or leave room.

Many hold a pencil or crayon with adult grip.

Able to take lids off jars.

Things still slip out of fingers.

Can draw vertical line.

Build a tower of five cubes.

Fine Motor, cont'd

Can visually distinguish small objects at a distance.

Can discriminate between small print letters.

LANGUAGE ACQUISITION

Vocabulary of more than 3 but less than 50 words; some have vocabulary of 200 to 300 words.

Join words together into two-word phrases (telegraphic language).

Pay more attention to what people say.

Understand longer sentences.

Still rely on facial expressions, gestures, body movement for communication.

Call themselves by own name; i.e., "Mary wants apple."

Also say, "I want."

Enjoy books; point to and name objects; turn pages.

Learn sounding of words.

Can sing phrases of songs (often not on pitch).

Imitate parents' tone of voice.

Timetables for Speech

Many children have quite intelligible speech without having mastered all the 23 consonant sounds.

By age	Sounds Mastered
3½ years	b, p, m, w, h
4½ years	d, t, n, g, k, ng, y
5½ years	f
6½ years	v, th (as in *that*), z (as in *azure*), sh, l
7½ years	s, z, r, th (as in *thin*), wh

Growth Chart—25th Through 30th Month

SENSORY POWERS/LEARNING

Understand simple cause-and-effect relationships; i.e., "Turn switch, light comes on."

Thinking starting to replace acting on objects (cognition).

Sense *oneness* vs. *many*.

Can distinguish one and two units, but can't go beyond (unless given special training).

Minimal understanding of time. Will respond to such phrases as "in a minute," "today," "pretty soon," but there is no concept of "yesterday."

Vague awareness of relationship between things: their number, quantity, weight, size.

Discriminate vertical from horizontal lines.

Attention span lengthening somewhat. Can concentrate better on manipulative and fitting toys: puzzles, nesting buckets or eggs, stacking disk toys, etc.

Learn by imitation of parents and peers.

Play with attributes of things: texture, shape, size, color, function.

Locate most parts of the body; emphasis then changes to *naming*.

Memory span improving.

Perceptual behaviors show finer discrimination.

SOCIAL DEVELOPMENT

Parents still on top of social ladder.

Imitate mannerisms of parents or primary caretaker.

Strong attachment to mothers. Will help mother put away groceries, do housecleaning, etc.

Increasing sense of independence.

Beginning to explore potential for influencing other people, especially parents.

Mainly interested in themselves (egocentric). Not apt to share or play with agemates.

Ready for participation in informal or formal playgroup.

Initial concept of a "friend" as a familiar peer.

Stare at others; like being looked at.

Call all other children "baby."

Call all women "Mommy" and all men "Daddy."

PLAY AND PLAYTHINGS

Play with patterns, sequence, order of magnitude (color cone, nesting toys, etc.).

"Parallel play"—two children playing near each other, but not together.

Mid-Twos able to play together.

Some Twos able to handle brush and poster paints to paint on paper.

Like to scribble with large crayons.

Enjoy repetition of familiar songs.

Run, gallop, swing to music.

Respond to musical rhythms by swinging arms, swaying head, tapping feet.

Growth Chart—25th Through 30th Month

PERSONALITY/ PSYCHOLOGICAL	HEALTH, SELF-HELP, AND ROUTINES
Fears and anxiety about separation from mother erupt.	Routines and rituals important. (There are bath routines, sleep routines, good-night routines, that must be strictly followed.)
Fears of short duration: strange objects, darkness, vacuum cleaner noise, bathtub drain, high places, wild animals, going to sleep, broken things (intactness), monsters, etc.	Ask to go to toilet.
	At 25 months can hold urine 1½ to 2 hours.
Fears learned from parents: mice, snakes, thunderstorms.	Enjoy bath.
Experiment with negativism ("No, no, no!") by being assertive, demanding, and strongly independent ("I do it myself!").	Like to wash hands, but never their faces.
	Ready for lessons in brushing teeth and rinsing the mouth.
Intent on doing things their way.	Weight and height gains reach a plateau.
Onset of contrariness (a healthy sign of growth; a sort of declaration of independence).	Appetites are smaller; less interest in eating; do not need as much food.
Learning self-identity vs. social conformity.	Dawdle at dinner table, in bath, while dressing (a form of negativism).
Awareness of self as a person with separate identity.	Help dress and undress themselves (learn to pull off pants and socks); some interest in buttoning and unbuttoning.
Self-concept enhanced when people react with approval and praise their accomplishments.	Sleep requirements vary between 8 and 17 hours a night for 2½-year-olds.
Consolidate sense of self by hoarding possessions.	
Learn that parents who are absent at the moment still exist and will return.	

Dear Parents:
   Do not regard this chart as a rigid timetable.
   Young children are unpredictable individuals.
Some perform an activity earlier or later than
this chart indicates.
   Just use this information to anticipate and
appreciate normal child development and
behavior. No norms are absolute.

CHAPTER FOUR

The 31st Through 36th Month of Life

When evening is come,
And father's at home,
Mother says that we may
Have a go-to-bed play.
A book he will bring us,
A song he will sing us,
A story he'll tell us.
We'll laugh and frolic away,
When evening is come,
And father's at home.

Father Is Home
(Anonymous)

It usually is at about two-and-a-half that Toddler-Twos become "Terrible-Twos." Of course, all Toddler-Twos do not attain this status at exactly the same time. Some are ahead, and some may reveal their erratic behavior nearer their third birthday.

"This is an age about which parents need warning," wrote the late Dr. Ilg, "because so much that the child now does naturally is directly contrary to what his parents would like to have him do." This change in behavior can be overwhelming not only to the child but also to the adults around him. Parents complain that they cannot do anything with this age level. However, if they understand the motivations and resulting behaviors of children during this stage of growth, they will find that maneuvering around defiant behavior is more successful than meeting it head-on. In *Infant and Child in the Culture of Today,* Dr. Ilg and her colleagues wrote, "The two-and-a-half-year-old is in a transition period . . . If he is managed rather than disciplined in terms of his peculiar limitations, he becomes tolerable and amiable."

Is there much difference in behavior and mental ability between a two-year-old and a toddler nearing her third birthday? Any teacher of two-year-olds and the parents of two-and-a-half-year-olds can tell you of the striking advances by the latter toddlers in physical growth and motor coordination, in social awareness, and understanding of themselves and their surroundings.

Louise Phinney Woodcock describes some of these differences in *Life and Ways of the Two-Year-Old:* "A parent or teacher rests for a moment in a children's swing. A young two-year-old frowns and demands that she get out because thus far the child has seen only children in the swing, and is not yet able to accept a digression from the simple pattern of swing occupancy she knows. An older two-year-eight-month child laughs, amused at seeing a grown-up using one of the children's playthings. Or again, the adult moves the block shelves and blocks from their accustomed side of the room to the other . . . the younger children either ignore the change or begin to build without comment. The two-and-a-half-year-olds look from the blocks in their new place across to the empty space where they used to be . . . near three-year-old asks at once, 'Why did you move the blocks?'"

The combination of improved locomotion skills and a strong drive for independence and separation from the mother make the two-and-a-half-year-old disturbingly assertive, demanding, and inflexible. He wants to go on doing what he did yesterday or at least hold on to it as long as he can. When you introduce a new musical record, for example, he will expect you to play it the next day, and the next, ad infinitum. He wants exactly what he wants when he wants it, cannot adapt, give in, or wait even a moment, perhaps because he is not able to think ahead. Everything has to be done just so and must be right in the place he considers the proper place. He gives the orders, decides which adult or child is to help him, and will accept no substitute. "Me do it myself!" is the battle cry of the day, and a kicking, screaming scene can ensue if someone intervenes.

Your toddler is struggling through a period of great turmoil and indecision. If you offer her two alternatives—a pear or a banana—you are letting yourself in for trouble. Ask your child what t-shirt she wants to wear, and her decision could take all morning. Obviously, the answer is for you not to offer confusing choices at this juncture.

Children are comforted when they are encouraged and helped (when necessary) to behave reasonably. Actually most little children appreciate guidance—although parents cannot always see this—and become attached to the adult most involved in their learning. Some parents overlook this when they permit their children to go too far in their negative behaviors, for fear of losing their affection.

Of course, reasonable behavior is not the Terrible-Two's goal; getting his mother to do his bidding is his purpose. If she ignores him, he screams or has a temper tantrum, knowing that this is an effective way to get what he wants. It is crucial to remember that most children are not being deliberately nasty or defiant; they are simply exploring relationships. They are now more aware of their increasing independence and need to experiment with their potential for influencing people, especially their parents. To the two-and-a-half-year-old, even discipline is something to be explored.

Children in the Terrible-Twos stage are more direct than others in their overt reactions to events. They move toward what they like and try to grab it. They respond with laughter and delight to their accomplishments. When they are afraid, they draw back, turn their head from what they fear, and cling to any person they can trust.

Usually their way of protesting is to cry, throw themselves on the floor, kick, hit, and bite. Some children resort to thumb-sucking for comfort. Others look for a reaction from adults; if it is sympathetic, they will put on a scene. If parents and teachers were taught to be aware of what prompts the rage and frustrations of Terrible-Twos, they would be able to intervene and perhaps forestall temper tantrums.

TEMPER TANTRUMS—STILL

"A temper tantrum is a young child's announcement that negotiations (with a parent) are over. Rather than recognize that he has already lost the battle, he finds a way to win," writes Dr. Louise J. Kaplan in her fine book, *Oneness and Separateness: From Infant to Individual* (New York: Simon & Schuster, 1978). "As he's hurling his body to the floor, shrieking, kicking, pounding, hitting, a part of the child wants desperately to stop . . . But he can't stop and he won't stop until all his tensions are gone—until he no longer feels vulnerable and helpless."

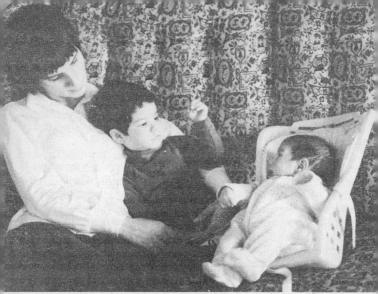

When a child recovers fully from her temper tantrum, she wants to "forgive and be forgiven." In most cases, parents are not able to quickly forget the frightening intensity of feeling displayed by their child during her uncontrolled lashing out. Dr. Kaplan suggests that humiliation and fear set tantrums off. A temper tantrum can be ignited, too, by acute anger, feelings of incompetence and inadequacy, etc.

The older Toddler-Two continues to want the affection and approbation of his parents, but is not usually adept at winning their confidence and wholehearted acceptance.

All things considered, your older Toddler-Two is more mature in many ways than she was at two. Although she can exasperate you and wear you out, if you contemplate her capabilities, limitations, and behavior in objective terms, you may be able to accept her as an interesting and even enjoyable member of your family.

Despite the desire and need of older Toddler-Twos to do everything by themselves, the parent is still the channel through which experience comes. Parents need to simplify what their children must discover, and bring the world down to their size by providing a carefully planned environment. As parents and teachers witness the wondrous growth of very young children, they need to steer them clear of too stern rebukes and frustrations, and know when to offer aid, when to provide stimulation, and when to retreat quietly.

GROSS-MOTOR DEVELOPMENT

The older Toddler-Two has a lot of energy and is constantly moving. He can run, jump, and climb, and enjoys walking sideways. He can alternate his feet going up stairs instead of using both feet on each stair, as heretofore. He probably jumps off the bottom step coming down.

Older Toddler-Twos have learned to jump straight up, getting both feet off the floor—a real gross-motor accomplishment. They bend their knees, swing their arms, and with great effort and puffing barely clear the floor. They expect and deserve adult appreciation for this prowess.

Your two-and-a-half-year-old is extending her range of activities and observations. She rushes hither, thither, and yon for fear of missing something. Her running is not as smooth as it will be in a few more months, and she cannot yet turn sharp corners well or come to a quick halt. Hence, she bumps into things, trips over them, falls, etc.

Older Toddler-Twos are learning to alternate their feet in propelling a kiddy car. They are also establishing a preference for using one hand rather than the other.

You will notice that your child has begun to enhance his walking and running with special feats: walking on heels or toes, changing to a stiff-kneed walk, trotting, moving in a one-sided gallop, etc. Improving their muscular skills is the most gratifying activity of two-and-a-half-year-olds.

Although the two-and-a-half-year-old is curious about everything, she does not yet have sufficient words to ask too many questions. This inadequacy drives her to try out everything for herself. She will attempt to climb anything that invites her efforts. She also climbs because she wants to see something better or to reach something she would like to examine.

Older Toddler-Twos do not like restrictions on bodily movement when these prevent them from reaching a goal. Frustration often besets them due to their inability to truly understand physical problems; for example, trying to bridge a space with too short a board. Adults can prevent anger, tears, and accidents by redirecting futile efforts and providing encouragement.

Children who have learned a new skill (riding a kiddy car, opening a door, jumping down a step, etc.) will resist any adult intrusion in their techniques.

From two-and-a-half-years onward, a child's physical

growth slows up. At the same time, her development in other areas is becoming more dramatic. Large muscles improve considerably during this period. Small-muscle control is also evident by smoother eye-hand coordination. She is learning now how to button her clothes, but still has difficulty tieing her shoelaces.

FINE-MOTOR DEVELOPMENT

Fine-motor control has also improved. Thirty- to thirty-six-month-old toddlers are able to manipulate more freely with one hand, and can alternate from one hand to the other. They can rotate their forearms, which permits them to turn a door knob. If tall enough, they are able to open doors. Unscrewing and screwing the lids on jars is a favored activity.

By now your child should know how to hold a crayon properly. Give him a thick one and plenty of paper for drawing pictures. (Avoid introducing coloring books at this time. They stifle free expression.) You can introduce a differently colored crayon at each drawing period until your child has been exposed to the various colors. Thirty- through thirty-six-month-olds are able to imitate a vertical and horizontal stroke and make a crude circular mark. If asked to make a cross, some toddlers draw two lines, but the strokes may not cross.

Better eye-hand coordination enables these toddlers to fit one thing into another. Among favored playthings are a stacking cone, nested boxes, cups, barrels, etc. Practice permits them to string one-inch multicolored wood or plastic beads on long, metal-tipped shoestrings. Stringing macaroni and other forms of pasta as well as assorted sizes of beads and buttons with large holes is another satisfying activity that strengthens fine-motor control. Also, you can make your own simple sewing cards of cardboard, or buy commercially produced sewing cards that are available in toy shops or the toy sections of department stores.

Simple jigsaw puzzles appeal to this age group because they offer quick results. While the two-year-old is apt to try to force a puzzle piece into any open space, the three-year-old will easily match the piece to the shape of the hole. For most thirty-month-olds, completing a puzzle becomes a test of memory. As children learn the spatial arrangements, they rotate the puzzle pieces smoothly. By their third birthdays, most toddlers can do twelve- to fifteen-piece puzzles, and fitting all the pieces into place enhances their confidence and self-esteem.

To refine your child's fine-motor coordination, you can let her help you fold paper napkins on the dining table. With a good deal of practice she will learn how to fold a piece of paper in half after she sees how you put the corners together. She can also help you fold the laundry. It might be a good idea to try with washcloths first, since their small size is more manageable. Helping you will make her feel competent and valued.

Some two-and-a-half-year-olds evince muscular incoordination and unawareness when they try to reach for a desired object. They relax their grip on one object while reaching for a second so that the discarded item falls to the floor unnoticed. More time and practice are in order here.

Visually, the eyes of children this age are as sharp as they ever will be. They move their eyes more freely and are sensitive to peripheral vision. They are able to pick out objects at a distance and distinguish between small print letters. They engage in long periods of looking.

LANGUAGE ACQUISITION

How two-and-a-half-year-olds learn as many words as they do before their third birthdays is a subject of much discussion among language specialists and educators. These toddlers must distinguish by name "radiator from radio, ventilator from elevator, escalator from percolator, etc."

Often mistakes occur from the misunderstanding of words. When told that a chair was "overhead," a child put her hand on top of her head and with wide eyes replied, "No, it isn't."

Words that sound alike but have different meanings cause difficulty. For example:

CHILD: "Are you busy?"
ADULT: "Yes."
CHILD: "Not too busy?"
ADULT: "No."
CHILD: "Only one busy."

The two-and-a-half-year-old has to learn not only the meaning of words, but their inflections as well. Nouns give him the least trouble for he easily learns the "s" ending for the plural. Sometimes he applies it too generally, as in "Has it got any foots?" Sometimes he omits the "s," as in "Sidney foot." Pronouns cause considerable problems: "Here come me." "I want to see she." "Take he away."

Sentence Formation

The average two-and-a-half-year-old has left behind her the time when single words were adequate to represent her protests, demands, etc. Now she can combine one idea with another thought in two-word sentences: "Sit down." "Boy hurt." At first her remarks consist of single ideas, but soon she embellishes a subject with considerable information and words.

Thirty- through thirty-six-month-old children can give their full names upon request. They are able to name simple pictures in a storybook. Most toddlers this age can follow three directions given at one time; for example, "Please pick up the book, give it to me, and sit down in your chair."

An increasing amount of talk is directed to other children in their play. However, most of these toddlers are more interested in what they say to others than in what others say to them.

Stimulating Conversation and Word Learning

Here are some recommendations by Dr. Genevieve Painter, as outlined in *Teach Your Baby* (New York: Simon & Schuster, 1971):

- When using a picturebook, ask your child, "Where is the dog?" "Where is the apple?" Show her how to point to the object in the picture.
- Give him a toy telephone to use for pretend conversations.
- Tell her stories using hand or finger puppets. Let her imitate what you do.
- Ask him to name objects he does not see around the house. ("This is a screwdriver." "What do you call it?")
- Teach her action words. When she throws a ball say, "Michelle throws a ball."
- Let him see the family photo album. Name each child and what each is doing.
- Play the game "This is the way we wash our clothes," etc.
- Sing and play finger games ("Put your finger in the air"); also nursery rhymes.

Very Young Children Are Linguistic Geniuses

Kornei Chukovsky, the outstanding Russian children's author and specialist in children's language, wrote a fascinating book, *From Two to Five* (Los Angeles: University of California Press, 1965), in which he considers two- and three-year-olds to be linguistic geniuses. "They have such a strong sensitivity to their language—its many inflections and suffixes—that the words they construct do not seem at all distorted and freakish

but, on the contrary, are extremely apt, beautiful and natural."
He extolls the mental dexterity of very young children learning
to speak.

These children create words that indicate some understanding of basic grammar, and they invent words which do
not exist in today's language.

"A big horse *hoofed* me."

"He *bulleted* me with his rifle."

"Mommy, how *balloony* your legs are!"

"Can't you see? I am *barefoot all over!*"

"Oh, look, *many* snows!"

Without any notions of the rules of grammar, young children
still employ "quite correctly all noun cases, verb tenses and
moods even when using unfamiliar words." It is not the fault of
children that adult language does not adhere to any logical
pattern. Often the words used by young children are more
"correct" than the grammar and, in fact, "improve" upon it.

Every Toddler-Two becomes for a short period a "genius" in
the creative use of language. Later, at five to six years of age,
this talent disappears since there seems to be no further need
for this exploratory type of word play. The exuberant feeling
expressed in "many snows" becomes the equivalent of "much
snow" in adult language.

It is mind-boggling how many grammatical principles have
to be mastered by two-and-a-half-year-old minds. Yet children
accept this gigantic challenge, and constantly sort out into
usable principles the "disorderly elements of the words they
hear without noticing." Surely two- and three-year-old linguists are the hardest working students in the universe!

The critical period for creative language expression is from
two to five, when the need and desire to learn how to speak is
so forceful. Should we constantly correct a child's inventive
grammar by substituting the adult version, or should we praise
the child's verbal creativity? Obviously, if parents constantly
correct grammatical and pronunciation errors, they repress
the child's free expression of his feelings and thoughts and,
according to Chukovsky, "risk fading the color out of the child's
speech."

This is the prime period for introducing the rhythm and
rhyming of poetry to children. Arranging words into patterns is
one of the ways that young children learn to speak. They "think
of words in pairs, assuming that every word has a 'twin'—an
opposite in meaning."

"Yesterday it was raw outside," someone noted.
"And today—is it cooked?" the child asked.

Young Children Love Nonsense Rhymes

Poems serve as a rhythmic accompaniment to the physical activities that all two- to five-year-olds initiate: clapping, hopping, jumping, galloping, marching. They cherish repetitive, two-line nonsense verse because it is inspired by merriment. They adore alliteration. One anonymous young poet wrote:

> Fuzzy Wuzzy was a bear;
> Fuzzy Wuzzy had no hair.
> So Fuzzy Wuzzy wasn't fuzzy,
> Was he?

This is the time to read poetry to children. After a few readings, children usually memorize the poems from beginning to end. The "poetic period" in the lives of young children helps shape their thoughts and feelings. It also inestimably enriches their speech as it increases their vocabulary.

When the two-and-a-half-year-old-going-on-three learns that words will serve him, he tries to expand his vocabulary and articulate all his observations and experiences. He compares one experience with another, and assigns explanations of his own within the limits of his vocabulary. As his knowledge increases, his understanding broadens, and he begins to speak about the relations he notices between things in his environment. Increasingly he draws his comparisons from memory as well as the visible setting. For instance, he will describe a block building as: "It stands like a tall building stands." He shows curiosity about phenomena: "The rain has stopped. Who stopped it?"

Picture Books

Toddler-Twos enjoy picture books with simple images, few details, and clear colors. They like to talk about the pictures. They are interested in sound and repetition, as in *Ask Mr. Bear,* a charming book by Marjorie Flack. They like to have stories simplified by the use of here-and-now experiences and vocabulary they know, and in which their own names can be substituted. They want to participate in the activity pictured.

Very young children derive considerable satisfaction from looking at picture books of transportation vehicles, animals and children, familiar household objects, flowers, birds, etc.

After you and your child have gone through a book several times, you can ask her to name some of the objects pictured. Praise her every time she correctly designates one. If she does not pronounce the name very well, repeat it properly without calling her attention to the error.

As your child gets older, his longer attention span allows him to sit through your reading of a picture book that has two or three sentences on each page. Think up ways for him to participate in this learning activity; for example, read part of a sentence and see if he can supply the missing word or words.

SENSORY POWERS/LEARNING

Very young children actively explore their environment not only visually, but also by full bodily play that incorporates their muscular and sensory abilities. They are ardent "touchers," and especially like the texture of fur (but not wool). It is up to parents to note the typical sensory responses of their particular children, and then to introduce play activities that will exercise their sensory aptitudes and extend them.

Two-and-a-half- to three-year-olds will employ their sense of touch to investigate enthusiastically all the available elements in their world. They will finger and stroke a fleecy sweater, corduroy jacket, silk blouse, etc. Buttons, washcloths, napkins, and the like are "felt" with the tongue and mouth.

Parents can suggest to their children that they pay attention to the sounds around them by making a game of identifying fire engine sirens, factory whistles, birds and animals, automotive noises, etc.

Sharpening all the senses does not end during childhood. Sensory awareness and responses operate throughout one's lifetime.

LEARNING AND INTELLECTUAL DEVELOPMENT

The early childhood years are years of rapid development. A child may attain as much as one-fourth of his intellectual growth in these years. Dr. Benjamin S. Bloom of the University of Chicago analyzed the growing-up patterns of hundreds of children. He pored over more than a thousand studies of youngsters, each of which followed up certain children and measured them at various points in their development. Although conducted by different people over the past half-century, these studies all showed such close agreement that Dr. Bloom began to see the emergence of specific laws of development.

For each human trait, he found there is a characteristic growth curve. Half a child's future height, for example, is reached by the age of two-and-a-half. Half of a male's aggressiveness is established by age three. Half of a person's "intellectuality" as well as general intelligence is formed by age four. According to Dr. Bloom, by the age of six, when a child enters first grade in elementary school, he has already developed as much as two-thirds of the intelligence he will have at maturity. Even with regard to purely academic achievement, at least one-third of the development at age eight has taken place prior to a child's entrance into first grade.

SOCIAL DEVELOPMENT

Two-and-a-half- to three-year-olds have a tough time in their social relations with their peers. They will gaze at other children, may cooperate momentarily, but function primarily in a solitary fashion. When playing with their agemates, they still tend to "rough them up"—pushing, poking, grabbing, and regarding them as things rather than people.

Thirty- through thirty-six-month-olds are not capable of putting themselves in anyone else's shoes. They will knock another toddler to the floor for no visible reason, but when the other child strikes back, they will be amazed and deeply aggrieved.

Although they push and hit, there is no devilish intent to hurt the other child. In fact, there appears to be a lack of consciousness of other children being present. As more interchanges take place, as language forges ahead, two-and-a-half- to three-year-olds may start playing together, and perhaps talk about what they are doing.

At this age, a "group" of two is common. The size of a group enlarges to three with increase in age, at three to four years. At five and six years, peer groups become extended to five children.

Fights for the possession of toys decrease as Twos become Threes, and gradually they learn to share and take turns. The leader in any playgroup is the child who has the ability to make a play scheme work as well as sufficient language to maintain harmony and peace.

Interactions with Parents

Between two-and-a-half and three years, your child will get along well with one parent. In fact, if the other parent intervenes, he may throw a temper tantrum. Children this age level want to do everything their own way. They do not like outsiders interfering. Parents should avoid confrontation by letting one parent handle this type of encounter crisis. Try not to take your child's abuse too seriously; it is his brash, immature way of showing his independence.

Being contrary and balky are other manifestations of wanting to have their own way. Some children even become aggressive and kick and bite their parents. Such unacceptable conduct must be handled firmly but calmly. You must let your child know that you will not tolerate hitting and biting. (*Remember: Hitting or biting back would bring you down to your child's level!*)

Sibling Rivalry

Children learn to be loving through their affectionate relations with their parents. All children will thrive on the assurance that their parents will care for them even after a new baby enters the family; that the parents have a generous fund of love for all the members of the family.

The quarreling and disputes that siblings engage in are due for the most part to the basic rivalry for the attention and love of their mothers and fathers. (Sibling rivalry may be sublimated later in life, but it is rarely or never completely overcome.)

Thirty- to thirty-six-month-olds are faced with the challenge of learning how to share their parents with others—their brothers and sisters, other members of the family, as well as various adults in their milieu. This is one of the facts of life that is very difficult for all children to learn and to accept.

Attendance at Nursery School

Participating in a nursery school is a major milestone in the life of a two-and-a-half- to three-year-old. Some make an easy adjustment; all they seem to want is reassurance that a grown-up is around when their parent leaves. To help a balky child, having the parents leave the child immediately and letting the teacher win the child to herself and her play offerings has positive and negative implications. Some children protest being "dumped." They need a little time to get started at play; then they are able to bid their parents good-bye. Some cry on being left, but will stop when parents are out of sight. Others cry when left and on being picked up in the afternoon. Still others protest by refusing to eat lunch at noon. Slight changes

in toilet habits sometimes occur (getting the opportunity to use the toilet at regular intervals can clear up this form of protest). When children finally make an adjustment to nursery school, they make the most of the experience.

Two-and-a-half- to three-year-olds especially enjoy swinging, being pulled in a wagon, climbing to the top of a slide, and pushing and pulling things. They enjoy scribbling, water painting with large brushes, etc. They also like singing and moving to music. They like to look at pictures and name them. They like to listen to stories.

Some words of caution are in order here: All two-year-olds must be protected from serious mishaps, discomfort from colds, hunger, and fatigue.

The thirty- through thirty-six-month-old can be a rigid despot, full of negative behavior toward his parents. His rituals take over much of his everyday routines, making family life unbearable most of the time. However, if parents understand that he is contrary and attention-seeking because he is passing through a stage of development that is typical of his age level, they may feel tired, but less harried, overwhelmed, and distraught.

In *Your Two-Year-Old: Terrible or Tender,* Louise Bates Ames and Frances Ilg write that two-and-a-half-year-olds "have need to make themselves felt; they act tough, doing all the wrong things. They will awaken in the morning before mother is up and put everything they can find into the toilet . . . they won't keep their clothes on, won't stay in bed, and will wander in the middle of the night."

PERSONALITY/PSYCHOLOGICAL DEVELOPMENT AT THIRTY-ONE THROUGH THIRTY-SIX MONTHS

To expand his self-image, the two-and-a-half-year-old uses the word *mine* to show his proprietary interest in things and persons. He is an incorrigible hoarder and collector of things. He hides toys to be sure he will have them on later occasions. His egocentric behavior shows when he peers into a mirror and says, "It's me." He finds it difficult to play with other children because he must be at the center of every play action, and there is no place for others. He seems satisfied to play by himself or to play next to other agemates, but not with them cooperatively. Playing with peers will come as he approaches his third birthday.

The thirty-one- through thirty-six-month-old is conscious of being a member of the family. She shows this in many ways. She displays affection spontaneously. She laughs contagiously, and indulges in elementary histrionics for the amusement of others. She is starting to express some feelings of pity, sympathy, shame, and modesty. She may pout when scolded, and feel guilty when she has had a toileting accident. She may even try to blame baby brother or the family dog for such a lapse.

Thirty-one- through thirty-six-month-olds are in transition from a presocial to a more socialized stage. They oscillate between dependency and self-sufficiency. They have not yet made complete the distinction between themselves and others. In their play with dolls or stuffed animals, they are prone to dramatize the mother-baby relationship and, in so doing, are beginning to demonstrate that they are aware of being separated from their mothers. Only by increasing this detachment can they achieve an adequate sense of self.

Interpreting the feelings of very young children is very complex. Inasmuch as these toddlers lack sufficient words, parents have to rely on each child's behavior to ascertain how each one truly feels toward the people and objects in her world. Each Toddler-Two is an individual who brings with her an approach or reaction based on her habits or prior experience. One child will react forcefully; another gently and timidly; still another will be demanding.

In *Oneness and Separateness: From Infant to Individual,* Louise J. Kaplan writes: "Experience of the self as good and holding together are no longer linked to a parent's actual presence in the world, but to the parent's approving and disapproving presence in the child's fantasies and thoughts. Although he will continue to rely on his parents' actual *yes's* and *no's, do's* and *don'ts,* admiration and admonition, permissions and restrictions for many years to come, the child will gradually convert these actualities into his personal and unique psychological style of getting along in the world."

Thirty-one- through thirty-six-month-olds broadcast their independence in their words and deeds. Often they express their ego in ways that create danger for themselves and others around them. They have no notion of the inner and outer controls needed to "stand on your own two feet." Parents are barraged with small decisions to be made about what their autonomy-bound children can or cannot do in exploring their limits and experimenting with their environment.

Reasonable rules and limits must be agreed upon and established by parents and others in the family; if this is not done, a child will play off one adult against another—to the distress of all concerned.

Self and Sex*

- Calls himself "I" and others "you."
- Calls a female "lady" and a male "man."
- Aware that he is a boy and that he is different from his mother.
- Cognizant of his genitalia, which he may handle when undressed.
- Differentiates sex of children by general terms "boy" and "girl."

More on Psychological Separation

When the time comes for you to enter your child in a playgroup or a nursery school, seeing how well separation has taken place will be reflected in whether she has trouble parting from you. If your child's psychological growth has proceeded well, you should be able to leave her in the care of the teacher because your child will feel sure that you will pick her up later in the day.

Some two-and-a-half-year-olds may not be ready for nursery school. However, research by Jerome Kagan of Harvard University indicates that many two-year-olds are able to accept such separation without any loss of bonding ties between themselves and their mothers. "Separation," writes Dr. Hiag Akmakjian in *The Natural Way to Raise a Healthy Child,* "is a psychological weaning and like weaning must be done gradually if problems are to be avoided. Implicit in the above is each parent's ability to *allow* psychological separation. Parents who have experienced fulfillment in their child nurturing are most often able to accept the blossoming independence of their offspring. At the same time, all early childhood separation situations require sensitive handling."

*Adapted from *The Child from Five to Ten* by Arnold Gesell, M.D., and Frances L. Ilg, M.D. (New York: Harper & Row, 1946).

Lost Child Syndrome

Combine locomotor ability with a relentless drive for independence and the unabating grip of curiosity, and you have to deal with the inevitable "lost child syndrome." This appears to be more prevalent at two-and-a-half years than any other age. There are many reasons for this, including the child's dawdling, running ahead of parents, darting in another direction, as well as the momentary distraction of parents who lose sight of their adventuresome offspring.

The caterwauling of the lost child usually arouses friendly attention from passersby who try to comfort him until his mother or father comes to retrieve him. Sometimes it takes quite a while to locate a child lost in a department store, zoo, park, or other crowded place. Of course, the child is greatly relieved to see his mother or father, but the parent is not necessarily relaxed because of the feelings of anxiety, fear, guilt, and anger that have been aroused by the child's disappearance.

Some Ways to Avoid Accidental Separations

- Keep your child in a stroller when in a department store or other large shop.
- Place your child in the seat of a shopping cart in a food market.
- The use of a child's harness can prevent the disappearance of your child. However, this unpleasant device should be resorted to only when you plan to be in very crowded places.
- Most two-and-a-half-year-olds need extended horizons, but only adventures that do not result in sudden separations from parents.
- Pin a tag on your child's jacket or sweater, with full name, home address, and phone number.

If your thirty-one- through thirty-six-month-old should wander away from you, your best precautions notwithstanding, try to remain calm and sensible. It would be helpful, too, if you taught your child to recite his full name and, if possible, his home address. Yes, at two-and-a-half! This knowledge could shorten the time to a reunion between a frightened child and a frantic parent.

EARLY CHILDHOOD ANXIETIES AND FEARS

The thirty-one- through thirty-six-month-old whose life has been generally protected can be timid about whatever is too large, too close, too loud, too sudden, or too hectic. This can include a large dog, boat, train, or fire engine whistles, strangers, anyone called "doctor," etc.

Most studies of childhood anxieties and fears point out that girls are more apprehensive than boys. It is not certain whether this tendency is the result of an innate difference between the sexes or whether it is the result of conditioning. It appears that the vast majority of childhood fears are learned. However, without some fear, a very young child could not survive by himself for any length of time.

For an in-depth presentation of the anxieties and fears of children, we recommend *Helping the Fearful Child: A Guide to Everyday and Problem Anxieties* by Jonathan Kellerman (New York: W. W. Norton & Co., 1981). Dr. Kellerman writes that "Anxiety is learned helplessness. . . . Sometimes anxiety affects a child's sense of control physically; for example, in bed-wetting, bladder control is lost due to tension . . . in stuttering, the speech muscles can tighten up so that fluency is impeded.

"By sharing how she feels about what scares her, a child is less likely to develop distorted ideas. In addition to conversation, nonverbal modes of expression such as drawing and playing can be ameliorating. A parent can observe and listen, provide realistic information, and help the child distinguish harmful situations from those that are not."

Nightmares and Night Terrors

Some children have bad dreams after eating certain foods or following a very busy day. Such nightmares almost always pass quickly. Nightmares are the most common childhood sleep disorders. When they persist, the child's daytime experience should be reviewed for evidence of stress.

Night terrors are most common in children under the age of six. Experts are not sure what causes this sleep disturbance. In most instances, night terrors do not last long and disappear without treatment. However, if they continue over a period of time, you should discuss this problem with your pediatrician.

Insomnia

Putting a child to sleep can turn into a nightly battle. The more the parent insists the child go to sleep, the harder the latter protests. This may lead to an ongoing pattern of wheedling, threats, temper outbursts, and punishment. To help a child accept bedtime and go to sleep peacefully, the parents should spend some time with her. The bedtime routine can include reading a pleasant story or making one up, playing a quiet game of short duration, and some comforting good-night hugs and kisses. Having become drowsy during the relaxing bedtime period, most children will fall asleep soon after a parent leaves the room. Other toddlers may test limits. However, once children see that their parents mean business, they will fall asleep.

In insomnia, tension prevents the onset of sleep. When faced with an anxious child who is insomniac, a parent should first try to find out what is bothering him. It may be something that will respond to parental reassurance.

Fear of Animals

The fear of animals can be the result of a firsthand experience; for example, a child may have been bitten by a dog. Indirect exposure to upsetting, animal-related events may also cause fear to develop. A child may see a friend being attacked or he may view material on television that is frightening.

To help a child with animal fears, do not force him to confront the large dog that horrified him. Instead find something related to dogs that is not fear-provoking (a young puppy or a photograph of a dog). At first, let your child watch as you handle the puppy or picture. Then gently guide him to pet the dog with you, and extol the dog's lovable qualities and your child's ability to be in control.

Fear of the Dark

Some young children associate the dark with being left alone or being lost. For the child who fears the dark, a night light can be used. She can learn to feel comfortable in the dark if a night light is left on in a nearby bathroom. Care should be taken that the child who fears the dark is relaxed at bedtime.

Fear of Water

Children who have experienced loss of control while in the bath or swimming may develp a fear of water. It is wise for children to be taught how to swim at an early age. This is especially important if the family has a pool; swimming skills will help prevent accidents.

Toddler-Twos find learning to swim easy and enjoyable. Fear of water is usually short-lived. The child who persists in his anxiety can be helped by having a trusted adult guide him gradually so that he experiences feelings of fun, relaxation, and ultimate mastery.*

Moving

Moving to a new home is an upsetting experience for toddlers. They do not like changes in their accustomed milieu and way of life. The following are some things parents can do to make moving more acceptable:

- If possible, let your child see your new home before you move in.
- Try not to move during the school year.
- Let your toddlers and preschoolers carry their favorite possessions from the old home to the new.
- Try to make your child's new room look as much as possible like the old one.
- Try not to be upset yourself. The pressure around moving time may make your children regress in their behavior; they will return to being themselves once they get used to the place.

Vacations Without Your Child

Taking vacations away from young children is a form of separation toddlers find hard to take. If both parents stay away for long periods, it is especially anxiety-provoking. Young children have no sense of time and are concerned whether their parents will ever return.

*Adapted from *Helping the Fearful Child* by Dr. Jonathan Kellerman (New York: W. W. Norton & Co., 1981).

This situation can be made somewhat easier while you are gone by having your children stay in their own home with someone they know well (a favorite grandmother or other close relative). You might try to prepare your toddlers for such separations by planning some short separation as a trial run. For instance, you can spend a few hours away from home; then extend your overnight stay away from home one to two nights. This will help your children realize that you will return to them.

Hospitalization of a Parent

If the hospital admission is a planned one, it would make life easier if you prepared your children beforehand. If the hospital stay is to be a long one, it would help the children if they could be brought to see the sick parent occasionally.

Death

Of course, death is the final separation. To a young child, the death of a parent is regarded as intentional abandonment. Dr. Hiag Akmakjian offers the recommendations below on how to handle the death of a parent.

Should one parent die when the child is very young, the latter will worry that the other parent might also be lost. As the surviving parent, you can counter this anxiety by reassuring your child that you will be there to take care of him.

It is a mistake to discourage or minimize a child's grief at the death of a parent. Mourning is the most natural response to death. Children should be allowed to feel the sadness that is there. Although mourning ends sooner when it is more deeply felt, it takes time for all of it to be resolved.

Parents can reassure their children that they have many more years left to live. At the same time, they should speak honestly, gently informing their children that eventually everything that lives dies.

Should your child attend a funeral? This very personal decision is up to you. Although death is not real to any child under the age of seven, there is no harm in having a child attend a funeral. According to Suzanne Ramos in *Teaching Your Child to Cope with Crisis* (New York: David McKay, 1975), children over the age of eight should be given the choice of attending funerals and other mourning rituals. And they should be encouraged to talk about their feelings of sadness—or anger—over losing a parent as well as the loss of attention, and their fears of abandonment and dying themselves.

PLAY, PLAYTHINGS, AND FANTASY

For the running and climbing thirty-one- through thirty-six-month-old, planning an environment for exploration requires not only body-building and ego-building equipment, but also opportunities for exploring space, size, cause-and-effect, etc. Knowing how to arrange or rearrange the environment for the maximum development of young children is an indispensable asset to parents and professionals alike.

Prerequisites for a Play Environment

Play, which is self-chosen by children, requires space and play equipment that make playing possible. At the same time, play challenges need to be integrated into the setting, with many alternative choices so that the child can find activities in which he can succeed more often than he will fail. The play area needs to be arranged to give the child the feeling of being apart from the ordinary world. What others do outside this milieu is of no concern to the child. Inside there are no adult-set rules of conduct or accomplishment. The rules of play are child-ordered. Within the bounds of safety, everything is permissible.

Buckminster Fuller wrote, in an article published in the November 12, 1966, issue of *Saturday Review,* "It is possible to design environments within which the child will be neither frustrated nor hurt, yet free to develop spontaneously and fully without trespassing on others. I have learned to undertake reform of the environment and not try to reform Man. If we design the environment properly, it will permit child and man to develop safely and to behave logically."

Materials of play do not have to be only toys and objects; they can be a setting that allows the child to create her own imaginary situations. Such an environment can define space in a very personal way, which the child can occupy and use at will. The space and its appearance suggest to the child how she can form her own play world. It can be a tent, a tree house, a gym frame, or it can be a playroom. However, the environment should be one the child can subvert to her own ends and control. Playthings should be in proper scale to the child's size so they will neither overwhelm nor thwart her. Much like the arrangement in the shop of a competent technician, the containers of play material need to be arranged and stored so that they immediately communicate to the child their availability and proper replacement locations.

Free physical activity requires lots of space. Besides the public playground (imperfect as it is for toddlers) or backyard, basements can be converted into large, open play spaces. Ingenious fathers can build excitement into the area by constructing platforms of various heights. A child-sized log cabin, indoors or out, can provide endless play hours. A playhouse might incorporate peepholes with colored plastic windows and differing wide-angle lenses to promote other ways of viewing the world. Only with sufficient space and appropriate equipment can young children learn to use their bodies smoothly in space.

Thirty-one- through thirty-six-month-olds are able to recreate an action someone else has performed, points out Dr. Catherine Garvey of the Johns Hopkins University. "The child first shows an ability to imitate certain actions he sees others perform; thereafter he will reproduce actions that he may have noticed several hours or even days before . . . He is able to construct mental representations of actions and events, remember them, and be able to call them up even when the model is absent."

Accordingly, two-and-a-half- to three-year-old children will imitate mother on the telephone, father standing with his hands behind his back, mother cooking dinner, father taking out the garbage, etc. As their language expands, their dolls, play people, and toy animals begin to walk and talk and come alive.

Mr. and Ms. "Big" demand "equal status" in the family hierarchy. They want to do what the adults do: drive the car, sweep the kitchen floor, run the vacuum cleaner, push the lawn mower, operate the television set, phonograph, hair dryer, sewing machine. Turning electric switches on and off makes Toddler-Twos feel masterful because it provides them with some feeling of control over their environment.

Of course, most adult tools and equipment are fraught with danger for very young children and need to be kept out of

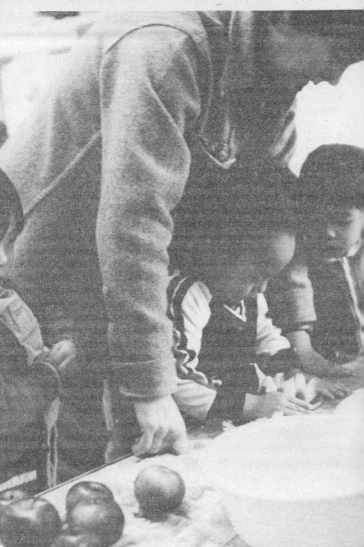

bounds. Luckily, there are available child-size play materials that are completely satisfying. Investigate the hardware store and paint shop in your community for simple adult tools that even youngsters can handle: a lightweight shoemaker's hammer, lightweight shovel or hoe with a cut-down handle, a child-size leaf raker, wide paint brush and painter's pail, an old-fashioned scrubbing board, wash basin, clothespins and clothesline, a table-top ironing board, etc.

Although thirty-one- through thirty-six-month-old girls and boys want to do anything and everything, most often their attempts reveal their lack of experience and poise. For example, should you invite your talkative child to speak to Grandpa or Grandma on the telephone, he may abruptly lose his voice and aplomb. When he insists on pushing the baby in the stroller, he soon discovers that he cannot maneuver the turns.

The Value of Construction Play

"Making a place in the world is so basic to young children that they start to build at around age two. And from then on they continue to map out territories—in the nursery school with building blocks, in playground sandboxes, and on beaches. Children in the country near fields use wood, rocks, and earth to construct their houses. Even in the city, with its limited open space and natural building materials, children make structures out of cardboard, boxes, ties, bricks, and other discards grown-ups no longer need.

"Unfortunately, as a child grows, a lot of this building instinct is gradually stifled. In our educational system we quickly replace 'childish' building blocks with pencils and looseleaf paper . . .

"Tests and studies show that children are much more sensitive and creative than grown-ups, but at around age eleven, a transition takes place. The child moves from being inventive to being inert."*

*From an article by Beverly Russell, "Why Children Must Build," in the Spring 1978 issue of the Alumnus Magazine of the New Jersey Institute of Technology.

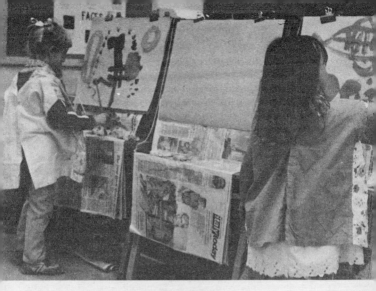

Painting Is an Enriching, Unstructured Activity

Children need varied art materials that are suitable to their developmental level. For example, if a child can handle a paint brush and would like to paint, he is ready for painting. The preschool years are especially appropriate for the introduction of painting because during this period children's painting is least representational. Their most direct response is to the material itself. When Toddler-Twos begin to paint, they paint their feelings, not things or people.

Experimenting with Paints

A child can paint with great blobs of color and feel he has created something wonderful. He finds he can invent colors, and mixing them is great fun. He can paint a shape and appreciate it as something *he knows*. As he continues to create other objects, his mental images grow stronger.

Each child paints in her own way. Some splash large strokes across the paper; others use staccato strokes; some paint in patches; still others make linear pictures. Gradually their paintings take form. As help is needed—and only then—the parent can show the child how to dip her brush into and against the paint jar so there is not too much paint on it. If adults keep in mind that painting is another form of play, they will let children go through their own stages of growth in painting. Parents do not walk and run for their children; they should not paint for them.

Supplies for Adventures in Painting

Poster paints are best for children because they flow easily from brush onto paper. Since poster paint is water based, it

can be washed off faces, hands, clothing, etc. Red, yellow, blue, black, and white are adequate because almost any color can be made by mixing two or more of these together. Three brushes (¾", ½", and ¼" wide) are all a young child requires. Long-handled, flat bristle brushes are best.

There are different kinds of paper suitable for painting. White drawing paper is the most expensive and the best, but 18" × 24" sheets of unprinted newsprint paper are adequate. Powder paint is less costly than liquid poster paint, and is almost as good when it is mixed with water to the consistency of heavy cream. Inasmuch as mixed powder paints spoil quickly, they should be prepared in small quantities for each use. Watercolors that come in hard little cakes lack the freeing quality of poster paint; they are not recommended for young children.

In painting (and drawing), a child's first recognizable symbol usually is a human being. Two circular shapes may be eyes; two lines may represent arms; two other lines may suggest legs. Representation of a body as such comes later. With slight variations, these symbols become animals.

Planning a Painting Corner

Young children can paint independently when the room arrangement and organization of materials permit this. The easel, single- or double-sided, should be sturdy and placed in an area that cannot be harmed by paint, with the floor protected by linoleum. The tray of an easel will hold small jars of poster paint; an empty jar will hold the paintbrushes. Pads of 18" × 24" newsprint paper can be held in place on the easel board by spring clips.

A wall easel can be made at home from a piece of thin plywood or beaverboard, about 20" × 26", and two blocks of 2"-thick wood. The blocks are screwed to the back of the board at the bottom corners to give a slight tilt to the easel. A narrow rectangular box can be attached to the bottom of the board to hold the paint jars. Two holes drilled at the top of the board will permit hanging it from screws driven into the wall.

A low table large enough to hold 18" × 24" sheets of paper and a tray for the poster paints are adequate for home use. One advantage of a painting easel, however, is that the child's paper is up where he can see his painting as he works on it.

Newspapers can be spread on table and floor to make cleaning up easier. A smock of plastic or cloth or Dad's discarded shirt (the sleeves cut short and the shirt worn back to front) will protect your child's clothing.

A child learns to paint, model with clay, and make constructions as she learns to talk—slowly, developing at her own pace. It is more important for young children to enjoy painting than to learn the correct techniques (which they will learn in due time).

Provision needs to be made so that fresh paintings can dry. This can be accomplished with a clothesline and spring clothespins. When paintings are dry, a large bulletin board should be available for displaying them. Since children and parents often wish to save paintings and drawings, portfolios are available for storing a growing collection.

A child's first painting is his initial step in learning a new language of expression, and all of his efforts call for your genuine encouragement and praise.

The Play of Older Toddler-Twos

Unlike the dramatic play of kindergarten children, the play of thirty- to thirty-six-month-olds is not planned. Very young children are unable to corral their agemates for the group activity involved in house, train, or block play. Their actual takeoff can be a physical happening, such as rolling down an incline. If it looks like fun, and offers a chance for testing one's daring, usually other children will join in. Some prop—a doll blanket, empty pail, or telephone—may become an incentive for acting out an experience. However, due to their crude socialization techniques and limited vocabulary, older Toddler-Twos have great difficulty starting a play project.

Should some interplay get under way, it rarely involves more than two children, who promptly imitate each other. Naturally, eating and going to bed are the most frequent activities. Such routines as having one's hair washed, going to the toilet, visiting grandparents, telephoning, turning on the television, or getting gas for the car are also subjects that get "dress rehearsals."

Doll play is enjoyed by very young children every day. The doll of the two-and-a-half-year-old is always undressed. Rather than try to dress a doll, a child of this age will carefully select pieces of colored cloth and cover the body and face of a doll in a box, not necessarily a bed. Generally two-and-a-half- to three-year-olds recreate with their dolls the routines and happenings that occur in their everyday lives. Sometimes they are not ready to use a doll in a make-believe play situation. Then they regard themselves to be the doll and will assume the role of the doll, even if the doll bed or doll carriage is too fragile to hold them.

A comparison of the play of thirty-month-old children versus sixty-month-olds reveals how much more of life's details have been noted by the older role players, and how many new dramatic skills have been learned in so short a period. Doll play for the older children involves bathing, dressing, undressing, feeding, combing hair, ironing, etc., in addition to an entire housekeeping program. Such activities are enacted easily in a setting furnished with a play stove and refrigerator, doll bed, doll cradle, and so on.

The play of very young children can suddenly and easily disintegrate into shrieking and running aimlessly. Their play activity is still mainly self-centered and on the solitary side. However, should one child throw a ball (or sand in a sandbox), all the nearby children will join in wild, mass imitation.

Fantasy in Child Play

The early childhood years are a period of assimilating a tremendous amount of information. It also is the time for consolidating maturing physiological and psychological needs. It is deeply frustrating for a thirty-month-old to learn to adjust to the restrictions imposed upon him by the adult world. Since this is coupled with his push to practice emerging selfhood, separateness from parents, and independence, life with a thirty-month-old can be extraordinarily trying.

"But young children have an insurance policy," writes Dr. James L. Hymes, Jr., in *Teaching the Child Under Six* (Columbus, Ohio: Charles E. Merrill, 1974). "They live a large part of their time in a private world, one they themselves plan, manage, and control beautifully. In their dream world things always work out as they should. In this inner world, each child can be as powerful and masterful as ego demands."

Because young children have a continuous need for settings in which they can make the rules, they exert real effort to control the outcome of their pretend play. They relish situations in which they are the masters: "I must be the doctor and

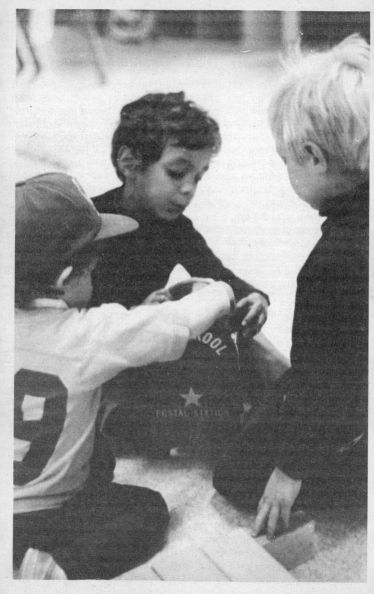

you must be sick." "This must be my birthday and you must bring me a present."

Sex-Typing Play

During the early childhood years, girls show an interest in dolls and doll play, and boys turn to building blocks, cars and trucks, jet planes, etc. Part of this may be due to the cultural mores which until quite recently dictated that boys should not be "sissies" and play with dolls, and girls should not be "tom-boys" and play football. Sex-typing play may also be due to the fact that this is the time when girls are expected to identify with their mothers and boys with their fathers.

However, as increasing numbers of mothers leave the home to go out to work, and as their lives begin to resemble those of the fathers, sex-role expectations for children may also become less rigid.

HEALTH, SELF-HELP, AND ROUTINES

In *These Are Your Children* (Glenview, Ill.: Scott, Foresman, 1975), Gladys Gardner Jenkins and Helen S. Shacter write, "How well children fulfill normal growth patterns will depend not only upon normal maturation, but on the kind of diet and physical care they receive. A lack of knowledge of diet, which may result in overfeeding at this age, may lead to obesity which can keep a child from running and playing in a normal fashion."

Although girls are ahead of boys in skeletal development, generally they are somewhat lighter and shorter than boys. Most girls are about one-half their adult height when they are two, and boys when they are two-and-a-half. Boys continue to have more muscle tissue; girls have more fatty tissue.

Most children have all twenty of their baby teeth by the time they are thirty months old.

Appetites and Nutrition

Appetites still fluctuate between good and poor. It is best to allow these swings to continue. If you need convincing, keep a chart to reassure yourself that good days balance poor days. Food preferences and refusals are like those of two-year-olds.

A child will prefer fruit and meat and dislike green vegetables. Some children will feed themselves the foods they like, and allow mother to feed them foods they are lukewarm about. They still go in for eating jags, and a food that was once preferred may suddenly be refused.

Thirty-one- through thirty-six-month-olds have a terrible time with food and eating. They do not like this or that food. Due to their diminishing weight gain, there is a lessening of appetite. At the same time, refusing food is a part of the toddler's declaration of independence from parental control. Many children resort to poor eating habits as one of the ways to express their individuality. You might let your child skip a meal occasionally, remembering that a hungry child always eats eventually. Do not serve reheated food to him once he has refused it. There is no place for a battle of wills at the kitchen or dining room table (or any place else, for that matter).

Allowing your thirty- to thirty-six-month-old choices in foods makes for great difficulty at mealtimes. It may be possible to offer a choice of one or two cereals or eggs at breakfast, and one or two sandwiches at lunch. However, in most homes, dinner is limited to what mother puts on the table. Finger foods may be tolerated at other meals, but not at dinner, when proper table manners are expected. Everyone is expected to sit through the evening meal until all have finished. These rules are impossible for an older Toddler-Two to comply with.

You need unbelievable patience in managing children this age. Parents have their own methods for coping—some of which work and some of which don't. Having children eat separately means cutting down on friction but also shortens time with father. Many parents compromise by permitting very young children to leave the table after the entree has been consumed.

Washing Up

Washing is a generally happy activity because children enjoy water play. Bathing is also fun because parents make provisions for play with boats, filling and emptying containers, etc. However, soap in the eyes is still a problem, and there is resistance to hair washing. You can help speed up the washing and drying procedures by serving as a model.

After you and your child wash your hands before mealtimes,

dry your hands first so your child can see how to do this. Let her use her own hand towel. If necessary help her at first. You can praise her efforts by saying, "I like the way you dry your hands."

Always keep your child's hand towel on a hook or bar near the sink within his reach. If your child cannot reach the sink, get him a sturdy stepstool and keep it nearby, but out of harm's way.

Dressing and Undressing

The physical control of the two-and-a-half-year-old has matured so much that he is able to undress himself completely, even down to his bare skin. Of course, it is easier to undress than to dress oneself, and it will be several years before your child will be able to do this himself. Most two-and-a-half-year-olds work hard at mastering the demands of dressing. For now, your child's dressing may be limited to putting on socks and shirt, and perhaps his pants and coat—still with some subtle help from you. Be patient. Always praise him for trying and succeeding, showing him calmly how to handle each step and article of clothing. Do not expect your child to master the entire process before he is six or seven years old.

Dressing can be speeded up if parents limit their thirty-one-through thirty-six-month-old's choice of clothing to be worn. Two-and-a-half-year-olds consider dressing to be an important adult procedure, and will take hours to decide what clothing to wear for special occasions. To smoothly accelerate the process, parents can share the dressing chore: "You do the socks, and I'll help with the shoes," etc.

Dressing time is an opportune time to start teaching tidiness in putting things away, clothing as well as toys. If you want a room to look neat, make sure you have specific places to hang or store things. If you can draw or paint, put pictures of toys on shelves, as well as footprints on the floor of your child's closet to indicate placement of shoes. It helps to put hooks down low for hanging clothing, towels, etc. Learning habits of orderliness takes a long time and much intervention by parents, but it pays off in later years.

Toilet Learning at Thirty-one Through Thirty-six Months

Although most children this age have better retention control (as much as five hours), are able to verbalize their toileting needs fairly consistently, express pride in their achievements, may be dry at night (if taken up), and some in full control of their bowel movements (though they need help in wiping themselves), child-care authorities counsel parents not to be disappointed if their children lag behind this timetable. It seems that in no area of functioning are individual variations more striking than in toilet learning.

Dr. Spock reports that "studies of average children show that most of them are still having accidents at two-and-a-half years, and plenty aren't able to take over full responsibility by thirty-six months."

Thirty-one- through thirty-six-month-olds begin to be uncomfortable when soiled or wet. They will want to be changed promptly, and will also wish to wear underwear like older children (instead of diapers like babies).

Patience, a relaxed attitude, and praise when your toddler is successful in using the toilet will add extra mileage to one of nature's "grand designs."

Bed-wetting

Bed-wetting is a problem only if it persists much beyond a child's fourth year of life. It may be a result of feelings of anxiety or hostility. Sometimes children are angry at their parents, but afraid to show their feelings openly or to express them verbally. Or they may feel unloved for a variety of reasons.

If enuresis persists beyond five years of age, a doctor should be consulted.

Constipation

Richard H. Granger, M.D., author of the 1974 edition of the U.S. Government's booklet, Your Child from One to Six, offers these words of caution with regard to the problem of constipation in Toddler-Twos: "One thing parents should not do to the child is manipulate the rectum. Times have changed. Equipment such as enemas, suppositories, even rectal ther-

mometers should never be used unless a physician has ordered them, and then for only the shortest possible time. If children cannot or will not have bowel movements on their own, parents should seek help from their doctor. Occasionally a physical problem may be present, but some psychological problem is far more likely to be the cause of constipation."

Negativism Gives Way to Indecision

Your child wants to have his cake and eat it, icing and all. He cannot make up his mind. You may have to struggle to get him into the bathtub, and once he is in, you may have to urge him to get out again. He wants to put on his coat and go outdoors, but as soon as you bundle him up, he decides to stay in the house.

Although your patience and fortitude will often peter out, it should comfort you to know that she will be easier to live with after her third birthday. At three, she will be eager to please, and will be better able to do so. She will profit by experience, share, take turns, and even make decisions that she will stick by—characteristics that are alien to thirty-one-month-olds.

Growth Chart—31st Through 36th Month

MOTOR DEVELOPMENT

Gross Motor

Stand on one foot for about 2 seconds.

Walk on 2″ line for 10 feet.

Run well, but unable to start and stop quickly.

Jump up in air with both feet; jump from chair to floor.

Hop on one foot for 2 or more hops.

Jump over string 8″ high.

Master small tricycle.

Jump from second stair step to the floor.

Walk upstairs alternating forward foot.

Walk downstairs alone with both feet on each step.

Anal sphincter muscles in control.

Fine Motor

Good hand and finger coordination.

Can move digits independently.

Build tower of 8 cubes.

LANGUAGE ACQUISITION

Rapid increase in vocabulary; average 50 new words a month.
(Most reach 900 words between 2nd and 3rd birthdays.)

Use "I" instead of proper name when referring to themselves; employ pronouns "I," "me," "you," in speech.

Use three- or four-word sentences; sentences have characteristic children's grammar.

Can give first and last name when asked.

Ask questions that begin with "what," "why," "where."

Make confused distinctions between *yes* and *no*, *come* and *go*, *give* and *take*, *push* and *pull*.

Frustrated if not understood by adults.

Enjoy picture books with 2 or 3 sentences on page. Can name items in pictures (dog, book, apple).

Interested in how words sound.

Enjoy rhyming words.

Begin to understand that words have a beginning, middle, and end sound.

Telescoping of words continues.

Growth Chart—31st Through 36th Month

SENSORY POWERS/LEARNING

Eager to learn; ask questions endlessly.

Understand concept of *one*.

Can match some colors—red.

Learning to concentrate.

Ongoing interest in exploring the world of objects.

Can remember 3 directions at a time without having them repeated ("Shut the door, get your cap, and sit down")

Sense of space more precise (here or there, under or over); can give fair answers to "where the birds and fishes live."

SOCIAL DEVELOPMENT

Discovering satisfaction from doing things for others.

Enjoy helping with household chores.

Relive their babyhood verbally (may even want to be a baby).

Call women "lady" and men "man," as distinguished from mommies and daddies.

Love to give orders.

Experience difficulty with siblings.

Social contacts fleeting due to short attention span.

PERSONALITY/ PSYCHOLOGICAL

Tend to be rigid and inflexible in their wants.

Cannot make up their minds.

Can be obnoxious in their demands; rebellious, violent in their emotions.

Frequent mood swings.

Conscious of own sex organs; beginning interest in physiological differences between males and females.

Can locate and name body parts and their functions (gender identity).

Know they are a boy like father and are different from girls, or vice versa.

Interest in watching others in bathroom or when undressed.

Greatly improved self-control.

Must be watched constantly due to unpredictable behavior.

Love and affection get mixed up with "pushes and pinches."

Growth Chart—31st Through 36th Month

PLAY AND PLAYTHINGS	HEALTH, SELF-HELP, AND ROUTINES
Beginning to play with other children.	Most Toddler-Twos achieve a measure of daytime bowel and bladder control. (Complete nighttime control seldom achieved before 3.)
Group play without adult supervision quickly deteriorates.	
Unable to resolve altercations with agemates without adult help.	Can feed themselves, at least part of meal, without too much spilling; may require help as they tire.
Enjoy use of telephone, but unable to sustain long talk.	Can manage spoon and cup, with some spilling.
Can put together 6- to 12-piece puzzles.	Can take off and put on their own shoes; cannot tie shoelaces.
Beginning of fantasy and pretend play.	Will cooperate while being dressed.
Like to finger-paint and model with clay; also to easel-paint.	Can undress themselves completely at 2½ years.
	Begin to be able to select and put on their own clothes at 3 years.
	Average amount of sleep required by 2½ is 13 hours.

Dear Parents:

Do not regard this chart as a rigid timetable.
Young children are unpredictable individuals.
Some perform an activity earlier or later than this chart indicates.

Just use this information to anticipate and appreciate normal child development and behavior. No norms are absolute.

CHAPTER FIVE

The 37th Through 42nd Month of Life

It was an old, old, old,
  old lady,
And a boy that was half-
  past three;
And the way that they
  played together
Was beautiful to see.
      Henry Cuyler Bunner,
      from *One, Two, Three!*

In the past twelve months, the maturing of your child's power of locomotion, her improved bodily control, and her burgeoning speech have fueled her strong, innate drive for independence and separateness from you, and for the gradual emergence of her feelings of autonomy. What looked like rebellious behavior was actually a reflection of your child's struggle to achieve self-confidence and a competent self-image.

Some child-rearing professionals call the third year the "golden age of childhood." At the age of three, what a child learns depends less upon what his body can do for him and more upon outside factors. The adults in the child's life and his relationships with his peers determine to a large extent the kind and amount of stimulation and challenge he faces. The thirty-seven- to forty-two-month-old's expanded vocabulary and verbal comprehension enable parents to communicate their sense of values and their way of life to their very young child.

The typical thirty-seven- through forty-two-month-old child is calmer, more conforming, and easier to manage. He has reached the stage in his emotional development where he

adores his parents and wants to be just like them. He wants to do what they do, imitate their language and their physical actions and gestures. The contrariness and anger of the two-and-a-half- to three-year-old appear to have subsided. At the same time, inevitably he still has to come to grips with the realization that he cannot and may not do everything he would like to do.

Three-year-olds are delightful most of the time, albeit exhausting on occasion. Their expressed affection for their parents makes them responsive and lovable. They are good company.

The infancy period has ended. Your child's transition to a new plateau of development is not abrupt. It reflects the previous stages, and heralds her entry into the play and fantasy world of the nursery school set. Her loyalty is to three- and four-year-olds, not two-year-olds.

Your three-year-old's personality and intelligence have grown so that he knows how to please or infuriate you. He can ride a tricycle and other vehicles. His imitative abilities enable him to participate in fantasy play with his older sister, speak to a stuffed dog, have a tea party with an imaginary guest, etc.

Your child easily memorizes nursery rhymes. She cherishes stories about herself when she was a baby and about the family. She seeks answers to unending questions about herself and everything in her universe. The three-year-old is a great conversationalist; she will talk to herself and everything and everyone in her world.

Insistence on bath and bedtime rituals is beginning to ease up. He will even be willing to sleep in an unfamiliar room with the lights off. The three-year-old is much easier to live with than heretofore. He has learned to make simple choices, among other behavioral strides forward.

GROSS-MOTOR DEVELOPMENT

The gross-motor mechanisms of three-year-olds mesh quite effectively. They walk erect, swinging their arms in adult fashion. Their shoulders too are more erect, and the typical toddler's protruding abdomen is decidedly reduced. They sit on a chair, with ankles crossed; stand briefly on one leg; and walk on tiptoe. They are able to hop on one foot a few times. They walk forward, sideways, or backwards. They can kick a ball hard, and catch a large ball between their outstretched arms.

The gross-motor movements of three-year-olds are no longer studied motion; they have become automatic. As the result of a year of practice, they run with greater smoothness; start and stop more easily; turn sudden corners and negotiate sudden stops with skill. They can go upstairs unaided, with feet alternating; coming down, most children put two feet on each step. They are able to jump down from the bottom tread, both feet together. Now they can jump about twelve inches off the ground.

Threes have mastered a tricycle and other ride 'em vehicles, using pedals smoothly. They are able to steer clear of obstacles in their way. They can get up easily from a squatting position, walk up an inclined plane, and climb on a jungle gym with some degree of self-assurance.

The Sense of Balance

The sense of balance is one of the achievements that neurologists examine when ascertaining the health of a child's nervous system. In *Perceptual and Motor Development in Infants and Children,* Bryant J. Cratty writes that "sometime during the third, fourth, or fifth year, a series of balance tasks are given, which include line walking, narrow beam walking with arms or body held in various positions, standing on one foot or toes, etc." The ability to walk a straight line is attained by children at about three years of age. A study conducted by Dr. Nancy Bayley many years ago showed that 50 percent of the three-year-olds who were tested were able to walk ten feet on a one-inch line without losing their balance. On a slightly raised balance beam, two-year-olds will walk with one foot on the beam and the other foot on the floor. Most three-year-olds are able to alternate the placement of both their feet part of the way. By their fourth year, children can slowly walk the entire length of a ten-foot balance beam.

Your energetic three-year-old can throw a ball overhand about ten feet, and catch a large ball between her extended arms. She kicks a ball vigorously.

FINE-MOTOR DEVELOPMENT

The three-year-old is interested in play projects that require more precise finger and hand manipulations than heretofore. His crayon drawings show that he can control movement. He uses both crayons and pencils effectively, and his strokes are firmer and less repetitive. He can copy a circle, and reproduce a cross if shown how to do it. He now draws a human figure showing a head and possibly two other parts.

His ability to build a tower of nine to ten cubes is the result of the maturing of neuromuscular skills rather than the growth of his attention span.

Although she can perform vertical and horizontal tasks, she appears unable to handle oblique tasks. Even with the aid of a model, she can fold a piece of paper lengthwise and crosswise, but not diagonally.

He is able to properly place a round, square, and triangular block in a formboard or a shape-sorting box. He can match two primary colors, usually red and yellow, but may confuse blue with green.

She can use scissors to cut paper. She will relish cutting pictures out of magazines the family is discarding.

Threes will try to turn an eggbeater for purposes of whipping cream or eggs.

The eye-hand coordination of the three-year-old is much smoother than the toddler's. He is able to pick up marbles, raisins, tiny pebbles, etc., with his thumb and forefinger, with each eye covered separately. He is adept at stringing large wooden or plastic beads on a shoestring.

LANGUAGE ACQUISITION

Twos acquire words; Threes use them. At three years, words become instruments for designating ideas, relationships, etc. Vocabulary reaches an average of one thousand words. The three-year-old can name most household items. Not all words are the carriers of serious meaning: some have melody value or humor value; others are meaningless chants, with sounds to be experimented with. Some are so new to the child that he uses them in soliloquies and dramatic play in order to convert them into words, sentences, and syntax (grammar). "He is," wrote Dr. Gesell, "both an actor and a talker and he uses acting to perfect his talking. He acts out the role of the plumber, the delivery boy . . . in order to practice spoken words and verbalized thinking. Most of it seems aimless and pointless, but it is the mechanism used by the three-year-old to achieve speech and give meaning to words."

Three-year-olds speak in short sentences (three words in an average sentence) and usually with animation. They pay great attention to adults, listen to their words, and watch their faces for clues as to their approval or disapproval. Most can easily name all the pictures in a familiar storybook. They like to listen to simple stories and nursery rhymes, and love to pretend being a bear, a dog, or a horse. They are extremely

curious about people and things around them and ask many simple questions.

The memory of the three-year-old keeps on improving. She can remember what happened yesterday even though she may not really understand the concept of "yesterday" or "tomorrow." She can recall three commands at a time without any hesitation: "Please shut the door." "Get your sweater." "Get down."

Some Good Books for Threes and Fours

Children differ greatly, so it is up to you to discover which books will be best for your child. Visit your local library with your child at least once a week. The children's librarian will be pleased to recommend suitable titles.

Alexander, Martha. *Nobody Asked Me if I Wanted a Baby Sister.* (Dial Press, 1971)
———. *Sabrina.* (Dial Press, 1971)
Beskow, Elsa. *Pelle's New Suit.* (Harper & Row, 1929)
Brown, Margaret Wise. *The Noisy Book.* (Harper & Row, 1939)
———. *The Runaway Bunny.* (Harper & Row, new edition, 1972)
Buckley, Helen E. *Grandfather and I.* (Lothrop, Lee & Shepard, 1959)
———. *Grandmother and I.* (Lothrop, Lee & Shepard, 1961)
Budney, Blossom. *A Kiss Is Round.* (Lothrop, Lee & Shepard, 1954)
Chess, Victoria. *Alfred's Alphabet Walk.* (Greenwillow, 1979)
Cohen, Miriam. *Best Friends.* (Macmillan, 1971)
Cole, William. *What's Good for a Three Year Old?* (Holt, Rinehart & Winston, 1971)
Duvoisin, Roger. *A For the Ark.* (Lothrop, Lee & Shepard, 1952)
———. *The Crocodile in the Tree.* (Alfred A. Knopf, 1973)
———. *The House of Four Seasons.* (Lothrop, Lee & Shepard, 1956)
Ernst, Kathryn F. *Danny and His Thumb.* (Prentice-Hall, 1973)
Ets, Marie Hall. *Gilberto and the Wind.* (Viking, 1963)
———. *In the Forest.* (Viking, 1944)
———. *Just Me.* (Viking, 1965)
———. *Play With Me.* (Viking, 1955)

————. *Talking Without Words.* (Viking, 1968)

Feder, Jane. *Beany.* (Pantheon, 1979)

Flack, Marjorie. *Angus Lost.* (Doubleday, 1941)

Freeman, Don. *Corduroy.* (Penguin Books, 1976)

Gág, Wanda. *Millions of Cats.* (Coward-McCann, 1928)

Gramatky, Hardie. *Little Toot.* (Putnam, 1939)

Green, Mary McBurney. *Is It Hard? Is It Easy?* (Addison-Wesley, 1960)

Hoban, Tana. *One Little Kitten.* (Greenwillow, 1979)

————. *Push, Pull, Empty, Full.* (Macmillan, 1972)

————. *Shapes & Things.* (Macmillan, 1970)

Holl, Adelaide. *The Rain Puddle.* (Lothrop, Lee & Shepard, 1965)

Hutchins, Pat. *Rosie's Walk.* (Macmillan, 1968)

Kantrowitz, Mildred. *Willy Bear.* (Parents' Magazine Press, 1976)

Klein, Leonore. *Mud, Mud, Mud.* (Alfred A. Knopf, 1962)

Klein, Norma. *Girls Can Be Anything.* (Dutton, 1973)

Krasilovsky, Phyllis. *The Very Little Boy.* (Doubleday, 1953)

————. *The Very Little Girl.* (Doubleday, 1953)

Lenski, Lois. *Davy's Day.* (Walck, 1943)

————. *I Like Winter.* (Walck, 1950)

————. *Spring Is Here.* (Walck, 1945)

Lionni, Leo. *Little Blue and Little Yellow.* (Astor-Honor, 1959)

————. *Swimmy.* (Pantheon, 1963)

Lobel, Arnold. *A Zoo for Mister Muster.* (Harper & Row, 1962)

McGovern, Ann. *Too Much Noise.* (Houghton Mifflin, 1967)

Moffett, Martha. *A Flower Pot Is Not a Hat.* (Dutton, 1972)

Munari, Bruno. *Bruno Munari's ABC.* (Collins, 1960)

Nakatani, Chiyoko. *My Teddy Bear.* (Crowell, 1976)

Parsons, Ellen. *Rainy Day Together.* (Harper & Row, 1971)

Paterson, Diane. *Eat.* (Dial Press, 1975)

Petersham, Maud and Miska. *The Rooster Crows.* (Macmillan, 1945)

Rand, Ann and Paul. *I Know a Lot of Things.* (Harcourt, Brace & World, 1956)

Rice, Eve. *Oh, Lewis!* (Macmillan, 1974)

Roche, P. K. *Goodbye, Arnold.* (Dial Press, 1979)

Rockwell, Harlow. *My Nursery School.* (Greenwillow, 1976)

Ruben, Patricia. *Apples to Zippers: An Alphabet Book.* (Doubleday, 1976)

Scarry, Richard. *Best Word Book Ever.* (Western, 1963)

Schlein, Miriam. *Shapes.* (Addison-Wesley, 1952)

Tresselt, Alvin. *Rain Drop Splash.* (Lothrop, Lee & Shepard, 1946)

Viorst, Judith. *Alexander and the Terrible, Horrible, No Good, Very Bad Day.* (Atheneum, 1972)

———. *Rosie and Michael.* (Atheneum, 1974)

Ward, Lynd. *The Biggest Bear.* (Houghton Mifflin, 1952)

Wildsmith, Brian. *Brian Wildsmith's ABC.* (Franklin Watts, 1962)

Wright, Ethel. *Saturday Walk.* (Addison-Wesley, 1954)

Zaffo, George. *The Giant Nursery Book of Things That Go.* (Doubleday, 1967)

———. *The Giant Nursery Book of Things That Work.* (Doubleday, 1967)

Zion, Gene. *All Falling Down.* (Harper & Row, 1951)

Zolotow, Charlotte. *The Storm Book.* (Harper & Row, 1952)

———. *William's Doll.* (Harper & Row, 1972)

SENSORY POWERS/LEARNING

In *Thinking Is Child's Play* (New York: Avon Books, 2nd printing December 1971), Evelyn Sharp writes, "To help your child develop his powers of thinking, you need to understand how a child thinks, so that you can meet him on the level where he is. Listen—really pay attention—to what he says, and you can get a clue. Children's misconceptions often provide a peek inside their minds."

We agree with Ms. Sharp that "children do not pass from one stage of development to another all at once . . . Rather, concepts are constructed, layer upon layer. The transition is gradual, and the boundary lines are blurred." Keep this in mind as your children move from one age and stage to the next.

Some of the games thirty-seven- through forty-two-month-olds enjoy are picture lotto games of animals, birds, flowers, fruits, etc., and picture domino games. Both kinds offer agreeable matching opportunities. Also good are appropriate jigsaw puzzles. A felt board (homemade or purchased) with felt people, animals, and objects invites sequential thinking and arranging. A deck of playing cards might promote awareness of numbers and beginning counting.

Ms. Sharp offers some pointers on ways of presenting learning games to young children:

Let your child think for himself. Give him enough time. If he doesn't succeed after several trials, you can give him a *hint*, but do not *tell* him the answer. Everything he is able to work out for himself gives him confidence, and can make the next challenge easier.

Let your child perform for herself whatever actions are called for. Let her do it even if she seems to take a long time.

Always make each game a pleasant experience for your child and you.

Learning games are less effective if continued too long at one time. Do not keep at it for over five or ten minutes with your thirty-seven- to forty-second-month-old.

Three-year-olds have begun to show a new sense of order (which is, of course, welcomed by all parents).

Most Threes cannot name colors, but they are able to match shapes. This explains their ongoing enjoyment of shape-sorting toys. They have begun to identify, classify, and compare the objects they encounter in the course of their daily activities.

The period from three to four years of age is punctuated by striking cognitive growth. Children this age are beginning to reason. They are learning how things are related to each other, and now they can create wholes out of parts and group things together.

It appears that these very young children are actually starting to feel somewhat in charge of themselves in their special universe.

SOCIAL DEVELOPMENT

The three-year-old knows that she is a person and you are a person. She uses words and mannerisms to express her feelings of affection, her desires, and even her problems. However, her sense of self is not always in tune. She is subject to fits of anger or jealousy. She can experience deep anxiety and frustration that are sometimes accompanied by a temper tantrum or a wild attack against a physical object. Luckily, her emotional outbursts are short-lived. Inasmuch as her emotional life can swing from high to low, and because she has a vivid imagination, she can fall prey to fantastic fears.

Threes (and Fours) devote a great deal of time and effort to making friends. They generally are clumsy at first, tagging after older children, or hugging younger ones. They are beginning to share, but not yet wholeheartedly. Slowly they are

learning what it means to take turns, to compromise and to relate to others. They do not have a real understanding of cooperation.

If their approach does not work, they will try playing the clown, repeating actions and phrases that attracted attention in the past. Most three-year-olds are delightful show-offs who like to make others laugh and love them.

It makes no difference to a thirty-six-month-old whether a friend is a girl or a boy. Children this age enjoy other children of both sexes equally well. Very young girls and boys play the same games.

Imaginary Friends

It is good when children enjoy being with other children their age. However, some may be slow to enjoy the company of other children and will withdraw for a while. In time, a child will have a natural liking for a "special friend." Two quiet children may enjoy each other; or two active children may like to play ball or ride their tricycles together. Some children change friends frequently. Others like to have several friends. Sooner or later, most thirty-six- to forty-two-month-olds wind up having two "good friends."

Some children who live in remote places imagine having a friend, or use carefully chosen stuffed animals or dolls as friends. They give them names and talk to them. They take them along wherever they go. Such children will even involve both parents in imaginary situations with their make-believe friends. Many parents enjoy the conversations and do not get annoyed; they think it takes imagination to create and enact all kinds of scenes. Other parents are annoyed; they believe their children should be enjoying *living* friends. Whichever kind of parent you are, try to retain your sense of humor and patience. When ready, your child will give up her inanimate friends. They did come in handy when your child had no nearby friends, and while she was feeling her way to becoming a member of a peer group.

The Loner

Some young children choose to spend too much time by themselves, or with siblings and adult relatives. Of course, solitary play or adult-associated play should not be totally condemned.

According to Dr. George E. Gardner, author of *The Emerging Personality, Infancy Through Adolescence* (New York: Delacorte Press, 1970), the loner, through fear due to an unfortunate past experience or shyness, prefers to be alone. She may lack basic social skills to reach out to others, and needs to be encouraged to be with her peers. On the other hand, there are children, usually firstborn, who genuinely enjoy solitary play but will also participate in group activities. Such children do not necessarily have any social problems.

Parents need to be sensitive to their children's feelings and should try to introduce them to their peers in situations where they are likely to feel most secure. Some aspects of socialization can go forward only through pleasurable relationships with other children. Very young children who are timid in the presence of their peers will learn social poise if they are given sufficient opportunities to be near or to play with children on a regular basis.

The Importance of Grandparents

The conviction of Arthur Kornhaber, M.D., and Kenneth L. Woodward, authors of *Grandparents/Grandchildren: The Vital*

Connection (Garden City, NY: Anchor Press/Doubleday, 1981), borne out by more than three years of in-depth personal interviews with some three hundred children and as many grandparents, is that "the bond between grandparents and grandchildren is second in emotional power and influence only to the relationship between children and parents. No matter how grandparents act, they affect the emotional well-being of their grandchildren . . . simply because they exist . . .

"Emotional attachments between grandparents and grandchildren are unique. The normal conflicts that occur between children and parents simply do not exist between grandchildren and grandparents . . . Grandparents and grandchildren do not have to *do* anything to make each other happy; their joy comes from *being* together . . .

"On becoming a grandparent, the impulse to nurture is reawakened, and earlier experiences of motherhood and fatherhood are relived . . .

"The complete emotional well-being of children requires that they have a direct, not merely a derived link with their grandparents . . . In their capacity as living historians, grandparents transmit ethnic heritage . . . and religious faith and values."

Baby-sitters

Teenagers do a lot of baby-sitting. They may or may not be experienced with the ways of young children, and will feel more confident if you show them how you care for your child. For that matter, any sitter will appreciate having full information about your way of doing things. As your child grows older, he is sure to announce "Mother always does it this way" or "Mother lets me have that." If you've talked your ways over with the sitter, she or he will be able to distinguish fact from your child's attempts to test how far he can manipulate things to suit him.

Among the items a sitter likes to know are: Does the child expect food or drink before bed? What time does he go to bed? Is he supposed to have any medicine? Should he have any medicine if he asks for it? What is his favorite toy? How do you arrange the covers? Does he go to the bathroom during the evening?

The sitter should also have other information: What is the telephone number where you, or some other responsible person, can be reached; the telephone number of your doctor, the fire or police department? How do you regulate the heat? Are there any extra jobs you have in mind? How about snacks, use of radio or TV? Do or don't you permit the sitter to invite a companion? What time will you return? People who are otherwise prompt are often careless in their time commitments to sitters. If you are to be delayed more than fifteen minutes, you should phone.

PERSONALITY/PSYCHOLOGICAL DEVELOPMENT

Their desire and ability to imitate their elders and to conform make three-year-olds quite obedient. Due to their enlarged usable vocabulary most Threes can be managed by reasoning and distraction. Three-year-olds are at peace with themselves and their world—much of the time. They rebel less frequently. Instead of using prior primitive methods of pushing, biting, and scratching, they now resort to the use of language to resist.

Thumb-sucking during the day occurs only when they are weary, thwarted, or ill. It can take place at night as a tensional outlet. Three-year-olds may wander around the house during the night.

Threes are still dependent upon adults for affirmation of their feelings of accomplishment. They respond positively to encouragement, praise, and consistent direction. They do not like anything new or unusual in their daily routines.

In their desire to please, thirty-seven- through forty-two-month-olds may want to help set the table, among other household chores. They now are more proficient at folding paper napkins. Most children this age are eager to help adults in the kitchen, doing marketing, etc. Let them!

Discipline

In *How to Parent,* Fitzhugh Dodson writes, "The right kind of spanking needs no special paraphernalia. Just the hand of the parent administered a few times on the kid's bottom. The right kind of spanking . . . clears the air, and is vastly to be preferred to moralistic and guilt-inducing parental lectures . . .

"A child can understand very well when you strike him in anger. He knows you are mad at him and he understands why . . . Too many mothers nowadays seem to be afraid to spank their children. They talk and nag a great deal as a substitute . . . The main purpose of spanking, although most parents don't like to admit it, is to relieve the parent's feelings of frustration."

The Excessively Shy Child

By the third year, one can spot a very shy child. We are not talking about the quiet, self-reliant child, nor are we referring to the shyness toward strangers that crops up at eight to ten months of age, and again at about fourteen to fifteen months. Rather, we are discussing the child who is terribly shy because she lacks self-confidence in social situations.

We are concerned about exaggerated retiring behavior that makes it difficult for a child to participate in play or other activities with his peers. "Such a shyness," according to the Canadian Mental Health Services of Ottawa, "is not a virtue, but usually a sign that something has gone wrong during the process of growing up."

Obviously, the very shy child needs to have a better opinion of herself. Somewhere along the way, such a child must have felt that she was neither loved nor valued. In their desire to raise a "perfect" child, there are parents who criticize too freely, overworking their *dos* and *don'ts*. Such parents often find that they are raising a child who is ill at ease and hesitant; who retreats from any kind of action, decision making, or involvement. The extremely shy child is unsure of herself and feels that she cannot do many of the things she would like to do.

Below are attitudes and actions that the Canadian Mental Health Services of Ottawa warns parents to avoid:

- Failing to let your child try to feed, wash, and dress himself even before he is able to assume full responsibility.
- Making all the decisions for your child.
- Making too many negative comments: "Don't touch." "Stop that noise!" "Can't you do anything yourself?"
- Expecting too much too soon in the way of manners, acceptable habits, and cleanliness.
- Humiliating or embarrassing your child at social gatherings because she spilled a glass of water or was otherwise clumsy.

How to Help a Shy Child

- Provide opportunities for more playmates.
- Gently ease your child into amiable social circles.
- Avoid the "spotlight" approach; i.e., too much comment when introducing your child to anyone. Give her ample time to make gains at her own pace.
- Redirect your child's attention from the things he cannot do to what he can do.

- Let your child know in your words and actions that you appreciate her and all her accomplishments.
- Seriously consider additional ways you can help your child to build a better opinion of himself.

All mothers (and fathers) take heart! In *Your Child Is a Person* (New York: Viking Press, 3rd printing, 1973), Drs. Stella Chess, Alexander Thomas, and Herbert G. Birch write, "It is no longer as fashionable as it was a decade ago [1955] to blame the mother for a child's behavioral and emotional difficulties . . .

"In our view, personality develops as the result of a constant interaction between the child, with his unique way of reacting, and his total environment, in which the parents are highly influential elements. Neither the child's characteristics alone nor the parents' practices and attitudes alone provide an adequate basis for understanding psychological development . . .

"The essential individuality of children is often overlooked in child-care books and in treatises on personality development . . . The fact that children are different is not a reason for parents to abdicate and let the young raise themselves as their individuality dictates . . . Any set of principles to help parents with child care can only be a compass and a guide and not a rigid blueprint or prescription."

The Effects of Moving on the Family

The *reason* for moving affects the family most. If parents welcome the change because it represents a promotion or a return to the old home town, the feelings they convey to their children will be positive and happy. However, if the move results from a job loss, death, or divorce, both the parents and children will be troubled.

Because a move is difficult under the best of circumstances, there is a tendency for children to be put aside. Preoccupied with a myriad of details, parents often do not take the time to discuss the move with their children. If not invited to talk about the move, children feel isolated and frightened just when they most need a supportive sense of family.

Reservations about a move are natural and you need not hide them. There is comfort for your child in knowing that you have qualms about moving just as he does. When he hears you admit that you will miss your friends, or job, or favorite park, he will realize that you understand the feelings he is struggling with. If you can overcome any ambivalence you may have with the conviction that the move is the right step for the family and that all will work out well, your child will also be likely to accept the change more easily.

It is the eighteen- to thirty-seven-month-old who has the greatest struggle to hold on to her sense of self. Much of her identity is tied to her parents, her accustomed surroundings, and a few favorite objects: a teddy, her crib, a beloved blanket. Deny her these personal possessions and she is apt to become upset. In the confusion of moving, the child may get the feeling that she is losing everything that is "her." She sees her toys being packed away, her crib dismantled, and wonders if she will ever see them again. During the commotion of moving day, she may even fear that she will be abandoned.

Include your thirty-seven-month-old on the trip to select your new house or apartment. If that is not feasible, return home with pictures of the house. A few snapshots of the park, neighborhood children, and nursery school will do much to help your child look forward to the move while realizing that life will continue much as before.

Use the colorful booklets provided by the moving company for storytime and as a basis for discussing the move. Familiarize your child with the movers and the van. Moving day can be played with dolls, a few empty cartons, and a wagon so that the whole process of packing, loading, unloading, and setting up can be enacted. After playing these games, one three-year-old joyfully pointed out every North American van the family passed on the highway, believing that each was the one containing their possessions. In this way, he felt the van was traveling along with them.

Include your child in farewell activities. Last visits with friends can be family affairs. A farewell party at home or at nursery school can be arranged for your little one. One mother sent a cake to school with "Good Luck, Mark" emblazoned across it. The teacher took her cue from the parent and part of the day was devoted to discussing moving and the child's new home and school.

If yours is a "company move," or if you can afford it, use a professional packing service. This will free you from the most time-consuming chore of moving. It will also concentrate confusion into just two days—packing day and moving day. If you must do your own packing, try to save most of it for evenings and when your child naps.

This is not the time to throw out your thirty-seven-month-old's scruffy toys. Pack her possessions last and be sure to leave a box of her favorites to accompany you in the car. This will help your child overcome her sense of dislocation and strangeness.

Although the temptation may be great, do not send your toddler to Grandma's or another relative during the move. It will do more for his peace of mind if he can stay with you.

Managing Moving Day

On moving day you will want to accept help from friends with meals and watching your child. Be sure to set aside luggage, food, toys, and other items that will accompany you. Ask the movers to load your child's things last, unload them first, and label them accordingly. This will help you reestablish her surroundings quickly.

If you can, make the journey to your new home a leisurely one and include some diverting activities in your schedule. Select a motel with a playground if you are traveling by car. A romp on the swings and slides will do wonders for your thirty-seven- through forty-two-month-old.

After your arrival, do not be in a hurry to set the whole house in order. Go slowly with any major changes in your customary household arrangements. Concentrate on the necessities. With your child or children in tow, explore the new neighborhood, find the park, the library, and the shopping center. Treat your family and yourself to dinner out.

Do not be upset if you notice changes in your toddler's sleeping habits or if she clings a little closer to you than before. She may ask for old friends. It is best not to underestimate her feelings and to deal with them openly. Now is the ideal time for you to admit that you miss your friends, too. Before long your child will be mixing the names of new friends with the old. Then you will know that you really are "home."

PLAY, PLAYTHINGS, AND FANTASY

When children enter their early childhood years their play is clothed in greater imagination and symbolism. They throw themselves wholeheartedly into role-playing, and it is out of this particular play that their conceptual schemes unfold. This free play, which has its own particular organization and structure, grabs a child's mind as no formal schooling can.

Most little boys and girls are avid "doers" and "talkers," and they have much to experience in order to extend their verbal skills and cognition. All children require and benefit from a sufficiency of imaginative play.

Young children come to understand themselves and the world through their dramatic play. They play with things and ideas in order to understand them more fully and come to grips with reality. In their dramatic play, children relive the different experiences they have had. "One of the functions of symbolic play," according to the late Jean Piaget, "is to satisfy the self

by transforming what is real into what is desired." It is a completely involving way for young children to plumb their feelings and broaden their knowledge.

Although thirty-seven- through forty-two-month-olds are ego-oriented, they are increasingly aware of interrelationships in their play. They use objects and ideas as a basis for their imaginative play. They can role-play and enjoy dress-up activities.

This is a prime period for confidence building ("Look at the tall building I made!" "See me ride my tricycle!"), of encouraging curiosity via all kinds of patterns of association: of learning differentiation through lotto games, jigsaw puzzles, etc.; of exploring city and country living through building block cities and farms; of thinking through kinship relationships by means of dolls and doll play.

This is the perfect time for giving young imaginations full sway (as in store play, puppetry, and other theater arts activities); for testing manual dexterity (with assorted construction sets); and for helping creativity flourish (by means of painting, clay work, music exploration, etc.).

Thirty-seven- through forty-two-month-olds delight in combining building blocks and all kinds of toy vehicles to make cities with roadways, bridges, tunnels, garages, etc. They enjoy playing house, "flying" jet planes, "driving trains," or being firefighters. They discover that it is more fun and more interesting when a few children engage in the play together.

Maneuvering wooden ride 'em trucks and trains on casters works well with a few children playing together. Pushing or pulling a wagon or doll carriage in which another child sits and building cooperatively with large hollow blocks likewise contribute to the establishment of agreeable social relations. Sharing a sandbox can enhance social awareness.

The child-sized wooden stove, kitchen cupboard, sink, table and chairs, and kitchen utensils permit a few children at a time to "cook food for a dinner party" and to set the table with appropriate dishes and cutlery. The child-sized doll bed and dresser and assorted dolls invite several children to play together. Boys and girls eagerly join forces to play at family living. Dress-up and theater arts activities also fully engage children in imaginative role-playing.

Although Threes continue to relish gross-motor activity, they are beginning to carry on sedentary play for longer periods. Rather than running aimlessly or throwing balls and other things, most prefer working on a puzzle, a shape-fitting box, or a formboard until they have mastered it. They like to play simple picture lotto and domino games. Thirty-seven- through forty-two-month-olds are more expert at putting jigsaw puzzles together. The number of pieces your child can handle at this age will depend upon his past experience with puzzles. Most forty-eight-month-olds can properly assemble up to thirty puzzle pieces. You can also introduce your child to the challenge and fun of making designs with multicolored parquetry blocks (triangles, squares, etc.).

Puppets, a punching bag, a giant push 'em ball, and other such playthings make it possible for young children to release their tensions by bringing their pent-up emotions to the outside. Thus, sometimes alone and sometimes with a few age-mates, very young children go about their momentous task of growing up and learning.

Planning a Child's Room

A basic consideration in designing a child's room is to make it a flexible environment to meet the changing ages and stages of child growth and development. The requirements of very young children and primary grade children are understandably quite different. Any room layout and furnishings must take into account the temporary and long-range specific needs and interests of the children concerned.

Scale is important. Because the ego of the very young child struggles in an environment built for giants (adults), furniture and furnishings need to be scaled down to the child's size. Chairs, tables, clothes racks, and book shelves can "grow" as a child grows. Legs of tables can be replaced; the brackets of a clothes rack can be adjusted; book shelves can have extra shelves added. Life is more manageable and pleasant in a "responsive" atmosphere.

All children need opportunities to exercise, especially on rainy days. At sporting goods stores or good toy shops you will find gyms that clamp onto a doorway that have a chinning bar, seat swing, rings, etc. Gym mats for very young children who like to turn somersaults or wrestle are usually available at school supply or sporting goods houses.

"As behavior changes so should the environment," writes Alexandra Stoddard, author of *A Child's Place* (Garden City, NY: Doubleday, 1977). "Make things movable . . . Not only

should the furniture be lightweight enough to move around, but the bigger pieces should be on heavy-duty casters so a child can move them. When there is a party, up goes the Murphy bed so there is room for people and play."

Parents should be able (figuratively speaking) to hose down the floors, walls, and even ceiling of their child's room. Practically, they should be able to use a sponge and a strong cleanser to make cleaning easier. There are all kinds of vinyl coverings, water-resistant enamels, and Fiberglas finishes today. When you think of flooring in your child's room, think of the approach of hospitals to maintenance and cleanliness.

Ms. Stoddard presents countless ideas on furnishing for each age level up to the adolescent years. We especially like the following of her recommendations:

- The use of adhesive-backed silver Mylar mirror paper to make distortion mirrors for children to see themselves in.
- Hanging a large horizontal sheet of shatterproof mirror on a wall so the bottom touches the floor—another opportunity to look at themselves.

- Making or buying a playhouse. Have a lumber yard cut four 4' × 4' plywood panels. Paint each wall a different color (with lead-free paint, of course). Join the walls together with removable pin hinges (available in hardware stores). Cut out windows and doors in circles, squares, and triangles.

Every playroom should have a large framed or unframed bulletin board (4' × 8') to display art work or other creative endeavors. Burlap-covered, soft Cellutex boards make excellent bulletin boards. Burlap can be purchased by the yard in assorted colors. Tack holes do not show in the burlap. Sliding hardboard doors with baked enamel finishes work well as washable chalk boards (use wax Cray-offs). Painted steel boards will hold magnetic letters for word play or for hanging pictures with strong small magnets, etc. They are available in most variety stores.

Another popular approach today is the use of "do-it-yourself" cork board squares. These give great flexibility since they can be cut to fit any wall space available and can be tacked and retacked without making holes in the cork.

Playroom Storage Facilities

If you want your child to play by himself at times, if you want the playroom to be orderly and easy to manage by you and your child, you will have to plan its storage facilities carefully.

In the 1950s, Creative Playthings designed and marketed a very versatile storage system—Hollow Box Furniture—which consisted of 12" × 12" × 12" boxes and 12" × 48" shelf boards. These boxes can be made of ½" plywood or white pine lumber (which can be ordered from any lumber yard). Each hollow box (one side was open) had ⅜" holes drilled in the center of five of its sides. Each shelf board had ⅜" holes drilled at each end. When grouped together in units of four, six, eight, or ten cubes, screws and nuts held each arrangement permanently in place. The cubes can be used with shelf boards to serve all kinds of storage needs. Boxes can be used for seats, to support tabletops, and—if casters are attached—to create a convenient mobile block cart.

As the child grew, four hollow boxes were joined together with a 2"-framed plywood or colored linoleum 24" × 48" tabletop to form a low toddler table; a school child's 24¾"-high desk was made with eight boxes. (Check your local unpainted furniture shop for the availability of boxes, shelf boards, and tabletops.)

If carpentry is one of your hobbies, you may enjoy making nursery school-type storage units for your home: a bookshelf and book display unit, a coat rack cubby, foldaway shelving, etc. Such units can be seen or purchased at school supply houses. You can see these in use at most well-equipped nursery schools and kindergartens. Ask the teacher for the source of such storage units. (Also check the Yellow Pages of your

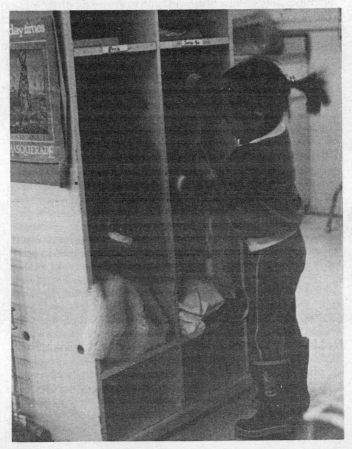

local phone directory under *School Furniture & Equipment*.)

Most of the above units will accommodate the 5½"-, 11"-, and 22"-long unit building blocks, all kinds of transportation toys, puzzles, fitting toys, farm and wild animals, play people, musical instruments, etc. When each item has its own visible storage space, it is easier to choose particular toys to play with and to put them back after use. It takes time to teach children to put back their toys. However, even very young children will try to cooperate if convenient storage facilities are available in the playroom.

Parents will question the repetition in the home of the equipment usually found in the better nursery schools. The hours spent at home are longer than those in the day-care center or nursery school. Most nursery schools are conducted on a half-day program. Moreover, children usually work in groups at these centers. At home, a child has time to work out her own new block building or dramatic play ideas that she may want to try out in school the next day.

Tables, Chairs, and Rockers

Every two-year-old (and older) child needs a play table with a washable surface. A Formica top will make it impervious to water, clay, finger paints, etc. Most playroom tables come as 24" × 48" rectangles or 30" to 36" diameter rounds. Preferred are those with legs that can be removed so the table will grow with the child. A two-year-old needs a table from 19" to 20" high; 20" to 22" high will serve three- to six-year-olds; 24" to 30" high are suitable for preteens and adults. Chairs come in 10", 12", 14", 16", and 18" heights from seat to floor. Allow an 8" to 10" height difference from top of table to top of seat for a toddler (10" to 12" for school-age children and adults). If you purchase more than two chairs, order stacking ones to save floor space. School supply houses or seating firms carry stacking furniture in all sizes. (Again, check the Yellow Pages of your local telephone directory under *School Furniture & Equipment*.)

Homemaking Play Equipment

It is natural for children to relive the activities of the world around them, and life is easier for them to understand when they have acted out the parts of the people in it. The items that follow are enjoyed in the home as well as early childhood centers:

- stove: 24″ high; cupboard: 43″ high; sink: 24″ high; refrigerator: 37″ high (bought or homemade)
- tea table: 30″ in diameter × 22″ high; 2 chairs
- housecleaning set (toy broom, wet mop, hand brush, dry mop, dustpan, etc.)
- stationary ironing board: 8″ wide × 20″ long × 24″ high (with shelf); adult-sized clothespins; wood or metal toy iron
- metal wash tub; scrubbing board; assorted baskets and boxes; empty spools
- accessories and props: aluminum tea set, pots and pans, cutlery set, kitchen utensil set, pitcher and tumblers, toy telephone, cookie cutters, measuring cups and spoons
- *Store or Post Office Play:* play store (wood or heavy corrugated); plastic fruits and vegetables, empty cans and labels, weighing scales, cash register (toy version), toy money

- *Dress-Up:* Mother's and Dad's shoes, washable plastic bonnets, floppy hats, costume box or suitcase, pocketbooks, gloves, scarves, jewelry, squares and lengths of colored cloth; stethoscope (adult-size), masks
- *Homemaking Play Furniture:* large wood doll carriage, large doll bed, cradle, 12″ rubber or vinyl drink-and-wet doll, assorted doll clothes, doll bath, soft Raggedy Ann and Andy dolls, dress-up mirror (12″ wide × 47″ high). Assorted stuffed animals (check the eyes); stuffed 30″ life-size soft dolls, mattress, doll blanket, bendable family figures

Those who like working in wood will find that making a child-sized doll carriage, doll bed, and foldaway doll house can be fun. There are good books on the market that provide blueprints for such equipment. One of the better ones is *How to Make Children's Furniture and Play Equipment* by Mario del Fabbro (New York: McGraw-Hill, 1972).

Children this age show keen interest in the immediate environment. Their play centers around family life, occupations of people, neighborhood events, and transportation and communication. They need adequate paraphernalia to clarify and recreate their new information.

Transportation Toys

Living in an age of rapid transportation and advanced space exploration, it is inevitable that much play activity will center around space capsules, jet airplanes, cars, buses, boats, trains, etc. Jumbo wooden transportation toys encourage active group play; small toys permit individual play. Children benefit from having a balanced selection of both. For this type of play you might consider Skaneateles wooden trains, tracks, and blocks set (including a semaphore, crossing gate, switches); wooden boat sets (tug and barge, ferry boat, freighter); transportation vehicles (dump truck, auto and horse trailer, fire-ladder trailer, truck, ambulance, bus, airplane); and, of course, unit building blocks (play people, assorted animals, and small vehicles).

Not all play is carried on with others. At times, a child expresses a desire for privacy. Playing alone, she can explore more intensively as she accumulates experience and knowledge. She also withdraws from the group for a time to organize her discoveries.

For use with miniature toys (of wood, metal, or rubber—try to maintain a scale), oil cloth play environments and miniature block or box environments are enjoyable.

Manipulative Toys

Manipulative toys and quiet activities are not "busy work." They have educational and self-entertainment values. They help children develop eye-hand coordination, sharpen their observations of likenesses and differences, and help them see relationships of parts to the whole. Here is a list of favorites:

pounding bench
jumbo beads & laces for stringing
lock box or lock board
shape-sorting box
parquetry blocks
gear toys
snap blocks
stacking toys
nesting toys (bowls, barrels, eggs)
pegboard and large pegs
embossed cubes
jigsaw puzzles (wooden or rubber)
formboard
sewing cards
adult tools (not make-believe), to be used under supervision: hammer, nails, soft lumber, hand saw, etc.
construction toys: Tinkertoys, Nuts & Bolts, Lincoln Logs, Lego and Brio blocks

Materials and Equipment for Arts and Crafts Activities

long-handled, flat bristle brushes: 1", ¾", ½", ¼"
liquid poster paints: red, yellow, blue, black, brown, white, violet (8-oz. or 16-oz. jars)
powder paints (sold by the pound; mix it yourself)
folding aluminum rack for drying children's paintings
newsprint paper, 18" × 24" (in reams)
moist clay (10- or 25-lb. can)
Play-Doh

bulk finger paint: 8-oz. or 16-oz. jars
finger paint paper: 16″ × 22″ (100 sheets)
aprons and smocks (to protect clothing)
large crayons, felt-tip pens (in assorted colors)
manila drawing paper: 9″ × 12″ (50 sheets)
glue, paste, paste brush
construction paper: 9″ × 12″ (50 sheets)
gummed paper: 10″ × 12½″ (50 sheets)
4½″ blunt-tipped scissors (left-handed ones for left-handed children)
assorted die-cut glossy colored paper shapes

Working with Wood

If you live in a large house, adults as well as young children welcome a good work bench with screw clamps and storage for tools. Make sure that the top is heavy enough (at least 22″ × 42″ × 1¾″ thick) to withstand hammering. A butcher block top is ideal. Make sure the height is between 24″ and 27″ to serve the growing child from kindergarten through high school. Get one with two vises if you plan to have two or more children. You may have to put up a pegboard storage unit to hold tools. Pegboard hardware is sold in every hardware shop and holds any tool. Lumber can be scraps from a lumberyard.

At first a child likes just to hammer nails into soft wood. Later boys and girls learn how to cut, sand, and construct crude boats, trains, doll houses, etc. Buy adult tools—do not waste money on "toy" tools. (Of course, adult supervision is essential until the child is skillful enough.)

For Quiet Play

Assorted picture lotto games, large wooden dominoes, and assorted jigsaw puzzles are favorites.

For Nature & Science Play

Your child will spend time enjoyably with a giant magnifier, giant magnet, ant farm, terrarium, kaleidoscope, binoculars, aquarium, rock collection, nature bowl (sea shells, acorns, stones, etc.), tinted plastic eyeglasses or plastic sheets, microscope, butterfly net, rabbit or hamster cage, etc.

For Music-Making and Dancing

Nursery school children rejoice in making music with their agemates and respond with enthusiasm to rhythmic activities. Favorite rhythm instruments are a hand drum, maracas, musi-

cal triangle with striker, tambourine, wrist bells, xylophone, tone block with striker, autoharp, etc.

Phonograph Records for Young Children

Since young children love to listen to stories, sing songs, and move to music, favorite recordings remain a satisfying alternative to television. One difficulty with locating good children's records is that most record or toy shops do not carry adequate or well-chosen stocks (the same applies even more to discount stores).

The following are some criteria to observe when purchasing records for children:

- There must be artistry and good taste because no child has time for mediocrity.
- The music should be simple—not cluttered with too-elaborate orchestration or big choruses.
- There should be a "catchy" tune or rhythm that has instant appeal.
- Story recordings should never talk down to children.
- Growth in musical appreciation comes from early listening to classical forms of music; avoid the "excerpt" type, and use instead selected adult recordings that are complete.

It is actually not possible to separate records for children according to specific age slots because of the broad range in musical backgrounds and interests of children. Hence, the listings that follow are suggested selections only. Please bear in mind, too, that all fine recordings will not necessarily appeal to all children.

Classical Music

Carnival of the Animals (Saint-Saëns)
Children's Corner Suite (Debussy)
Clair de Lune (Debussy)
Eine kleine Nachtmusik (Mozart)
Firebird (Stravinsky)
Golliwog's Cake Walk (Debussy)
Die Moldau (Smetana)
Peer Gynt Suite (Grieg)

Peter and the Wolf (Prokofiev)
Moonlight Sonata (Beethoven)
The Flight of the Bumble Bee (Rimsky-Korsakov)
The Nutcracker Suite (Tchaikovsky)

Folk Music

The United States is rich in folk music because such people as Moses Asch (founder of Folkway Records), Pete Seeger, Burl Ives, Woody Guthrie, and many others have spent their lives recording and promoting it. Folk singers are especially popular with all children because their voices are natural and clear in their renditions of work, play, and humorous subjects.

Selected folk song recordings include:

The Baby-Sitters: Folk Songs for Babies, Small Children, Parents and Baby-Sitters (Vanguard)

Joan Baez: *Farewell Angelina* (Vanguard)

Charity Bailey: *Music Time* (Folkways)

Woody Guthrie: *Songs to Grow On: Nursery Days* (Folkways), and *Songs to Grow On: School Days* (Folkways)

Sam Hinton: *Whoever Shall Have Some Good Peanuts?* (Scholastic)

Burl Ives: *Burl Ives Sings* (MCA), *The Best of Burl's for Boys and Girls* (MCA)

Jean Ritchie: *Marching Across the Green Grass, etc.* (Folkways), *Southern Mountain Children's Songs and Games* (Folkways)

Peggy Seeger: *Animal Folk Songs for Children* (Scholastic)

Pete Seeger: *This Land Is My Land* (Folkways), *American Folk Songs for Children* (Folkways), *Birds, Beasts, Bugs and Little Fishes* (Folkways), *Abiyoyo and Other Story Songs for Children* (Folkways)

The Weavers: *The Weavers at Carnegie Hall* (Vanguard), *The Weavers on Tour* (Vanguard), *The Weavers' Greatest Hits* (Vanguard)

Recordings for Rhythms, Body Movement, and Dance

Ella Jenkins: *Counting Games and Rhythms for the Little Ones* (Scholastic), *Rhythms of Childhood* (Scholastic), *Songs and Rhythms from Near and Far* (Scholastic)

Children's Singing Records

Charity Bailey: *More Music Time and Stories* (Folkways)
Tom Glazer: *Music for Ones and Twos* (CMS Records)
Poems and Songs for Younger Children (Spoken Arts)

Storytelling Records

Hans Christian Andersen's *The Ugly Duckling and Other Tales* (Caedmon)
Carol Channing: *Madeline and Other Bemelmans* (Caedmon)
Nonsense Verse of Carroll and Lear (Caedmon)
Carlo Collodi's *Pinocchio* (Caedmon)
Puss in Boots and Other Fairy Tales from Around the World (Caedmon)
Claire Bloom: *The Tale of Peter Rabbit, etc.* (Caedmon)
Paul Tripp: *Tubby the Tuba, Adventures of a Zoo, The Story of Celeste* (Wonderland)

You may wish to write to the record-producing companies below for their catalogues in order to see the range of subjects each one covers:

Caedmon Records, 1995 Broadway, New York, NY 10007
Capitol Records, 1370 Avenue of the Americas, New York, NY 10019
CMS Records, 12 Warren Street, New York, NY 10007
Enrichment Materials, 50 W. 44 Street, New York, NY 10018
Fantasy Records, 733 Ninth Avenue, New York, NY 10019
Folkways Records, 43 W. 61 Street, New York, NY 10023
MCA, 10 East 53 Street, New York, NY 10022
Pathways of Sound, 102 Mt. Auburn Street, Cambridge, MA 02138
Pickwick Music Corp., 445 Park Avenue, New York, NY 10022
R & J Records, 108 Sherman Avenue, New York, NY 10034

Scholastic Records, 906 Sylvan Avenue, Englewood Cliffs, NJ 07632
Spoken Arts, 310 North Avenue, New Rochelle, NY 10801
Vanguard Recording Society, 71 W. 23 Street, New York, NY 10010
Warner Brothers Reprise Records, 3 East 54 Street, New York, NY 10022
Weston Woods, Weston, CT 06883
Wonderland Music Co., 477 Madison Avenue, New York, NY 10022

Outdoor Equipment and Props

5′ wood or steel climbing ladder
play boards (¾″ × 5½″ × 44″)
hollow boxes (2 sizes: 5½″ × 11″ × 11″ or 5½″ × 11″ × 22″)
wooden barrel
pails, pulley, rope
walking teeter-totter board (10′ long × 7″ wide × ¾″ thick)
fabric tunnel (for crawling and obstacle races)
pail, shovel, sand sifter, wooden spoon, etc., for sand play; sand machine
gardening tools (child-size)
rope ladder
climbing rope
utility balls (6″, 8½″, 10″)
cable spool (utility companies give them away)
28″-diameter wooden hoop
fire bell
rubber tires for swing, climbing wall (try neighborhood gas station)
3-way wooden ladder (4′ high × 8′ long × 20″ wide)
rope cargo net
used packing box or crate
log cabin playhouse
fireman's gym and platform (slide attached to climber)
wooden saw horses (12″ and 18″)
wooden or steel sandbox or sand table (27″ × 72″ × 5½″ deep)
water play basin or enameled tray; watering can, 3″ painter's brush, paint bucket
metal or wooden wagon
double-wheel wheelbarrow

ride 'em tractor, trailer, train
rocking boat
tricycle

HEALTH, SELF-HELP, AND ROUTINES

Most pediatricians will test vision and hearing as soon as a child is old enough to understand and cooperate. Also available are child health clinics and organizations that can give such tests at reasonable cost. Parents should see to it that their thirty-seven-month-old (and older) children undergo periodic seeing and hearing evaluations. Should there be any irregularities in the functioning of a child's eyes or ears, get prompt medical attention.

Dressing and Undressing

Thirty-seven- through forty-two-month-old children will help with dressing as well as undressing themselves. Sometime between three and four years, they usually learn to unbutton buttons. Inasmuch as little girls develop somewhat more rapidly than little boys, some thirty-seven-month-old girls are able to dress themselves with very little assistance. Boys this age still have trouble with shoelaces, back buttons, zippers, and some snappers. However, they can pull their trousers and underpants up and down.

If they have hooks within easy reach, children this age can hang up their own coats and caps after being outdoors. To encourage your thirty-seven-month-old's growing sense of orderliness, it would be a good idea for you to install low hooks in his closet on which he can hang his clothes. You might also lower the hanger rod in his closet so that he will be able to reach the hangers by himself.

Washing Up

In order to make your child's self-help efforts more appealing and easier for her, place a sturdy stepstool below the bathroom sink so that she can reach the faucet and get the soap. Thirty-seven-month-olds can wash their hands, but require some supervision for drying them. They can put their towels back on their own racks or hooks.

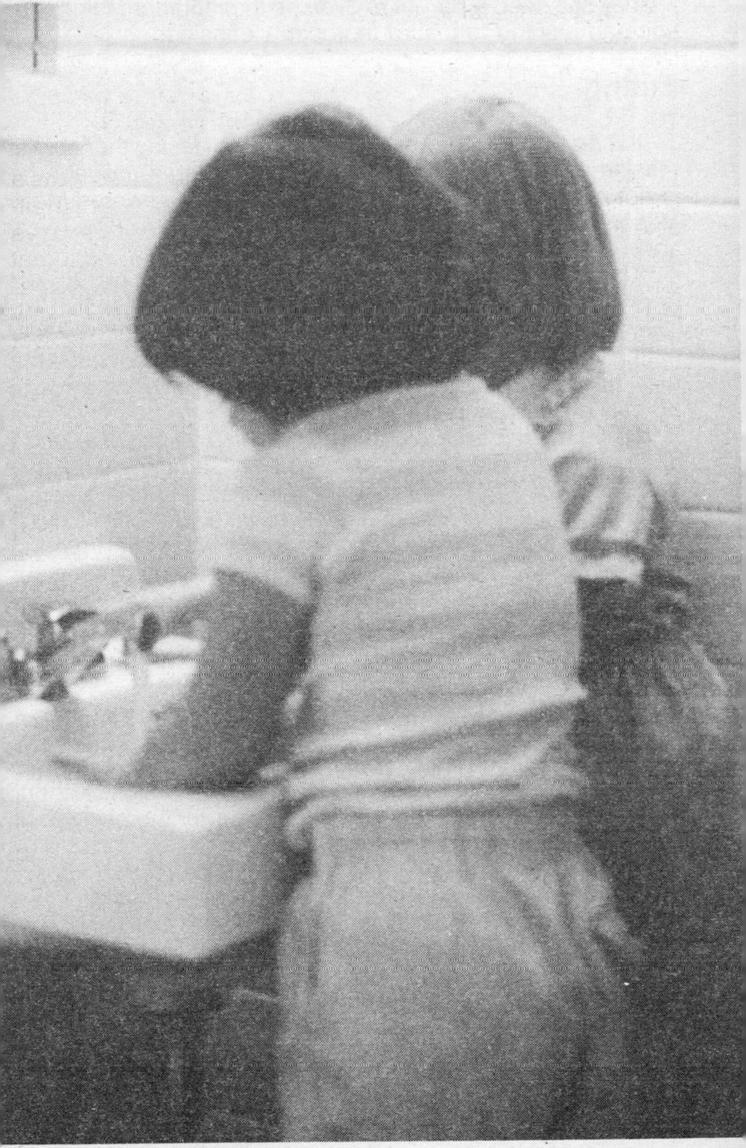

They still need a parent to oversee their toothbrushing routine and bathing to insure thorough cleansings.

Eating

"It is reasonable to expect your child to sit facing the table at mealtime. If he keeps turning away from the table, probably he is not hungry, and it is best to end the meal," writes Molly Mason Jones in *Guiding Your Child from Two to Five* (New York: Harcourt, Brace & World, 1976).

"After you have put your child's plate in front of him do not urge him to eat. When eating time is almost over, tell him so. Twenty-five or thirty minutes is likely to be long enough for any meal in a setup just for children . . . Never give your child the idea that you are either pleased or displeased by the amount he eats or leaves on his plate."

Thirty-seven-month-olds are efficient in their use of a spoon or fork and can eat without spilling. They can drink smoothly from a cup or small glass and can pour well from a pitcher.

As a special treat you might like to take your child to visit a friend for lunch, or go to a restaurant where very young children are welcome. This will be high adventure for your thirty-seven-month-old, and will foster her awareness of table manners and the social as well as gustatory pleasures inherent in eating.

Daily Routines

Most thirty-seven-month-olds have bowel and bladder control during the daytime and sleep through the night without wetting the bed. They can go to the toilet by themselves (if helped beforehand with buttons).

Nursery school-age children will take a nap of an hour or so.

Bedtime should be a cheerful, peaceful time. Parents need to be clear as to *when* they think it should be. It appears that dreams, nightmares, and night wanderings are common in both boys and girls at this age level.

Growth Chart—37th Through 42nd Month

MOTOR DEVELOPMENT

Gross Motor

Most can stand on one foot, with momentary balance; also on toes.

Can climb up an inclined board.

Like to climb on a jungle gym.

Can walk a straight line or curbstone; walk backwards.

Run, jump, and climb with finer coordination.

Swing arms freely while walking or running.

Walk well, without close visual inspection of moving feet.

Get up from a squatting position without help.

Can catch a large ball with their arms extended forward; throw without losing balance.

Can kick a ball.

Use pedals riding a tricycle; can steer to avoid obstacles.

Enjoy sliding down a not-too-steep slide.

Gallop, jump, walk, run to music with abandon.

Alternate feet when going upstairs; not necessarily when going down (2 feet per step).

Jump from a bottom stair to floor.

Shoulders held more erect.

Protruding abdomen much reduced.

Fine Motor

Increasing control of fingers.

Adept at picking up small objects.

Can handle scissors to a degree.

Can copy a circle from a drawing of a circle; reproduce a cross if shown how.

Control of a pencil improving.

Can place round, square, triangular blocks in formboard.

Can build a tower of 9 small blocks.

LANGUAGE ACQUISITION

Enjoy new and unfamiliar words.

Average vocabulary 900 words.

Can repeat three numerical digits.

Most are good talkers.

Use language to get what they want.

Most starting to ask "how," "what," "why," "when" questions.

Respond to simple directions; i.e., to put a ball on or under a chair.

Name pictures of familiar things in picture books; can tell what the people or things are doing.

Interested in animal stories, alphabet books, here-and-now stories.

Love to play with words (as in silly rhyming). Know a few rhymes.

Remember words of many songs.

Final consonants appear more regularly.

Voice is generally well controlled.

By 42 months, verbal responses are comprehensible.

Use plurals in speech; use personal pronouns "I," "me," "mine."

Still use their own rather than accepted adult grammar.

Growth Chart—37th Through 42nd Month

SENSORY POWERS/LEARNING

Sort objects by color and size.

Eyes coordinate well.

Show facility in moving their eyes.

Can follow a moving target without losing attention.

Can talk about what they see in books.

Can differentiate a boy from a girl.

First interest in TV viewing (commercials, cartoons, "Sesame Street").

Growing understanding of time intervals: *yesterday, today* and *tomorrow.*

Count by rote up to 10 but no awareness of quantity beyond 2 or 3.

SOCIAL DEVELOPMENT

Value mother most of all; love to do things with her.

More orderly.

Some begin to share their toys.

Average are friendly and agreeable.

Will cooperate in putting toys away.

Can deal with and benefit from a playgroup or nursery school.

Enjoy being with peers; mutual responsiveness; beginning to learn to take turns.

PERSONALITY/ PSYCHOLOGICAL

Interest in different postures for urinating of boys and girls; girls try to urinate standing up.

Interest in babies; may want family to have one.

Subject to fits of anger or jealousy.

May have bad dreams but are easily quieted.

Growth Chart—37th Through 42nd Month

PLAY AND PLAYTHINGS	HEALTH, SELF-HELP, AND ROUTINES
Sustained attention up to 20 minutes.	More susceptible to the common cold; other communicable diseases.
Enjoy block play; may combine blocks with toys to create roadways, garages, etc.	Appetite fairly good.
Fascination with sand and water play continues.	Self-feeding with little spilling.
Like blowing soap bubbles; "painting" with water; washing clothes; sailing boats, etc.	Using both hands, can pour water, juice, or milk from a pitcher into a glass or cup with little spilling.
String large wooden beads on a tipped lace.	Most fairly skillful in handling feeding utensils.
Like to do jigsaw puzzles.	Cup now hold by handle in adult fashion.
Doll play, hospital play, community play more imaginative.	Wash hands; require supervision for drying.
Easel painting, finger painting, crayoning enjoyed.	Better at undressing than dressing.
Match 2 or 3 primary colors; confuse blue with green.	Can put on own shoes, slacks, underpants or take them off.
Enjoy manipulating clay or Play-Doh.	Need help with hard to reach buttons, zippers, and tying sashes or shoelaces.
Noticeable musical advance in use of voice.	Many sleep through the night.
	Generally, afternoon nap is a quiet play time or rest period.
	Control bowels and bladder during daytime.

Dear Parents:

Do not regard this chart as a rigid timetable.

Young children are unpredictable individuals. Some perform an activity earlier or later than this chart indicates.

Just use this information to anticipate and appreciate normal child development and behavior. No norms are absolute.

CHAPTER SIX

The 43rd Through 48th Month of Life

I keep six honest serving-men
  (They taught me all I knew);
Their names are What and
    Why and When
  And How and Where and
    Who.
I send them over land and
    sea,
  I send them east and west;
But after they have worked
    for me,
  I give them all a rest.

I let them rest from nine
    till five,
  For I am busy then,
As well as breakfast, lunch
    and tea,

For they are hungry men.
But different folk have different
  views.
  I know a person small—
She keeps ten million serving-
    men,
  Who get no rest at all!

She sends 'em abroad on her
    own affairs,
  From the second she
    opens her eyes—
One million Hows, two million
    Wheres,
  And seven million Whys!
    Rudyard Kipling,
    The Elephant's Child

There are differences even within a specific period of maturation, but knowledge of the general ways of typical growth can
facilitate parental understanding and management of their
very young children.

Modes of behavior become increasingly complicated as
children mature. Although each child moves forward in conformity with well-nigh universal sequential ages and stages of
development, it is always according to his or her own timetable
and style; *timetables of maturation are not rigidly fixed.* All
children, normal or atypical, are faced with pressures and
problems in the course of growing up.

Forty-three-month-old boys and girls can behave unpredict-
ably and be rather withdrawn. They appear cherubic some of
the time, but can spoil the appealing picture with sudden outbursts. The whining of forty-three-month-olds can be un-
believably annoying. They can be bossy, insist on immediate
attention, and feel terribly unsure and unloved.

Although the parents may not cause the negative responses in their uncertain children in most instances, they
need to stand by them with understanding and patience. Ambivalence appears to be part of normal behavior for forty-
three- through forty-eight-month-old girls and boys.

Three is a conforming age; three-and-a-half is just the opposite. He expresses strong resistance to adult requirements.
Although he believes that adults are all-powerful, he is not
afraid to challenge that power. This child will make up fantastic
tall tales when so motivated because he has very little concept
of truth or untruth. Unreality and fantasy are part and parcel of
his behavior. Since much of his boasting and storytelling is to
impress and please you, try not to make big issues of his
fantasizing and fibs.

Refusing to obey appears to mothers to be the chief difficulty of forty-three- through forty-eight-month-old children.
They are strong-willed, and are forever testing their willpower
by opposing their mothers or fathers. Even the simplest chore
can bring on total rebellion. Dressing, eating, going to the
toilet, going to bed—each can precipitate violent disagreement.

If one were to describe the forty-three-month-old in a few
words, it would be that she is anxious, unsure, and self-willed.

Her feelings of insecurity can be seen in physical ways—stuttering, stumbling, even trembling on occasion. Prevalent, too, among children this age are thumb-sucking, nose picking, nail biting, chewing on their own clothing, etc. They may appear excessively shy at one time and unbearably aggressive the next.

GROSS-MOTOR DEVELOPMENT

The forty-three-month-old often gives the impression of being physically uncertain, and even helpless. His feelings of insecurity may prompt him to seek the hand of an adult even though a railing may be there to support him. However, despite his sense of inadequacy, he can jump high and far. He navigates stairs one foot on a step at a time, and can balance well on a walking board. He is able to hop on one foot as well as hop in place on both feet. He can touch his toes without bending his knees.

Both girls and boys begin to explore a variety of catch-and-throw ball games. They love to run on their toes, and can walk smoothly on a straight line. On their "good" days, they enjoy climbing on a jungle gym, sliding down a slide, riding a seesaw with a peer, and going up in the air on a swing. At other times, they may be so tense as to stumble or fall.

By forty-three months of age, most children can hop from one to three steps on their preferred foot. By forty-eight months, most can hop from four to six steps on one foot.

Most boys and girls this age can walk a distance of ten feet on a straight one-inch-wide line. However, it is not until nearly four years of age that children can walk a circular line. Forty-three-month-olds can walk on a balance beam for a short distance. They can throw a ball about ten feet.

FINE-MOTOR DEVELOPMENT

Boys and girls this age may show a mild tremor in their fine-motor coordination due to their uncertainty. Parents should not pay any attention to this transient condition. Older siblings must not be permitted to make fun of their younger brothers and sisters.

During this period, both boys and girls may use their preferred handedness while drawing, stringing beads, and so on.

Scribbling and Drawing

By the time a child reaches his forty-third month, he may play with squares in his drawings; he may also "square-off" circles. Another child may try to make squares by following the sides of his paper with straight lines.

Many forty-eight-month-olds are able to recognize, name, and draw a single square.

LANGUAGE ACQUISITION

Talking vocabulary grows from an average of 900 words at three to 1,500 at four years of age. A forty-three-month-old can ask as many as 400 questions a day. Some mothers we know asked, "Is that all? We think it is more nearly 1,000 questions a day!"

Obviously he is eager to practice his extraordinary talking ability. Do not ignore his questions; instead, try to answer all of them simply even when he asks questions to which he already knows the answers. This appears to be one of his ways to start and continue a conversation.

Due to the ongoing improvement in your forty-three-through forty-eight-month-old's vocabulary and memory skills, you will have less trouble understanding her, and she also should understand you better. Now she can promptly place an object *on, under,* or *in back of* a sofa. She uses a great variety of expressions spontaneously that designate the *past, present,* and *future,* as well as many complicated expressions relating to time ("for a long time," "for years," "a whole week," "in the meantime"). However, she may refer to a future happening as if in the past: "I'm not going to take a nap yesterday." Before too long, such confusion will be self-corrected. Children this age can be put off "until later" or "when it's time," another mark of improved understanding and increased patience.

The forty-three- through forty-eight-month-old is starting to realize that words represent feelings and ideas as well as things—for example, when using such words as *good, tired, cold, hot, warm.* Your child will now understand the difference between many words that sound alike: the plane *flies;* the *flies* buzz around the pail.

Forty-three- through forty-eight-month-olds have learned to use *I* instead of *me* at the beginning of a sentence. They continue, however, to exercise their own rules of grammar by saying *rided* instead of *rode, hided* instead of *hid;* calling all men *mans,* etc. Most still have trouble pronouncing the letters *b* and *f, th* and *k;* for instance, they will say *baf* instead of *bath.*

Language development is the high point of forty-three-month-old children. This is especially true of some late-talking boys whose language acquisition at two years appeared backward, but which now suddenly bursts into bloom. At the same time, parents should be aware that the speech of some forty-three- through forty-eight-month-old children can lapse temporarily into stuttering and stammering. Educators and linguists tend to label the stuttering at this age as mere "preschool nonfluency." Their advice to parents is that unless it goes on for several months, they should regard it as a passing phase of normal awkward speech production.

Each child's maturation timetable is wholly individual. Some are ahead and some behind the so-called average. This age is an ideal time for language acquisition because children naturally combine their play and language. They make up words, love silly rhymes, and begin to use such auxiliary verbs as "would," "could," "be," "have," and "can." They use negatives effectively. Sentences grow longer; formal grammar is gradually being mastered.

Because their attention span is growing, children this age can listen to stories for as long as twenty minutes. They thoroughly enjoy being read to, and will request their favorite stories. They want to look at the pictures in each book while being read to.

By forty-eight months of age, most children recognize important capital letters; for example, "D" as in "Daddy," "M" as in "Mommy," "L" as in "Larry" or "Lois," etc. Many are also able to identify some capital letters in alphabet books, on alphabet blocks, and on familiar street signs.

Parents can use words when trying to control their forty-two- to forty-eight-month-olds. They will listen when reasoned with. In fact, most children this age will respond positively to reason. They may even do something they dislike if given a good reason. ("Brushing your teeth should keep you from having cavities.") Most children this age are able to give their full name, the street on which they live, as well as the city or town, when asked to do so.

When a Child Uses "Bad" Language*

All children pick up words and phrases that offend adults. Unflattering names seem to be the order of the day: "dope," "rat," "stinker," "stupid," etc. In addition to having to put up with rather mild derogatory adjectives ("dirty," "silly," "sloppy," etc.), parents may suddenly be affronted by the appearance of taboo four-letter words. Toilet talk is also par for the course as well as such aggressive taunts as "I'll shoot you," "I'll cut you up and eat you up," and so on. Any child from any background will on occasion use these objectionable words, even when he does not understand their meaning.

When young children cannot get something they want very much, they usually become angry. They may let off steam in physical actions or in nasty words. Many parents regard the ugly words of their children as personal attacks. They are embarrassed because they fear that others will think their children's language reflects what they hear at home.

What should a parent do? First of all, do not worry! The use of "gutter" language is another passing phase most children go through without any damage. Unruffled parents will ride out this particular storm just as they are able to handle the other less-than-admirable behaviors of their growing children.

Never scold or punish your child for saying "bad" words. Instead you might show her how to make up new words, or offer her funny word substitutes. Sometimes a simple substitute like "darn" will do. Of course, no one approach will always work. You will have to use your own judgment.

When your child uses language that offends you, he may merely be teasing you. If you do not overreact, he will soon get the message that there is no fun in this for him.

A Language Acquisition Checklist

The following questions for parents of forty-eight-month-old children to consider were formulated by members of the Developmental Language and Speech Center in Grand Rapids, Michigan:

1) Does your child use three words in an average sentence?

*Adapted from *Some Special Problems of Children Aged Two to Five Years* by Nina Ridenour and Isabel Johnson (New York: Child Study Association of America, 1969).

2) Is your child beginning to understand simple number concepts; i.e., *one* and *many*? Does he understand "Get me one block" or "Get me lots of blocks"?
3) Does your child listen to longer stories?
4) Can your child identify seven pictures by hearing their names when you say "Find the _____" (such items as a dog, cup, shoe, house, flag, clock, star, leaf, basket, book)?
5) Can your child organize her thoughts and words to tell a simple story, share her ideas, or express her feelings?
6) Does your child refer to himself by the word *I*?
7) Is your child understandable to people outside of the family even though her speech is not perfect?
8) Has your child's memory improved? Can he remember what happened yesterday (even though he may not completely understand such words as *yesterday* and *tomorrow*)?
9) Can your child count to three?
10) Does your child learn from what she hears?
11) Can your child tell you his first and last names?
12) Does your child know how old she is, and the name of the street where she lives?

SENSORY POWERS/LEARNING

This period is highlighted by increased cognitive growth. Learning in all areas is moving forward swiftly. The forty-three-month-old is beginning to discover how things are related to each other. He is trying to control the world he lives in by "ordering his universe."

She can build with blocks, model with clay, create wholes out of parts, and group things together. She is able to play simple matching lotto games (a broom belongs in the kitchen, a pig belongs on a farm, a jet plane belongs in a hangar, etc.). Her thinking is becoming more sophisticated, and her imagination prompts her to fantasize and make up stories.

Children this age seek answers to endless questions about bodily functions, sexuality, and how the genitals and the bowels function. Parents are called upon to provide uncomplicated answers couched in clear language; the simpler the information supplied, the better. This is no time for embarrassment or for self-conscious evasion.

Forty-three- through forty-eight-month-olds have good perceptual ability; their eyes coordinate well. They are able to follow a moving target without losing their concentration. Most forty-eight-month-old boys and girls become aware that there are two sides of the body, although they cannot label the left or the right side. However, they can identify the thumbs, index, and little fingers of their hands. Now they have greater awareness of more body parts, including their knees, elbows, and sometimes their shoulders. Many can point to parts of the face, including the eyes, eyebrows, nose, mouth, and ears.

Forty-three-month-old girls and boys can count up to ten (and even beyond) by rote, but they have no notion of actual quantity beyond two or three. They may or may not start with one when counting. However, they can proffer "just one" or two objects upon request. Most can properly count two or three things.

Trips as an Educational Tool

One way to extend the horizons of three-and-a-half- to four-year-olds is through simple excursions. These should be strong in sensory experiences, and what the child sees must concern something that he can reproduce in his own way at a later time. In planning trips remember too that young children relate with enthusiasm to people or things in action.

To young children everything is new, nothing is commonplace; for example, the casting of shadows by the sun, how rain falls and sounds, and so on. Sensations that are accepted casually by older children and adults are fresh and exciting to children this age.

Below are some trips that boys and girls of three and four will enjoy:

- The kitchen of a restaurant to see how food is prepared.
- A bakery to see the ovens, the preparation of baking mixtures, and finished baked goods.
- A supermarket to see the many assorted items that are displayed and sold.
- A new building going up.
- The local shoemaker, laundry, barber shop, pet shop, bank, post office, pizza parlor, etc.

Some Games and Activities to Increase Sensory Awareness*

Is your child a "looker," a "toucher," a "hearer," a "sniffer," or a "taster"? Is he responsive to all kinds of sensory experiences? Once you determine your child's sensory behavior patterns, you can enhance and extend his awareness. Below you will find several suitable sensory games and activities for your child and you to enjoy together.

Body Movement Activities

- Make a list of whatever moves in the house, in the park, on a city street, at a farm, at a doctor's office, etc.
- Walk like a robot; crawl like a baby; gallop like a pony; jump like a kangaroo.
- Move like an old man, a dancer, a lion, an elephant, etc.
- Swim like a fish; fly like a seagull; conduct an orchestra.

Touch Games

- Touch parts of your body; touch items of clothing (zipper, button, sock, etc.).
- Show and tell what you can do with your hands (bounce a ball, hammer a nail, etc.).
- Make a "texture box." Collect two each of textured items (sandpaper, square of terry cloth, felt, lump of sugar, sample of wool carpet, piece of vinyl) and insert all of them in the handhole you cut into a small, closed corrugated box. Select one texture; name it, then match it with the second unit. Remove both items from the box.

Visual Awareness Games

- Ask the child: "Look around. What do you see?" Have her pick out specific *shapes* (circles, squares, triangles); *colors*

---

*For complete descriptions and lists of necessary props as well as instructions for many learning games and activities, we recommend *Partners in Play* by Dorothy G. Singer & Jerome L. Singer (New York: Harper & Row, 1977) and *Your Child's Sensory World* by Lise Liepmann (New York: Dial Press, 1979).

("Which do you like best?"); *light and dark areas; stationary and moving objects.*

- Conduct a visual memory game: Have your child describe with as much detail as possible a place she especially likes.

Hearing Games

- Identify indoor sounds (clock, eggbeater, doorbell, running water); outdoor sounds (cricket, frog, airplane); harbor sounds (foghorn, water lapping, seagulls calling); animal sounds (roar of lion, meow of cat, quack of duck).
- Rhythm play: Listen to and practice the rhythms of a washing machine, typewriter, popular song, etc.

Vocalizing and Speech Play

- *Learn, recite, and act out in pantomime the rhymes and actions of poems and stories ("Little Jack Horner," "Little Boy Blue," Caps for Sale, The Story About Ping, etc.).*
- Recite opposites: If I am not small, I am _____ (big); If I am not hot, I am _____ (cold); If I am not happy, I am _____ (sad).

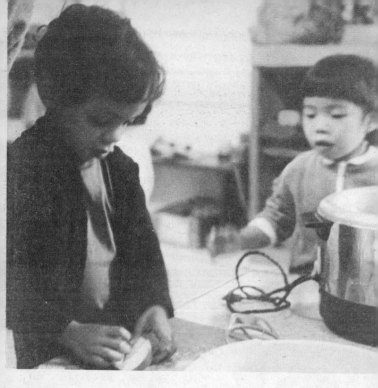

Increasing Awareness of the Senses of Taste and Smell

- Identify by taste, with eyes closed, various foods: potato chip, salted nut, diced apple, grape, peach, banana, etc.
- Identify foods that are sweet, salty, sour, and bitter.
- Identify differences between a nectarine and a peach, sweet and bittersweet chocolate, etc.

Sorting, Classifying, Naming

One of the ways adults process information and store it in their minds for future use is by first sorting it out and distinguishing it from other things they have seen. For example, if we notice a dog, we recognize it first by its shape, its four legs, and a tail. After establishing the *category* of animal, we identify and "sort it out" by its different features—floppy ears, silky hair, short legs. Then we classify and code it, and label it as a specific breed of dog—a "spaniel."

A very young child lacks sufficient knowledge and language to classify and name an object by its features and code name. For example, all cars are cars. But some are called "Fords," and only one car is "Daddy's car." How is the child to know whether a word is a name or a way of referring to a sort of thing?

One of the important mental skills that a child perfects by forty-eight months of age is sorting objects by their appearance, feel, and use. She learns to recognize and discriminate things that are alike from those that are not alike. When she begins to use language to label these processes or code them by name, she has acquired not only a way of saying something, but a powerful instrument for organizing her thoughts about things.

Initiating sorting games during the quiet times of the day is a way of practicing the sorting and classification of objects while providing entertainment. (They should not be set up as "academic lessons.")

To sort objects by how they look, start with two different objects—color-cube blocks, buttons, corks or bottle caps, spools, balls, forks and spoons, etc. When two different objects have been sorted, go on to three; then four and five. Vary this by cutting out different pictures from magazines. Sort pictures of trucks from pictures of passenger cars; farm objects from city objects; birds from fish.

Next, try sorting by color: red blocks from blue blocks, green buttons from white buttons, etc. Do not expect your child to name the colors correctly right away. You can introduce the activity by saying, "Look, here is a red block. Can you find another one like it?" Repeat, using other colors.

Then encourage your child to sort by size: "Let's put all the little ones here and big ones there."

You can enhance the activity on another day by introducing your child to sorting by shape: help her distinguish blocks from balls, circles from squares, and so on.

Forty-three- through forty-eight-month-old girls and boys like to have coins to put in their banks. They appear to know that money is used to make purchases at the supermarket, shoe store, toy shop, etc. Of course, they have no real idea of how much things cost.

SOCIAL DEVELOPMENT

A child learns to relate to life and people when she is not isolated from the world and its goings-on. Her first attempts at wider socialization come when the family includes others in its activities. People of varying ages, temperaments, occupations, and relationships stimulate a child's feelings, her curiosity, and her thinking. Parents and teachers who are alert to the need for building social relationships between different age groups take steps to initiate amiable social ties. One nursery school director insisted on fostering close relations between the different grade levels in the school community. The twelve-year-olds, for instance, made toys for the three-year-olds, and the eleven-year-olds read to the four-year-olds stories that they themselves had written and printed.

Because the growth of vocabulary enables three-and-a-half- to four-year-old children to recruit their peers for their playgroups, they also now have verbal means for excluding children not wanted. This can make life miserable for the shy child, and might call for sensitive adult intervention. During this time span there may be a temporary and shifting attachment to some one playmate, often of the opposite sex. Generally girls are the initiators of such attachments.

Leadership in the group life of children from three to six years of age is given to the child who has ideas, skills, and resources that facilitate play.

Young Friends Can Battle

The more social contacts a young child has with her peers, the greater the likelihood of quarreling. Friends appear to be more prone to arguing than children who do not play together on a regular basis. Most disputes at this age start over possessions. Older children appear to have fewer disagreements than younger ones. However, when older children quarrel, the conflicts last longer and involve more aggressive behavior and talking. Parents take note—children settle most quarrels by themselves! They almost always recover quickly and show little or no resentment.

Fathering

Fathers have become more deeply involved with their young children, to the benefit of the entire family. With more and more mothers working outside of the home, both parents are now juggling their jobs and parenting responsibilities more equitably.

Certainly mothers and fathers are different individuals, and having more than fleeting exposure to each of them is especially enriching and satisfying to children. Boys and girls need mothers *and* fathers as role models and to set standards for their children's comfortable functioning in a very complex world.

Most fathers appreciate their small children more after they are in good control of their bodily functions and have sufficient language for meaningful interchanges of feelings and ideas. That is not to say that nowadays most fathers avoid sharing in the feeding, bathing, and other tasks that are part of nurturing young children. On the contrary, these past years have seen fathers take time off from work in order to be actively involved in child care and in helping with ever-present household chores. Indeed, fathers can be—and are—as competent and sensitive caregivers as mothers.

As toddler boys and girls enter the phase of separating from their mothers in their striving for autonomy, they turn naturally to their fathers. They come to see their fathers as important beings, who also are the source of active physical fun, interesting storytelling, adventuring in the community, and so on.

By the time children reach their third birthdays, they note the differences in the way men and women behave. Fathers become the pattern for male behavior while mothers show the children what females are like. This awareness of sex differences is highlighted by the little boy's wish to marry his mother and the little girl's desire to wed her father, after they have grown up. Little girls practice their femininity on their dads; little boys fall in love with their moms.

Current Views on Fatherhood

In an article in the New Jersey Section of the June 27, 1982, edition of *The New York Times,* Sandra Friedland presented the latest figures of the U.S. Department of Labor with regard to working parents. According to these, both parents were in the work force in nearly half of the American families with children under six, as compared to one in three in 1974. There is every indication that the percentage of working couples with very small children will continue to increase.

Although more fathers want to become involved in the care of their children, our society has not made many allowances to help advance this movement. This finding is the result of a privately financed survey of how American institutions have responded to the changing roles of fathers. However, James Levine, director of the survey, found more support for men who want nurturing roles than had been anticipated. Mr. Levine believes that more positive attitudes are gradually evolving and this interim period is an exciting, albeit difficult, time for men.

Sibling Rivalry

Jealousy is inevitable between children, and the term "sibling rivalry" is used by psychologists and child specialists when they speak of it. The term *sibling* simply means a brother or sister. Whether a child is a firstborn who is replaced by a

new baby or a newborn who finds older brothers or sisters when she arrives, she will have to come to grips with feelings of jealousy.

The extent of sibling rivalry is related to the age difference between children. If your child is eighteen months of age when a new sibling is born, obviously he has to share you a great deal while he is still extremely dependent upon you. The most open forms of rivalry between children at ages three, four, and older are taking, breaking or hiding the sibling's toys, as well as tattling, teasing, and fighting.

The great amount of time you must devote to your newborn will seem less threatening to your older child if she is at least three years old. If the age difference is five years, and the older sibling has already established contacts in the outside world (especially through school or preschool), she is less keenly aware of having to share you with the new sibling. It would be a mistake, though, to think that jealousy does not exist in the older child. She, too, needs consideration and visible reminders of love from both parents, especially in the beginning of the new family constellation.

Sometimes jealousy is so subtle that it is almost overlooked, as in the classic example of the small boy who hugs his baby sister so hard that she cries. Other times the hostility is more overt, and can take the form of verbal abuse in addition to physical punishment.

Another type of child may express jealousy by withdrawing into herself. This child may mope around the house, refuse to go out to play, become very quiet and depressed, and perhaps even seem obsessed with the baby. In such a case it may be useful to consult a child psychologist so the jealousy can be brought to the surface instead of smoldering in the child.

How Parents Can Deal with Jealousy

Although some jealousy is to be expected, there are things parents can do to minimize it. Most important is to understand your child's feelings. A firstborn needs the help of his parents to realize that even though there is a baby in the house and he now has to share his parents, he is not loved less than heretofore.

Be good-natured when your firstborn demands extra attention. Try to meet her needs, even if they seem unimportant to you. For example, when you are changing the baby, your older child may insist that you rub some baby powder on her, too. Set aside some time every day to do something special with your older child. This can be as simple as playing a game together or reading a story. Do not put off her reasonable requests with a steady "In a minute," "Later," or "I'm busy with the baby." Arrange time in your busy schedule to take your firstborn places your baby is too young to visit.

Often when the older child sees the attention his rival is getting, he will slip back into baby ways, such as wetting his pants or wanting a bottle. Cheerfully fix a bottle for him; he probably will not enjoy it very much! When your older sibling feels secure enough, he will relinquish his temporary regression.

Of course, you should not tolerate overt resentment in the form of hitting, grabbing, or pulling the baby. Instead, reassure your older child that you love her very much, but will not let her hurt the baby.

Prepare your child fairly early in your pregnancy for the new arrival. It helps considerably if you handle the "introduction" properly. Include your child in what is going on and when the baby comes let him help you whenever he safely can.

Many children feel grown-up and important if they are allowed to help with the baby. Even a three-year-old can hand you powder or help put diapers away. A four-year-old can safely give the baby a bottle if he is sitting in a large comfortable chair supported with pillows. It might also be a good idea to provide your older child with a large rubber doll that will allow him or her to act out safely how he or she feels about the new baby—either by feeding the doll baby or bopping it over the head.

If your child wants to touch or hold the baby, let her. There is no quicker way to fan the flames of jealousy than to tell the other sibling: "Do not touch the baby, you might hurt him."

How to Minimize Jealousy Between Your Children

Although parents cannot eliminate jealousy, they can try to teach their firstborn ways of coping with it, encouraging her to verbalize her feelings, offering understanding, and diverting some of her energy and impulses into building-up and knocking-down play with blocks, clay, paints, etc. Pounding toys and properly directed play are especially satisfying outlets to lessen the accumulation of hostile emotions. Planning so that your firstborn has playmates of her own age also helps.

You must take your cues from your firstborn to help him overcome his negative reactions. Nevertheless, he will have to come to terms with the baby himself. As your children grow they will work out their own relationship.

PERSONALITY/PSYCHOLOGICAL DEVELOPMENT

The forty-three-month-old appears to be riddled with all sorts of fears. He is still afraid of the dark and has not overcome his distrust of large or strange animals. He dislikes having his parents go out at night even when left with an accustomed and friendly sitter. Grotesque faces also upset him.

You will find that your child may whine if her wants are not fulfilled promptly or if she has nothing interesting to do. It may be that her vivid imagination catapults her into fearful situations. At the same time, she tries to control the behavior of others: "Don't talk!" "Don't laugh!"

Mothers, be prepared! Forty-three-month-olds may resist your authority both verbally and physically. (It seems that fathers do not get this treatment.) Children this age respond best to specific suggestions. They are not affected by generalizations, from whatever source.

This appears to be a time of "new unsettledness." Parents are well aware of this when their forty-three-month-olds withdraw from them, or imperiously demand, "Hold my hand!" Yet there are agreeable times even in the midst of turbulence. Children this age freely express their feelings of affection for their parents through words and physical means.

Forty-three-month-old children are now much better at making choices so that dawdling is less prevalent. They can pick the color shirt or socks they want to wear without exhausting the patience of their attending parent.

Ego Building—Learning About Me!

"I looked in the mirror and what did I see?
I saw somebody and it was ME.

I looked in the water and what did I see?
I saw my reflection and it was ME.
I stood in the sunshine and what did I see?
I saw a shadow and it was ME.
I looked in an album and what did I see?
I saw a picture and it was ME.

"A child needs to have a clear, complete image of himself before he can relate himself to others and the world around him. These activities are designed to increase your child's understanding of his physical self and to help him develop an image of his own body:

This Is ME

"Introduce your child to herself in a full-length mirror. 'This is Jennifer Jones.' Say, 'Hello, Jenny.' 'Hold out your hand to the child in the mirror.' 'What is she doing?' 'Put your hand on your head, your shoulder; touch your nose, elbow, etc.' Then ask, 'How many elbows do you have? heads? toes? Let's count them and see.'

How MY Body Works

"Talk to your child about the different things the parts of his body can do. What are his ears used for, his eyes, his feet, etc.? Why is his head hard rather than soft? Help your child make a scrapbook of pictures of hands doing all kinds of things; of feet; of faces; etc.

The Parts of ME

"Have your child point to each part as it is named. She will enjoy repeating this until she can say parts of it from memory:

Here are my EARS,
Here is my NOSE.
Here are my FINGERS,
Here are my TOES.
Here are my EYES,
Both open wide.

Here is my MOUTH
With TEETH inside.
Here is my TONGUE.
It helps me speak.
Here is my CHIN,
And here are two CHEEKS.
Here are my HANDS
That help me play.
Here are my FEET
That walk today."*

Self-Discipline†

It is evident that young children develop exceedingly close relationships with their parents, and want and need their love and approval. If parents have been consistent, their children will grow increasingly responsive to their example and counsel. However, if parents confuse their children by letting them get away with something one time and punishing them the next, they will not know what is expected of them. Hence, such children are not able to draw the line between acceptable and unacceptable behavior.

Everything a child sees and hears in his home in his early years is firmly imprinted in his mind, and his parents are responsible for what these things are. A forty-three-month-old may not understand the subtleties of things, but he sees what is happening around him. What you say and what you do are at the base of his values, attitudes, beliefs, and behaviors.

One of the goals of mature behavior is self-discipline. Parents are not preparing their children for the realities of life when they continuously tell them what to do and what not to do. Parents need to give their children freedom to exercise their own judgment as they grow older (starting at four years and up), remembering always to keep expectations and limits within their children's current abilities.

If your child learns that the rules of the family are just and that disobedience may lead to serious problems, he will try to adhere to the limits and goals you set.

*From *Parents' Home Activity Guides,* Issue #1 (Ferguson, MO: Ferguson-Florissant School District, 1975).
†Adapted from *Better Late Than Early* by Raymond S. Moore and Dorothy N. Moore (New York: Reader's Digest Press, 1977).

PLAY, PLAYTHINGS, AND FANTASY

The adult world is too large, too complicated, and often too threatening to the very young child. Therefore, he focuses upon the microcosmic world of play, a world he can master through toys and play materials. To these he imputes his childish beliefs and expectations as well as his feelings, and through repeated explorations he gradually relinquishes some of his more fantastic beliefs.

When the child tries to make the world conform to *her* childish beliefs, she is confronted over and over with the actuality of situations and events, ever-present threats, and sometimes painful consequences. She comes to understand herself and the real world only if she is permitted and encouraged to try, to persist until she learns what she can and cannot do. Play in early childhood presents a minimum of risks and penalties for mistakes. Play is a child's way of learning by trial and error to function with confidence in the actual world.

Pretend and Fantasy Play

When young children find the real world overwhelming—when they are unsure and words fail them—when their smallness, their ignorance, and their limited capacity bring them face to face with the stunning fact that they are still very little and cannot do very much, they resort to play and fantasy as a way out of their frustration.

To counteract their fears of the grown-up world, they escape to their pretend play, performing roles in "scripts" that cannot be countermanded in the real world. Their vivid imaginations create monsters, wild animals, and fearsome situations. To counteract them they take a toy animal or play doll to the doctor, hospital, or nursery school, or for a walk on a dark night. Some young children suffer more than others; for security, they need to hold on to a security blanket, a miniature car, a favorite stuffed animal.

Make-believe play is the way very young children sort out their impressions and try out their ideas. They find it hard to separate fantasy from fact at this age. They do not have the logical skill of the adult. Hence, reality and fantasy merge into their "child's-eye view" of the world. Some of their fantasies come from movies, television, and their immature thinking.

This is not the time to impose adult logic or to dampen playful spirits. Creativity thrives when parents appreciate this special period of pretend play and supply their children with some of the needed props. A list of appropriate items includes:

- *play people*—wedge-shaped painted wood type, stationary plastic type, or bendable rubber figures. All come in the form of family members (scale 1″ to 1′) or community workers (police officer, fire fighter, doctor, nurse, construction worker, etc.).
- *farm and zoo animals*—of vinyl, rubber, or wood.
- *performing arts characters*—hand puppets, finger puppets, shadow play figures.
- *doll play accessories*—doll, doll bed, blanket, carriage, mattress, baby bottle.
- *homemaking play accessories*—nonbreakable child-size tea set, pots and pans, broom, etc.
- *social play props*—telephone, tea table and chairs, playhouse.
- *dress-up play props*—large mirror, hand mirror, gaudy costume jewelry, vests, lengths of fur, colorful remnants for skirts, fake moustaches, wigs and hats, aprons, dress-up clothes, handbags, scarfs, grown-up shoes, and such accessories as a stethoscope, binoculars, goggles, an umbrella, and badges.

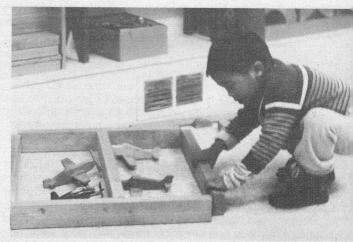

There are some roles which appear completely dependent upon having the right hat. How can you be a police officer without a proper cap decorated with a shiny badge, or a fire fighter without a bright red helmet?

As three-and-a-half-year-olds approach their fourth birthdays, a period of striking imaginative play unfolds in which reality hardly exists. They recruit all available objects as props for their dramatic homemaking, transportation, and city and country play. The ingenuity and resources of parents and nursery school teachers who wish to give these young imaginations full scope are brought into play. Trips, group discussions, storytelling, and visits to the library enrich the role-playing of these children.

Aggressive behavior is one facet of the play activity of forty-three-month-olds. "War games" can break out without warning in the nonviolent nursery school or the most pacifist of homes. While it is best to let children settle their quarrels, parents and teachers need to be prepared to intervene should real violence or destruction ensue. Intervening properly is a skill to be mastered by both parents and teachers.

Overly aggressive children will soon learn that they must compromise and "get along" with the other children if they wish to continue in their dramatic play. Should a "war" break out and the artillery is firing "salvos" of building blocks or barrels against the defenseless other side, the nursery school teacher will have to intervene promptly and diplomatically, perhaps with a "Yo, ho, I see a whale yonder!" and hope that the drama will quickly be directed against the imaginary mammal, not one another.

Cooperative Play Starts in Earnest at Forty-three Months

At this age, much of the children's play is conducted in groups of two or more in long periods of elaborate cooperative, self-initiated pretend scenes. The children get along well with preferred friends, but may exclude, push, or hit unwelcome children. There is less squabbling over possessions and play materials and less hoarding of toys, however. Boys and girls enjoy doll play and playing house with some peers and child-sized items of household equipment. At this age, children enjoy the process of construction more than play with a finished product. They build all kinds of block structures, using assorted shapes and sizes. Now action play is combined and held together with lively and imaginative conversation. As varied and enthusiastic as the playing may be, quarrels and fatigue do set in, and sensitive adult arbitration is in order.

Piaget on Play and Fantasy

In studying the play of young children, Piaget concluded that there are three main divisions. The first includes *practice games,* such as throwing balls, pitching pebbles, stringing beads, or building with blocks. One of their functions seems to be the sharpening of motor skills. *Symbolic games,* in which blocks may represent a launching pad and flight capsule inhabited by astronauts, develop next. The last to appear are *games with rules,* which may provide the clue to what happens to children's play in later life. Many of them phase out in favor of socialized games, baseball for one.

Piaget described the emergence of make-believe or symbolic play, by the end of the sensorimotor period of development, in which an object becomes the symbol for something else it may remotely resemble. Between the ages of two and four symbolic play is at its peak. There is also a special kind of play, called *compensatory play* by Piaget, which involves doing in make-believe what is forbidden in reality.

Piaget's emphasis on the importance of symbolic play has stimulated considerable research among cognitive psychologists. Jerome L. Singer of Yale University has published considerable work on the creative functions of make-believe play and daydreaming. He believes that the ability to fantasize helps children explore different possibilities, control aggressive impulses, increase storytelling skills, etc.

Starting Nursery School*

Starting to go to a nursery school *is* a brand-new experience, and parents and teachers understand that it can be very trying for some children. Therefore, they take steps to avoid or to ease any tensions. The child's first day is planned to be brief

*Parts of pages 298–299 adapted from *Living and Learning in Nursery School* by Marguerita Rudolph (New York: Harper & Brothers, 1954).

and in the company of a parent or other consistent caregiver. No activity is urged upon the child.

With the cooperation of the parents, the teachers gradually introduce the children to nursery school life. During the first weeks of school the teachers get to know the parents and learn about the background of each child, which helps them in guiding each child's adjustment to nursery school. For the majority of children adjustment to a good nursery school involves no lasting difficulty. For other children, starting nursery school presents problems that require special understanding and patience on the part of parent and teacher alike.

Individual cubbies are provided for children in nursery schools for the orderly care of their belongings. To each child, his cubby is a symbol of his belonging in the room. It can also be a place of refuge when the going is rough.

Being accepted as they are, nursery school children gain confidence in themselves. Gradually they become interested in others and learn how to become members in good standing in their group. As children experience a teacher's friendship and help, they also find out about her or him as a person and learn the meaning of authority. Nursery school children learn physical and emotional self-control, among other things.

Adjusting to the Nursery School Group

At the beginning of the nursery school year, when children are new to the group, their ways of adjusting to one another are generally gauche and crude. Some children feel amiable but do not know how to express themselves. Others behave aggressively to hide their fear and uncertainty. Children have to learn how to defend themselves almost as often as they have to be kept from fighting. In time, most of the children are able to resolve their battles with little or no interference by the teacher. Besides aggressive children, there are those who try to adjust to others by resorting to bribery or cajolery. Still others will use temper tantrums as an attention-getting device.

Some children are fearful and anxious and cannot function smoothly until they are helped to overcome their negative feelings. Others are completely at a loss when it comes to initiating activity and adjusting to other children because they have been over-controlled at home. These are the silent, unobtrusive youngsters who withdraw from the nursery school group. Nursery school teachers are aware of the strengths and weaknesses of their charges, and usually are successful in helping a shy child integrate into the group as he learns to build up his self-confidence.

Typical Full-day Nursery School Routine

The average full-day nursery school routine is simple and understandable. The children arrive at 9:00 A.M. and stay until 3:00 P.M. (Some schools operate on a half-day schedule, from 8:00 A.M. to noon.) There is a midmorning snack of crackers and juice and a well-balanced hot meal at noon. Lunch is followed by a rest period of at least an hour, during which several children may sleep.

Periods of indoor play alternate with play outdoors. The children take turns in using the play yard, which is equipped with simple swings, packing boxes, sturdy wood or steel climbers, hollow blocks, barrels, five- and six-foot ladders, pails, wagons, and a large sandbox. The children have ample

opportunity for vigorous climbing, swinging, balancing, jumping, pulling, hauling, and running.

Indoors there are unit building blocks, floor trains, dolls, a child-sized stove, cupboard, sink, pots, pans, dishes, crayons, paints, clay, and other plastic materials, as well as a workbench, pieces of soft wood, and simple tools for construction activity. There is a music period for singing simple songs, use of free body rhythms, skipping and leaping to music, and so on. Another period is devoted to storytelling, or the teacher reads to the group. Ample time is allowed for children to talk things over together.

From the beginning, rules of acceptable conduct are set by the teacher. For instance, children cannot destroy the products of others in the nursery school group; building blocks cannot be thrown or used as weapons; clay cannot be ground into the floor; finger paints may not be smeared on other children, etc.

Adult Participation in Play*

Adult involvement in child's play is a delicate matter. Most children like to have parents or other familiar adults play with them. It is not only the attention they enjoy; they sometimes also expect them to join in their play.

Consider the challenge of making a tall block building. All sorts of measurement and balancing decisions have to be made. A child will resolve many obstacles by himself, but his experience is not broad enough. This is where sensitive adult intervention may be helpful.

A child who has every detail spelled out for her will become just as frustrated as a child who is left too long to struggle by herself. The balance between sensitive encouragement and overeagerness to do all the thinking for a child is much like walking a tightrope. Suggestions are usually better than specific directions. An approach of "Do you think it might work this way?" is actually more helpful than swift accomplishment by the adult. Sensing your know-how, the child will follow your suggestions. However, she will not learn or enjoy herself if she is not allowed a chance to try to put her own ideas into play.

It appears, too, that the extent to which children learn by

*Adapted from *The First Seven Years* by Eric Trimmer (New York: St. Martin's Press, 1978).

doing depends in large measure upon the play possibilities made available to them by their parents.

The Child's First Art Experience

In *The Art of the Young Child: Understanding and Encouraging Creative Growth in Children Three to Five* (New York:

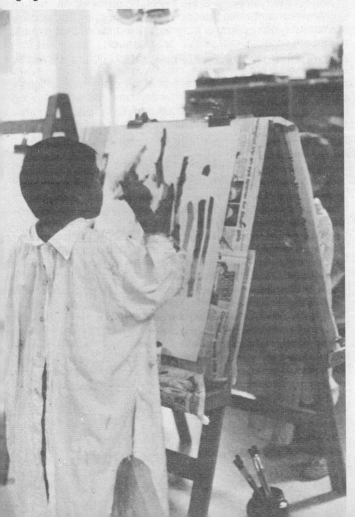

Museum of Modern Art, 1968), Jane Cooper Bland writes, "Parents are the child's first art teachers because the child has his earliest art experiences at home. Not only the casual things surrounding him, but particularly his toys, books, and playthings have tremendous influence upon the young child's developing taste and should be chosen with an eye toward their potentialities for creative play."

Art teachers believe that the materials out of which children create are important to their sense of satisfaction and accomplishment. Often parents provide art materials that are too advanced or elaborate. Basic art materials, discussed in a prior chapter, will spark interest in creating with paints, crayons, clay, etc.

Mrs. Bland recommends the use of large sticks of soft chalk which come in many colors. They can be used when it is too difficult to set up the poster paints or to introduce another medium. The best kind of chalk is lecturer's chalk, which is approximately half an inch square. Crayons should not be confused with chalks.

Even though finger painting is often a freeing experience, it is not a demanding one. Therefore, it offers little opportunity for growth. However, finger painting can satisfy the child who has the need to be messy.

Many forty-three-month-olds can cut with scissors and handle paste adequately on their own level. However, if a child is not able to use scissors until he is four or five, then that is when he ought to start.

Mrs. Bland advises parents to be aware of the fact that "When a child feels that what he has been making is not respected, he is likely to try to do something that he thinks will be acceptable. If this happens, he probably will never again feel quite as free or confident in his own expression."

Enrichment: Singing

Singing is the most elementary form of music. Beatrice Landeck, in her book *Children and Music: An Informal Guide for Parents and Teachers* (New York: William Sloane, 1952), suggests that parents find their own voices and fill their homes with music. She writes that "Either your own or your husband's mother (or father) will remember the songs, singing games, or rhymes each knew as a child. When you have exhausted your own, your family's and your friends' repertory of songs, you can widen your choices of songs by investigating the traditional songs of your country—our American folk songs." Lilting, rhythmical international folk songs offer additional opportunities for making music by singing.

Constant repetition will help you and your children to learn the words and the music easily. You can introduce phonograph records that have good rhythms and easy-to-learn words, as performed by Woody Guthrie, Burl Ives, Tom Glazer, Pete Seeger, and others.

In *Toys & Playthings: A Practical Guide for Parents and Teachers* (New York: Pantheon Books, 1979), John and Elizabeth Newson present these succinct thoughts on play and playthings: "Play comes first; toys merely follow. We do not play as a *result* of having toys; toys are no more then pegs on which to hang our play. In theory, toys are not needed; the child could happily wander through her fantasy world, her imagination supplying all that was wanted. Perhaps *because* the human imagination is so extensive and complex, children seem to look for tangible reference points, as it were, from which to range the more freely. Just as language makes subtle and complicated thought possible, perhaps toys do the same for play . . . Toys which persist are those which satisfy the child's wish to grow in skill and in power, which feed his imagination, absorb his emotion and seize his curiosity, and which purely and simply amuse him, surprise him and make him laugh."

HEALTH, SELF-HELP, AND ROUTINES

Routines appear to give forty-three-month-old boys and girls the most trouble, with mealtime and dressing two of the most troublesome ones. Bothersome whining is common. During smoother parts of the day—between routines—your child may be affectionate and amusing, cooperative and confiding; in short, a completely delightful companion.

Dressing and Undressing

Children this age can undress rapidly, and also put on their underpants, socks, shoes, shirts, pants, dress, or sweater. However, most are more uncooperative than helpful with regard to getting dressed. It will be a while longer before most are able to tie their own shoelaces or unbutton back buttons. They can unbutton and button front and side buttons.

Forty-three- through forty-eight-month-old boys and girls love getting new clothing, which they enjoy showing to others—peers, relatives, other adults.

Eating

Forty-three-month-olds can feed themselves well, with much less spilling than at thirty-six months. They are more adept at pouring milk, juice, or water from a pitcher that is not too large for them to handle. Many children this age may dawdle when allowed to dine at the family table. Try to be patient when your child is more interested in objecting to the procedures of eating than in demonstrating her increased control of utensils and foods.

Sugar and Hyperactivity

We cannot overstress the devastating effects of sugar-laden foods on the health and behavior of young children. In addition to being responsible for causing tooth decay and obesity, sugar in the diet can exacerbate the already disruptive behavior of hyperactive children. Hyperactive behavior can be ameliorated in many instances by placing afflicted children on diets that are free of sugar (dextrose, fructose, glucose, maltrose, and sucrose), as well as artificial colorings and artificial flavorings.

Fears and Dreams

There are episodes of wakefulness and crying at this stage that are caused by dreams and nightmares. Fears and frightening dreams are on the rise. Your child may suck his thumb at night, using his "lovey" for solace and reassurance.

Childhood Accidents and Safety

Although prevention is the best protection against childhood accidents, parents and other caregivers need to know how to cope with any emergency that may arise. In *A Sigh of*

Relief: The First-Aid Handbook for Childhood Emergencies (New York: Bantam Books, 1977), Martin I. Green writes, "Children are more likely to have serious accidents than adults because they are not only the victims, but often the unconscious perpetrators . . .

"Some toy-related injuries have less to do with any defect in the toy itself than with the way it is used. Parents sometimes forget their children's inexperience . . . Give your child the guidance his age requires: two- to four-year-olds are most susceptible to toy-related injuries . . . This is especially true of boys, who are statistically more likely than girls to have accidents."

Playground Safety

Fortunately, most playground accidents consist of minor cuts, abrasions, and bumps. However, even in the best playground, whenever several children climb, swing, run, and jump, there is the chance that someone may be grievously injured.

Climbing and swinging apparatus is safely embedded in concrete in most public playgrounds. Equipment anchored with pegs in backyards should be checked regularly to make sure they do not loosen. All anchoring devices should be buried so they cannot be tripped over. Exposed hardware should fit flush or be capped, and any protruding parts covered with tape. Metal structures need to be kept rust-free, and wooden equipment restored or replaced as needed.

A *slide* should be no higher than six feet for children under eight, and shaded from the sun. A *sandbox* should be shaded from the sun while in use. The sand should be raked frequently. It should be covered at night to keep it free of moisture and animals. *Chain swings* are best for children under five.

Water Safety

Close adult supervision is the best safeguard against drowning accidents. Of course, the single best safety precaution is knowing how to swim. Most children are able to learn this at a very early age.

Bathtubs and wading pools filled with water are potential hazards. Small wading pools should be emptied after each use and turned over to keep rain from collecting in them. All pools need to be covered during the months when they are not in use. Teach your child never to play in any pool without your permission; one-third of childhood drownings occur in the pools of neighbors.

Growth Chart—43rd Through 48th Month

MOTOR DEVELOPMENT

Gross Motor

Run smoothly.

Can tiptoe for a distance of 10 feet.

Can balance on a walking board.

Can hop 1 to 3 steps on preferred feet; hop in place on both feet.

Stumbling and falling due to lack of coordination of flexor and extensor muscles.

Can jump rather high.

Like to try catch-and-throw ball games.

Can ride tricycle without bumping into things.

May seek support of a holding hand ascending and descending stairs.

Fine Motor

Hand tremors of many 3½-year-olds indicate temporary lack of coordination.

Use thin, uncertain lines in their drawings.

Eye blinking and poor visual coordination part of growth changes.

Can trace diamond on large piece of paper.

Can cut with scissors.

LANGUAGE ACQUISITION

Love to play with language and make up new words.

May stutter and stammer due to temporary incoordination.

Sentences grow longer.

Use 4 to 5 words to express thoughts.

Beginning of correct grammatical usage.

Average vocabulary at 3½ is 1,000 words; grows to 1,500 words at 4.

Follow directions with two prepositions; i.e., *on top of, under,* etc.

Beginning to use auxiliary verbs: "would," "could," "be," "have," "can."

Use negatives effectively: "I don't want to go."

Create own grammar: *rided* for *rode, wented* for *went,* etc.

Begin to talk about imaginary conditions. "Suppose that . . ."

Enjoy listening to stories for as long as 20 minutes or more.

Adore silly rhyming.

Growth Chart—43rd Through 48th Month

SENSORY POWERS/LEARNING

Able to count to 3.

Develop perfect size perception.

Begin to match pictures in simple lotto games.

Can point correctly to 6 common geometric shapes.

Memory improves.

Can recall events in recent past.

Beginning to think problems through with ideas in their minds.

Understand *heaviest, longest*.

SOCIAL DEVELOPMENT

Use words to get other children to play with them; also use words to exclude other children.

Exclusion is enforced verbally, for the most part.

Beginning to grasp concept of sharing.

Temporary attachment to one playmate, often of the opposite sex (girls may be the initiators).

Demonstrate affection for other children and adults.

PERSONALITY/ PSYCHOLOGICAL

Learning to cope with anger and fear, phobias, nightmares, excessive thumb-sucking.

Sibling rivalry (competitiveness among brothers and sisters) appears and needs parental intervention.

Sexually show-offs about organs which distinguish boys from girls.

Are developing self-restraint and self-control.

Growth Chart—43rd Through 48th Month

PLAY AND PLAYTHINGS	HEALTH, SELF-HELP, AND ROUTINES
Active jungle gym and ladder climbers.	Eager to help with real family chores (water plants, wipe table, etc.).
Enjoy using a slide; welcome a helping hand at bottom of high slide.	Will help with housecleaning and keeping things neat.
Like to toss bean bags into holes in target.	Can go to toilet unassisted.
Capable of cooperative play; may need adult help in interactions with peers.	Able to use fork and spoon.
Can put together large and simple jigsaw puzzles.	Able to put shoe on correct foot.
Advancing toward make-believe play.	
May have difficulty distinguishing fantasy from reality.	
Ready for simple cooking and baking experiences.	
Enjoy painting with large brushes; cover entire paper; name pictures when finished.	
Enjoy manipulating clay.	
Can carry a tune and move to its rhythm.	
Enjoy playing "What floats?" with sponge, soap, plastic cup, wooden spoons, etc.	

Dear Parents:

Do not regard this chart as a rigid timetable.

Young children are unpredictable individuals. Some perform an activity earlier or later than this chart indicates.

Just use this information to anticipate and appreciate normal child development and behavior. No norms are absolute.

CHAPTER SEVEN

The 49th Through 60th Month of Life

The greatest poem ever known
Is one all poets have outgrown.
The poetry, innate, untold,
Of being only four years old.
Christopher Morley,
To A Child

Fours are no longer babies. They have developed beyond their toddlerhood, the stage in their lives when closeness to mother was the only thing that mattered to them.

They have grown a little bigger physically during the past year, and have more stamina and improved physical coordination. Boys and girls at forty-nine through sixty months are quite active physically and mentally. They talk "a mile a minute" because their words and ideas are boundless and demand unending practice.

Four-year-olds appear less in need of approbation for everything they do or say, although a pat on the back or a hug is always in order. They seem more confident than they were only a few months ago. They are eager for everything that is new—new sounds, new sights, new words, and new skills and accomplishments of every sort. They have many ideas of their own to express—if parents will listen! Fours have countless ideas to communicate in painting, dramatic play, and block building; in this they need encouragement, materials, space, and time.

Forty-nine- through sixty-month-old boys and girls ask many and more complex questions, in part because there is so very much they want to know, but also to garner attention. If parents understand that their seemingly overwhelming waves of queries permit children to exercise their growing listening and talking skills, they can try to be more patient and responsive.

Fours use more building blocks and accessory playthings in their increasingly intricate block structures. Sometimes Fours enjoy planning and building with a few agemates.

The most noticeable musical advance made by four-year-old girls and boys is in the use of their voices. With increased control, they find it easier to sing on pitch. They can remember the words of many songs, and enjoy singing alone or in a group.

Child-care specialists indicate that forty-nine- through sixty-month-old boys and girls seem quite advanced so that parents often make too severe demands upon them. For example, they fuss about their children's noisiness and sloppiness, and continually attempt to correct their language and manners. Young children are turned off by the everlasting *do's* and *don'ts* with which they are bombarded by their well-meaning parents. One of the results can be a plethora of defiant name-calling and a less than pleasant relationship between parents and children.

Whereas most forty-nine- to fifty-four-month-old children are outgoing and sometimes even out of control, fifty-four-through sixty-month-olds are usually composed and agreeable. The latter are just beginning to be able to make some distinction between fact and fantasy.

Middle-Fours tend to be more self-motivated. Most can concentrate longer on undertakings than Early-Fours. Although they can tolerate frustration better, the emotions of Middle-Fours are still unsure and can swing without warning from laughter to tears.

Fifty-four- through sixty-month-old children are aware of the distinction between "good" and "bad." They make unhappy faces when they are scolded by their parents. They especially relish stories of how their parents were good but also bad while they were growing up.

Of course, there are decided differences in all children. Hence, not all Fours are wild and not all Fives are calm. Try to appreciate and enjoy the liveliness and zest for learning by doing of your child during this period, despite some perfectly normal behavior that you may find neither delightful nor pleasing.

GROSS-MOTOR DEVELOPMENT

Fours are in good control of their bodies. They run well, turn sharp corners smoothly, and can make a fair running broad jump. However, they still skip in only a so-so fashion. Although they cannot hop, skip, and jump in sequence, they can balance on one foot for several seconds. Most Fours are able to hop from four to six steps on one foot. Their improved body balance is indicated by their ability to "walk the plank" on a walking board. They are able also to jump down unaided from a two-foot height.

Keeping their legs straight, Fours can bend at the waist in order to pick up objects on the floor. They are able to bounce a ball and will try to strike one with a bat. They can execute a strong overhand throw. Fours enjoy climbing trees and ladders, and especially relish acrobatics. For example, they delight in hanging upside down by their knees on the rung of a jungle gym, turning somersaults, jumping, and so on. Some Fours are starting to roller-skate, and most can pump themselves on a swing. It is not until four years of age that children can walk a circular line without losing their balance.

In brief, Fours have boundless energy, and are challenged

into attempting physical feats that are arduous and sometimes reckless.

FINE-MOTOR DEVELOPMENT

Fours can thread a lace into a sewing card, button clothes (if the buttons are easily accessible), and lace shoes.

In their drawings, they may give concentrated attention to the representation of an isolated detail. At this time, a typical drawing of a human figure consists of a head and two appendages, and possibly two eyes. The body as such does not appear until five years of age. Fours can copy a circle and a cross, but they cannot as yet draw a diamond shape from a model. When Fours paint, they hold their brush between thumb and forefinger, often providing a running commentary on what they are depicting.

VISUAL-MOTOR DEVELOPMENT

Fours can build a tower of ten or more blocks. Boys and girls are able to match shapes in a formboard, which includes triangles, circles, and squares. They are better able to use scissors now; for example, they can cut along a line fairly well. Many Fours are beginning to try to print letters and numerals. Children this age are able also to string small beads to make a necklace.

LANGUAGE ACQUISITION

Fours carry on a love affair with words—all kinds of silly words and sounds. Forty-nine- through sixty-month-olds make up their own words, use slang, and swear (not only for the sake of the sounds, but for the response as well). Most are beginning to add words to their vocabulary that shock their parents and nursery school teachers. Many talk openly about elimination and use toilet words—"poopie pants," "dirty pee pee," "smelly poop," etc. You may also have repeated back to you questionable words that appear in your own speech. The best recourse for parents is to pay no attention to the offensive words their children are using, and at the same time to get them engaged in some other activity. If not belabored, this phase usually is of limited duration. When parents fuss over

children's play with unacceptable words, the latter are apt to use them whenever they wish to get a rise out of their parents.

Imaginative Fours start to tell stories of their own creation, which they are eager to share with their parents and other children. When their imaginations get out of bounds, they embroider actual events with make-believe details. Some adults believe such children are not being truthful and should be reprimanded. The demarcation between fantasy and reality is still hazy at this juncture.

Talking vocabulary will have increased to about 1,550 words by forty-nine months, and to about 2,200 words by the time children are sixty months old.

A four-year-old is usually able to repeat his name, age, and address upon request. His speech is completely intelligible, except for some minor mispronunciations. The grammar of the four-year-old is essentially correct. He knows the meaning of such spatial expressions as *on, under, in back of, beside, in front of.*

Some Language Activities

What Is Missing? Place five or six cards with pictures your child can name in the center of a table. Ask her to close her eyes while you take one away and hide it. She must then open her eyes and tell you what object or picture is missing. If she guesses right, she gets to take an object or picture off the table while you close your eyes.

A variation of this game is to cut off some part of a picture (a wheel, leg, arm, or hat, etc.) and have her guess what part is missing.

Concentration. Place eight or ten picture cards face up on a table. Name each picture while your child listens carefully. Then shuffle the cards and turn them upside down on a table. Players take turns pointing to a card and guessing what it is. When your child turns the card over and guesses correctly, he picks up the card and keeps it, and takes another turn. If he is wrong, the card is placed face down on the table.

Word Games. To further enhance language skills, you can purchase go-together lotto cards (the object being to match fronts and backs, etc.), A to Z lotto, or assorted picture lotto sets (animals, birds, flowers).

Fours like to listen to stories and nursery rhymes; especially enjoyed are nonsense verses. Stories that they love they want to hear repeatedly, with nary one change in wording. Silly language is at its height. The following are some good books for Fours and Fives. However, since children differ greatly, it is up to you to discover which books will be best for your child.

Allard, Harry. *The Tutti-Frutti Case.* (Englewood Cliffs, NJ: Prentice-Hall, 1975)

Anglund, Joan Walsh. *A Friend Is Someone Who Likes You.* (New York: Harcourt, Brace, 1958)

Benton, Robert. *Don't Ever Wish for a Seven-foot Bear.* (New York: Knopf, 1972)

Berger, Terry. *I Have Feelings.* (New York: Human Sciences Press, 1971)

―――. *I Have Feelings Too.* (New York: Human Sciences Press, 1979)

Bond, Michael. *A Bear Called Paddington.* (Boston: Houghton Mifflin, 1960)

Brenner, Barbara. *Bodies.* (New York: E. P. Dutton, 1973)

―――. *Faces.* (New York: E. P. Dutton, 1970)

Brinckloe, Julie. *The Spider Web.* (Garden City, NY: Doubleday, 1975)

Brooke, Leslie. *Johnny Crow's Garden.* (New York: Frederick Warne, 1903)

Brown, Marc T. *One, Two, Three: An Animal Counting Book.* (Boston: Little, Brown, 1976)

Brown, Margaret Wise. *The Important Book.* (New York: Harper & Row, 1949)

―――. *The Indoor Noisy Book.* (Harper & Row, 1942)

Bruna, Dick. *I Can Dress Myself.* (London: Methuen, 1978)

Brunhoff, Jean de. *The Story of Babar.* (New York: Random, 1937)

Burton, Virginia Lee. *Katy and the Big Snow.* (Boston: Houghton Mifflin, 1943)

―――. *The Little House.* (Houghton Mifflin, 1942)

―――. *Mike Mulligan and His Steam Shovel.* (Houghton Mifflin, 1939)

Carle, Eric. *The Very Hungry Caterpillar.* (New York: Collins, 1969)

Clifton, Lucille. *Everett Anderson's Year.* (New York: Holt, Rinehart & Winston, 1974)

Crews, Donald. *Freight Train.* (New York: Greenwillow, 1978)

De Regniers, Beatrice Schenk. *Little House of Your Own.* (New York: Harcourt, Brace, 1955)

————. *May I Bring a Friend?* (New York: Atheneum, 1962)

Fassler, Joan. *Don't Worry, Dear.* (New York: Human Sciences Press, 1971)

Flack, Marjorie. *Ask Mr. Bear.* (New York: Macmillan, 1971)

————. *The Story About Ping.* (New York: Viking, 1970)

Galdone, Paul. *The Frog Prince.* (New York: McGraw-Hill, 1975)

Goldsmith, Howard. *Toto the Timid Turtle.* (New York: Human Sciences Press, 1980)

Gramatky, Hardie. *Little Toot.* (New York: G. P. Putnam's Sons, 1939)

Hoban, Russell. *Bedtime for Frances.* (New York: Harper & Row, 1960)

Hoban, Russell and Lillian. *A Baby Sister for Frances.* (New York: Harper & Row, 1964)

————. *Bread and Jam for Frances.* (New York: Harper & Row, 1964)

Hoban, Tana. *Circles, Triangles & Squares.* (New York: Macmillan, 1974)

————. *Count & See.* (New York: Macmillan, 1972)

————. *Over, Under & Through.* (New York: Macmillan, 1973)

Hutchins, Pat. *The Wind Blew.* (New York: Macmillan, 1974)

Johnson, Crockett. *Harold and the Purple Crayon.* (New York: Harper & Row, 1955)

Joslin, Sesyle. *What Do You Say, Dear?* (Reading, MA: Addison-Wesley, 1958)

Keats, Ezra Jack. *Peter's Chair.* (New York: Harper & Row, 1967)

————. *The Snowy Day.* (New York: Viking, 1962)

Kessler, Ethel and Leonard. *The Big Red Bus.* (Garden City, NY: Doubleday, 1964)

————. *The Day Daddy Stayed Home.* (Garden City, NY: Doubleday, 1971)

Krasilovsky, Phyllis. *The Man Who Didn't Wash His Dishes.* (Garden City, NY: Doubleday, 1978)

————. *The Shy Little Girl.* (Boston: Houghton Mifflin, 1972)

Krauss, Ruth. *A Hole Is to Dig.* (New York: Harper & Row, 1952)

————. *The Carrot Seed.* (New York: Harper & Row, 1945)

————. *I Want to Paint My Bathroom Blue.* (Harper & Row, 1956)

Kuskin, Karla. *Roar and More.* (New York: Harper & Row, 1956)

Lionni, Leo. *The Biggest House in the World.* (New York: Pantheon, 1968)

———. *In the Rabbit Garden.* (New York: Pantheon, 1975)

———. *Inch By Inch.* (New York: Astor-Honor, 1962)

McCloskey, Robert. *Make Way for Ducklings.* (New York: Viking, 1941)

———. *Time of Wonder.* (New York: Viking, 1957)

Maestro, Betsy. *Harriet Goes to the Circus.* (New York: Crown, 1977)

———. *Where Is My Friend?* (New York: Crown, 1976)

Milne, A. A. *Winnie-the-Pooh.* (New York: E. P. Dutton, 1954)

Minarik, Else. *Little Bear.* (New York: Harper & Row, 1957)

Montresor, Beni. *Bedtime!* (New York: Harper & Row, 1978)

Newberry, Clare Turlay. *Barkis.* (New York: Harper & Row, 1938)

Nodset, Joan L. *Go Away, Dog.* (New York: Harper & Row, 1963)

Piper, Watty. *The Little Engine That Could.* (New York: Platt & Munk, 1954)

Potter, Beatrix. *The Tale of Peter Rabbit.* (New York: Frederick Warne, 1903)

Preston, Edna M. *The Temper Tantrum Book.* (New York: Viking, 1969)

Rey, H. A. *Curious George.* (Boston: Houghton Mifflin, 1941)

Rey, Margret and H. A. *Curious George Goes to the Hospital.* (Boston: Houghton Mifflin, 1966)

Rockwell, Anne and Harlow. *The Supermarket.* (New York: Macmillan, 1979)

Scarry, Patsy. *Big Bedtime Story Book.* (New York: Random House, 1980)

Schlein, Miriam. *Fast Is Not a Ladybug.* (Reading, MA: Addison-Wesley, 1953)

———. *Heavy Is a Hippopotamus.* (Addison-Wesley, 1954)

Sendak, Maurice. *In the Night Kitchen.* (New York: Harper & Row, 1970)

———. *Where the Wild Things Are.* (Harper & Row, 1963)

Seuss, Dr. (Theodor Geisel). *The Cat in the Hat.* (New York: Random House, 1957)

———. *The Foot Book.* (New York: Random House, 1968)

Slobodkin, Louis. *Magic Michael.* (New York: Macmillan, 1944)

Slobodkina, Esphyr. *Caps for Sale.* (Reading, MA: Addison-Wesley, 1947)

Spier, Peter. *Crash! Bang! Boom!* (Garden City, NY: Doubleday, 1972)

———. *Fast-Slow, High-Low.* (Garden City, NY: Doubleday, 1972)

———. *Gobble, Growl, Grunt.* (Garden City, NY: Doubleday, 1979)

Stevenson, Robert Louis. *A Child's Garden of Verses.* (New York: Platt & Munk, 1977)

Tester, Sylvia Root. *Sometimes I'm Afraid.* (Elgin, IL: Child's World, 1979)

Tobias, Tobi. *Moving Day.* (New York: Alfred A. Knopf, 1976)

Tresselt, Alvin. *White Snow, Bright Snow.* (New York: Lothrop, Lee & Shepard, 1947)

Udry, Janice May. *A Tree Is Nice.* (New York: Harper & Row, 1956)

Ungerer, Tomi. *Crictor.* (New York: Harper & Row, 1958)

Watson, Jane W. *My Friend, the Baby Sitter.* (Racine, WI: Western Publishing, 1971)

Williams, Margery. *The Velveteen Rabbit.* (Garden City, NY: Doubleday, 1958)

Yashima, Taro. *Umbrella.* (New York: Viking, 1958)

Zolotow, Charlotte. *Big Sister and Little Sister.* (New York: Harper & Row, 1966)

———. *The Quarreling Book.* (Harper & Row, 1963)

SENSORY POWERS/LEARNING

Fours have a greater capacity for quiet play than they had a year ago. They possess quite rudimentary powers of generalization and are starting to order their experiences. Now they can name and match several colors.

The four-year-old is beginning to sense herself as only one among others. Her mind is alert and far-ranging. However, from a strictly academic point of view, her mental processes are still narrow in concept. She has only dim notions of the past and the future. She shows minimal interest in the plot of a story.

Although the forty-nine- to fifty-four-month-old child can count to four or more, his number concept barely goes beyond one and two. His mind is packed with all kinds of details: big and little, pretty and ugly, small and tall, light and dark, and so on.

"Thinking is very concrete at Four," writes Agnes de Lima in *The Little Red School House* (New York: Macmillan, 1942). Fours appear to be sharply observant in matters that concern them. For example, in a nursery school group, four-year-olds were naming the children who were absent, and there was one child's name no one remembered. However, when this particular child's blanket was shown, the others suddenly shouted out the name of the missing child in unison. Then all the children's blankets were brought out, and each child in turn named the rightful owner of each blanket without the slightest pause.

In *Survival Handbook for Preschool Mothers* (Chicago: Follett Publishing Co., 1977), Helen Wheeler Smith suggests many activities parents can initiate with their four-year-olds, some of which follow:

For spatial perception—Use two pegboards and golf tees. Make a design and have your child copy it. Then put in different numbers of tees and have your child match yours.

For whole-part concepts—Use puzzles, measuring cups, take-apart toys, etc. Make a circle and square on a piece of cardboard. On colored paper, make a circle and square of the same size, and cut them into one-half, one-third, and one-quarter parts. Have your child match the pieces to the whole units.

For classification and grouping—Use several different kinds of dry beans. Ask your child to put similar kinds in sections of egg cartons or cups. Vary this by using animal picture cards, asking your child to sort them to find look-alikes. Or play card games (Old Maid or regular cards), grouping them by colors, numbers, etc. Use dice or dominoes to find dot groupings.

CREATIVITY

Rose Mukerji, author of "Roots of Early Childhood for Continuous Learning" (in *Early Childhood Education Readings Rediscovered,* edited by Joe L. Frost, New York: Holt, Rinehart & Winston, 1968), believes that "The early childhood years are particularly fruitful and have great potential power for improving education, for four reasons:

"These are the root years during which children meet the challenge of knowing who they are in relation to people outside the unique confines of the family . . .

"The early childhood years are the root years in concept formation . . . [Each child's] primary strategy for intellectual growth is active, manipulative, and sensory . . .

"The early childhood years are the root years for language development . . . Language becomes a highly efficient way to store information, to recover information, and to solve problems . . .

"The childhood years are the root years for creativity."

Children Thrive on Encouragement

A study by the University of Chicago of the lives of one hundred internationally famous musicians, mathematicians, and athletes indicates that responsive parents and an encouraging home atmosphere were the prime elements in producing these outstanding performers.

"The old saw that 'genius will out' in spite of circumstances is not supported by our findings," reports Dr. Benjamin S. Bloom, Director of the Development of Talent Project at the University of Chicago.

Creativity in Children

Little is known about the origin, nature, and blossoming of creativity. Even today our society has too little regard for those who are inventive of mind and playful of spirit. Most of our schools train for conformity.

If you could survey the outstanding creative leaders in science, business, art, government, and so on, you would find that most had a lonely time from childhood throughout their fruitful years. You would find that many of them were *only* children who created a fantasy world of their own making. If there were second children, they were left to their own devices most of the time, and they had to make use of their own resources to amuse themselves. Most had parents who cared as much about their early play life as their later formal learning. In fact, in many instances, their parents encouraged and entered into their early play life and sought to provide the kinds of play materials that stimulated creativity and fantasy in their offspring.

At a conference in childhood and creativity held in 1979 at St. Vincent College in Latrobe, Pennsylvania, psychoanalyst Erik Erikson stated that Albert Einstein (whose parents did not interfere with his uniqueness) "retained the quality of childlikeness, as opposed to childishness, ascribed only to rare persons in history." Erikson believes that "Einstein's whole development confirms the vital importance of the right to play and the unique relationship between play and the development of creativity." Einstein's mother and father gave their special son free rein throughout his childhood and adolescence. Apparently they were sensitive parents who were able to recognize and accept their son's right to follow his own instincts.

At the same conference, Dr. Peter H. Wolff, Professor of Psychiatry at Harvard Medical School, commented, "We prize children's budding creativity, but if it gets out of hand, it becomes uncomfortable for us, and we try to crush it into the conventional mold. The processes and products of creativity tend to disrupt the order of things, and we are not comfortable with disruption."

SOCIAL DEVELOPMENT

Fours are very sociable. Often they relish companionship to such a degree that they do not like to play alone at home in the afternoon, even when they play with other children on a regular basis in the morning. Four-year-olds are likely to chatter endlessly when playing together.

Three four-year-olds at play may encounter difficulties be-

cause two of them have a tendency to gang up against the third. Most often when a third child tries to enter the play of two other children, exclusion and unhappiness are the outcome for one of them. If they are accustomed to group play and have had some experience in how to handle a dispute, Fours generally can settle most of their disagreements effectively. Nonetheless, adult supervision of forty-nine- to sixty-month-old children is still recommended.

In a playgroup or nursery school, Fours will share possessions brought from home. Although they may suggest taking turns in their play, this is not always orderly. Sometimes a child will deliberately initiate disruptive behavior, which may be more a crude attempt to evoke social response in other children than merely the expression of antisocial impulses.

The dramatic play of Fours is often hectic and uncontrolled in its wild shifts of place, pace, and characters. The sense of humor of four-year-old girls and boys is reflected in their wonderful silliness.

Increasing self-reliance in their personal habits, rugged determination, and an inclination to be domineering give Fours the mien of self-sufficiency—which is not necessarily so.

Fours can develop sudden new and strong likes and dislikes for certain people, foods, clothing, or even playthings. The best pal of yesterday may be shunned today without apparent reason. An erstwhile favorite food may be abruptly rejected.

Agemates are more exciting to Fours than grown-ups. Although they will still play with either boys or girls, a best friend is likely to be of the same sex (perhaps because they enjoy the same activities).

Fours boast and brag and make lots of noise. Although they love being with their peers, it doesn't take long for them to engage in quarreling and name-calling. Sometimes they do battle verbally; at other times, they resort to hitting. When thus embroiled they can be heard to shout, "Go away! I don't want to play with you!"

Four-year-olds will fight with their older, demanding siblings. Aware that such quarreling and in-fighting are normal and sometimes even enjoyed by all siblings, parents can separate the children if the going gets too rough. They also can try to find out what it is that provokes these outbursts.

Since the behavior of four-year-olds toward a new baby in the family is unpredictable, they should not be trusted alone for any length of time with an infant sibling. Fours are likely to be impatient and rough with younger brothers or sisters.

It is fun to have a conversation with an animated four-year-old. Fours are inordinately proud of their parents and often quote them as authorities. At the same time, Fours frequently challenge the power of their mothers, both verbally and physically. They relish particularly new adventures and times alone with their fathers.

PERSONALITY/PSYCHOLOGICAL DEVELOPMENT

Four-year-olds seem to have a built-in mechanism for getting out of control. When frustrated or angry, they may kick and spit, and even threaten to run away from home. Four-year-olds require firm parental guidelines in order to remain on a more even keel. Reasoning can often be useful when dealing with a recalcitrant four-year-old; otherwise physical restraint may be the answer.

Despite their critical capacities and improved reasoning ability, Fours continue to be beset by unreasonable fears—fear of the dark, of monsters, of physically exceptional people, of animals, feathers, cotton, and on and on. This may be due to the growth of their imagination and fantasy. Fours can turn the tiniest fear into an overwhelming giant.

It seems that the gradually maturing social insights and behavior of four-year-olds are at the root of an increase in their alibis, fabrications, assertiveness, and clowning. They are not yet able to separate truth and fantasy. If their deviations from the truth and reality are handled with patience and sensitivity by their caregivers, Fours are bound to pass through this stage of confusion without any emotional scars—and to the great relief of their mothers and fathers.

Fours have begun to realize that other children are separate entities, like themselves in some ways but different in others; that other children also have mothers and fathers, and thoughts and feelings of their own.

Although four-year-olds love a great deal, their hates can be equally strong. Giving a book, record, clothing, or other gift to a four-year-old evokes genuine enthusiasm and appreciation. Fours can be utterly charming and beguiling. But they can be downright obnoxious as well. Their mercurial emotional swings make rearing Fours hectic and even horrible at times; parents never quite know what face or mood their four-year-old will turn up.

Fours may be jealous when their mothers and fathers exhibit closeness. At this stage, strong family feelings are being established.

Four-year-olds are especially interested in becoming five-year-olds.

Distasteful Personal Habits

Nail-biting, nose-picking, thumb-sucking, and the like usually cause excessive parental concern and distress. Often, though not always, they may indicate a deep-lying insecurity that may be hard to ameliorate. Ignoring behavior of this kind is usually the best approach. The use of encouragement in an attempt to help the four-year-old feel at ease is usually the most successful method in alleviating such habits.

Nail-biting

Many Fours bite their nails at one time or another. If your child is one of these, you might review her daily routine and recent happenings in her life to see whether you can ascertain any reasons for her feeling unduly anxious at this time. Many children who bite their nails show no other signs of insecurity. They merely find it an easy activity to resort to when they are bored or fed up, and expedient if they happen to have a rough nail or two. You will not stop this habit—or any other one for that matter—by nagging. However, you may be able to reduce it by making sure that your child's fingernails are kept smooth (you can teach your child how to use an emery board). Colorless nail polish may induce your girl or boy to have neat nails.

Thumb-sucking

There seems to be less thumb-sucking among four-year-olds. However, many Fours may still suck their thumbs when feeling especially insecure, or upon going to sleep at night. In most instances, the thumb-sucking subsides before the fifth or sixth birthday. Parents would be advised not to make too much of this transitory tensional outlet. Examples of deformity of the teeth from inordinate thumb-sucking are relatively rare.

Swearing

Fours usually pick up swear-words from older children or adults by imitation. Most interesting is the fact that the tendency to use language that is objectionable to adults is caused by the reaction of the parents. If the parents show anxiety or irritation, or punish the child for using such words, they will most likely be repeated, even if the child does not know their meaning. Casualness in dealing with this behavior will bring the best results. The child should *not* be punished. Instead, he or she might be reminded that others do not like swearing. Repeat performances, if any, should be ignored.

Though parents should learn not to respond to every negative behavior of their rambunctious four-year-olds, a better approach would be to encourage all acceptable behaviors and to try to use consistent guidelines in dealing with their Fours. One clue as to how successful parents are is how much more they and their children are enjoying their daily life together than when there is a great deal of ongoing wrangling among them. Parents need to remember that children really want to be family members in good standing. They fail in this when they are not able to find enough chances to be "good."

Lying or Stealing

Lying and taking things that belong to others are normal in four-year-olds. Such experiences often are the prelude to the incorporation of honesty in a slowly evolving conscience. Like all the other values that collectively make up an inner system of control, honesty is an abstract concept that a young child gradually internalizes through her interactions with the world around her. Conscience building is a learning process that will take all the first five to seven years of your child's life. Only so much can be expected of a child at any point in the process.

In *On Being Human* (New York: E. P. Dutton, 1967), Ashley Montagu writes that ". . . a child may be able to understand the distinction between what belongs to him and what belongs to others, but this does not mean that he really understands honesty. Knowing that a new ball is his sister's does not decrease his desire for it; acquiring it in any way he can is likely to be more important to him than any abstract idea about honesty."

In order to put your expectations in realistic perspective, it might be helpful to look at how a child's view of honesty changes as her conscience develops. At first, a child sees "good" and "bad" solely in terms of herself, with no awareness of the needs and rights of others. Whatever gives her pleasure is good and what gives her pain is bad. As the child advances in her behavior, she may know that certain acts are right or wrong because of the approval or disapproval of her parents. However, she does not yet understand the broader implications of good or bad behavior. Around age four, the child's curiosity—characterized by her favorite word, *why*—sets the stage for her becoming increasingly conscious of the reasons for the behavior expected of her. Between five and six, she begins to learn ethical behavior at a somewhat abstract level.

Fours Are Neither Thieves Nor Liars

Pediatricians and child psychologists maintain that when one-, two-, and three-year-olds take things that do not belong to them, it is not stealing. They take things because they want them very much, and do not have a clear sense beyond this. "A four-year-old is no more a thief than he is a liar," writes Fitzhugh Dodson. "The four-year-old has no sense of property. At this age, possession is ownership."

How should parents approach this situation? Most child-rearing authorities agree that this is an opportune time to teach the four-year-old in a pleasant but firm manner that he is not permitted to take things that do not belong to him. Making any child feel "wicked" is harmful and inappropriate.

Separating the "real" from the "pretend" is impossible for very young children. Usually when a four-year-old tells a made-up story, she is not lying. She is being carried away by her vivid imagination. However, if such stories make up a major part of her life, it raises the question as to whether your child's real life is satisfying enough. Perhaps the remedy would be to help her enjoy companionship with children her own age and to have more time with you.

How a Conscience Is Built

Conscience is generally defined as a set of standards of acceptable behavior and prohibitions adopted by the personality to govern from within, and resulting in guilt when violated.

Your growing child exhibits his developing conscience when his behavior, formerly so daring and extreme, becomes more cautious and prudent. As Hamlet put it, "Conscience doth make cowards of us all."

Most researchers agree that an internal system of standards that functions without the need of an external "police officer" does not emerge until about the fifth or sixth year. What immediate relevance, then, has a discussion of conscience to parents of preschoolers?

Selma Fraiberg comments that the modes of parental control that are established in the earliest years of life serve as the patterns of conscience in later years. Thus, we can speak of conscience building in the early years before a conscience has even appeared. Freud regarded the development of a conscience as a product of identification. Most authorities view conscience as developing through a child's relations with other people whom she loves, depends upon, and takes on as models—usually the parents.

Understanding the origins and workings of a conscience and maintaining an awareness of their own attitudes will enable parents to facilitate the development of a sound conscience in their children.

A child develops a conscience as he incorporates the customs and values of his family, his neighborhood, and his culture into his own inner monitor. Dr. George Gardner, in *The Emerging Personality* (New York: Delacorte Press, 1970), explains, "We think of the superego or conscience as that process of our inner self which reviews our primitive impulses and evaluates them against the demands of our society."

Children attain a reliable conscience at different ages. A conscience may be solid in one situation, but shaky or nonexistent in another. Vacillation is to be expected. The preschooler's conscience is similar to a microscopic form of life that after bulging in one direction may shrink in another.

Most values are instilled through a small child's observation of the manner in which the parents handle situations in their own lives. Tolerance for the feelings and views of others, for instance, grows out of seeing and identifying with the forbearing behavior of the parents during and after an encounter with someone whose beliefs are different from theirs. The development of a healthy conscience in children is facilitated when adults carry out their responsibilities without fussing about them.

At first parents need to be present to guide their child. As time goes on, he can curb forbidden actions by himself. He knows what you want him to do and tries to do it. This is the beginning of what is called a conscience. A little boy refrains from raiding the cookie jar when his mother is in another room. A little girl shouts "It's mine!" instead of pinching or kicking her playmate. Such restraints on behavior are evidence of real growth.

Fours learn what is acceptable behavior by being told, even more by observation, and to some extent by praise or punishment. Unfortunately, some parents spend more time scolding their children for errors than praising them for acceptable behaviors.

In their efforts to understand the confusing world, small children sometimes become burdened with guilt feelings over trivial incidents. Parents can help their children reduce such feelings by not making them feel foolish. Such statements as "You did something to feel sorry about and it's okay now" or "Now that you have talked about it, you will feel better" can help a child feel unburdened of guilt and respected for her attempts at testing her budding conscience.

The following are some of the ways in which parents can lend support during the various stages of their children's conscience formation: Show faith in each child's ability to take a new step and become more mature. Be consistent in the exercise of firm but reasonable discipline. Avoid being self-righteous when your child does or says something of which you do not approve. Steer clear of the trap of unrealistic expectations.

No one wants a child's conscience to be so overstrict that she loses joy in simply being alive—in her body, in her feelings, in herself.

Sexuality in Children

Sex in the early childhood years is concerned with interest in the body. Sometime after the first year or early in the second, children are taught the names and locations of parts of their bodies: hair, eyes, ears, nose, mouth, chin, arms, hands, fingers, chest, legs, feet, toes, etc. Associated with this teaching is a lot of touching and pointing to various parts with obvious pleasure.

However, very few parents include in these discussions the male and female genitalia (penis, testicles, clitoris, vagina, labia). Young children must eventually reconcile the sensations that make the genitals significant with the fact that adults do not seem to think that genitals are important—maybe they should not feel good; maybe they are "dirty" or "bad." They learn not to talk about these parts because their parents do not want to, and they begin to feel uncomfortable because they have discovered that touching and rubbing their genitals give them special pleasure.

Masturbation

The subject of masturbation is cloaked in untruths that have caused psychological harm to young children and great distress to uninformed parents. Some of the untruths are that masturbating will cause blindness, insanity, impotence, or sterility; that masturbation is a nasty perversion.

The fact of the matter is that *all* young children, including infants, do a certain amount of handling or rubbing of their genitals. Casual, infrequent masturbation should arouse no concern on the part of parents and nursery school teachers. However, when it is practiced immoderately, and to the exclusion of play with peers, it may indicate that the child is deeply troubled. One answer is to find the cause of the child's behavior. According to child psychologists and child-rearing specialists, it is not the masturbation itself that is harmful, but the anxiety and woe it can cause both children and parents.

All young children naturally handle their genitals. Normal children are interested in exploring all parts of their bodies. When they touch their genitals and find that this produces an agreeable sensation, they are likely to repeat the action.

Many adults are not aware that young children do indeed have sexual feelings, and that by manipulating their genitals they experience a degree of sexual pleasure. They also fear that young children who show sexual feelings may grow up to be overly sexed. To repeat: A moderate amount of handling of the sex organs is perfectly normal in young children and should be ignored.

Parents who believe that masturbation is shameful and unhealthy are bound to be troubled when they find their child so engaged. Their response is to try to curb it at once. Actually the first thing they need to do is to stop fretting about masturbation.

Parents who make a scene and tell their children that they are doing something "bad" are merely implanting in them feelings of guilt and poor self-esteem. It has been found that the more children are forced to think about masturbation due to parental emphasis on it, the harder it is for them to curb the impulse. It is best to use casual distraction rather than scolding, threats, punishments, or rewards in efforts to make a young child cease masturbating. A more positive approach would be for parents to keep their children active, to provide the toys and activities their children enjoy the most, and to make sure they have one or two agemates with whom they can play often.

Masturbation causes nothing more serious than an occasional mild genital irritation, except when a child has been made to feel ashamed or guilty about it. Children may masturbate out of boredom, or because they are unhappy and need to console themselves, or just because it feels good. Masturbation in public is embarrassing. It is up to parents to divert their four-year-olds *before* they make it a habit.

Children begin to ask questions about adult sex during their early years. Their questions are normal ones about the differences between boys and girls, where babies come from, etc. How you reply will depend upon the age of your child and the nature of the question. Some four-year-olds may think a baby is born through the navel. It is best to give as concise and accurate an answer as possible.

If you are ill at ease and have trouble answering, your child will get the message that there is something "not nice" about sex. Hence, it is a good idea for you to check whether you have sufficient information to answer such questions in an informed and relaxed manner. If you are uncomfortable with the subject and think you need help, check with your doctor, a child-care authority, or a local librarian as to the many excellent books and pamphlets on sex education written for the parents of children of various ages.

Sex Play

Most parents are perturbed when they discover that their young children are engaged in some form of sex play with their peers. Instead of being upset, parents need to know what their children are doing at all times. This may be an opportune time for parents to discuss bodily functions with their children on a level that is commensurate with their children's stage of maturity.

Children learn very early that sex is a secret matter, that people do not display their sexual urges in public, and that sex is not a topic for open discussion. Hence, sex acquires for them a somewhat hush-hush quality, regardless of parental attitudes.

Role Play During Early Childhood

Role play refers to any activity in which young children assume identities that are different from their own. For example, a forty-nine-month-old boy boasts, "I'm Superman!" Or a fifty-four-month-old girl interrupts her housecleaning play to say to her male playmate, "Don't forget to take your lunch." Or, "You be the policeman and I'll be the nurse."

Spontaneous sex-role activities occur when children are in free-play situations. Not only are sex-role patterns acquired at an early age, they actually are practiced throughout the early childhood years. Role play is clearly a social activity.

A study of sex-role play has revealed that across the age groups of three-and-a-half to four-and-a-half to five-and-a-half, the average amount of sex-role play was 5 percent for younger children and 22 percent for older children.

PLAY, PLAYTHINGS, AND FANTASY

Girls and boys this age can initiate their own play activities. The things and people they see and hear at home, in nursery school, and in the community spark their desire to dramatize all their experiences. In their dramatic play, they usually reveal their confusion about what is real and what is make-believe. Their fantasizing is one way in which they experiment with all kinds of ideas, feelings, and situations.

Fours can assume any number of roles, and as they play, they begin to get a glimmer of understanding of complex social situations. As they build community settings they come to apprehend environmental interdependence. If the toys are large and require cooperation from peers, forty-eight-month-

old children learn that there are basic social amenities to master, as well as tolerance for different personalities and respect for the needs of others. They find that they can be followers or leaders, and they change roles easily. This is the power of play in action.

Fours need many of the play materials at home that are available in a well-organized and supplied nursery school. The push to be active in the adult world is so overwhelming that children of this age group literally act out every family and community worker's role with whatever play materials are at hand. If they do not find the toys or play materials they need, they will create their world with paper boxes, cans, bricks, pieces of wood, etc. However, cans and bricks are not always conducive to play, and paper boxes fall apart when roughly handled. Hence, it is up to parents to provide in the home some of the accouterments a child needs for her fantasy to go to work—a toy world that offers full opportunity for being free and daring.

Construction Play of Four-Year-Olds

This period heralds even more improved manipulative skill so that Fours can undertake all kinds of constructions. Snap

Blocks, Tinkertoys, Lego and Baufix sets, Lincoln Logs, Play-skool Bristle Blocks, and other put-together toys are available for the practice of "engineering" techniques. Fours also enjoy such expressive activities as painting, modeling with clay, making string sculptures, and simple woodworking. They experiment freely with shape, line, color, pattern, form, and distance.

A word of caution is in order here. If children are made to feel that their efforts do not meet adult standards, they may withdraw from trying anything new, and some may develop a deep-seated sense of inferiority.

Dramatic Play of Four-Year-Olds

Make-believe play appears to be at its zenith at this time. Boys especially enjoy chasing games, as personified in Cowboys and Indians, for which only a few suggestive props are required (a three-gallon hat, a coil of rope, colorful bandana, headband, some feathers, etc.). Girls and boys participate happily together in the roles of doctors and nurses. For this pretend play, a real stethoscope, Band-Aids, and some tongue depressors are all that are needed.

Four-year-olds thrive on variety. Parents can spark other forms of make-believe play by introducing novel props when their children want to transform themselves into various characters. For example, a folding fan, castanets, and a shawl will be appreciated by a young Spanish dancer. Barber shop play will be enhanced with a comb, brush, shaving cream, bladeless shaver, paper towels, etc.

A log cabin, corrugated carton playhouse, or cloth tent will spur hours of backyard fantasy play. Providing some pieces of furniture (a small table, stools, etc.), a non-breakable child-size tea set, and plastic tumblers, along with real cookies and fruit juice, fosters unlimited play possibilities.

Play with Puppets

Fours begin to really breathe life into hand and finger puppets, though they are not yet able to properly manipulate stringed puppets (marionettes). You can purchase a simple puppet stage or make one yourself out of a sturdy corrugated carton. Coloring faces on brown lunch bags is an enjoyable and inexpensive way to make lots of paper hand puppets.

More Involved Block Play

At this age, boys and girls extend their play with building blocks to include acting out community worker roles. Their block constructions are limited only by the amount of blocks they have on hand. In-scale toy transportation vehicles, play people, and animals serve to extend their imaginative endeavors.

When playing with a friend or two at home, block play can degenerate into the flinging of blocks because Fours often go out of bounds. Parents will know the time has come for them to intervene when they hear wild laughter, or crying, or other unusual noise emanating from their children's playrooms. The comforting thought here is that it is possible for parents to restore peace and order because most four-year-olds will respond positively to the admonitions of adults.

Playing with Dolls

Fours love to play with dolls, for the most part putting them to bed, but also dressing and undressing favorite dolls or teddy bears. (At some time during the forty-nine- to sixty-month period, girls begin to want to play with little girl dolls rather than baby dolls per se.) Housekeeping activities often are dovetailed with doll play, and include reenactments of the caregiving Fours have experienced or still see being carried on by their parents for a baby sibling.

Fours are not yet really interested in dollhouse play. However, miniature dollhouse figures and furniture (if sturdy and simple) are fine accessories for enhancing block-built houses and furthering family-life play.

Outdoor Play Environment

These children flirt with danger. They will climb over walls, up trees, and over one another, often managing to get into awkward and even hazardous predicaments in the process. They use equipment in unorthodox ways; for instance, they will walk up a slide and not use it just for sliding down. Therefore, outdoor equipment for Fours needs to be challenging, but relatively free from danger. One answer is a balanced assortment of portable wood or metal equipment that would pose challenges and provide fun, as well as a wide margin of safe manageability by the children. When children are in control of the hollow blocks, planks, ladders, sawhorses, etc., they are in control of themselves, too.

When Fours want to test their balancing skill, for example, they put a plank on top of two low hollow blocks and then gradually increase the height to that of two sawhorses or packing crates. They learn from experience how to avoid hurting themselves and others.

Means of mastering potential danger can be incorporated into physical play equipment. Ladders and slides without handrails will teach a child physical coordination and competence. A cut-down tree trunk with the bark stripped off and placed horizontally on or near the ground is a relatively safe challenge. Good sense and courage need to be inculcated in children in their early years. That is why nursery schools deliberately provide this kind of "adventure" equipment.

Portable outdoor equipment can serve as well for the imaginative play of Fours. The girls and boys combine the pieces in ingenious ways to form a large boat, a playhouse, etc., thus making the play environment work for them.

Most public playgrounds are a disaster area for young children. It would appear that they are designed by adults who do not know the needs of preschool children. Often they are bleak, open spaces paved with asphalt, offering no protection from sun or wind. There rarely is a toilet facility close at hand. Usually there is no water in a drinking fountain. Some playgrounds boast a few metal pipe structures for gymnastics surrounded by a wire fence. Dramatic play and appropriate physical explorations do not flourish here. The movements of swings are unpredictable and unsafe. Boredom from doing the same thing repeatedly often leads a child to attempt some dangerous variation. Instead of being a safe and pleasant atmosphere for physical play and social interaction with peers, such a playground can become a battleground where each child is on his or her own.

In the small towns of yesteryear, a young child could go everywhere—to the blacksmith's, a milking barn, the town grocery, or the hardware store. As adults worked at their occupations, the child would be there watching and, if old enough, sometimes even pitching in to help. Children did not need a "special" place for playing—they had woods and fields, the backyard, and safe pathways on which to adventure. The arrangement of today's cities permit the young child very little direct contact with the dynamics of the adult world. For this reason, there is an urgent need for dramatic changes in our public playgrounds.

The Importance of Nursery School

A nursery school offers four-year-olds a wide variety of playthings and opportunities for group play. Fours are stimulated socially and intellectually by their contact with agemates, the nursery school teacher, and the activities and events that are built into the nursery school schedule.

Block building sessions also provide opportunities for pretend play. As the result of a trip to an airport, for instance, a few

children may recreate an airport with an observation tower, runways, hangars, jet planes, etc., and they may play at being pilots for several days. Four-year-olds become increasingly adept "architects." Their block structures indicate some pre-planning and careful execution. As several Fours cooperate in building an extensive layout, each one is actually practicing tenets of sharing and helpfulness.

During daily group discussions in nursery school, four-year-olds are alive with talk and questions. They may discuss a simple phase of science, perhaps nature study or zoology. There usually are a few small animals in the nursery school room—gerbils, rabbits, turtles, fish, snakes, etc. Or they may review their individual reactions to what they saw and heard on a group trip. The children also take turns talking about their weekend experiences at home.

In the nursery school, no child sits or stands about unoccupied. Fours enjoy painting, clay modeling, very simple weaving, and elementary woodworking. Most four-year-olds concentrate longer than three-year-olds. Fifteen minutes to half an hour is an average; a few children will concentrate for almost an hour. They like handling all kinds of expressive materials and enjoy the ability to change what they are making as they go along.

Fours create more defined forms in their drawing and painting. They paint masses of color next to each other instead of over one another. A circle may suggest a head to a four-year-old, who may embellish it by putting facial features in it. Fours tend to use the whole sheet of paper. They may start a painting with a definite notion of what they wish to create, or they may improvise as they go along.

Four-year-olds try to make specific things with clay, shaping and adding clay rather than taking apart and starting again. They have more definite designs in mind when they select materials for making a collage. Fours like to form wire or pipe cleaners into mobiles or other constructions. Most require help with tying or joining loose parts.

In addition to drawing, painting, clay modeling, and collage making, four-year-olds enjoy such other forms of creative expression as music, dance, and mimicry. In fact, their most important activity at this time is their spontaneous imaginative play.

In *Children Are Artists* (Stanford, CA: Stanford University Press, 1953, revised edition 1963), Daniel M. Mendelowitz writes, "Uninhibited children participate eagerly in all forms of artistic expression. They sing, dance, draw, paint, model, and build naturally and unself-consciously . . . If a child hesitates about expressing himself . . . it is because some adult has done something to inhibit his free participation in these forms of play."

Many young and older children become inhibited from expressing themselves in the various art media because there still are parents and teachers who place too much emphasis on neatness and adult standards of artistic perfection. Mr. Mendelowitz believes that "Inadvertently we often say or do things which make a child feel that he cannot paint or draw or build or make things with clay . . . As time passes, this negative attitude solidifies into what is known as a lack of ability or talent."

No one is born a talented artist. "The talented child . . . is a child who has received . . . sufficient satisfaction from a certain kind of activity to participate in it more frequently and with more intensity than do most of the children in the same age group, and so has developed his capacities beyond the average of his group."

Trips Extend Horizons

Fours have ever-widening interests. They want to see new things they have heard about and find out more about familiar objects. Visits to an airport, farm, kennel, garage, fish market, police station, firehouse, even a museum, are likely to give

them much pleasure, and add to their fund of information. They like especially to go behind the scenes. Such experiences pave the way to social studies programs later on in kindergarten and first grade.

TV—the Electronic Baby-Sitter

Almost all four-year-olds watch television. For the parents, it is an electronic baby-sitter; for the children, it can become too passively engrossing. The parents and not the children should decide which programs their Fours should watch. (Incidentally, this is a good time for you to arrange for your four-year-old to have a thorough eye examination.)

IQ and Reading

Parents should not worry about increasing the IQ scores of their four-year-olds, but they can provide understanding, sincere interest, and appropriate stimulation. To satisfy the insatiable curiosity of Fours, parents need a wealth of readily available information upon which to draw.

There are so many different points of view as to when a child should start learning to read and by what method that parental confusion is inevitable in this area. Many experts agree that most children before the age of seven do not possess the relationship-thinking abilities, patience, and self-discipline that are demanded by the techniques of reading. Of course, there are precocious children who learn how to read with some understanding of content by their fifth birthdays.

The watchword is: Don't push!

This is a prime time for children to develop initiative and daring. Girls and boys who have had lots of positive experiences are the ones who will feel confident to handle the new and the different now and in their ongoing years. They will have the assurance that they can start anything from scratch, and they will not fear the possibility of making mistakes. Above all, they will not be afraid to play with ideas.

Fours are eager to try anything. They have a special love affair with everything that is novel to them. Most childhood educators believe in postponing counting, reading, and other academic learning at this time in favor of countless opportunities for free creative play.

Fours seek recognition from adults for their play and art creations. Their paintings and drawings should be hung on a bulletin board for everyone to enjoy. Building block constructions might be kept intact a few days until Dad and Mom have had a chance to acknowledge their child's very real accomplishments. A child's stories or poetry should be set down on paper by the parent (if so inclined, the child can also illustrate these) and the finished work read and enjoyed by the whole family.

The play of four-year-olds can be creative or chaotic, depending upon how parents prepare the environment and the kinds of play materials they provide. Parents need to keep in mind that four-year-olds can be rough and careless with toys.

There is a tendency to change the decor of a child's room only once, and the furniture only twice—from a crib to a bed, from a low table to a desk. A change of play equipment and of the use of space are indicated each time a child has passed a landmark in development. Skimping in this area shortchanges a child.

The Child Who Does Not Play: Play Therapy

Childhood appears to be a trial run when children are given the time they need to find out about themselves, other people, and the universe in which they live. In the course of growing up some children develop different kinds of emotional problems: fears of many kinds, feelings of hostility, aggressive behavior, lack of self-esteem, anxieties, poor social adjustment, intense jealousy, extreme shyness, showing off, and withdrawal being the most prominent among them. Disturbed children suffer, too, from unconscious feelings of guilt.

Since no one can determine exactly what goes on in a child's mind or get a child to talk like an adult, specialists who work with distressed children have found that much can be learned about them from watching them at play, during which most children reveal both their imaginary and their real lives. As the most natural form of expression of young children, play can also expose their inner conflicts and immaturity.

One of the most striking characteristics of an anxious child is a strong inhibition of play activity. Often such a child is not able to play at all. Even in a relaxed, well-equipped nursery school, she may remain tense and incapable of doing anything with any of the playthings. Other traits of the neurotic child are lack of constructiveness and an overpowering impulse to destroy. When she does play, the disturbed child (whether emotionally ill or mentally retarded) acts as if she were younger than her chronological years.

Every small child recreates a world of fantasy for himself at some time. Some children, however, sink too deeply into the world of their own thoughts and feelings, and so lose contact with reality. At some point the healthy child grasps the difference between fantasy and reality, and at eight or nine years of age becomes involved in explorations of the world of real people, things, and situations. The normal child wants to understand himself and the adult world; the disturbed child cannot make this transition.

The nature of a child's play can indicate the type of disturbance that underlies it. Children who are meticulously clean and avoid "dirty" or "messy" play, who arrange toys in neat patterns only, who dislike painting and shun finger painting, whose drawings are "dominated by rulers and compasses,"

who play silently and alone, or keep up a constant unintelligible chatter to hide their deepest feelings during their obsessional play, indicate a rigidity that can mask a serious problem.

Constant reversion to an earlier level of maturity and the compulsion to use materials that are charged with symbolic significance (sand, water, or fire) might signify some early unresolved conflict or overly strict home training.

The child who aimlessly handles every toy in a playroom without playing with any one thing, and who starts half a dozen games only to drop each one moments later, is also indicating some grave problems. The child whose play is accompanied by explosive excitement and who loses control of whatever she may be doing (for example, throws clay about wildly or destroys the constructions of her playmates) may be signifying deeply buried inner turmoil. Such conflicts can only be uncovered by careful professional observation and analysis of the child as she is helped to play and to talk in the ameliorating atmosphere of the play therapy room or clinic.

It was the late Dr. Anna Freud, one of the pioneers of psychoanalysis for young children through the use of play therapy, who recognized that "the daydreams of children and activity of their fantasy in play is equivalent to the free associations of adults in analysis."

The denial of reality is one of the particular features of play in general and especially in games of make-believe. The elements for constructing a pleasurable world of fantasy and play are readily available to children. The task of the child analyst is to get the emotionally disturbed child to separate fantasy from fact, and to help him assimilate reality into his personal scheme of things. Fantasy is the name given to a kind of daydreaming that is the opposite of controlled thought.

For severely troubled children from three years of age and up, regular visits to a play therapist have proved effective in

relieving them of emotional conflicts that often find expression in excessive temper tantrums, bed-wetting after five or six years of age, withdrawal, or general destructiveness. By bringing out into the open the fears or anxieties that are distressing or immobilizing the child, and by sharing them with a tolerant grown-up (the play therapist), her terrors usually become less terrifying, and frequently will subside.

"Lack of ability to play is not natural and is not an inborn characteristic," writes Margaret Lowenfeld in her book, *Play in Childhood* (New York: John Wiley & Sons, 1967). "It is a neurosis and should be reckoned with as such. Children who fail in their ability to play with their fellows are children with characteristics that will make them unable to combine with their fellows in later life." She goes on to say that "Play is an essential function of the passage from immaturity to emotional maturity. Any individual without the opportunities for adequate play in early life will go on seeking them in the stuff of adult life."

HEALTH, SELF-HELP, AND ROUTINES

Fours who attend nursery school may have one cold after another throughout the winter. Children from about two to six years of age appear to be especially susceptible to cold germs. Their colds can last three days or up to three weeks. Young children are also likely to have throat infections. Frequently they have a high fever when ill. Bed rest depends upon the nature of the cold and the age of the child.

Nose and throat irritation can be ameliorated by having the child breathe warm, moist air. Nose drops should *not* be used unless prescribed by the doctor; the same applies to the use of cough medicine. Most often, unless fever is present, parents see their children through mild colds without seeking medical help. Although colds are usually not critical, sometimes young children may develop such complications as bronchitis, sinusitis, or ear infection.

Many four-year-old boys and girls can experience disagreeable stomachaches when they are tense or overly upset. Their distress is real, not imagined. Some children may even throw up. When calmed by the ministrations of their caring parents, such stomachaches tend to pass away.

Inasmuch as Fours are veritable whirligigs and daring acrobats, they are accident-prone. Their front teeth are highly vulnerable. When they fall on their faces, often one or two of their front teeth are knocked out. If a tooth is knocked out, take your child—and the tooth—immediately to your dentist. Baby teeth can sometimes be put back into place so that they reattach themselves if you secure dental help speedily enough. If the tooth cannot be put back into position, your dentist must decide whether to leave your child with a gap until the second teeth come in or whether to replace it with a temporary false tooth.

Four-year-olds may cry or whine when they feel insecure and unsure of themselves. "Growing pains" is an apt descriptive. Each age and stage of growth and development present their own stresses and strains, challenges and problems. Luckily, there are countless delights and satisfactions along the bumpy way for both children and their parents.

Dressing

Four-year-olds require less supervision in their home lives. They can dress and undress themselves with minimal assistance. They can lace their shoes, but not tie shoelaces or bows. They are able to tell the front from the back of their clothing. Some Fours are adept at buttoning buttons if they are not too small or in hard-to-reach places.

If their interest in taking off and putting on their clothes has been encouraged all along, young children will be able to do a creditable dressing job by the time they are four. However, they will still require help with snowsuits, tight rubbers, boots, etc.

Bathing and Washing

Fours are able to wash themselves with only minimal supervision. They have a tendency to wash the same part repeatedly.

Boys like to sail boats while they are bathing. Girls like to wash rubber dolls. Both like to let the water in the tub run down and gurgle away. They will try to clean the tub. Their drying of themselves is so-so, which calls for parents to finish the job.

With "no-tears" shampoos, hair-washing need never become an unhappy tussle. Girls and boys can comb their hair, albeit not up to the standard of neatness of their parents.

Four-year-olds cannot cut their fingernails or toenails, but parents can give them a role in the process. Let your child use an emery board to smooth his or her nails. Toenails need to be cut straight across. Children can clean them with an orange stick.

Care of the Teeth

Four-year-olds can brush their teeth at bedtime and before breakfast in the morning.

To insure good dental health, young children need an adequate diet, proper care of the teeth at home, and regular dental checkups, with cleaning and, when required, dental repair. The pedodontist (a dentist specializing in the care and treat-

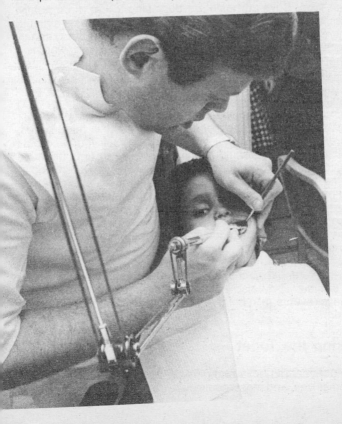

ment of children's teeth) should be capable and friendly with children.

Four-year-olds like to use a dental "disclosing tablet" that harmlessly stains red those teeth that are covered with plaque. Brushing the red off the teeth is a challenge. When the red is gone, children and parents know that the teeth are clean. The dentist will show you and your child the proper way to use dental floss between all the teeth.

Eating and Table Manners

Forty-nine-month-old children are quite efficient with spoon, fork, and glass or mug, but they are not able to cut up their food. Boys and girls are beginning to eat more neatly. Inasmuch as handling utensils has become less difficult, Fours can talk and eat at the same time. However, they sometimes get carried away with their own storytelling or watching other people. As their attention gets directed elsewhere, glasses of juice, milk, or water can be spilled.

You can teach your young children acceptable table manners by example rather than by nagging. Eventually they will behave at the dinner table as the other family members do.

With the best of intentions, but needlessly in most cases, parents worry about the amount of food their four-year-olds consume. There should be no fussing by parents because healthy children eat what their bodies need, provided wholesome, balanced meals are presented to them every day.

Fours like to select their own menus. They are apt to go on food jags, wanting the same foods again and again. They may also flatly refuse certain foods. If any midmorning or early afternoon snacks are made available, they should consist only of nonjunk food items: carrot or celery strips, apple or banana slices, cubes of natural cheese, etc.

Understandably, children eat less when they are overtired or excited. They also eat less before, during, and after an illness (even a mild cold). As children recover, their appetites return.

Using the Toilet

Four-year-old boys and girls are able to go to the toilet by themselves, and most require little help. Although intrigued by the bathroom activities of others, they may insist on privacy for themselves. Parents can gradually promote the idea that grown-ups prefer to be alone while in the bathroom, and that older children also have a right to privacy.

In a distressful situation, a four-year-old may suddenly feel the need to void. If a toilet is not close at hand, an accident may follow. Some children may lose control of their sphincter muscles when they are especially perturbed.

Fears

Fours are quite fearful, due in part to their vivid imaginations. Boys and girls may be afraid of monsters, ghosts, witches, goblins, and so on. Fours who are afraid or timid require wholehearted reassurance, not adverse criticism or derision. Parents must never reproach their fearful children, nor permit siblings to make fun of them. With sufficient experience and considerate nurturing, the fears will go away.

Napping

After lunch, Fours will take a play-nap of an hour or so, whether at home or at nursery school. This involves rest or looking quietly at picture books or playing with some toys on their beds. Some children may actually fall asleep.

Although four-year-olds will try to put off going to bed at night, most fall asleep in a short time. They like to take a favorite stuffed animal or soft doll to bed with them. Boys and girls will express affection for their parents at bedtime with a goodnight kiss and a big hug.

Nightmares

Nightmares are relatively common with four- and five-year-olds. They are not abnormal unless they occur night after night, or are accompanied by night terrors. Generally, nightmares disappear for most children by the time they are about six or seven years old.

A nightmare may be an indication of a temporary normal anxiety. All children are deeply concerned about certain things, and sometimes their fears will manifest themselves in this manner.

The best way to treat a nightmare is to get to your child without delay after he first cries out, and to turn the lights on in his room. Your calming presence will comfort him. However, when children are allowed to scream themselves fully awake, restoring them to peace and quiet takes extra affectionate patting and reassurance. It is best to remain in the room with your child until he starts to sleep again.

Night terrors are rarer than nightmares. Most four-year-olds never experience them. Actually only a few children have them more than once in a great while. The first signal of a night terror is the same as a nightmare—frightened crying or screaming. When you reach your child, she will appear to be in a trance, neither asleep nor awake. Put on all the lights in the room at once. Do not try to reason with your terror-stricken child. Just try to remain on as even a keel as you possibly can because this is a frightening episode for the child.

If your child gets out of bed during a night terror, try to pick him up gently and then soothe him back to relaxation. Should your child wake up from a night terror, just tell him that he had a bad dream. Usually the terror goes away, and the child returns to normal sleep without knowing what has transpired.

No one knows why some children have night terrors and others do not, or even where a nightmare ends and a night terror begins. Parents need to try to find the underlying cause (or causes) of the child's tension and to remove it. If the origin is not evident, talking the matter over with your doctor may provide you with some helpful insights and answers.

Thumb-sucking

Many four-year-olds may suck their thumbs when they are fatigued, bored, or very sleepy; also when they are hungry or not feeling well. Some Fours suck their thumbs when they are reprimanded, lonesome, or otherwise unhappy.

When children feel that they are valued and loved, turning to thumb-sucking for solace usually disappears. Nagging, punishing, teasing, or bribing are of no more avail with this nervous habit than with any other behavior triggered by insecurity, lack of self-esteem, dejection, and so on.

Growth Chart—49th Through 60th Month

MOTOR DEVELOPMENT

Gross Motor

Most can hop on one foot from 4 to 6 steps.

43% of 4-year-olds accomplish rudimentary galloping (skipping on one foot, walking on another).

Locomote skillfully; turn sharp corners.

Run, roll, climb ladders and trees.

Sit with knees crossed.

Motor driven: take pleasure swirling, swinging, somersaulting.

Can jump down from a two-foot height with feet together.

Use hands more than arms in catching a small ball.

Ride tricycle and manipulate U-turns efficiently.

Walk up and downstairs one foot to a step.

Fine Motor

Can use blunt-nosed scissors well.

Can cut on a line with scissors.

At 4, draw picture of human figure with head, body, arms, legs.

At 4½, add eyes, hair, ears, hands, feet to drawing of human figure.

Can copy following capital letters and forms: O, V, H, T, +

Thread small beads to create necklace; can't thread needle.

LANGUAGE ACQUISITION

Talking vocabulary reaches 1,550 by 4 years; 1,900 words by 4½ years.

Can name a penny, nickel, or dime as they point to them.

Can say "hello," "goodbye," "thank you," "please."

Increasing interest in TV.

Able to clearly say first and last names.

Know own sex.

Use sentences of 5 to 6 words.

Love to play with words.

Still have difficulty adding correct endings to words.

Begin to learn the rules for making plurals (one bird, two birds).

Ask why, when, how questions and word meanings constantly.

Can argue with words as well as fists.

Still use forbidden words learned from peers: "dirty pee pee," "poopie pants."

Can be violent in their storytelling: stress death, killing, objects that crash, fall down or break, etc.

Confuse fact with fiction in children's books.

Can identify 10 objects from a picture.

Enjoy jokes, silly or funny books, silly language.

SENSORY POWERS/LEARNING

Can count 3 objects with correct pointing.

Can count to 30 by rote memory.

Can develop the order of magnitude of heaviest to lightest of five blocks.

Can demonstrate biggest and longest of three things.

Beginning to grasp a sense of the seasons and activities related to each season.

Can name and match 4 primary colors.

Distinguish between lateral, vertical, and horizontal lines.

Mastering use of space words (back and front, under and over, in, on, up, etc.).

Growth Chart—49th Through 60th Month

Sensory Powers/Learning, cont'd

Developing a sense of time (as expressed in the words *days, months, minutes, time to go to bed,* etc.).

SOCIAL DEVELOPMENT

Strong feeling for family and home.

Concern for younger children in distress or baby sibling.

Can be aggressive with older sibling.

A glimmer of cooperation.

Understand need to share and take turns.

Respond to verbal and physical limitations: "As far as the corner." "It's a rule that we do not hit other children."

Interested in and ready for group activity.

Play groups become larger; competition emerges between groups.

Love to whisper and have secrets.

Prefer companionship of children to adults.

Play with imaginary playmates.

Tendency in play groups for a division along sex lines: boys play with boys, girls with girls.

PERSONALITY/ PSYCHOLOGICAL

Sensitive to praise and blame.

Tend to go "out of bounds"; tell tall tales.

Are very noisy.

May take objects that are not their own.

May still suck thumb on going to bed.

Boys may clutch their genitals when overanxious.

Interest in marriage and marrying; propose to opposite-sex parent.

Cling to notion that babies are purchased.

Questions about how babies get out of mother's stomach.

Extremely conscious of navel; think babies are born through navel.

Brag, boast, exaggerate (expanding sense of self).

Beginning awareness of "good" and "bad."

Exhibit some self-criticism.

Growth Chart—49th Through 60th Month

PLAY AND PLAYTHINGS	HEALTH, SELF-HELP, AND ROUTINES
Enjoy active outdoor play.	Seem to have colds all winter, aggravated by nursery school attendance.
Enjoy water and sand play in and out of doors.	Wash hands, face; brush teeth (need some supervision).
Can play outdoors without too much supervision.	Verbal play about elimination, such as "you old bowel movement."
Enjoy construction toys: Lego, Tinkertoys, miniature blocks, etc.	Interested in other people's bathrooms; demand privacy for themselves; curious about bathroom activity of others.
Like to do jigsaw puzzles.	
Enjoy performing arts projects: finger puppets, shadow plays.	Most dry during the day, but accidents occur.
Enjoy sewing cards; "sewing" on cloth with long needle.	Majority dry all night if awakened at midnight.
Like to dress up in adult clothing and role play.	One bowel movement after breakfast or lunch common.
Dramatic play themes may continue for 20 minutes or more.	Appetite at 4½ years to 5 years increases.
Active doll and homemaking play.	Handle fork and spoon skillfully, but not a knife.
Painting, drawing, coloring more successful.	Can pour milk from a pitcher without spilling.
Enjoy finger painting, clay modeling.	Dress and undress if supervised.
Interested in snakes, frogs, and especially turtles, that can be cared for in a terrarium.	Some lace their shoes.
	Sleep 11 hours or longer.
	Most have play-nap or no nap at all.
	Night waking and wandering disappear.
	At 4½ years, troubled by bad dreams (wolves, etc.).
	The brain, spinal cord, nerves reach almost full adult size by 4 to 6 years, with little growth thereafter.
	Genital tissue does not grow rapidly in early years.
	Respond well to "E" eye test.

Dear Parents:

Do not regard this chart as a rigid timetable.
Young children are unpredictable individuals.
Some perform an activity earlier or later than
this chart indicates.

Just use this information to anticipate and appreciate normal child development and behavior.
No norms are absolute.

CHAPTER EIGHT

The 61st Through 72nd Month of Life

When I was One,
I had just begun.
When I was Two,
I was nearly new.
When I was Three,
It was hardly Me.
When I was Four,
I was not much more.
When I was Five,
I was just alive.

But now I am Six,
I'm as clever as clever.
So I think I'll be six
Now and for ever and ever.
　　　A. A. Milne,
　　　The End
　　　(from *Now We Are Six*)

Most professionals agree that the early childhood years end at the seventy-second month of life, and that *average* five-year-olds may not be ready for the demands and complexities of reading, writing, and arithmetic for another year or two. Nonetheless, our culture, by law, has stipulated a child's sixth birthday as the entrance date into the world of academe, when a child begins formal instruction in the three R's in the first grade of elementary school.

"Five years," says David Melton, author of *How to Help Your Preschooler Learn . . . More . . . Faster . . . & Better* (New York: David McKay, 1976), "is all the time parents have to give of themselves in the education of their young children before outsiders—teachers, peer groups, television—take over the hours of their day. Hopefully, as a result of your intensive personal efforts during this short period, your child has developed into an active, inquisitive child, eager to learn and, better still, to function as a loving, caring, intelligent, creative human being throughout his adult life."

"Five is a nodal age," according to Drs. Gesell and Ilg, "which marks both the end and the beginning of a growth epoch . . . [the child] has come a long distance on the upward winding pathway of development . . . Although by no means a finished product, the five-year-old already gives token of the adult he or she is to be."

Fives are relatively free of their mothers' hovering. Most appear to enjoy the separation caused by attendance at kindergarten. Five-year-olds have a better understanding of the world, both physical and social, and their own place in it. They are no longer as completely dependent upon their parents as they were even a year ago. They are commencing to pay attention to the opinions and expectations of other children, in addition to those of their parents.

Their social world has expanded. Fives are able to spend many hours away from home with adults other than their parents. As their facility with language forges ahead, their play with peers takes on characteristics that presage the interpersonal relationships they will form later in life. By the end of this period, children are capable of a higher level of reasoning and learning.

"To parents," wrote the late Dorothy H. Cohen, author of *The Learning Child* (New York: Pantheon Books, 1972), "five is at last the age when reason and dialogue promise the long awaited behavior that is close to the adults' own; to children, Five is power and strength, to be tested and expressed with as full a measure of autonomy as they dare take."

Physically, by age five, the child's body proportions, although still immature, increasingly begin to resemble those of the adult. She no longer looks like a baby. The brain of the five-year-old has reached 75 percent of its ultimate weight. Muscles and bones have grown stronger, too, permitting greater control of motor skills. Fives can use their hands and legs competently. They walk, run, skip, hop, jump, and climb easily and naturally. They can traverse straight and circular lines, descend stairs alternating their feet, as well as alternate their feet while skipping. Most mid- or older Fives are exploring the

techniques of balance on a two-wheeler. They climb with sure-ness from one object to another. Although they evince interest in stilts and roller skates, Fives are not able to really manage them.

Handedness is usually set by age five. Ninety percent of all children in the United States are right-handed; twins com-monly are left-handed. (Heredity *may* be a factor in handed-ness.) Left-handed children usually require special help in learning to write. It is best not to interfere with a child who clearly indicates preference for the use of the left hand. Five-year-olds are able to distinguish the right from the left hand in themselves—but not in others.

The eye-hand coordination of Fives is not yet in complete control. They may have trouble trying to get at things beyond arm's length. They can unintentionally spill or knock things over.

Five-year-olds normally are farsighted. Therefore, they should not be allowed to spend too much time examining small things at close range.

Intellectually, Five is a voluble talker with a vocabulary of around 2,000 words. His articulation has improved. He uses connectives more often to describe an event. In their dramatic play with friends, Fives conduct a "kind of collective dialogue." Most appear to ramble out of bounds. It may be that this type of language use permits five-year-olds to fantasize and avoid some of the bonds of reality.*

Fives are able to match ten colors, and can correctly name at least four primary colors.

Almost all Fives are ready for simple principles of science and mathematics. Although their interest can be sparked by hearing stories in these areas, they also require lots of opportunities to watch and take part in simple experiments. They appreciate nature stories, and enjoy watching and caring for animals, plants, fish, and insects. Taking nature walks and collecting natural objects are very popular with five-year-olds.

A few Fives are ready to read, and some do so. Others pretend that they can read by telling a story as they turn the pages of a picture book. If a five-year-old wishes to be able to read, the chance to learn should be granted. Physical development as well as mental ability of each child needs to be taken into account before a formal reading program is started in kindergarten.

Socially, Fives are pleasant to live with. They are cooperative and will help with household tasks. They give and receive love from both parents. They thrive on affection and praise and like to be told how well they are doing. Fives play well with siblings because they are less bossy. Most are devoted to a younger sibling.

Fives play best with children their own age. Generally they accept both sexes in their kindergarten and home play. They

*Adapted from *The Child from Five to Ten* by Arnold Gesell, M.D., and Frances Ilg, M.D. (New York: Harper & Row, 1946).

still function best in a group of two. With supervision, they are able to accept a third member in the group.

Five-year-olds seek adult help and guidance. They get along fairly well with parents and teachers, at least for the first six to eight months of the fifth year. Inasmuch as most Fives are more at ease, they transmit a feeling of stability and competence.

Emotionally, Fives "don't go off on wild tangents" as do Fours. They are more deliberate, and most think before they speak. Five-year-olds may continue to have fears and anxieties about strange noises, darkness, wild animals, being alone, separation from mother, etc. However, these concrete fears are temporary and go away. Fives are just beginning to be able to differentiate between fact and fantasy.

PLAY AND FANTASY

The eye-hand performance of Fives is practically that of an adult. Fives handle well all kinds of puzzles and other manipulative and construction toys. They are avid players and users of the construction toys and raw materials of play available in a kindergarten. They paint, draw, color, cut, and paste with enthusiasm and a good degree of skill. Unit building blocks are the preferred play materials of both boys and girls. Fives like to build "big" and will stand on chairs to make sure that their structures are taller than they are. Girls continue to engage in domestic play. Although most boys will join in this type of play, others prefer more active games.

In their dramatic play, Fives can identify more easily with adults. They create both realistic and imaginative characterizations and develop these parts into far more involved play schemes than they could only a year ago.

Many five-year-olds cease chasing from one activity to another. They know what they want to do on a specific day, and will even carry a project over to the next day. An increase in perceptual awareness is indicated in their drawings and paintings. Many have passed the stage of just daubing paint; they want to create something, and they have a real feeling of accomplishment when they complete a picture. They like to show their products to their teachers and take them home for their parents to admire.

Kindergarten teachers do not experience difficulties with

the sex questions and exposure problems that are rampant among four-year-olds. Fives are more modest and will rarely expose their genitals.

All in all, it can be said that five-year-old boys and girls are a delight to their mothers and fathers.

GROSS-MOTOR DEVELOPMENT

Five-year-olds may be expected to grow two or three inches during the year and to gain from three to six pounds. Of course, they vary in the amount they gain, depending partly

upon their total body size. Although boys are often slightly taller and heavier than girls, five-year-old girls are usually about a year ahead of boys in their physiological development. A strong correlation exists between height at preschool age and in adulthood; a child who is taller than average at five years has a 70 percent chance of becoming a tall adult.

The physical growth of Fives is uneven. Their legs lengthen more quickly than other parts of their bodies, their lungs are still relatively small, and their hearts are developing rapidly. Their large muscles are more developed than the small muscles that control the use of the fingers. Hence, many five-year-olds are not ready for the demands of writing.

Fives are active and noisy, but less restless than a year ago. They run faster, climb higher and more freely, and are full of vigor and the joy of life.

Fives keep time to music when they dance, and they are more mature in their sense of balance. Five-year-old boys and girls enjoy dancing and gymnastics, and show advancement in these areas.

By five, girls and boys can run with reasonable speed. Studies indicate that five-year-old children can travel approximately 11.5 feet per second. They are able to broad-jump a distance of 2 to 3 feet. They can clear a height of about 1 foot when asked to jump over a low hurdle. By five years, children have achieved sufficient balance, strength, and endurance to be able to hop the distance of 50 feet in eleven seconds (girls excel boys in this type of physical feat). Fives are able to balance on one foot for 4 to 10 seconds, and can bend and touch their toes without bending their knees. They are able to walk a narrow line without falling off for a distance of 10 feet.*

Five-year-olds are competent riding a tricycle, and many are ready to learn to ride a small bicycle. Before their seventy-second month, most children will have learned how to mount, start, balance, and stop on two-wheelers that are scaled to their sizes.

Five-year-old girls and boys like to do all kinds of acrobatics and stunts, including somersaults, handstands, jumping from two- to three-feet heights, climbing *up* a slide, sliding down head first, swinging up in the air, etc.

Fives have learned to catch, throw, and kick adequately

*From *Perceptual and Motor Development in Infants and Young Children* by Bryant J. Cratty (New York: Macmillan, 1970).

enough to play many kinds of ball games with their agemates. They are adept at catching a large playground ball.

FINE-MOTOR DEVELOPMENT

Five-year-olds can hold a pencil or crayon between the thumb and first two fingers, essentially an adult grasp. They can copy in recognizable form a circle, cross, square, and, by five-and-a-half, a triangle. They still have trouble drawing the oblique lines in a diamond shape. They now draw a human figure with a head, trunk, legs, arms, and facial features. There will be a door, windows, and a chimney on a house. A tree may also embellish the picture. Now they say what they are going to draw before they begin: "I'm going to make a garden."

Fives can copy their names. They are able to form the capital letters *V, T, H, O, X, Y, U, C,* and *A.* They can now thread a large needle and sew real stitches.

LANGUAGE ACQUISITION

Fives usually speak clearly and are well understood. They use plurals, pronouns, and tenses correctly, and in well-constructed sentences. They love to talk and carry on long conversations (which, however, reveal considerable naiveté). They are great at telling stories, and like to tell their teachers what happened at home, and their parents about the day's events in kindergarten.

Although Fives still like to be read to, they also like to get off in a corner and look at books or even to "read" on their own. They like to pick out words they know. They will memorize whole pages and, in some cases, a whole book. They relish humor, and are especially fond of stories in which animals "act like people."

Five-year-olds like to recite or sing lilting rhymes and jingles. Television commercials, "Sesame Street" jingles, and the like are favorites. Sunday School and kindergarten songs are rendered with or without encouragement.

Fives are able to define nouns by their uses; for example, milk is to drink, a wagon is to pull, an apple is to eat, a ball is to throw, etc. New words intrigue them, especially abstract ones. They are constantly asking the meaning of words they do not know. Fives ask questions to garner information. They are less frequent than their four-year-old attention-seeking queries, and they are more relevant. The investigations of five-year-olds are meaningful: "What is this for?" "How does this work?" "What does it mean?"

In *Childhood and Adolescence: A Psychology of the Growing Person* (New York: Random House, 1957), Joseph L. Stone and Joseph Church write of the five-year-old, "Now he is bringing language to bear on his busy taking in and digesting of the world—its colors and flavors and textures and implications. He is even preparing to branch out into the world of vicarious experience provided by written literature."

Some Effects of Learning Language*

In addition to being open to what people tell him, the child also becomes able to formulate his own experience and thus

*Parts of pages 373-374 adapted from *Child's Eye View* by Carol Tomlinson-Keasey (New York: St. Martin's Press, 1980).

to teach himself. Language is not simply an instrument of communication, but also a medium of thinking and feeling. Without language we could not learn to read.

The thought patterns of five-year-olds, despite the presence of language, are very vague and immature. There is little evidence of their use of logical operations to understand the world.

Adults have classified most of the world into small subcategories. There are seven days in a week, twelve months of the year, four seasons of the year, and so on. Such classifications help adults deal with the world. Five-year-olds are not clear about precise adult groupings. For example, when asked what the days of the week were, one five-year-old replied, "Sunday, Monday, Yesterday, Wednesday, and November." To a young child, it is logical for "yesterday" to be included because it has the word "day" in it. His birthday is in November, which explains why he included this in the list!

The time, geography, animal, and other classifications that young children verbalize tend to mask the naive system they use to organize the world.

Classification systems exist in our numbering system, in our knowledge of science, in the grammar of language, in music notation, in all of life. A strong foundation of language and a wide variety of experiences will make it easier for preschoolers to come to understand the world. Parents can help by explaining how events and words fit together.

Below are some good books for Fives and Sixes. However, since children differ greatly, it is up to you to discover which books will be best for your child:

Adler, David. *A Little at a Time.* (Random House, 1976)
Aliki. *My Five Senses.* (Crowell, 1972)
————. *The Two of Them.* (Greenwillow, 1979)
Anderson, C. W. *Billy and Blaze.* (Macmillan, 1962)
Anglund, Joan Walsh. *Love Is a Special Way of Feeling.* (Harcourt, Brace, Jovanovich, 1960)
Association for Childhood Education. *Told Under the Green Umbrella.* (Macmillan, 1930)
Babbitt, Natalie. *Something.* (Farrar, Straus & Giroux, 1970)
Barrett, Judi. *I Hate to Take a Bath.* (Four Winds, 1975)
Bate, Lucy. *Little Rabbit's Loose Tooth.* (Crown, 1975)
Behrens, June. *How I Feel.* (Children's Press, 1973)

Bemelmans, Ludwig. *Madeline.* (Viking, 1939)
———. *Madeline's Rescue.* (Viking, 1953)
Berenstain, Stan and Jan. *The Bears' Almanac.* (Random House, 1973)
Bishop, Claire Huchet. *Five Chinese Brothers.* (Coward-McCann, 1938)
Boden, Alice. *The Field of Buttercups.* (Walck, 1974)
Brenner, Barbara. *Amy's Doll.* (Alfred A. Knopf, 1963)
———. *Barto Takes the Subway.* (Alfred A. Knopf, 1961)
Brown, Margaret Wise. *The Dead Bird.* (Addison-Wesley, 1958)
Bulla, Clyde Robert. *Daniel's Duck.* (Harper & Row, 1979)
———. *The Stubborn Old Woman.* (Crowell, 1980)
Burningham, John. *Come Away from the Water, Shirley.* (Crowell, 1977)
Carle, Eric. *The Grouchy Ladybug.* (Crowell, 1977)
Cleary, Beverly. *The Mouse and the Motorcycle.* (Morrow, 1965)
Cohen, Miriam. *The New Teacher.* (Macmillan, 1974)
———. *When Will I Read?* (Greenwillow, 1977)
———. *Will I Have a Friend?* (Macmillan, 1967)
Daugherty, James. *Andy and the Lion.* (Viking, 1938)
D'Aulaire, Ingri and Edgar Parin. *Abraham Lincoln.* (Doubleday, 1957)
De Regniers, Beatrice Schenk. *Everyone Is Good for Something.* (Houghton Mifflin, 1980)
———. *Laura's Story.* (Atheneum, 1979)
Duvoisin, Roger. *Crocus.* (Alfred A. Knopf, 1977)
Ehrlich, Amy. *The Everyday Train.* (Dial Press, 1977)
Emberly, Ed. *Klippity Klop.* (Little, Brown, 1974)
———. *The Wing on a Flea: A Book About Shapes.* (Little, Brown, 1961)
Farber, Norma. *As I Was Crossing Boston Common.* (E. P. Dutton, 1975)
Fassler, Joan. *Howie Helps Himself.* (Albert Whitman, 1975)
Fatio, Louise. *The Happy Lion.* (McGraw-Hill, 1964)
———. *The Happy Lion and the Bear.* (McGraw-Hill, 1964)
———. *The Happy Lioness.* (McGraw-Hill, 1980)
Greene, Laura. *Help: Getting to Know About Needing and Giving.* (Human Sciences Press, 1980)
Hader, Berta and Elmer. *The Big Snow.* (Macmillan, 1948)
Hall, Donald. *Ox-Cart Man.* (Viking, 1979)
Hazen, Barbara S. *The Gorilla Did It.* (Atheneum, 1974)

Heller, Linda. *Alexis and the Golden Ring.* (Macmillan, 1979)

Hickman, Martha Whitmore. *My Friend William Moved Away.* (Abingdon, 1979)

Hoban, Tana. *Is It Red? Is It Yellow? Is It Blue?* (Greenwillow, 1978)

Hoff, Syd. *Danny and the Dinosaur.* (Harper & Row, 1958)

Hutchins, Pat. *Happy Birthday, Sam.* (Greenwillow, 1978)

Ipcar, Dahlov. *The Biggest Fish in the Sea.* (Viking, 1972)

Iverson, Genie. *I Want to Be Big.* (E. P. Dutton, 1979)

Kahn, Joan. *You Can't Catch Me.* (Harper & Row, 1976)

Keats, Ezra Jack. *Goggles!* (Macmillan, 1969)

———. *The Little Drummer Boy.* (Macmillan, 1968)

Kraus, Robert. *Whose Mouse Are You?* (Macmillan, 1970)

Krauss, Ruth. *Backward Day.* (Harper & Row, 1950)

Kuskin, Karla. *A Space Story.* (Harper & Row, 1978)

Leaf, Munro. *The Story of Ferdinand.* (Viking, 1936; Penguin, 1977)

Lionni, Leo. *Geraldine the Music Mouse.* (Pantheon, 1979)

Lobel, Arnold. *A Treeful of Pigs.* (Greenwillow, 1979)

———. *Frog and Toad Are Friends.* (Harper & Row, 1970)

Manushkin, Fran. *Shirleybird.* (Harper & Row, 1975)

Payne, Emmy. *Katy No-Pocket.* (Houghton Mifflin, 1944)

Peet, Bill. *Cowardly Clyde.* (Houghton Mifflin, 1979)

———. *How Droofus the Dragon Lost His Head.* (Houghton Mifflin, 1971)

Petie, Haris. *Billions of Bugs.* (Prentice-Hall, 1975)

Provensen, Alice and Martin. *The Year at Maple Hill Farm.* (Atheneum, 1978)

Sazer, Nina. *What Do You Think I Saw?* (Pantheon, 1976)

Seuss, Dr. (Theodor Geisel). *Horton Hatches the Egg.* (Random House, 1940)

―――. *The 500 Hats of Bartholomew Cubbins.* (Vanguard, 1938)

Sharmat, Marjorie Weinman. *What Are We Going to Do About Andrew?* (Macmillan, 1980)

Shulevitz, Uri. *Dawn.* (Farrar, Straus & Giroux, 1974)

Simon, Norma. *I Know What I Like.* (Albert Whitman, 1971)

Steig, William. *Amos and Boris.* (Farrar, Straus, & Giroux, 1971)

―――. *Sylvester and the Magic Pebble.* (Simon & Schuster, 1969)

Stein, Sara Bonnett. *A Hospital Story.* (Walker, 1974)

―――. *Making Babies: An Open Family Book for Parents and Children Together.* (Walker, 1974)

―――. *That New Baby.* (Walker, 1974)

Thompson, Jean. *I'm Going to Run Away!* (Abingdon Press, 1975)

Turkle, Brinton. *Rachel and Obadiah.* (E. P. Dutton, 1978)

Van Allsburg, Chris. *The Garden of Abdul Gasazi.* (Houghton Mifflin, 1979)

Yashima, Taro. *Crow Boy.* (Viking, 1955)

Zindel, Paul. *I Love My Mother.* (Harper & Row, 1975)

Zolotow, Charlotte. *Hold My Hand.* (Harper & Row, 1972)

―――. *Mr. Rabbit and the Lovely Present.* (Harper & Row, 1962)

SENSORY POWERS/LEARNING

Fives are just beginning to combine what they know and what happens to them in the immediate present with what they have experienced before. They are commencing to be able to look forward to "tomorrow." In extremely uncomplicated situations, Fives are on the way to understanding the meaning of cause and effect. Memory is increasing. They still need countless opportunities to employ their five senses in manipulating ideas and objects and discovering through concrete experiences. They cannot cope with abstract ideas. Kindergarten can provide the materials and activities that are not always available to children in their homes.

THE IMPORTANCE OF PRE-PRIMARY EDUCATION

"Fives who go to a good kindergarten live the fifth year of their lives with more vigor. They work harder, see more, do more. They are happier, and get more from life. They also give more of themselves . . .

"You can say why good schools for this age are so important in four words: *The children are ready.* You can say it in three words: They are *popping, bursting, eager.* They have reached a new time in their lives, a time when stimulation, adventure, ideas, challenge, companionship have begun to be of prime importance . . .

"Kindergarten children begin to know and understand more about the world about them. The horizons of their world are extended with each experience. They learn about the nature and the properties of things. They increase their vocabulary with its attendant meanings. They learn to express themselves verbally as well as through various art mediums. They develop greater motor coordination. They begin to take responsibility for themselves and to help in the housekeeping activities of the school. They grow in their acceptance of limitations and controls. They make progress in learning how to get along with other children and how to work independently as well . . .

"Fives are our most eager scholars. They don't tolerate school; they beg for it."*

School systems in the United States automatically accept children for enrollment on the basis of chronological age: four years and eight months to five years for kindergarten, and six years for first grade. None of the rules will help parents know what is best for their particular child, however. Not every child is ready for kindergarten at five or first grade at six. For those children who are not ready, school can be a nightmare of failure and pressure to learn material for which they are not developmentally ready.

*Excerpts from a talk by James L. Hymes, Jr., Ph.D. (retired Professor of Education at the University of Maryland) at a conference of the Association for Childhood Education International held in Indianapolis in 1962.

Dr. Richard Granger, author of HEW's publication, *Your Child From One to Six* (Washington, DC: HEW, Children's Bureau Publication, 1974 edition), offers these guidelines for assessing maturity before starting school:

- Physically, the child must be healthy and strong enough to enjoy the challenge of going to school and to bear up under the increased stresses involved.
- The child must be able to separate from you and spend a number of hours each day in a place that is unfamiliar, with adults and children who are largely unknown at first.
- In most schools the child must be able to obey directions even when not watched every minute.
- The child must have a long enough attention span to be able to sit still for fairly long periods and concentrate on one thing at a time, gradually learning to enjoy the practicing and problem-solving activity involved.
- The child must be able to tolerate the frustration of not getting immediate attention from the teacher or others, and to wait for and take turns.

- The child must have some of the basic eye-hand skills necessary to the learning of reading and writing, such as handling a pencil, turning pages, recognizing shapes and colors, and so forth.

Dr. Granger writes that no single rule or test can help you decide whether your child is ready or not. What, then, can you do? One thing is not to push your child into school at the earliest possible age your school allows. Although a few children who are very bright and mature socially may be ready, many are not. One year of age difference in the four-to-six-year age group is an enormous amount of extra living and learning time on a percentage basis. It amounts to one-fourth to one-fifth of the child's entire life. That amount of extra time between the start of one school year and the next may be exactly the amount of time your child needs to get it all together—to integrate physical, psychological, and social skills to the point where entering school becomes exciting instead of frightening.

Beyond this, many people would advise that you think about

helping your child to get ready for school even before the four-to-six period. One way is to have your child spend some time in a preschool program of some sort—a parent-child center, nursery school, or day-care center.

The good kindergarten provides opportunities for Fives to meet their needs and interests: for large and small muscle development, dramatic play, manipulation and matching, manipulation and construction, for exploration, testing, and discovery, and for experiences to develop perceptual skills. The following are the types of play materials and equipment that work best with kindergarten children:

Blocks—wooden blocks of various sizes and shapes; floor blocks, hollow blocks

Transportation Toys—interlocking trains, boats, trucks

Picture Making—material for drawing and painting; easels, tables, floor space

Homemaking—suitable furniture and layout; materials that suggest the roles of the father, mother, and children in a home, including cooking utensils, toy telephones, small tools, dolls, etc.

Library—picture books and simple reference books; tables and chairs

Dressing Up—clothing and materials to suggest various characters for dramatic play, including hats, scarves, shoes, junk jewelry, etc.

Make-Believe—puppets, stage, etc.

Store—a counter, toy money, etc.; from time to time children might convert this area into a post office, hospital, doctor's office, veterinarian's office, etc.

Construction—boxes, cartons, scrap material, paper, string, scissors, glue, paste, etc.

Family and Community Play People—wedge-type or bendable standpatters, etc.

Music Making—rhythm band instruments, drums, autoharp; dance props, such as hoops, scarves, etc.

Sand—sandbox with sand, containers, spade, sieves, spoons, etc.

Water—container, bottles, measures, funnels, siphon, etc.

Modeling—clay, plasticine, containers with covers; adequate work space

Individual and Small Group Occupations—educational toys, including puzzles, beads, pegboards, wool, large needles,

unlined paper, pencil, scissors, record player, suitable records

The World About Us—small animals, plants, flowers, collections, magnet, compass, magnifying glass, scales, thermometer, prism, wheels, globe; space for children to contribute items of interest

Woodwork—workbench, hammer, nails, soft wood, handsaw, sandpaper, glue

TEACHING THE CHILD UNDER SIX

James L. Hymes, Jr., in his excellent book *Teaching the Child Under Six* (Columbus, Ohio: Charles E. Merrill, 1968; second edition 1974) pleads for the removal of any academic teaching in the kindergarten. He strongly disapproves of workbooks, coloring books, and excessive teacher talk. He resents the practice of having five-year-olds kept sitting rigidly in their chairs during teacher presentations.

According to Dr. Hymes, much that is wrong for children under six is done in the name of *reading readiness*. He wants kindergarten teachers (and their parents) to give five-year-old boys and girls only as much reading activity as they are willing and eager to learn.

Above all, "Kindergarten must get rid of the pressure of preparing children for first grade."

Reading Readiness

In reading, as in the other language arts, the parent actually is the pacesetter. If you read a lot, you are saying to your child that reading is important and enjoyable to you. However, it is your reading to your child that is paramount to his learning.

There is a sharp distinction between speaking and reading. To speak, the child learns a vocal symbol for a concept. When the child is ready to read, she has to associate a visual symbol with her previously learned vocal symbol. Reading instruction should be given only when a young child is interested and is able to hear and speak the language with success, and only if she is herself motivated to learn.

Language Acquisition

Impression precedes expression, and intake precedes outflow in every aspect of language learning. It is only after a child is able to recognize symbols for sounds that he is ready to learn to make the latter.

Language encompasses receiving and transmitting. We receive when we listen and read, transmit when we speak and write. A child needs to learn that writing is "talk put on paper." To forward this concept, ask your child to tell you a story, write it down in large letters, and then read it back to her.

Although listening, speaking, reading, and writing occur in this order, they also overlap. The interrelationship of all facets of the language arts continues throughout one's lifetime.

More on Reading Readiness*

Parents can involve their interested five-year-olds in all kinds of activities at home to help them build basic skills for reading. However, they should be treated as play and games and not as an academic subject to be taught.

The following are some of the developmental steps a child goes through before and during the process of learning to read:

Coordination: the ability to control the movements of one's body (walking, running, jumping, hopping, skipping, balancing). There are psychologists who believe that some children have reading difficulties because they missed important physical development stages—crawling, for example.

Visual-motor control: good control of the movements of one's small muscles (as in stringing beads, piling small blocks, copying shapes, cutting, etc.).

Visual perception: being able to match shapes, colors, sizes, etc.

Visual memory: the ability to reproduce shapes, letters, etc., from memory.

Auditory perception: being able to identify sounds, hear the difference between words, match rhyming sounds, etc.

*Parts of pages 385–388 from "Steps to Reading," a pamphlet by Kaye Foremaster of the Escondido Union School District, Escondido, California, 1977. Reprinted with permission.

Auditory memory: the ability to recall sounds, being able to respond to directions, etc.

Oral language production: being able to express oneself verbally.

A Sampling of Coordination Activities

- Have your child hop on his left foot, then on his right; also on both feet while you count to ten.
- Together with your child, jump forward and backward over a line.
- Run with your child on tiptoe, then stand on tiptoe while you count to ten.
- Play Simon Says with your child, including *right* and *left* actions in your directions.
- Play throw-and-catch ball with your child.
- You can create your own physical coordination activities, taking cues from your child.

Visual-Motor Control Activities

- Cut pictures out of a magazine, cutting each picture into different shapes. Have your child put the parts of each picture together and paste them on paper.
- Hold up your right and left hands; ask your child to look from one to the other as you say *right* and *left;* ask which hand is *up* and which is *down,* etc.
- Your child may enjoy stringing pieces of small pasta or assorted beads.
- Draw a circle, square, triangle, and cross on a piece of paper; ask your child to copy the shapes.
- Draw simple zigzag lines and curves on a piece of paper; ask your child to cut along the lines.

Visual-Perception Activities

- Place blocks or buttons on the floor; ask your child to arrange them according to size, then according to color.
- Talk about the colors of your child's clothes, pictures in storybooks, magazines, etc.
- Have your child sort teaspoons and tablespoons, forks from knives, etc.

- Measure amounts of water with your child, using containers of various sizes, pouring the water back and forth.
- Make two sets of numbers on cards; ask your child to match the numbers.

Visual-Memory Activities

- Using a newspaper or magazine, ask your child to circle all the words beginning with a letter you specify.
- Give your child an old magazine and ask her to cut out as many similar objects as she can find in it.
- Arrange three shapes in a certain sequence; mix them up; ask your child to arrange them in the original sequence.
- Open a storybook to a certain page; let your child look at it for a moment, then close the book. See if he can find the same page again.
- Draw two houses; put a door on one. Cover the picture; ask your child to draw a door in the same place on the second house. Then continue with windows, a chimney, etc.

Auditory-Perception Activities

- Indoors or out, listen for sounds with your child. In your home, ask your child to indicate the sources of specific sounds; for example, the motor of the refrigerator.
- Clap out a pattern of sounds; ask your child to repeat it. Suggest that your child clap out a pattern for you to repeat.
- Say several words that start with the same sound; ask your child to repeat the sound heard at the beginning of the words—for example, *hat, house, hot, horse.*
- Say two words that rhyme—for example, *cat* and *pat.* Ask your child to say as many more as she can.
- Say three words that end with the same sound—for example, *hand, band, sand.* Ask your child to name the ending sound. (You can create your own sounding games; have your child try to suggest some.)

Auditory-Memory Activities

- Give your child three or four differently colored crayons. Call out the colors and ask her to arrange the crayons in the order you call them.

- Name three body parts; ask your child to touch them in that order. (It will please your child if you take turns in switching director and learner roles.)
- Tell your child a very short story; then ask him questions about it.
- Say three letters; ask your child to repeat them forward and then backward.
- Whisper a short message to your child; ask him to repeat it.

Oral Language Production

- Name a familiar animal; ask your child to try to describe it. (You can interchange common farm and wild animals in this game.)
- Make a paper bag puppet; ask your child to make up words for it to say. (Suggest that your child make his own paper bag puppet.)
- Put something in a paper bag; have your child reach in, feel the object, and then describe what she feels.
- Pantomime some action; ask your child to describe your action in words.
- After your child has watched a TV program that you selected for her, ask her to tell you what happened in it.

No learning game or activity should be permitted to become a boring routine either to children or to their parents. A change of subject and pace is always refreshing. It is up to parents to determine the interest and attention span of their young learners. At the same time it is important for parents (and teachers) to help strengthen learning and playing skills that will make it possible for young children to spend time on their own without adult supervision or pressure.

Communicating Projects

Now that your child can follow directions, she needs opportunities to give directions and to carry simple oral messages to others. Let your child express herself without interruption or correction. Nothing is more discouraging than perpetual criticism of pronunciation, grammar, etc.

If your child wants to learn how to write, teach him his name, using a large pencil to print capital letters on a big sheet of paper. Whatever he asks about and wishes to learn, teach him in a casual but direct way. However, never push him beyond his current capacity.

Family conversations at mealtimes offer opportunities for your child's increasing language development, as well as agreeable interchanges of events, ideas, feelings, etc.

Teaching Beginning Reading

The early progressive school teachers believed that delaying the three R's until children were seven or eight years old would enable them to provide experiences much more suited to the children's current interests and needs. In her book, *The Little Red School House* (New York: Macmillan, 1942), Agnes de Lima, who was a teacher at the Little Red School House, wrote, "Interestingly enough, these various experiences make it easier for children later on to acquire the academic tool subjects."

In progressive schools, children are encouraged to use words that vividly describe what they see, feel, smell, hear, and taste. Specifically in the Little Red School House, which is still in operation in Greenwich Village in New York City, five-year-olds become aware of the importance of signs and printed directions as they go on trips about the city. "Reading readiness is thus gradually increased until many children are reading almost without knowing it." The approach is to make certain that children want to learn to read, and that their beginning reading experiences are relaxed and pleasant. (At the Little Red School House, too, children begin to learn to write at the same time as they learn to read. They are taught manuscript writing because it appears to be a more natural form for them to learn to use. The teachers make sure that the writing is clear and legible.)

In the words of Agnes de Lima, "A child may take a picture of a boat or a train and he or the teacher may say, 'It is a big boat' or 'It is a big long train.' The picture then may be hung on the wall and under it the teacher may write on a strip of paper level with the children's eyes, 'This is a big boat.' The teacher reads the words aloud. The children read them, too. Next, the other picture may be put up with a strip which says, 'This is a big long train.' The teacher reads this also, and so do the children. Then the teacher asks the children if they can pick out the parts on the two strips of writing which are alike . . . Besides matching words or sentences, we may match words and pictures, sentences and pictures, or complete a sentence by choosing one word from a group of words phonetically related."

When the children are ready, books that are not readers are introduced in the classroom—simple, attractive books that include here-and-now stories, poetry, animal stories, etc.

Learning Arithmetic

Arithmetic learning goes on regularly long before children are ready for formal study because quantity and numbers are a part of every young child's life. The clock regulates routines at home and in the school. It is amazing how early in life a child gets to know the difference between one or more cookies. Going to the supermarket is also a quantity- and number-learning experience. Buying an ice cream cone or a new ball entails an elementary arithmetic procedure.

Miss de Lima writes that when a child is six years old, "we have him count and group in tens with concrete objects. Thus, by grouping in tens the six-year-old begins to get through direct experience a sense of our number system."

MUSICAL EXPRESSION

Children like music of all kinds, especially music to which they can respond with their whole beings. Body movements and rhythmic interpretations are natural accompaniments to the musical activities of kindergarten-age children. The impulse to dance and to give physical response to music is inherent in most children. Kindergarten teachers and parents need only give children opportunities to respond freely to slow, fast, heavy, and soft types of music. Rhythmic activities may be an outgrowth of almost any experience. They can be stimulated by a bunny hopping, a plane or bird flying, ducks swimming, etc. Simple rhythm band activities offer very satisfying musical experiences, and promote the social value of learning to cooperate with agemates in a group.

PRE-MATHEMATICAL LEARNING

"Reciting the names of the numbers in order has about the same relation to mathematics that reciting the alphabet has to reading," writes Evelyn Sharp in her book, *Thinking Is Child's Play* (New York: Avon Books, 2nd printing, December 1971).

In the manipulation of simple objects, five-year-olds can learn methods of reasoning that are of greater use than merely learning to count. Children need to become familiar with the concepts of classification and seriation (arranging things in order), which are at the base of all kinds of logical thinking.

"*Classification* requires the ability to recognize likenesses and differences between objects and to group them accordingly . . . *Seriation* calls for arranging objects in a series according to some specified order. Because this concept is based on comparison, it is harder for children than classification."

Children learn not from objects per se, nor from what they are told about them—they learn only from their own manipulations of things. To this end, Miss Sharp presents a series of pre-mathematical thought-provoking games that deal with the techniques of classification and seriation. The games can be made with cardboard, tape, babyfood jar tops, playing cards, paper plates and napkins, string and spools. Playing these enjoyable learning games with your child will give you insight into how your child thinks and, without any pressure, allows you to stimulate her cognitive growth.

The Concept of Time

Time is another complex numerical ordering system that takes understanding, experience, and maturation before a child can master it. Slowly children learn that a regular ordering system exists between seconds, minutes, hours, and days. Learning to attach specific numbers to the gross ordering of the passage of time will also extend their mathematical thinking.

By the time children are seven to nine years of age, their ability to order the world of time and to describe its many elements with appropriate numbers becomes evident. In short, they really know how to tell time and understand the ramifications of the passage of time.

SOCIAL DEVELOPMENT

Fives are comparatively independent. They feel protective toward younger siblings and playmates. However, a five-year-old can experience pangs of jealousy when a younger (or older) sibling is receiving all the attention. They are capable, too, of blaming some of their own negative acts on a perfectly innocent younger sibling.

Their friendships are becoming firmer. Five-year-olds actively choose to engage in associative play with one or more peers. They want and need playmates, and enjoy all kinds of group play projects. Choosing friends in the kindergarten goes beyond availability, common interest, or like-sex. It is more nearly in the province of children serving each other's special needs.

With advancing chronological age during the preschool years, there is an increase in all forms of social interaction, and the proportion of acceptable to unacceptable methods of

social behavior tends to increase. Some of this may be due to the fact that the older child relies more on verbal than on physical actions.

Some of the skills that are acquired as a child learns to relate to others are giving, receiving, and sharing; expressing feelings and ideas; making choices. Social competency also includes techniques for expressing interest and friendship, for welcoming and including others in play, and for initiating and carrying on group activities. No child enjoys a satisfying social life unless he learns how to play with other children. Every child wants to be part of a group of children his own age. He achieves stature only as he is accepted and respected by the group members; as he plays or works with them in the attainment of mutual goals; as he makes contributions to group projects; as he learns that group life calls for initiative as well as conformity.

Children, if left alone, will seek play and playmates as if their lives depended upon it—and perhaps they do!

Throughout her social development, a child spends less and less time with her family and more in play with children her own age. This trend, which extends gradually over several years, is a major process in a child's social sophistication. Positively, there is more independent behavior and increased participation in peer group activities. On the negative side, it expresses itself in a growing revolt against parental control and often in a critical attitude toward parents and the home. The peer group is a child's very own social milieu, with its special language, mode of interaction, loyalties, values, and acceptable forms of behavior, many of which the grown-up cannot understand. The child has equal and at times even superior status with others in this child-sized dominion, not the subordinate role he invariably has with his parents and other adults.

Sociality in the Kindergarten

Learning to function well as a social being presents difficulties for most five-year-olds. They are making a major social adjustment from the security of the family and home to a strange environment with a teacher and a large group of unknown agemates. One child will differ from another in the amount of time, experience, and guidance she requires to enable her to interact with others. All children need sufficient time and experience to learn how to participate reasonably in a group and to share without fighting, withdrawing, or forfeiting their own rights.

There are times when the kindergarten teacher intervenes to limit or to direct the social behaviors of five-year-olds, especially when they go out of bounds. The kindergarten teacher is the key factor in the development of a feeling of security within the classroom. As a person who enjoys young children and accepts them as they are, the kindergarten teacher helps them become accepting of one another.

In addition, there are routines that need to be followed in the kindergarten in order to facilitate the use of limited space, facilities, equipment, and supplies by several five-year-olds. Sharing and cooperating usually cause some curtailment of personal wishes and the freedom to do as one pleases, and all children do not react with equal geniality to this fact of life. "Parents need to be aware that a child's happiness or unhappiness at school may have to do with his inability to give up some of his individual desires for the greater good of the group," writes Dorothy Cohen in *The Learning Child* (New York: Pantheon Books, 1972).

Five-year-olds who are over-talkative, disruptive, or destructive in the kindergarten, who harm other boys and girls in the classroom or on the playground, indicate that they are not prepared for this type of group living and learning. Helping such children become attuned to the give-and-take of play and work in an organized program becomes the responsibility of the parents, with some guidance from the kindergarten teacher. Fortunately, most Fives adjust quite smoothly to kindergarten attendance.

Most five-year-olds would have little trouble communicating with adults if lost in a city or town. Most are relatively calm in a crisis (which may be due to the fact that they are not yet able to express complex emotions). In unusual but uncomplicated situations, five- to five-and-a-half-year-old children show amazing emotional stability, which adults find admirable. Most five- to five-and-a-half-year-old boys and girls evince a good degree of patience, politeness, generosity of spirit, and friendliness in their manner of functioning.

Fives Love Their Mothers and Fathers

Life with five- to five-and-a-half-year-olds is much easier than at any other age level because they are intent on pleasing their mothers and fathers. Mother is the center of the child's universe at this time.

Fives like to have their mothers at home when they return from school. They enjoy holding long talks with their mothers. They especially want mother close at hand at bedtime, when they are sick, and when they are upset about something.

Fives are also very fond of their fathers. They are inordinately proud of them, and love having the company of their fathers whenever possible.

They are "amusingly manly or womanly" in the way they mimic the daily routines of their parents in their make-believe play. Their imitations of the behavior of adults will never again be quite so exact and engrossing.

Fives lump parents, grandparents, relatives, and others into a category they call "grown-ups," who are set apart from their agemates.

Generally, five-year-olds get along and play well with their brothers and sisters.

Interaction with Relatives

Fives will react to relatives they rarely see as they do to other visitors—observing them from a safe distance before deciding how to respond. Parents or the relatives must not try to force the children to kiss the relatives or to say "I love you."

Such pressure will usually make a five-year-old even more ill at ease.

Another matter concerns disciplining when parents and children go to visit grandparents or other relatives. These other family members must never be given the opportunity to undermine the authority of the parents. At the same time, parents need to protect their young children from any unrealistic expectations that relatives may have for them.

Racial Awareness

In *Non-Sexist Childraising* (Boston: Beacon Press, 1977), Carrie Carmichael writes, "All children come out equal, but quickly race is noted, sex is checked, and the world begins the process of imprinting on that baby what it wants from a brown girl, a black boy, a white girl, a yellow boy. The expectations vary for each race, sex, and social class."

Almost all Fives make friends on the basis of similarity of interests, not because of economic status, color, race, or religion. Even at five, a boy or girl may be heedless of the skin color of the child he or she enjoys playing with.

Many studies indicate that prejudice and racial misunderstanding harm all children. They hurt the prejudiced child (and the adult later on) by making such a child oppressive in action and dogmatic and narrow-minded in outlook. They scar the child who is the object of the denigration by teaching self-hatred and misplaced identity.

How Prejudice Develops

Each child becomes more aware racially as she grows older. Certainly by the age of three, a child senses her parents' racial attitudes. Incidents occur and the child observes her parents' reactions to them. A three-year-old black child stands with her mother near a slide in a park playground. A three-year-old white child comes over to play near the black child. The white mother pulls her child away. Both children quickly learn the significance of this action.

Or a black child looks at the white mother of an interracial child and states, "You can't be her mother because she's black and you're white." She goes on to say that she does not like the white mother because her grandmother told her that "white people are bad."

How can parents raise their children not to be prejudiced?

Identifying with One's Own Racial Group

A child must first identify with his own racial group to get his bearings on himself and the world. For most white children, this is not a problem. The white child sees his white parents and the white society around him and identifies with them. However, the white child must learn that there are other people in the world who may look different, just as there are people who have different values, but who should not be suspect because of this.

The black child sees her black parents and most often the black society around her, but as she grows older, she becomes increasingly aware of the many white people, too. She sees them on television, in stores, as teachers, and so on. (It is more likely for a white child never to have met a black person than vice versa.)

By nursery school age, the black child may have sensed a double standard in the society around him. Often he equates good things with being white. He needs to be taught that being black is something to be proud of, not ashamed of. All parents in our multiracial society must be aware of the "sinister" connotations of the color "black" and the "pure" connotations of the color "white" in the English language.

You need to be especially aware of this as you choose books to read to your children. Try to find books that mirror your child's own image. Look for books about children of differing racial groups coming together in the same story.

Interracial Marriages and Adoptions

If you are the biological parents of an interracial child, your child may have special identity problems. She may be confused as to which group she actually belongs. Have your child examine her skin, look at her mother's skin, and her father's skin. Teach your child that black/yellow/brown/red are good, and white is good; they merely are *different*. If you do not live in an interracial neighborhood, make sure your child comes in contact with people of the racial backgrounds of both parents, and that she also has playmates from both groups.

White parents who adopt a child who is other than white need to give him special attention. In addition to the careful choice of books, and the teaching of pride in himself, his appearance, and his racial background, such adoptive parents must make a special effort to see that their child has a chance to play with other children and to associate with adults of the same racial background. He should not be isolated in a white world as "one of a kind."

At about two-and-a-half, given the opportunity of contact, a child will probably start noticing differences in other children, such as hair texture, differently shaped eyes and noses, and assorted skin colors. Parents need to try to answer their children's questions or explain their observations by telling them about the different people who live on the earth. If parents are not derogatory, their children won't be. Above all, parents need to try not to say one thing and act another way.

It is important for children to play with agemates of other

races so that when they become adults, they will be better able to live and work together with mutual respect and tolerance.

In this regard, three especially sensitive books for preschoolers are:

- *Black Is Brown Is Tan* by Arnold Adoff. Illustrated by Emily Arnold McCully (New York: Harper, 1973). This is a delightful story-poem of an interracial family whose skin colors range from a brown-skinned mother to a white father and varicolored children.
- *Spin a Soft Black Song* by Nikki Giovanni. Illustrated by Charles Bible (New York: Hill & Wang, 1971). A black poet and a black artist tell of childhood experiences with the open charm of all children.
- *Stevie,* written and illustrated by John Steptoe (New York: Harper, 1969). A small boy in Harlem tells of his difficulties when cry-baby Stevie is added to the household.

A positive self-image brings a strong sense of identity and feelings of self-worth. Parents need to fight bias with truth. To be a fine white or black, American Indian, Puerto Rican, Chicano, Chinese-American, or a Nisei is to be a fine human being. To be Christian, Jewish, Muslim, Hindu, Buddhist, atheist, or agnostic is to exercise freedom of religious belief. The whole world is enriched by the variety of its races and cultures!

PERSONALITY/PSYCHOLOGICAL DEVELOPMENT

Although Fives can experience anxiety and unreasonable fears, by and large they are stable in their emotional lives and intellectual outlook. Self-confidence and social conformity appear to be par for the course at five to five-and-a-half years of age. While these children cry less than Fours, they may still caterwaul when angry, tired, or they cannot have their way.

The Importance of a Positive Self-Concept

Some researchers gave two different tests to a group of kindergarten children. One was an IQ test; the other measured self-concept. The results of these tests were tabulated while the children were in kindergarten. Two years later, the same group of children took an achievement test in elementary school to determine how well they were reading, writing, spelling, and doing arithmetic. The outcomes of the tests indicated that the measure of self-image was a better predictor of future school achievement (from kindergarten through second grade) than was the gauge of intelligence. This and similar studies bear witness to the importance of children's estimations of themselves to their learning and well-being.

Most five-year-olds are well-adjusted and dependable. Secure within themselves, they are outgoing and relatively undemanding in their dealings with others. They will attempt only what they believe they can accomplish. Since they usually finish what they set out to do, their successes enhance their feelings of self-worth.

Fives like to show their parents how they print their names, write numerals from 1 to 5, spell some of the simple words in their favorite books, and so on.

Learning "Right" from "Wrong"

Fives are capable of occasional falsehoods, and they are aware of untruthfulness in other children. Although they really try to tell the truth, most Fives are not always able to do so. Sometimes they cannot resist taking things that do not belong to them (perhaps because their sense of other people's property rights is still on the vague side).

While taking things should not be ignored, parents should not be surprised if it occurs. Some Fives indicate that they know they have done wrong by hiding or breaking objects they have "lifted." Calm, objective talks between parent and child about "right" and "wrong" are in order when such incidents occur. At the same time, parents need to make it clear that they do not believe their child to be bad or valueless.

When Older Children Continue to Suck Their Thumbs

Most children stop sucking their thumbs by the time they celebrate their fifth or sixth birthdays. It seems that their association with agemates or older children initiates their wanting to be less babyish. Older children frown upon thumb-suckers.

They think fingers can be put to better use playing games, climbing on playground equipment, playing ball, etc.

Of course, casual and limited thumb-sucking should not concern the parents of five-year-olds. However, children who suck their thumbs almost continuously may be telling their parents that something is amiss, and some help is needed to find them more satisfying pastimes. In this same vein, there are children who have ceased thumb-sucking only to start it again. Here, too, parents need to try to find out what is disturbing their children. Above all, parents need to try not to resort to perpetual nagging or punishing the child who continues to derive solace from sucking his thumb.

In *Some Special Problems of Children Aged Two to Five Years* (New York: Child Study Association, 1969), Nina Ridenour and Isabel Johnson offer parents some suggestions for handling thumb-sucking:

- Do not use force to restrain your child in any way. (The sucking won't be harmful, but the remedies might be.)
- Do not put disagreeable substances on your child's thumbs that are supposed to stop thumb-sucking.
- Do not punish, scold, or coax.
- Do not threaten that teeth will be made crooked.
- Avoid bribes or rewards.

When five- or six-year-old children appear to be trying to rid themselves of their thumb-sucking habit, parents can be supportive and reassure them that they will succeed. At the same time, parents can make sure their children have "as many as possible of the essentials for a full, secure, comfortable life," according to Ridenour and Johnson.

Fears

Thunder, heavy rain, and sirens deeply disturb five-year-olds, and the dark and solitude continue to trigger timidity.

Fives are more adept at verbalizing their fears and anxieties. Sometimes they will talk freely about what is troubling them. At other times, a parent or teacher may be able to help a child discuss what is at the root of his or her distress.

Fear of Death

Many five-year-olds experience a fear of death. It is important for parents to help their children accept, without being overwhelmed, the fact of death at some time for all living things. Many parents tend to steer away from the unpleasant reality of death.

Children who lose a parent, sibling, close relative, playmate, or pet can be spared severe and lasting emotional turmoil if they are helped to express their feelings at the time of the bereavement. There are child-rearing authorities who think children should learn about death before it actually touches their lives, and that the learning process should be gradual.

The death of a pet dog or cat, or even the discovery of a dead squirrel in the park or backyard, might provide the first learning experience. The parents can help their child express his sadness and sense of loss by being genuinely sympathetic and understanding.

Talking About Death

It is suggested that parents tell their five-year-olds that they will be together for a very long time to come. Eric Trimmer, author of *The First Seven Years* (New York: St. Martin's Press, 1978), writes, "If [your child] is afraid of illness as a prelude to dying, talk about people he knows who have been very ill, but have gotten better." On a more personal note, he says, "As a child I can remember my father saying to me, probably to answer my questions: 'Never be afraid of dying. Most people welcome death when their turn comes.' I found this most comforting when I was at this worrying stage, and when his turn came it was proved true."

Sex Education

Be prepared for some startling misconceptions during your first attempt to really talk about sex with your child. In *Sex Without Shame* (New York: William Morrow, 1978), Dr. Alayne Yates writes, "My six-year-old thought that babies resulted from kissing. My five-year-old wondered if boys have to pull on their penis in order to start the stream of urine. My sophisticated ten-year-old had once assumed that girls had a retractable penis they pushed out at will, like a bowel movement. At first, the parent learns more than the child . . .

"Parents who have been raised in sexually repressive homes may sense acute anxiety when they speak about eroticism. This can be inadvertently communicated to children by a slight frown, phrases rapidly repeated, or a higher pitched voice."

"There is nothing more natural in children of any age than sexuality," writes John Killinger in *The Loneliness of Children* (New York: Vanguard Press, 1980). "Yet there is no area of development that causes children more anxiety about themselves, or leads to more repression from parents, than sexuality . . . Children's earliest worries about sex apparently occur without provocation from the parents. Freud identified these as becoming vaguely conscious in children between the ages of three and five. During this period children become aware of their genitalia, recognize sexual differences between males and females, and begin to have erotic feelings about persons of the opposite sex, especially parents . . ."

John Killinger asks parents not to hesitate being physically responsive to their children, suggesting that they "snuggle them, carry them, roll on the floor with them, dance with them, embrace them, kiss them—and don't stop when they become three or six or twelve years old."

Sooner or later—generally toward the end of the fifth or sixth year—your child will pop the question that you have been dreading, usually having to do with the father's role in baby-making. For this, you may wish to rehearse your answer aloud to "see" how it sounds and how *you* feel while you are saying this. Try out your little talk while you are alone in the car or in the house until you feel completely comfortable with it. Then sit back and wait—chances are that you will be "on stage" sooner than you thought you would be.

Joae Graham Selzer, M.D., in *When Children Ask About Sex* (Boston: Beacon Press, 1974), writes, ". . . the way you live your life is the most effective way to teach sex education to your child. Your attitudes and behavior have a very great influence indeed. If you want your child to conduct his sexual life along lines that you believe are satisfying and fulfilling, your hopes will have a much better chance of being realized if you demonstrate in your own life what a loving relationship is."

Some Books on Sex Education for Young Children

- *Where Do Babies Come From? A Book for Children and Their Parents* by Margaret Sheffield (New York: Alfred A. Knopf, 1973). An informative book for very young children who are curious about sex. The descriptions of anatomy, conception, and birth are simple and clear, and the pastel illustrations by Sheila Bewley create a gentle mood.
- *Making Babies: An Open Family Book for Parents and Children Together* by Sara Bonnett Stein (New York: Walker & Co., 1974). *Making Babies* is part of a series of "Open Family" books, all of which include two texts on each page, one in large print for children and one in smaller print for parents. The text for children is very general; the parents' text presents ways to supplement discussions of the pictures. The success of the book depends largely upon the ability of parents to extend the children's text. The book is illustrated with photographs, mostly of children and animals. (Two stark photos of a fetus might be difficult for children to grasp.)
- *How Babies Are Made* by Andrew C. Andry and Steven Schepp (New York: Time-Life Books, 1968). This book is geared to children three to ten. Reproduction is described in plants and animals first (chickens and dogs), then in humans. The unusual color photographs of paper sculptures may not please some parents.
- *Let's Find Out About Babies* by Martha and Charles Shapp and Sylvia Wilde (New York: Franklin Watts, 1969). Relationships between parents and child—male and female—and reproductive similarities among humans and other animals are clearly and simply explained.

PLAY AND PLAYTHINGS

Five-year-olds are inventive, energetic players. They enjoy block building and easel painting. Their modeling with moist clay or Play-Doh is nicely executed. As mentioned previously, five-year-old boys and girls can carry a play project from one day to the next. When they paint or draw they have a preconceived idea of what they want to render on paper.

Fives are dramatic "here-and-now" players who are stimulated by the life around them in their homes and communities.

They are actively interested in every kind of worker, in the interdependency of city and farm, in the output of factories, the contents of big boats on the docks, where electricity comes from, and so on. They also show their interest in the exciting world in which they live by acting as jet pilots, astronauts, doctors, etc. They expect to produce something concrete with all their strokes on paper. The increased attention span of Fives permits their concentrated endeavors at home or in kindergarten.

The dramatic play of five-year-olds reveals what transpires in the home, supermarket, farm, or factory, as well as ideas about such natural phenomena as the sun, moon, wind, clouds, etc. In their make-believe impersonations, there is much talk to help clarify their ideas. Their scenarios dealing with death, killing, sickness, or accidents are factual, not necessarily fanciful. At the same time, Fives enjoy a rich fantasy life. Television productions add vicariously to their knowledge of the world.

Five-year-olds like to cut, paste, draw, trace, string beads, make things with bits of paper and cloth, etc.—all activities that are available in the kindergarten.

Boys and girls build with blocks: the girls construct houses for their dolls; the boys build skyscrapers, garages, roadways, bridges, tunnels, etc.

Doll play continues apace at five. Both boys and girls will play house with dolls—dress, feed, and put them to bed. "Doctor" play is less prevalent than it was a year ago.

Kindergarten children can work on most of the Montessori geometric and size-relation formboards without using the trial-and-error methods employed by four-year-olds. They use their sense of perception to complete twenty-six-piece jigsaw puzzles without the need to force pieces into place. They are able to quickly put nesting boxes into proper sequence.

Kindergarten boys and girls like to use such simple science objects as a magnifying glass, magnet, flashlight, and stethoscope.

Most Fives enjoy playing all kinds of picture lotto games.

Five-year-old girls and boys like to make up dances to music, and participate happily in singing and rhythmic games. They enjoy playing in a rhythm band. They love dramatic play, and are ready to act out a story they have heard, with lots of spontaneity and movement.

Kindergarten children can take part in large-group activities if they are well supervised, but they function more smoothly in small groups of two or three children, and preferably with just one other child.

Most often adults can remain in the background while five-year-olds iron out problems as they play together. Intervention is needed, of course, when one child is being mistreated, or if there is a possibility of physical harm.

Art Expression

Five-year-olds sometimes draw, paint, model, or construct for as long as an hour, but usually from fifteen minutes to half an hour. Some kindergartners still tend to change their work by painting one color over another. This is especially true of children painting for the first time.

Their drawing of a human figure shows awareness of the different parts from head to feet. Now they also include such features as eyes and ears. When they draw the American flag, they delineate the pole and the stars and stripes. Their houses have roofs, doors, windows, and chimneys.

In clay modeling, Fives combine forms and create better-constructed objects than they did when four years old. They make more complicated objects, and select whatever they apply to the clay (such as swab sticks, buttons, straws, etc.) to decorate it as a part of the piece rather than merely to stick things in and take them out again.

Fives choose materials for collage with care. They cut them into all kinds of interesting shapes. They use scissors with increased skill. They like to make constructions and mobiles, and are better able to fasten materials together with wire, pipe cleaners, paper clips, or yarn. They have begun to be able to balance one shape with another.

As with adults, five-year-olds have their good days and their bad days. They know that some of their things turn out better than others. Insincere commendation disconcerts them and impedes the growth of their realistic measurements of achievement for themselves.

Creativity During the Early Childhood Years

The spontaneity and originality that characterize the language and art of young children spring from their fresh experiences with the world in which they live, and their exciting discovery that they can communicate their feelings and ideas about people and things through many different symbolic forms.

According to Howard Gardner, co-director of Harvard's Project Zero, which is studying creativity in children, five- and six-year-olds can not only understand and use the symbols of language, painting, music, numbers, and so on, but often are able to combine them in ways that adults find novel and striking.

If you would like to experiment at home with various mediums of expression with your five-year-old, you will find many useful suggestions in *Buttons Are to Push: Developing Your Child's Creativity* by Milton A. Young (New York: Pitman, 1970) and *Guiding Your Child to a More Creative Life* by Fredelle Maynard (Garden City, NY: Doubleday, 1973).

The Appeal of Games

Free play is unrestricted; games have rules. Play may merely be the enactment of a dream, but in each game there is some kind of contest. When young children play games in the street, they are usually extremely simple.

Young children seldom need an umpire. They rarely trouble to keep score because little significance is attached to who wins or who loses. It does not seem to worry them if a game is not finished. Fives enjoy games that restart almost automatically, so that everybody is given a chance to play. Choosing leaders, picking sides, and deciding which side will start first is almost a game in itself.

The games of young children appear cumbersome to adults. When invited to participate, they may find themselves becoming impatient and wanting to speed things up.

Play and Playthings for Kindergarten Children

Enjoyable playthings that are not toys can be found in all kinds of shops:

Stationery Store
hole punch
small stapler and staples
magnifying glass
gummed stars, labels, flowers
scissors
number and letter stamps and pads

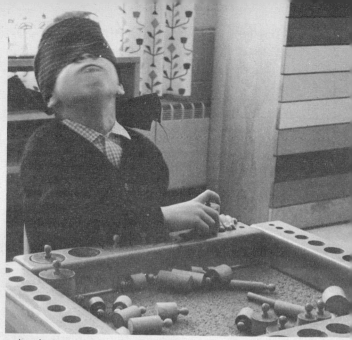

animal stamps
sturdy printing set

Hardware/Housewares Store
padlock and key
magnet
flashlight
small trowel
seeds and a flower pot
meat baster
watering can
clothespins
wind-up alarm clock
egg timer
egg beater
cookie cutters
rolling pin
plastic squeeze bottles

Discarded household items, in safe working order, can also serve admirably for manipulative and exploratory play. Such items include soft margarine tubs, berry baskets, cans of all sizes (with smooth rims), grocery store food trays, empty Band-Aid cans with flip-top lids, plastic bottles and jars with screw-on lids, and so on.

The following is a list of other useful items for make-believe play at this age:

• giant mirror
• dress-up materials: adult clothing, grown-up shoes, gloves, discarded handbags, assorted hats, bracelets, necklaces; also men's shirts, sweaters, caps, fans, fur pieces, etc.
• puppet stage (handmade or purchased)
• assorted hand puppets and finger puppets
• doctor's kit: real stethoscope, tongue depressors, gauze, Band-Aids, etc.

Television as a Tool for Stimulating the Imagination*

"In more than 90 percent of American homes," write Dorothy G. Singer and Jerome L. Singer in *Partners in Play* (New York: Harper & Row, 1977), "the television set is practically a member of the family."

With TV sets turned on from two to six hours a day, a vast parade of informational material and people in all walks of life (from baseball players to African dancers) compete for the attention of the child. Toddlers up to five-year-olds see a wide array of models engaging in adventurous activities they seek to imitate and emulate. Superman, Spiderman, and the Incredible Hulk perform impossible feats that affect the fantasy and play of young children. These and cartoon characters are tied in with action-packed violence and destruction, accompanied by spicy language. One researcher estimates that the average American child will have seen 18,000 televised murders by high school graduation time!

In the past several years, behavioral scientists have been studying how television affects the growing child. Psychologists and parents organized into citizen groups such as Action for Children's Television (ACT) "have called attention to the

*Parts of this page adapted from *Partners in Play: A Step-by-Step Guide to Imaginative Play in Children* by Dorothy G. Singer and Jerome L. Singer (New York: Harper & Row, 1977).

possibility that children will be encouraged to become overly aggressive as a result of the violence shown on television . . . a number of the research studies have demonstrated quite conclusively that young children, especially *those who have been active in hitting other children,* will increase their aggressive behavior." Since there are no studies reporting any good effects on preschoolers viewing violence, parents should be persuaded that the less violence seen, the better.

Even though monster movies and the supernatural appeal to many youngsters, the fact is that "what is exciting and enjoyable to an older child may trigger nightmares in a younger one." Fives do not have adequate information or thinking ability to deal with terrifying events and phenomena. Parents have reported increased nightmares, night terrors, and fear of the dark caused by such viewing.

Of course, there are also some positive aspects of television. Researchers indicate that preschoolers have obtained reading and number skills from watching programs such as "Sesame Street." "Mister Rogers' Neighborhood" appears to have encouraged children to be more considerate and friendly. Many make-believe games that children play in nursery school use characters and themes from television shows.

For five-year-olds (and younger children), TV viewing should be a shared experience with the parents. The TV show should be paced slowly enough to permit young children to follow the theme. It should encourage imaginative play, something a child may want to imitate. Programs for young children must be devoid of frightening scenes. Concerned parents who want to lead their children to the "healthiest kind of television viewing" might monitor certain programs and set definite times for TV watching.

Dorothy and Jerome Singer urge parents to guard against programs that involve great danger to animals, young children, or to parent figures; that feature supernatural characters and monsters engaged in frightening activities; that show characters torn apart or mutilated (as in cartoons); or that feature acrobatic and stunt activities (for example, Evel Knievel jumping across a canyon) that children might try to imitate with their tricycles.

Instead, the Singers and other early childhood educators would like to see children exposed to realistic animal stories that tell how animals are raised with love by children; fairly realistic cartoons involving stories of children who band together to deal with adventurous circumstances, to make things, or to help others; and programs that introduce children to music, dance, and puppetry.

Parents and teachers must be forceful in counteracting deceptive advertising in television toy and food commercials. They must provide consumer education for children by telling them about the pros and cons of highly touted toys and foods that really do not serve the best interests of children.

HEALTH, SELF-HELP, AND ROUTINES

On the average, five-year-olds will gain about four pounds during the year and grow about three inches. Their development is seen partly in this increased weight and height, but also in their ability to do more things by themselves and to express themselves well.

The health of Fives is quite good, with the exception of the colds and communicable diseases attendant to going to kindergarten. When stomachaches occur, they are most often related to the intake of food and to the need to have a bowel movement. Sometimes if a child does not enjoy going to school, the problem may express itself in stomachaches.

Five-year-olds generally have one bowel movement a day, usually after a meal. Children who function erratically need to be encouraged to sit on the toilet long enough to empty their bowels. Some Fives still require help in being wiped. Although they urinate infrequently, five-year-olds may need to be reminded to go to the toilet "before it is too late" because they find it hard to leave their companions and interrupt their play. Night accidents are rare at this age.

Five-year-old boys and girls like to do for themselves, especially if they have not been pressured by their parents to perform too early. They are almost completely reliable in washing themselves and bathing, but parents still need to assist in hard-to-reach places. Fives can brush their teeth and comb their hair, but usually require some reminding.

Most Fives eat well. They can feed themselves with little messiness. Although they like to eat with their fingers, they are quite adept with spoon and fork. Many are beginning to use a knife for spreading; most cannot use it for cutting meat. Inasmuch as Fives do not fidget as much as toddlers they are better company at the dinner table. Five-year-olds have definite food likes and dislikes. However, they will accept a greater variety of foods now.

Fives can dress themselves, but most cannot tie their shoe-laces or bows. Both girls and boys like to dress up, but they are not interested in taking care of their clothing. Neatness will come with ongoing encouragement and practice.

Sleep

Five-year-olds will benefit from a rest period, if not a nap, during the day, and at least ten hours of sleep at night. Some Fives appear to need eleven or twelve hours of nighttime sleep.

When they are very tired, some five-year-olds may ask to go to bed early. Getting ready for bed goes smoothly for the most part. Some Fives still take a favorite stuffed animal or doll to bed.

Many five-year-old boys and girls sleep through the night; others may have to go to the bathroom. The sleep of still others may be disturbed by frightening dreams in which wild animals are more prominent than people. Generally, these children return to sleep soon after being comforted by their parents.

Getting Five-Year-Olds Ready for First Grade

The shift from the informality of the nursery school and kindergarten to the formality of first grade in elementary school requires mid-Fives up to seventy-two-month-olds to prepare themselves for a brand-new "ball game."

It means learning to meet new sets of expectations, to assume responsibility for homework, put forth their best efforts, pay attention to the teacher, etc., as well as attending to their self-help routines at home.

Parents need to encourage their kindergarten children to do many things for themselves, including putting their soiled laundry in the hamper, keeping their room tidy, helping set the table and clearing away the dishes at the end of the meal, etc. It is not always convenient or easy, but parents need to resist the impulse to take over and do too many things for their young children because they can do everything faster and often better.

Actually, parents have been getting their children ready for formal schooling for several years, consciously or otherwise. They have been preparing their children by challenging them with suitable, increasing responsibilities. Parents have been getting their children ready by arranging for consistent health supervision, including all recommended inoculations and regular attention to their eyes, ears, and teeth.

Especially during this period in your children's lives, you can teach them to listen carefully and to follow instructions. While teachers at school work to strengthen this ability, it helps when children have had a head start at home.

Another skill that can be taught five year olds by their parents is awareness of all safety requirements when crossing streets. Children should know how to obey traffic lights and crossing guards in order to get safely to school. Even where children are bused, they should be familiar with all the rules of the road.

First Grade Blues

Many parents feel that no teacher will see how special their children are, especially in overcrowded classrooms. Parents who are unhappy about the possibility of having their children ignored will want to work with parent-teacher associations toward improving teacher-pupil ratios, classroom size, quality of teaching, and so on.

Even if the school is ideal, parents may feel somewhat let down after the first day or two. This may occur whether or not the child likes school. Parents feel they have lost their children, who either tell them nothing about school, or present scattered bits and pieces that reveal very little of each day's events.

Parents need to be prepared, too, for some tension in their children. During the first four or five weeks, almost all first grade children show signs of strain. Many may be irritable and cry easily. Others may return to bed-wetting, begin to chew their nails, eat little or no breakfast or lunch, etc. If such signs of stress do not disappear after a few weeks, you need to make an appointment with your child's teacher to discuss the situation. All parents find close contact with their children's teachers and school informative and beneficial.

Growth Chart—61st Through 72nd Month

MOTOR DEVELOPMENT

Gross Motor

Can stand on either foot up to 10 seconds; hop distance of 50 feet in 11 seconds.

Can walk a straight line without stepping off for a distance of 10 feet; stand and run on tiptoe for several seconds.

Skip alternately.

Skillful in climbing, sliding, swinging; smooth bodily control.

Bend and touch toes without bending knees.

Can broad-jump from 2 to 3 feet, using 2-foot takeoff.

Attempt all kinds of physical feats.

Learning to throw, kick, catch a ball; understand rules and scoring in game.

Skillful on tricycle; ready to learn to ride small bicycle. (By sixth birthday, will have mastered getting on, starting, balancing, stopping a two-wheeler.)

Descend stairs, alternating feet.

Move rhythmically to music; keep time when they dance.

Fine Motor

Handedness well established.

Able to distinguish right from left hand in themselves, but not in others.

Hold pencil, brush, or crayon in adult grasp between thumb and first finger.

Draw a recognizable human figure with head, arms, legs, trunk.

Drawing of house has door, windows, chimney, roof. Say what they are going to draw before they begin.

Can copy a circle, cross, square; by 5½ years, a triangle in recognizable form.

Can copy capital letters V, T, H, O, X, L, Y, U, C, A.

Can thread large needle.

Can "sew" wool in tipped laces through holes in a card.

LANGUAGE ACQUISITION

Speech is fluent and grammatically correct, except for some mispronunciations: s, v, f, th.

Define concrete nouns by their uses.

Interested in new words; constantly seeking their meaning.

Average vocabulary of 2,200 words.

Language facility can hide immaturity.

Use plurals, pronouns, tenses correctly in well-constructed sentences.

Can give full name, age, address when asked; may know birthday.

Love to be read to; memorize favorite stories; may act them out with friends or alone.

Recite or sing rhymes, jingles, or TV commercials.

SENSORY POWERS/LEARNING

Like to practice intellectual abilities; show parents how they can print their names, write numbers up to 5, spell words from favorite books.

Can correctly count fingers of one hand with index finger of the other and tell how many.

Can match numeral with quantity of objects.

Some comprehension of size and quantity words half–whole; big–little; more–less; tallest–shortest.

Begin to see relationship between capacity of different shaped containers.

Learn relationship between written and spoken numbers.

Can copy capital letters of given name.

Can sort objects by size, color, shape, and what goes with what.

Enjoy picture lotto games, picture dominoes, and other association group games.

Sort and match objects by texture (feel of things), smell, taste, etc.

Growth Chart—61st Through 72nd Month

Sensory Powers/Learning, cont'd

Match 10 colors; name at least 4 primary colors.

Vocational interest may be envisioned and discussed ("I want to be a doctor").

SOCIAL DEVELOPMENT

Intent on pleasing parents and other adults in family group.

Lump all adults as "grown-ups" who are set apart from agemates.

Relationship with father smooth, may obey father better than mother.

Like to please mother; take punishment better from mother than father.

Boys talk of "marrying mother."

Protective toward younger siblings and playmates.

Great drive to make friends.

Learning to share leadership, ideas, materials, and companions.

Can assume social amenities when necessary.

Acquiring social skills of giving, receiving, sharing.

Mastering techniques for expressing interest, friendship, feelings; for including others in play.

Like to impress their companions.

Learning concept of fair play.

Less time spent with family; more in play with agemates.

More independent behavior.

Growing revolt against parental control.

Demonstrate sense of humor.

PERSONALITY/ PSYCHOLOGICAL

Can experience fears (heights, dogs, death, etc.).

Better able to put fears and anxieties into words; may tell spontaneously what is troubling them.

Push for autonomy; want to be treated as adults.

Like to finish what they start, whether in play or assigned task.

Show greater intent and decisiveness.

Less dawdling.

Can accept fair punishment.

Contradictory behavior commonplace.

Can wail when frustrated or disappointed.

Impulsive behavior on occasion.

Cannot resist taking things that belong to others; may hide or destroy a stolen object.

When tense pick nose, bite nails, twitch nose, blink eyes, shake head, clear throat, etc.

May suck thumb before sleep or when tired.

Tension in kindergarten may result in pulling at clothes, scratching arm or leg, nasal discharge.

Curious about birth, marriage, death.

PLAY AND PLAYTHINGS

Highly imaginative, creative players.

Expert builders with building blocks; know in advance what they plan to construct.

Girls build houses for dolls.

Boys build skyscrapers, airports, garages, etc.

Can play alone, or with one to three companions, from 15 minutes to an hour daily.

Can solve most Montessori geometric color and size relation formboards.

Can complete 26-piece jigsaw puzzle.

Growth Chart—61st Through 72nd Month

Play and Playthings, cont'd

More interested in "here-and-now" themes than fairy tales or frightening fantasy.

Recreate roles of "doers" in pretend play; train engineer, doctor, boat captain, astronaut, etc.

Impersonation play accompanied by much talk to help clarify ideas.

Enjoy easel painting; pre-plan drawings and painting; mix colors with greater sureness.

Choose materials for collage work thoughtfully; balance one shape with another.

Can make mobiles and stabiles, incorporating original designs.

Use scissors more skillfully.

Strive for realism in their drawings; copy what they see; some children stop drawing.

Accompany music with bodily movements: slow, heavy, soft; walk like a bear, an old person, etc.

Interested in science and nature materials.

HEALTH, SELF-HELP, AND ROUTINES

May have one or two colds all winter; beginning to build immunity.

Occasional headache or earache.

Occasional stomachaches related to school adjustment or disliked food.

Increase in whooping cough, measles, chicken pox.

Wash themselves completely.

Attend to own toilet needs.

Oversensitivity to face, neck, and hair washing.

Definite likes and dislikes in foods.

Self-feeding with little mess.

Skillful with fork and spoon; may use knife for spreading, not cutting.

Can manage most dressing procedures (lace shoes, fasten large visible buttons, etc.).

Cannot tie shoelaces or bows well, or get into snowsuit.

Small buttons or fastenings in hidden places a problem.

Quite independent in daily routines.

Most have bad dreams or nightmares (wild animals, monsters, etc.).

Dear Parents:

Do not regard this chart as a rigid timetable.

Young children are unpredictable individuals. Some perform an activity earlier or later than this chart indicates.

Just use this information to anticipate and appreciate normal child development and behavior. No norms are absolute.

CHAPTER NINE

Special Parenting Topics

ADOPTION

The most frequent path to adoption remains the traditional one—an approved public or private adoption agency. Which agency to choose is a question that can be answered by the Bureau of Children's Services, operating in most states as part of the U.S. Department of Institutions and Agencies. This bureau can direct interested people to locally approved agencies.

The adoption process is a detailed procedure in which a trained caseworker learns about and assesses applicants, and the latter learn about adoption in general and a great deal about themselves. The focus is on matching the needs of a waiting child with the needs of applicants. No one passes or fails; children and prospective parents either do or do not match.

"The adoption procedure can be tedious or smooth, depending on the particular agency, part of the country, and availability of children," writes The Boston Women's Health Book Collective in *Ourselves and Our Children* (New York: Random House, 1978). "It can involve time-consuming and emotionally intense meetings and discussions with social workers and administrators. As many adoptive parents say, you really have to want to be parents to survive the waiting, wondering and soul-searching that can be part of the adoption experience."

A formal application is required outlining the medical history and information on the emotional stability of the prospective parents, which must be signed by a physician. Although a couple need not be childless or infertile to adopt, most applicants are in fact childless.

In a Public Affairs Pamphlet, *So You Want to Adopt a Child*, Ruth Carson writes, "No child will ever be urged upon you. You may want more than one meeting to decide. There will be no obligation built up. And there will be plenty of opportunity for you and the child to get acquainted before you make your decision. Perhaps the most important preparation for adoption is coming to terms with your own feelings. If you believe that you are comfortable with the idea and go through the adoptive process, your adopted child will be as much your child as if he or she had been born to you instead of for you." The prevailing standard for adoption remains the "best interests of the child."

The Final Steps

Adoption is primarily a state matter. Each state decides who may adopt, who may be adopted, and how adoptions are finalized. The great variations in each state's adoption laws make it imperative for prospective adoptive parents to study the most recent adoption rules and regulations in the state where they seek to adopt a child.

State laws usually require six months to a year before an adoption may become legal. When the adoption becomes legal, a new birth certificate is issued with the child's new name and your names as parents. The original birth certificate is sealed and filed. It may be opened by the state registrar only upon demand of the adopted person (if of legal age), or the adoptive parents by a court order.

Another way to adopt a child is through independent or "gray market" arrangements by third parties, usually doctors or lawyers. These placements are not made for profit. The fees paid are for legal and medical services connected with the adoptive process. No fee is paid for the baby per se, and the adoption is entirely legal.

"Gray market" adoption is not to be confused with "black market" placements; the latter depend only upon a customer's readiness to pay. Fraud and perjury are often encouraged in black market adoptions. *They are to be avoided!*

The basic difficulty with the gray market procedure is that most licensed adoption agencies and public welfare officials believe that adoptions should be in their domain. They challenge the judgment of outside lawyers or physicians who are active in handling adoptions, even though many of them have had extensive, successful records. In independent adoptions, as in agency adoptions, anonymity on both sides is maintained.

Hard-to-Place Children

Although there is a dearth of newborn infants available for adoption, there are many other children who are hard to place but equally in need of adoptive homes. These include handicapped children, older boys and girls, and minority and interracial children.

The adoption of a black or interracial child by a white person was practically unheard of not too many years ago. Nowadays it is the answer for many adults wanting to adopt a child, and for children who would otherwise go homeless. Blacks and whites both worry about the ability of adoptive white parents to equip black children with sufficient racial and personal identity to survive and function well in a prejudiced world. To date, most interracial adoptions appear to be working, but as of this writing there is no research data to confirm this.

There are homeless children all over the world. If you are interested in or want information about adopting a child from abroad, write to the International Social Service, American Branch, Inc., 291 Broadway, New York, NY 10007.

Most people do not want to adopt an older child who is no longer "cute" and "pliable." However, there is nobody who more desperately needs and longs for affection and belonging to a family than an abandoned older child. Although the adjustments in adopting an older child are greater for all concerned, the rewards can also be greater.

Many children are hard to place due to handicaps. Such children also think, feel, and react as other children do, and especially need to be nurtured and loved. In *A Parent's Guide to Adoption* (New York: Sterling Publishing Company, 1979), Robert S. Lasnik writes, "The recent focus on adoption of hard-to-place children has led to an increase in single-parent adoptions." Today both single women and single men are successful at adopting children and bringing them up.

Among the organizations that will provide information on single-parent adoption and adoptive parent groups are the following:

Commission for Single Adoptive Parents
Box 4074
Washington, DC 20015

New York Council on Adoptable Children
125 East 2nd Street
New York, NY 10010

North American Council on Adoptable Children
250 East Blaine Street
Riverside, CA 92507

According to Mr. Lasnik, one of the great breakthroughs in bringing together adoptive parents and children is the Adoption Resource Exchange of North America (ARENA). "ARENA operates a clearinghouse where licensed agencies in all fifty states, the District of Columbia, seven Canadian provinces, and the possessions of the United States can match families with hard-to-place children. Operated by the Child Welfare League of America's North American Center on Adoption, ARENA groups publish books featuring pictures and biographies of available special-needs children."

Colette Taube Dywasuk, herself an adoptive parent, has written an objective, helpful book, *Adoption—Is It for You?* (New York: Harper & Row, 1973), that will answer many of your questions about adoption. Another useful book, if you are considering adoption, is *The Adoption Advisor* by Joan MacNamara (New York: Hawthorn Books, 1975).

In *The Joys and Sorrows of Parenthood* (New York: Charles Scribner's Sons, 1973), The Group for the Advancement of Psychiatry writes, "A significant part of the preparation to be a parent is making the jump from a self-image of a nonparent to that of a parent. During a natural pregnancy, the internal change of the self-image is a central experience. The adoptive couple must wait until the baby responds to their care before they feel they are parents."

Adoptive parents should get as much information as they can about the background of their adoptee to do a good parenting job. This should include the medical background of the child and his or her biological mother and father, and data concerning their work, interests, skills, etc.

Adopting a Child from a Foreign Country

"While a child of another race will become a true member of your family, he or she can never be fully assimilated," writes Vicki Lansky, author of *Best Practical Parenting Tips* (Deephaven, MN: Meadowbrook Press, 1980). "It's unrealistic to let such a child think he or she is just like you." She suggests that adoptive parents of foreign-born children learn as much as they can about the other country's family relationships, cultural and religious celebrations and observances, and so forth, so that they will be better able to help their child maintain a feeling of racial pride and cultural identity.

It is a good idea, too, to keep in mind that if your child seems less than completely well upon arrival, most illnesses are treatable and reversible. In fact, according to Ms. Lansky, "Seeing your child through to full health can deepen your bonds with each other."

It is also recommended that a medical checkup be delayed for a day or two after your child's arrival because a thorough examination might be upsetting.

Adoptive parents of foreign-born toddlers may have to face such negative behaviors as their loss of appetite, lack of toilet control, temper tantrums, and excessive clinging or seeming indifference and withdrawal. The lack of a common language makes it impossible for the child to communicate his needs and desires, which exacerbates the already difficult initial period of adjustment.

When to Tell Children They Are Adopted

There is no accord among child-care specialists as to when it is best to tell children they are adopted. This uncertainty is upsetting to some adoptive parents. However, most parents sense when the child is ready for this information. The Group for the Advancement of Psychiatry indicates that "a most natural time to bring adoption up is when the child asks where babies come from. He can then be told that he came from the uterus of another woman."

There are professionals in the field who think the years between seven and ten are a propitious time to tell a child of her adoption and to assist her in accepting it. Other professionals suggest early discussion and recognition of the adoption; i.e., as soon as the parents are ready to talk about it and think their child will be able to understand and adapt to the fact.

Although the optimum time for both the child and the parents remains an individual parental decision, parents need to make sure that they are helping their adoptee to build secure feelings about his identity and about why he was adopted.

Everyone is in agreement that a child's introduction to the fact of adoption should be presented in the affectionate atmosphere of his home. He must never learn the news from taunting peers or in other distressful ways later on.

According to Dr. David M. Brodzinsky, child psychologist at Douglass College in New Brunswick, New Jersey, "The adoption revelation process is a stressful event. Parents are afraid of questions the child might raise, such as 'Why did mommy give me up?' The parents feel that the sooner they get it over with, the better. They terminate the dialogue too early because they think the child understands before he really does." Research indicates that abruptly or permanently closing the discussion about a child's adoption may create problems.

Very young children do not understand what adoption is. When they say they are adopted, they are just mouthing words. Child psychologists believe that a child has to know something about the birth process as well as what it means to be part of a family in order to understand something about what it is to be adopted. However, even a gradual, straightforward explanation of the process of adoption may not satisfy an adopted child. For example, a five-year-old may want to know why her biological parents gave her up for adoption. Dr. Brodzinsky and other child specialists think this may be an unresolved question that adoptees ask themselves throughout their lives. Actually, in many cases, the "acceptance of adoption is not complete unless a person becomes a biological parent herself."

More Research on Adoption Needed

Ongoing research is needed to determine how adopted children make adjustments to other children in the family, whether the latter are adopted or biological offspring. Also helpful would be more specific data on the outcomes for all concerned of interracial adoptions by white families of minority-group or foreign-born children.

Robert S. Lasnik succinctly expresses one of the basic frustrations involved in all cases of adoption, as follows: "Although parents can plan for all legal and psychosocial circumstances, the actual coming together of the child who is meant for that family and the parents who are meant for that child defies all logic and all rules."

CHILD ABUSE

A strictly legal definition of child abuse, according to Nathan B. Talbot, M.D., editor of *Raising Children in Modern America: Problems and Prospective Solutions* (Boston: Little, Brown, 1976), is the following: "Where a child under the age of sixteen is suffering from serious physical injury or abuse inflicted upon him by other than accidental means or suffering harm by reason of neglect, malnutrition or sexual abuse, goes without necessary and basic physical care, including medical and dental care, or is growing up under conditions which threaten the physical and emotional survival of the child . . .

"It is an interesting paradox that within the American legal system we have a precedent of premarital blood examinations of both partners to detect syphilis so as to prevent the scourge of congenital syphilis . . . as a compulsory health measure under the laws of all fifty states, we instill silver nitrate into the eyes of newborn infants to prevent gonorrhea . . . On the other hand, we do not provide basic health screening for possible child abuse and other disturbances in the child under six years of age."

Child abuse is not a clear-cut instance of hurtful interaction between the abusing parent and target child. According to Dr. Vincent J. Fontana, medical director of the New York Foundling Hospital and director of pediatrics at St. Vincent's Hospital and Medical Center in New York, "child abuse is a family affair involving the active abuser, neglector, the passively cooperative if unseeing mate, and the other children in the family, who may or may not be active participants but are certainly observers." He thinks that child battering is probably one of the most common causes of death in young children. Dr. Fontana maintains that "child abuse is a symptom of the violence running rampant in our society and we as a society are unable to control its existence."

In her Introduction and Overview to Volume 1 of *Families Today* (1979; one of a series of science monographs published by the National Institute of Mental Health), Eunice Corfman writes, "Child abuse seems inexplicable to most of us, a cruelty beyond comprehension. The 1975 national survey of family violence conducted by Murray A. Straus, professor of sociology of the University of New Hampshire, and Richard J. Gelles, associate professor of sociology at the University of Rhode Island, reveals an astonishing level of it, even when pushing, slapping, shoving, strapping, caning, and paddling are excluded—all acts that done to strangers could be considered illegal. Generalizing the survey's findings, which the investigators regard as an underestimate, about 3.7 percent of the nation's children between three and seventeen and living with both parents were repeatedly punched, kicked, bitten, beaten up, and otherwise physically abused."

In an article by Laurie Beckelman entitled "Why the Cry of the Beaten Child Goes Unheard" (*The New York Times Magazine,* April 16, 1978), Dr. Eli Newberger, director of the Family Development Study at the Boston Children's Hospital Medical Center, is quoted as saying: "Our society upholds a tradition of family autonomy. Children's rights have never been defined because we believe in the inviolability of the family and feel that we shouldn't wrest control from parents who have the right to discipline their children."

In 1974, the Child Abuse Prevention and Treatment Act was signed into law. The National Center on Child Abuse and Neglect acts as a clearinghouse for information on public and private programs related to child abuse. The agency develops training material for professionals working with abused children and their families, and awards grants to public and private organizations for the purpose of setting up centers to provide needed services.

All children are dependent upon adults for their survival and well-being. Certainly every child's birthright should include good physical, nutritional, and emotional care. Abuse of children by the adults who are supposed to protect them appears to span all ethnic backgrounds and income levels. For various reasons, doctors and the general public are loath to report cases of battered and otherwise abused children to the proper authorities—the police, family service agencies, etc.

Studies indicate that 60 percent of child abusers are men; about three-fourths of the incidents occur in cities and only one-sixth in suburbs. About 51 percent of *known* abusers have incomes below $8,000 per year. Estimates of the number of abused children in our country range from 800,000 to over 1 million annually; accurate figures cannot be compiled because all cases are not reported. (Authorities suspect that child abuse or neglect among the rich and middle class is frequently not reported. Most child abuse reports come from hospital emergency rooms that are used by the poor. The rich take their battered children to family doctors, who are less likely to file reports of child abuse.)

Herbert Yahraes, also writing in *Families Today,* states in his chapter on "Physical Violence in Families" that "Physical punishment starts with infants. An infant crawling on the floor picks up something dirty and puts it in his or her mouth, so you tell the child not to do that. The child, of course, doesn't really understand, puts the thing in his mouth, and mommy or daddy slaps his hand. Now that's something done for the child's own good, but it's also something that teaches the child that love and violence go together; that those who love you are also those who hit you."

Abusive parents or guardians are usually under stress (suffering from unemployment, inadequate housing, alcoholism, drug addiction, unpreparedness for child-rearing, marital or other family tensions, etc.). It is common for child abusers to have been battered children themselves. Often such parents believe that their beatings merely represent strict and proper discipline. Here is where family counseling can be especially helpful.

There are times when a parent loses control to the point of striking or humiliating his or her child. Such an incident is almost always followed by a sense of guilt and even remorse on the part of the abusive parent. Unfortunately, there are many children whose parents, despite their feelings of guilt, abuse them to an extent out of all proportion to the "offense"— often so severely that the helpless victim must be taken to a hospital.

"Husbands and wives who treat each other violently punish their children physically more often than other couples, and their children act violently against siblings more often than do the children of other couples," writes Herbert Yahraes.

The Fate of Abused Children

Julius Segal, in an article entitled "Child Abuse: a Review of Research in Volume 2 of *Families Today*," wrote that "Clinical observations have long suggested that abuse can seriously alter a child's physical resources—not only the ability but even the willingness to survive . . . For many abused children, lingering physical disabilities merge with intellectual and emotional ones in a pattern that invites lifelong problems."

Harold P. Martin, an early child abuse researcher, reported in 1974 the results of a five-year follow-up of fifty-eight abused children. While these particular youngsters did not suffer extremely severe injuries, about one-third evidenced poor physical growth and over half suffered neurological abnormalities. More than 60 percent had personality problems, including low self-esteem, poor social relationships, learning disorders, and behavior difficulties.

Dr. Brandt F. Steele, professor of psychiatry at the University of Colorado Medical Center, and a staff member of Denver's National Center for the Prevention and Treatment of Child Abuse and Neglect, reported in 1977 on some effects of abuse on the psychological development of children. He was concerned not only with children who had suffered fractures, burns, bruises, and internal injuries, but with those who were enduring emotional deprivation, nutritional neglect, sexual exploitation, and the complete lack of stimulation—especially in the early months and years of life. His conclusions were clear: "Maltreatment during this period not only results in immediate damage, but can also lead to deficits which affect the entire course of the child's life and distort all of his later psychological, emotional, and cognitive development."

Child abuse is a complicated, serious, national problem whose solution must involve many different professionals working with children and parents: pediatricians, psychiatrists, nurses, psychologists, family court judges, social workers, etc. Today more and more emphasis is being placed on the prevention and early identification of possible child abuse situations.

If you are one of those parents who cannot control an impulse to hurt or shame your child, or if your have ever had to get medical attention for your child after an abusive act on your part, *you need help!*

Parents Anonymous

Several years ago a mother on the West Coast found herself in the above position. After looking for someone who could help her overcome her harmful behavior and learn to understand her motivation, she and a social worker friend established Parents Anonymous. This national organization operates in much the same way as Alcoholics Anonymous. If you think you may need such support, write to Parents Anonymous, 22330 Hawthorne Boulevard, Torrance, CA 90505. The New York office of Parents Anonymous is at 250 West 57 Street, Room 1701, New York, NY 10019.

Child Abuse Prevention Program

The National Committee for the Prevention of Child Abuse, 332 South Michigan Avenue, Suite 1250, Chicago, IL 60604, conducts a child abuse prevention program to study and develop useful techniques for identifying parents who are possible child abusers. It attempts to intervene in cases of actual child abuse and to prevent potential abuse. A free copy of its booklet, "You Can Prevent Child Abuse," is available (in English and Spanish) upon request.

The National Institute of Mental Health has issued a reading list on the subject of child abuse in another free booklet. Write for DHEW Publication No. (HSM) 73-9034 to the U.S. Department of Health, Education, and Welfare, Mental Health Administration, 5600 Fishers Lane, Rockville, MD 20852.

The organizations listed above will be happy to provide you with information *wherever* you live, so do not hesitate to write or phone for help.

All authorities in this field believe that with improved circumstances, some battered children can lead relatively normal lives. However, very severely damaged children are never able to develop adequate skills of learning and living.

Luckily, most parents have sufficient self-control to curb their angry and/or unreasonable feelings. Part of the problem of child abuse lies in the fact that the aggressive impulses parents may experience during their years of child-rearing are in sharp conflict with the social ideal of unfaltering parental love and devotion.

In all cases of child abuse, each family member needs help. Everybody is harmed psychologically when a fist is raised, when emotional support is denied, or when caring communication ceases.

DYSLEXIA*

The existence of reading-disabled children of normal and superior IQ who manifest reversals and related "scrambling" difficulties in reading, writing, and spelling, despite adequate emotional and educational stimulation, was first recognized in 1898 by two British physicians, J. Kerr and W. P. Morgan.

What makes these dyslexic children special is their inability to read, write, speak, and spell correctly. For reasons not yet known, the brain jumbles the information it receives from the child's senses, causing difficulty in concentrating, in using symbols (letters and numbers), in grasping the concepts of time, distance, direction, etc.

Dyslexia is a rather variable learning disability. Some cases are quite slight and respond to relatively simple therapy; others are so severe that they require highly specialized multidisciplinary treatment.

Samuel T. Orton observed the systematic errors in the reading and writing of dyslexic children in Iowa City, and found that they tended to read words from right to left. The children also had difficulties with letters whose orientation contributed to their identification (for example, *p* and *q, d* and *b*), and they often "mirror-wrote" (*b* for *d* or *p* for *q*). Some of the children read as efficiently upside-down as right-side-up; others wrote with either hand.

Orton surmised that by the time most children start learning to read, cerebral lateralization has already occurred. This means that one hemisphere of the brain, in most cases the left (which controls movement on the right side of the body and is normally responsible for language functions), has established dominance over the other, usually the right. The right hemisphere controls movement of the left side of the body, and normally plays a minimal role in language function. The two

*See also Learning Disabilities, p. 448.

sides of the brain then work in concert, with the dominant hemisphere leading the other. Orton suggested that in dyslexics, the two hemispheres may still be competing for dominance. He believed that dominance was necessary for consistent left-to-right reading; that incomplete dominance could result in a tendency to read right-to-left.

Recent research indicates that dyslexics show less unity between the two hemispheres of their brains, and more rapport within each hemisphere. Bernard Sklar, working at UCLA's Brain Research Institute, endorses the theory that dyslexia is related to incomplete cerebral dominance. Paul Rozin and his associates at the University of Pennsylvania think that the dyslexic's principal problem is blending a sequence of letters into an English word, due perhaps to a neurological deficiency. Rozin recommends that dyslexics be taught a system of easily recognizable characters that represent words rather than individual sounds. There are other researchers who believe that reading should be taught to dyslexic children solely by the "look-say" method, drill in phonics, tactile involvement with letters, teaching machines, etc.

Check Your Child for Dyslexia

If your child is having serious trouble reading, consider having him or her tested for dyslexia—especially if you or other relatives are decidedly slow readers. Dyslexia is a perception disorder that may be either genetic or perhaps the result of a childbirth trauma, such as inadequate oxygen, etc.

The term dyslexia has become a catchall for reading retardation based on any number of factors: psychological, educational, or cultural. Basically, however, it is a *neurological problem* that may occur in children of all socioeconomic levels. One hemisphere of the brain supposedly controls language ability; dyslexics use both hemispheres when they read. Hence they confuse symbols in space and sounds in time; for instance, *24* comes out as *42, was* is read as *saw,* etc. Dyslexics have trouble following a sequence of words or lines. They may not hear sounds correctly, confusing *b* for *v, th* for *f,* or they may mispronounce words. Hand and eye coordination is a problem as well.

The following are some of the dyslexic's problems: poor awareness of body movement; inadequate combination of motor and visual ability; visual inefficiency; poor listening ability; difficulty in integrating several sensory abilities; poor grasp of sequence; poor sense of rhythm; difficulty mastering concepts of time, number, and space; difficulty with the learning process; gaps in general knowledge.

Visual-motor exercises, such as walking on a balance beam, bouncing a ball, and tracking a moving object with the eyes are often prescribed. However, owing to controversy in the field over the efficacy of such techniques, it is recommended that they be used only as a supplement to a child's remedial academic learning program.

Incidentally, a dyslexic child may be clumsy at skipping rope or riding a bicycle.

Children with dyslexia appear normal enough for the problem to go undetected. Often they are branded as underachievers and put in remedial reading groups, where—unfortunately—their problems may only worsen.

Some schools are set up to diagnose and treat dyslexia. A local university may have a learning-disorder center that is equipped to help your child. Although diagnosis is difficult, more and more educators and specialists are beginning to recognize the symptoms of learning disabilities. Eventually all affected children will receive the benefits of the new educational approaches.

Where to Get Help

The Association for Children with Learning Disabilities (ACLD) is a parents' organization that can provide information on diagnostic clinics, special schools, and tutoring services in your area. If you cannot find a chapter of ACLD in your area, send a self-addressed, stamped envelope to The Association for Children with Learning Disabilities, 4156 Library Road, Pittsburgh, PA 15234, for referral to the closest chapter.

The Orton Society offers a list of publications to parents of dyslexic children. Founded in 1949, this organization devotes its energies exclusively to the "promotion of the study, treatment, and prevention of the problems of dyslexia." You may request materials from The Orton Society, 8415 Bellona Lane, Towson, MD 21204.

The New York Institute for Child Development, 205 Lexington Avenue, New York, NY 10016, is a national center for the medical diagnosis and treatment of learning-disabled children. The Information Center of the National Easter Seal Society, 2023 West Ogden Avenue, Chicago, IL 60612, is another helpful resource. Write for their list of publications on learning disabilities.

"Can't Read, Can't Write, Can't Talk Too Good Either"

A readable and revealing account of one mother's experience in dealing with her son's perceptual problem is presented in *Can't Read, Can't Write, Can't Talk Too Good Either* by Louise Clark (New York: Penguin Books, 1974). The author details her successes and failures in handling her son's severe language problem from age two upward. A state-by-state listing of agencies and services for the dyslexic is included in her book.

Outstanding Dyslexics

Some dyslexics have made substantial contributions in their fields and one, Hans Christian Andersen, became a masterful writer even though he never learned to spell. Other notable dyslexics included Leonardo da Vinci, George Washington, John D. Rockefeller, Jr., Nelson A. Rockefeller, and Albert Einstein.

There continues to be considerable disagreement among those who study reading problems about what causes dyslexia and how it should be treated. Although several new treatments are helping some children, the real breakthrough will come only when neurologists and other researchers discover the precise connections that link visual forms and meaning.

GIFTED CHILDREN

Federal guidelines define giftedness as demonstrated talent in one or several of the following areas: general intellectual acuity, specific academic ability, leadership, creativity, and ability in the visual or performing arts.

"Parents can and do identify gifted children," says Dr. Jack Cassidy, associate professor of education at Millersville State College in Pennsylvania. In an article in the August 23, 1980, edition of *The Trentonian,* he cited some guidelines to enable parents to recognize possible giftedness in their children.

These include a high degree of verbal fluency and advanced vocabulary (Dr. Cassidy believes, however, that the notion that all gifted children learn to read before entering first grade is erroneous; in fact, only 20 percent of all gifted children are early readers); a great deal of curiosity about all parts of the environment; a high degree of problem-solving ability in both verbal and nonverbal challenges; prolonged periods of attention and concentration to a given task. The four criteria included here can be recognized before a child enters school.

Unfortunately, Dr. Cassidy leaves out exceptional creativity in the visual or performing arts and special musical aptitude—which also are signs of giftedness.

We believe that all children possess innate potentials, but some are more gifted or get more encouragement than others. Parents need to be aware of and nurture any special talents in their children. Some toddlers may have perfect pitch and an ear for rhythm to which they respond with their whole bodies. Other young children may be mechanically adept, building and analyzing their world with Lego construction sets, building blocks, or Tinkertoys. Then there are verbally precocious children who express their feelings and thoughts poetically or dramatically.

In the past, popular euphemisms for a gifted child were "egghead," "brain," or "genius," all of which alluded to a high IQ. Today the definition of the gifted has been broadened beyond the purely intellectual realm to include children who are talented in many areas, including the creative and performing arts.

At one time a gifted child was caricatured as being unattractive, bespectacled, skinny, and uncoordinated, sitting off by himself reading a book on quantum physics, or practicing the piano for hours on end while his peers were playing out of doors or generally having fun. The facts gathered over a period of more than fifty years indicate otherwise. The gifted child is healthier than average, better coordinated, usually more attractive personally, and enjoys a full, rich life.

All is not well, however. The plight of the gifted child in the United States is part of the neglect to which all minority groups are exposed socially and educationally, and it is exaggerated by our society's allegiance to the so-called virtues of adjustment, sociability, conformity, and convergent thinking. Success in school (according to the middle-class value system) favors the high achiever and looks less favorably upon the atypical child, the loner, or the rebel.

Needs of the Gifted

According to a report of the U.S. Office of Education, there are about 2.5 million gifted children in our country. However, such children stand *less than one chance in four* of even being identified as gifted; and probably no more than one in twenty is being helped by some kind of program for the gifted.

Gifted children require special programs if they are to benefit fully from their schooling. Unfortunately, there is still a widespread attitude that gifted children, because of their special endowment, already have an advantage over their other classmates and so should be able to "make it on their own." Many educators believe, however, that without *extra* attention these children may never realize the full extent of their giftedness. Without sufficient and proper cultivation, giftedness can wither much as flowers do in an untended garden. When a gifted child goes unnoticed, his or her potential is lost forever.

Today's programs for the gifted vary, but all have in common the attempt to stimulate creativity, allow in-depth exploration of a subject, and encourage progress according to ability and interest, not age alone.

Who Are the Gifted Children?

According to the American Association for Gifted Children, a gifted person is one "whose performance in any line of socially useful endeavor is consistently superior." The range includes those talented in arts and crafts, music, drama, and mathematics; those who possess exceptional mechanical or social skills; and those with a superior degree of abstract verbal intelligence.

Gifted children share certain characteristics. They are *mentally superior* in the sense that they perceive relationships with great ease, and are able to learn and remember new things, solve problems, speak fluently, and read with quick comprehension. Nevertheless, they resemble other children their age emotionally and socially in their play styles. Gifted children come from all kinds of family backgrounds. Environmental factors, especially values espoused in the home, are of great significance in fostering their talents.

Helping Your Gifted Child by Dr. Ruth Strang (New York: E. P. Dutton, 1960) is a classic. Her analysis of the different types of giftedness, the special problems gifted children face, and the parents' and schools' cooperating roles in developing their talents remains valid and important today. Especially meaningful is her concern with developing a balanced and responsible *whole* personality and guarding against one-sided development. Another interesting book is *Education of the Intellectually Gifted* by Milton J. Gould (Columbus, OH: Merrill, 1965). Dr. Gould outlines steps to take in identifying the gifted, followed by a thorough program of curriculum enrichment.

Creativity and Intelligence

Have you ever known a child who made adults uncomfortable by endlessly asking questions, testing rules and regulations other children accept automatically; a child who stood apart and often alone because of her strong sense of individuality? Such a child may fall into the category of an undetected "gifted misfit"—undetected because today's standardized IQ tests do not measure imaginative or unusual responses. Such a child may be considered "difficult" because many gifted children can resort to disruptive, hostile behavior when they are not given challenging tasks.

In *Creativity and Intelligence* by Jacob W. Getzels and Philip W. Jackson (New York: Wiley, 1962) the authors contend that cognitive intelligence is promoted in the classroom and then measured by tests that completely ignore imagination and creativity. It is a sad commentary on the problems of the gifted that this exploration into the relationship between creativity and intelligence (school success) is still timely twenty years after it was published.

Our society pays lip-service to creativity but does very little in fact to foster it. We respect and admire such qualities as openness, enthusiasm, the ability to take risks, playfulness, and the urge to discovery, yet our teachers reward conformity. Educational programs in general are based upon tests that measure IQ only, and in almost all cases school curricula revolve about rote memorization and comprehension.

In an address he presented at the Fourteenth Annual Meeting of the National Association for Gifted Children (held in Hartford, Connecticut, in May 1967), Dr. Stanley Krippner (former Senior Research Associate at the Community Mental Health Center, Dream Laboratory of the Maimonides Medical Center, Brooklyn, New York) outlined his "Ten Commandments That Block Creativity."

"1) *Everything thou doest must be useful.* America's emphasis on practicality has produced many worthwhile results, but often it has been carried to extremes, with deleterious effects upon our children. (Today's toys do not allow a child's imagination free rein.)

2) *Everything thou doest must be successful.* In our achievement-oriented culture, the foremost idea is that one should be competent in everything he does. Children steeped in this tradition will hesitate to display imagination, ideas, or creative products, for fear of ridicule and censure.

3) *Everything thou doest must be perfect.* A child who is criticized for work she has done is apt to regard this as an attack on herself rather than on her work. An adult who attempts in this way to stir a child to further efforts will find that the child ends up deeming herself a failure.

4) *Everyone thou knowest must like thee.* The need for universal acceptance is instilled in our children at an early age. This prevents them from forming their own concept of self-respect, and instead substitutes a fear of being unloved. Children will forfeit their creative ability to be 'one of the gang.'

5) *Thou shalt not prefer solitude to togetherness.* The classroom overemphasizes group interaction. Adults often regard solitude as a sign of emotional instability. However, many types of creative performance must be done individually, according to the whim of the gifted person, not the rules of society.

6) *Remember concentrated attention and keep it holy.* Western civilization has learned to use a mind as a spotlight rather than a floodlight. The floodlight mind leads to discovery, and increases perceptions of relations and details. This floodlight mind is almost totally ignored in American schooling. It is not just the children, but the entire society that suffers from this lack.

7) *Thou shalt not diverge from culturally-imposed sex-role*

norms. Creativity is a sensitive and independent attribute. In our culture, sensitivity is considered a feminine trait, and independence a masculine one. If parents teach healthy attitudes, they will produce children who are secure in their sex roles.

8) *Thou shalt not express excessive emotional feeling.* Creative people are likely to be highly emotional because access to their feelings also fuels their imaginations. Often creative children have a reputation for rebellion, although it is independence of thought and feelings that they are showing, not disruptive behavior per se.

9) *Thou shalt not be ambiguous.* Americans find it difficult to accept paradoxes, but the creative child is torn by choices. She sees advantages in all possible alternatives open to her. When circumstances require it, creative children are capable of making the best, most responsible decisions.

10) *Thou shalt not rock the cultural boat.* Children who are too inquisitive or have very vivid imaginations are often told to 'turn it off.' Therefore, many creative children will decide that the best thing to do is to leave their thoughts hidden rather than risk ridicule."

Programs for the Gifted

The basic problem facing the parents and teachers of gifted children is whether to provide acceleration, enrichment, or some combination of both. Mrs. Owenita Sanderlin has written an insightful book that reviews this subject, *Teaching Gifted Children* (New York: A. S. Barnes, 1973). The author presents pro-and-con points of view on such important issues as grouping students by ability and accelerating or enriching their courses of study.

The following are some special provisions for gifted children that are being made in various school systems:

- After-school, summer school, and weekend workshops sponsored by the school or community.
- An extra period for library use and book discussion.
- An extra subject—foreign language, music, mathematics, etc.
- Special homogeneous classes (sometimes called "honors programs").

- "Rapid-advance" or "special-progress" classes in which junior high school students are grouped homogeneously in order to complete three years of academic work in two.
- Special schools—an enriched program for children from all parts of a city or region who can demonstrate a high degree of abstract verbal, quantitative, musical, or artistic ability.
- Innovative curricula for both students and teachers that update and enrich existing programs.

Finally, it is up to parents to read widely and seek out unusual special-interest programs in order to enhance the life of their gifted child.

How to Determine If Your Child Is Gifted*

Many gifted children indicate their abilities early, which increases the probability that their particular needs will be accommodated. However, many others do not reveal their giftedness until the middle elementary grades or later. Without proper identification and support, gifted children may hide their capacities by kindergarten age.

The following are some easily recognizable characteristics of gifted children:

- Keen observation and curiosity.
- Early accurate use of a large vocabulary.
- Early use of entire sentences.
- Retention of a variety of facts.
- Periods of intense concentration.
- Ability to perceive relationships.
- Capacity for abstract thinking.
- A wide range of interests.
- Unusual skill in music, rhythms, drawing, or other art forms.
- Ask questions about subjects that do not interest their agemates.
- Early interest in clocks and calendars and ability to understand their function.
- Early ability to tell or reproduce stories and events with great detail.

*Parts of pages 441–442 adapted from *Somewhere to Turn: Strategies for Parents of the Gifted and Talented* by Eleanor G. Hall and Nancy Skinner (New York: Teachers College, Columbia University, 1980).

- Ability to carry on intelligent conversations with older children and adults.
- Learned to read early.

In addition, creative children are likely to have one or more of the following traits: a sense of playfulness and relaxation; a strong tendency to be nonconformist and to think independently; a reputation for having "far-out" or "silly" ideas.

If you would like to secure resources on gifted children, you can write to the following organizations:

National Association for Creative Children and Adults
8080 Springvalley Drive
Cincinnati, OH 45236

Association for the Gifted, a division of
The Council for Exceptional Children
1920 Association Drive
Reston, VA 22091

American Association for Gifted Children
15 Gramercy Park
New York, NY 10003

Office of the Gifted and Talented
U.S. Office of Education
400 Sixth Street, SW, Room 3835
Washington, DC 20202

THE HYPERACTIVE CHILD*

Many children with learning disabilities are *hyperactive.* They are restless, inattentive, easily excitable, and disruptive in class, and most often unable to play with other children. However, there is reason to believe that a number of hyperactive children, especially those whose only manifestation is behavioral (without learning difficulties or neurological findings), are merely children who have unusually high stimulation or activity levels.

Most of the children who will later be diagnosed as "hyperactive" will seem somewhat different to their parents during the first two years of their lives. Others will appear quite normal

See also Learning Disabilities, p. 448.

and will not perturb their parents until they go to nursery school, or even until they attend grade school.

Not all learning-disabled children are hyperactive, but almost all hyperactive children have learning disabilities. The learning-disabled child is not to be confused with the *slow learner,* who may require extra help, but who can eventually learn to perform.

Constantly hectic, impatient, overactive, impulsive, and highly distractible, hyperactive children are a persistent problem to themselves and to others. They cannot stop moving, talking, making noise. They may also have sleep problems and be bad-tempered. They are rambunctious, aggressive, and chaotic in school, disrupting class activities. At home, they are unpredictable, stormy, and annoyingly sloppy. Parents, peers, and teachers find it hard to like them. Even worse, hyperactive children are often inclined not to like themselves!

In *Raising a Hyperactive Child* (New York: Harper & Row, 1973), psychiatrist Mark A. Stewart and Sally Wendkos Olds point out that hyperactive children usually do not have friends because other children cannot cope with their hitting, show-off behavior, and failure to finish any game—a few of their other many disagreeable behaviors.

In *Parenting the Difficult Child* (Radnor, PA: Chilton Book Co., 1979), Florence K. Rogers writes, "Most writers on the subject of hyperkinesis [another word for hyperactivity] neglect one very important aspect, the parent-child relationship, which is usually the first thing that falls apart when a child behaves inappropriately or does not live up to expectations . . . No one else can help him if his parents cannot or have given up and won't try . . . Parents of hard-to-manage children need to rid themselves of many of their guilt feelings before they can realistically appraise themselves in relation to their child."

In *No One to Play With: The Social Side of Learning Disabilities* (New York: Random House, 1982), Betty B. Osman and Henriette Blinder write, "It has taken professionals a long time to recognize what parents have always known—that the learning-disabled child often just doesn't fit in . . . Living disabilities can become far more anxiety-provoking for the child and his family than his problems with reading or mathematics . . . Unfortunately very little information is available on how to help LD children succeed socially. However, social skills, like academic subjects, must be learned and can be taught."

Safeguarding Hyperactive Children

Hyperactive children are especially accident-prone due to their clumsiness, lack of attention, and impulsiveness—strong factors in children's accidents. Parents of hyperactive children particularly, and all young children generally, need to make sure their homes and backyards are as safe as possible. (See our section on Safety.)

Drugs for Hyperactive Children

Drug therapy for hyperactive children is increasingly frowned upon. Many doctors find it objectionable because there may be deleterious side effects in the long run, and because the drugs may create a totally false sense of well-being. "When the drugs wear off, the child is right back where he started."

Nutrition and Hyperactivity

Drug-free nutritional therapy for hyperactive children is gaining wide support. At The New York Institute for Child Development, a statistical analysis of laboratory tests on 265 hyperactive children revealed that 75 percent had abnormal glucose (sugar) tolerance. Other children exhibited allergies to certain food additives. Among hyperactive children, a diet completely free of sugar and color and chemical additives can produce dramatic positive behavioral results.

Soda, candy, cookies, cupcakes, jellies, fruit punches, flavored gelatin, and highly processed snack foods are decidedly harmful to hyperactive children. In fact, they are not good for children generally. All too often they rob children of the essential nutrients they require to maintain good health.

Hyperactive children need to be fed wholesome snacks between meals. The meals themselves should include complex carbohydrates—rice, potatoes, wholegrain breads, cereals, and crackers; fresh fruits and vegetables; and protein in the form of milk, natural cheeses, plain yogurt, eggs, lean meats, fish, chicken, turkey, nuts, seeds, and dried peas and beans.

Of course, no diet alone can alleviate a child's hyperactivity or learning disabilities, nor will every LD child respond. However, hyperactive children have had some improvement in their behavior as a result of careful nutritional therapy. *Note: No special nutritional program should be prescribed by anyone except a qualified physician who is intimately aware of each child's problems and special needs.*

The contention of Benjamin F. Feingold, M.D., pediatrician and allergist, and author of *Why Your Child Is Hyperactive* (New York: Random House, 1974), is that behavior disturbances and learning disabilities are caused by artificial flavors and color additives. (He does not discuss the effects of excessive sugar intake.) Dr. Feingold and other professionals agree, however, that although medical and psychological tests continue to play a considerable role in the clinical evaluation of the hyperactive child, their precise role and utility remain matters of sharp controversy.

Synthetic Color Additives to Avoid in Foods, Beverages, and Medication

Blue #2 (indigotine)
Red #2 (amaranth)
Red #3 (erythrosine)
Violet #1 (benzyl violet)
Yellow #5 (tartrazine)
Yellow #6

In addition, it is a good idea to avoid the following synthetic flavors, flavor enhancers, and preservatives in foods and beverages:

Alumina
Ammonium Sulphate
BHA (butylated hydroxyanisole)
BHT (butylated hydroxytoluene)
Cyclamates (noncaloric sweeteners)
Disodium Guanylate
Disodium Inosinate
MSG (monosodium glutamate)
Potassium Sorbate
Salicylates

Sodium Chloride
Sodium Nitrate
Sodium Nitrite

Dr. Feingold categorizes flavor enhancers as flavor *intensifiers,* flavor *modifiers,* flavor *potentiators;* also *imitation flavorings* and *artificial flavorings*—even *flavor enzymes.* "Only an expert can keep up with the categories and specific uses," writes this concerned doctor. We all need to try to avoid as many of the above as possible.

Dr. Feingold created the Feingold K-P Diet for hyperactive children which excludes *all* synthetic food colorings and flavorings. According to The New York Institute for Child Development, "The most valuable result of Dr. Feingold's work has been to bring attention to the fact that food sensitivities and allergies are important factors in evaluating and treating hyperactivity."

In an article in the August 24, 1980, edition of *The New York Times Magazine,* Joseph R. Hixson (a freelance writer specializing in medical topics), wrote: "It has been fifteen years since the allergist Benjamin Feingold developed his theory that an additive-free diet is a key weapon in the treatment of hyperactive children. Recently Dr. Sydney S. Gellis of Tufts Medical School, one of the acknowledged deans of childhood medicine in the United States, looked into some new research that has been done on children who were found to benefit from a diet free of the synthetic colorings, flavorings, and preservatives so prevalent in the American menu. He concluded his summary of the research with these words: 'Well, there you have it. The Feingold diet is in with a bang. It seems quite clear that artificial food dyes will have to go.'"

Dr. Gellis's statement is of concern to all parents whose children are suffering from a disorder that inhibits their ability to learn because they are hyperactive, or cannot focus their attention, or control their behavior for sufficient lengths of time.

The New York Institute for Child Development, founded in 1968, is a national nonprofit center that specializes in the diagnosis and treatment of learning disabled, hyperactive, and underachieving children. The Institute concerns itself with the investigation of the biochemical, nutritional, and functional disorders that are believed to cause hyperactivity and learning disabilities, as well as the development of a treatment that combines sensorimotor exercises and nutrition management.

The terms *hyperactivity* and *learning disabilities* describe subtle, seemingly nonorganic problems that interfere with a child's ability to learn to read, write, spell, and compute. Although these terms describe symptoms rather than causes, they have gained wide acceptance. It is estimated that hyperactivity and learning disability affect up to 20 percent of North American schoolchildren.

In *Treating Your Hyperactive and Learning-Disabled Child,* written by The New York Institute for Child Development with Richard J. Walsh (Garden City, NY: Anchor Press/Doubleday, 1979), these professionals state that "the difficulties of most hyperactive/learning-disabled children are caused by many different conditions. It appears that there is a combination of biochemical, metabolic, nutritional, or allergy disturbances, together with motor and perceptual inadequacies. Hence, treatment must be on an individual basis, and usually requires a combination of therapies."

For general information about securing medical and other professional tests and evaluations of your child, see the sections on Dyslexia and Learning Disabilities in this chapter. You will also find there a listing of helpful agencies and organizations.

Sensorimotor Therapy for Hyperactivity

Therapists and other professionals working with hyperactive children use exercises, games, and other techniques that specifically reinforce weak or nonexistent basic development skills. Once these elementary skills are strengthened, the children go on to concentrated training of their sense of perception, balance, eye-hand coordination, etc.

When Is Professional Advice a Good Idea?

Dr. Stewart and Ms. Olds, in their previously mentioned book, *Raising a Hyperactive Child,* write that "There is no precise criterion for telling when it is wise to seek a professional opinion about a child. The most important measure is how the parents feel. You may take your fears to a professional only to be told that whatever has been distressing you is merely a normal stage of growing up. Or you may be told that you do have a problem, but one whose solution is in your own hands. On the other hand, your child's behavior may be symptomatic of a deeper problem that requires evaluation and treatment by an expert."

LEARNING DISABILITIES*

Many children are born with or may acquire physical and/or mental conditions that interfere with their normal development. Fortunately many of these conditions can be helped or

See also Dyslexia, p. 432; The Hyperactive Child, p. 442.

completely corrected if parents are able to recognize the problem early and get prompt professional assistance. Otherwise an unnecessary lifelong handicap may be the outcome. If you suspect that your child may have special needs, do not wait until he or she enters school before you begin to deal with the difficulty.

Talk with your pediatrician, family doctor, or other competent professional in the field. Wherever you live, there are governmental agencies and parent organizations that will try to assist you if your child has special needs. Professionals working in your local Health Department and public schools can often put you in contact with those who are best able to help you and your child.

Any child with a learning disability, whatever term is used to identify its many forms, has a real handicap. The uninformed teacher may criticize the child for sloppy work or laziness when, in fact, he is doing the best he can and growing increasingly frustrated at the ease with which his classmates master the skills of reading, writing, spelling, and arithmetic. Continuing scholastic failure often leads to emotional difficulties as well. The end result may be even less productive work and more distress for both the child and his parents.

Recent studies suggest that about one of every ten children may suffer from some kind of learning disability. (As with color blindness, hemophilia, enuresis, and autism, boys seem to be affected more often than girls.) Some simple types of early learning disability are eventually outgrown; others may never be resolved or relieved.

Learning disabilities take many forms; the most common are *perceptual* and *motor malfunctions* and *hyperactivity.*

Margaret Golick, a senior psychologist at the McGill University Children's Learning Center in Canada, and a contributor to *The Child Health Encyclopedia* (New York: Delacorte Press, 1975), points out that there are myriad reasons for learning difficulties, not the least of which can be that the school does not "fit" the particular child, emotional upsets in the school or home, overcrowded classrooms, physical illness resulting in prolonged absences from school, or difficulty in hearing and seeing. These problems, despite normal intelligence, sensory stimulation, and adequate teaching, may result in the inability of the child to acquire the academic skills of reading, writing, spelling, and arithmetic. In short, although they appear normal, such children are quite "disabled."

The child who is hyperactive ("Can't sit still." "Always on the go." "Disruptive." "Clowns a lot." "Fidgety") suffers because these manifestations can seriously interfere with classroom learning.

Developmental Deficiencies

Growth and development, which start before birth and progress through a series of orderly ages and stages, are influenced by heredity and bodily makeup as well as by the effects of the environment parents provide. Physical growth is easily measured by increasing weight, height, and head size. If head size remains smaller than the usual norms as general growth goes forward, there is cause for concern because it may indicate a deficiency in brain development.

Intellectual skills and the capacity to use them in problem solving and decision making are also part of the growth process. Such skills include perception, memory, imagination, and conceptualizing, and depend upon the maturity of the brain and the early development and stimulation of sensorimotor powers (seeing, hearing, touching, and smelling). If the environment does not provide adequate stimulation and there are no opportunities to practice increasing powers, learning deficiencies may ensue.

Language acquisition is another indicator of the growth of intellectual abilities. The child's ability to respond to the verbal requests of others, to communicate feelings and desires in words, and to use words in thought and reasoning are indispensable to the basic skills required in reading, writing, spelling, and so on.

The early years are also a critical time for emotional development. Giving and receiving, loving and being loved, developing a positive self-image and self-confidence, and respect for others—all are learned skills that affect adaptation and social competency. Children who are unwanted, unloved, or cared for in depersonalized institutional settings suffer from emotional deprivation.

Deviation from normal development in the form of delays in physical, sensory, mental, emotional, and social growth may well create learning disabilities. Children affected by such delays are labeled as having developmental problems. They may be rated as borderline, mild, moderate, severe, or profound retardates; or they may be diagnosed as brain-damaged, overactive, hyperactive, or hyperkinetic, indicating excessive distractibility and a short attention span.

It takes several professionals to plan programs for children with learning disabilities, among whom can be the pediatrician, psychologist, social worker, educator, speech pathologist, ophthalmologist, or play therapist. In any planning, difficulties that are treatable must be tackled first. The purpose of a thorough study is to ascertain each child's weaknesses and strengths.

It is evident that to provide proper help for learning-disabled children, parents need to detect the problem ideally *before* the child enters school. Some cities and states are instituting programs of home visitation and individualized learning therapy. (Brookline, Massachusetts, and Clayton, Missouri, are among actively concerned cities.) You can write to your State Superintendent of Education for a listing of such programs.

Between six and ten million preadolescent children in the United States are thought to have some form of learning disability. The wide variation in estimates is explained by the relative newness of the field and differences in defining and labeling the various types of learning disabilities. Since the early 1960s, over one hundred specific kinds of learning disabilities have been identified. Besides learning disabled, such troubled children can be labeled perceptually handicapped, dyslexic, or subject to minimal brain dysfunction.

Although researchers and educators disagree on exactly what learning disabilities are, they concur on what they are *not.* They do not stem from mental retardation or such environmental factors as poverty or family strife; nor from such physiological problems as nearsightedness or astigmatism; nor from emotional and psychological problems (although the latter two may arise as the child tries to cope with the disability).

The Causes Are Unclear

Theories on the causes of learning disabilities are as diverse as the labels. The factors of race, social class, and intelligence have been ruled out. However, the sex of a child has not: for reasons that remain unclear, it appears that three out of every four learning disabled children are boys.

At present, the largest group of possible causes seems to

be physiological, which includes heredity, viral illnesses during the mother's pregnancy, her prolonged labor, the lack of oxygen during birth, head injuries, allergies, and poisoning. Some of these factors can result in a very slight neurological disturbance most frequently designated as minimal brain dysfunction.

"Whatever the problems, they rarely show up until a child is in the first, second, or third grade," says Darral Chapman, Chief of Therapy at The New York Institute for Child Development, which specializes in studying learning disabled children. "That is when a child is called upon to really use those written and spoken language skills intensively and, compared to the so-called normal performance of his classmates, he begins to fall behind." Besides trouble with reading and writing, other symptoms may appear, including clumsiness at sports, inattentiveness, restlessness, and poor coordination.

Although some learning disabled children can copy words and sentences, they are unable to produce them unaided; or they may reverse letters, print them backwards, or jumble the letters (for example, writing *heors* for *horse*). Similar problems may occur with speech. A child may be unable to sound out words, may still use baby talk at an advanced age, or may consistently mispronounce certain words. Some learning disabled children encounter difficulty distinguishing between such abstract ideas as today and tomorrow, left and right, many or few.

It is estimated that only half of the learning disabled children in the United States are ever diagnosed and treated. "Most parents do not know what to look for," says Dr. Sidney Walker of the Southern California Neurological Institute. "Many teachers trained fifteen or so years ago are unfamiliar with the field. Also, if your pediatrician seems baffled, it is probably due to the fact that the subject of learning disabilities is just a tiny part of the vast wave of new medical discoveries he (or she) has to keep up with. As it stands today, the burden of finding help rests most heavily on a child's parents."

Most children with learning disabilities will always have some problems and will always have to work harder. There are no easy answers. However, through careful diagnosis, doctors, educators, psychologists, and parents are learning to create specific educational therapy whereby special teaching techniques in reading and arithmetic can help children who have difficulty learning by traditional methods. Physical therapy provides exercises for eyes, limbs, and fingers to help improve perception and coordination.

"Could Your Child Be Learning Disabled?," a questionnaire compiled by The New York Institute for Child Development, lists warning signals of physical conditions which may or may not be interfering with your child's achievement in cognitive and social areas. If you can answer "yes" to at least five of the questions below, your child *may* have a learning disability.

1. Is your child easily distracted?
2. Is your child's performance inconsistent (performs task well one day, can't the next day)?
3. Is your child unusually sensitive to light, noise, touch, or certain clothing material?
4. Is your child a bed-wetter?
5. Did your child have trouble learning to lace, button, and tie items of clothing?
6. Was your child colicky?
7. Does your child avoid sports or activities that involve catching or throwing a ball?
8. Does your child walk or run clumsily?
9. Does your child confuse right and left?
10. Does your child use one hand for some things and the other hand for other things?
11. Does your child have trouble clapping or dancing rhythmically?
12. Does your child seem to "tune out" at times?
13. Does your child frequently trip or walk into things?
14. Does your child have a short attention span?
15. Does your child get frequent stomachaches?
16. Does your child frustrate easily?
17. Does your child have a history of allergies?
18. Does your child always crave sweets?

If you are or think you are having trouble with a learning-disabled child, write The New York Institute for Child Development, 205 Lexington Avenue, New York, NY 10016, for its checklist of symptoms, information on its special program of sensorimotor exercises and nutrition management, and latest research findings.

If you suspect that your child has a learning disability, the following steps are recommended:

- Get a thorough examination of your child, including blood chemistry, neurological testing, and visual perception and coordination testing. (A complete family history may be requested because learning difficulties often run in families.)
- Make sure that medical test results are analyzed along with the educational test scores, IQ tests, psychological evaluations, and school records. This means that all the professionals must confer in order to get a whole picture of your child. (Tests and diagnoses can be costly. New education laws stipulate that all handicapped children must be provided for in school systems.)
- Work with doctors and teachers to devise a helpful educational and therapeutic program. Ask how you might help your child at home. Insist on a complete explanation of the planned educational program in school. Make sure that your child will be reevaluated regularly.

PARENTING

Ira J. Gordon, Ph.D., former director of the Institute for the Development of Human Resources at the University of Florida, has aptly written, "If you recognize that a [child-rearing] book is not an expert and cannot displace you, if you see it as providing ideas from which you can select what makes sense to you (and with which you are comfortable), then it can help you move more smoothly and more naturally into the most fascinating (and demanding) role in the world, that of parent."

We agree with Dr. Helen De Rosis, author of *Parent Power/Child Power* (Indianapolis: Bobbs-Merrill, 1974), that parenthood is the single most important job in the world, and that more needs to be done in offering courses in child growth and development and parenting to first-time mothers and fathers. In almost all areas of child-rearing, too much appears to be left to chance.

According to Dr. De Rosis, "Parents are quick to point out their shortcomings, to wallow in guilt, and to hate themselves for their limitations . . . My experience has shown me that people are often stronger than they realize, wiser than they believe, and more effective than they even imagined.

"Parents know that children need food, shelter, and clothing. Most of them know that children also need warm and affectionate relationships. What many of them do not know is that qualities of warmth and affection do not thrive in tension-bound parents . . .

"Sometimes parents are good for and to their children; sometimes not. Most times, they are in-between, with occasional excursions to the extremes. But whatever you are, you will exert a powerful impact on your children . . ."

Non-Sexist Child-Rearing

Parents who wish to rear liberated, non-sexist children will try, from the very beginning, to help them become independent boys and girls who will be able to make choices as adults that will be free of sex stereotypes.

"Non-sexist child-raising . . . means providing a child with a world full of options in the form of toys, books, learning materials. It means working within the family and in the schools and other institutions for active sexual equality," writes Carrie Carmichael in her book, *Non-Sexist Childraising* (Boston: Beacon Press, 1977).

According to many child-rearing specialists today, girls and boys who are brought up in families in which both the mothers and the fathers are liberated have a greater chance of becoming liberated adults themselves. Fathers who do not play an active role in the care of their children and who do not participate in the daily chores of family life are in effect perpetuating sexism.

Non-sexist parents who permit their children to pretend to be whatever they fantasize resist the passé supposition that toys must be either girls' toys or boys' toys. Unfortunately, what are termed girls' toys are confined to the doll/home/crafts sphere; boys' toys include everything but dolls. Yet dolls play an important part in teaching young children of both sexes how to be nurturing and non-sexist when they themselves become parents.

In the nursery school, girls and boys are encouraged to play with *all* available toys and equipment. In the kindergarten, too, boys and girls are free to play without the need to choose only sex-related playthings or to assume sex-defined pretend roles.

Sex Stereotyping in Picture Books

Picture books are the first exposure of very young children to the literary world. Unlike television, with its transient visual and auditory stimulation, books offer treasured interactions between children and parents, and pictures children can repeatedly return to for pleasure and learning. Thus children tend to identify with storybook characters—all the more reason to be concerned if the characters represent offensive sexual stereotypes.

The following picture books have a definite sexist bias:

- *What Do People Do All Day?* by Richard Scarry (Random House). Animal characters portray different occupations. Females are poorly represented with regard to professional jobs. One section of the book, "Mother's Work Is Never Done," shows Mommy Pig cleaning house, caring for the family, and cooking a large meal. Daddy Pig comes home from work, is served like a king, and eats too much.
- *The Bears' Almanac* by Stan and Jan Berenstein (Random House). This book deals with the months and seasons of the year. Springtime shows Mamma Bear cleaning, brother and sister sweeping, and Papa Bear sleeping. Summertime shows Mamma making lemonade while Papa lounges in the swimming pool.
- *Let's Play House* by Lois Lenski (Henry Z. Walck). In this picture book two little girls perform all the household functions of unliberated mothers. Their friend Peter is called in to eat their supper, move furniture, and act as "doctor" when they pretend to be nurses.

Some nursery rhymes, "Little Miss Muffet" for one, suggest that girls are weak and frighten easily. Perhaps if Little Miss Muffet had shooed away the spider many years ago, fewer females would tremble at the sight of a harmless insect today (and perhaps males would feel free to express *their* fears!).

Numerous authors have tried to reverse the sexist trend in children's literature. Some excellent non-sexist books include:

- *Mike Mulligan and His Steam Shovel* by Virginia Lee Burton (Houghton Mifflin Co.). This beloved story shows that males and females can successfully work together.

- *The Man Who Didn't Wash His Dishes* by Phyllis Krasilovsky (Doubleday). A man who lives alone, with no wife to look after him, eats and eats without ever cleaning up until he runs out of dishes and utensils. (The moral is that procrastination does not pay, and that a man is perfectly capable of doing his own housework.)
- *Papa Small* by Lois Lenski (Henry Z. Walck). Mamma and Papa happily share family chores in this book. During the week Mamma cooks and Papa returns home from work and rests. On the weekends, Papa cooks and Mamma rests. (Bravo!)
- *Mommies At Work* by Eve Merriam (Alfred A. Knopf). New horizons for females are shown: Mommies are not only capable of mothering, but also can perform jobs that heretofore were labeled "For Men Only."
- *Katy and the Big Snow* by Virginia Lee Burton (Houghton Mifflin). Katy the tractor is the heroine of this picture storybook. Katy demonstrates her power and importance by saving a snowed-in city.
- *Boys and Girls—Girls and Boys* by Eve Merriam (Holt, Rinehart & Winston). Here girls and boys are seen together—performing the same skills, enjoying the same things, sharing similar ambitions and dreams.

Understanding Child Development

In *Between Generations: The Six Stages of Parenthood* (New York: Times Books, 1981), Ellen Galinsky writes, "Understanding child development can give parents more age-appropriate expectations . . . The emphasis is put on behavior as communication. Discipline is thus seen as problem solving. The child is helped to learn a more acceptable manner of communication . . .

"Just as in all aspects of parenthood, sometimes parental expectations are flexible, sometimes hard and fast; and sometimes they are met, and other times they are not, causing the parent to hold on tightly or to grow . . .

"Often parenthood is written about as if it takes place on a stage set, isolated from the rest of life. But life, with its ups and downs, very much affects parenthood."

Psychologist Haim Ginott, in *Between Parent and Child* (New York: Avon Books, 1973), attempts to tell parents how they can treat their children with understanding and sympathy. His basic principles of parenting espouse the use of communication of feelings between parents and their children. Included among his tenets are the employment of effective forms of praise and criticism, setting limits of acceptable and nonacceptable behaviors, and parental modeling, especially with regard to positive ways of handling feelings.

Rudolf Dreikurs, M.D., author of *Coping with Children's Misbehavior: A Parent's Guide* (New York: Hawthorn Books, 1972), thinks that children have innate capacities to develop in healthy, effective ways. Children have a built-in push to grow and to be competent. One of the main tasks of parents is to provide an environment that permits this development to occur. Dr. Dreikurs suggests that parents use encouragement to help children attain their optimal potentials. He defines encouragement as a "continuous process aimed at giving the child a sense of self-respect and a sense of accomplishment."

Dr. Dreikurs believes that parents need to learn to accept the mistakes of their children as well as their own, and to work for improvement—but never for perfection. He recommends letting natural and logical consequences teach children to change their behavior.

In *Mothering: The Emotional Experience of Motherhood After Freud and Feminism* (Garden City, NY: Doubleday, 1978), Elaine Heffner writes, "When women make a full-time commitment to the care of young children, this is a professional choice as important as any other they might make . . . They take the major share of the stress of child-rearing, and have a right to expect both the practical and emotional support that will enable them to do the kind of job that can give them the self-esteem they deserve. The help and involvement of fathers is part of that support, and is important for children as well as mothers . . .

"Guiding a child through all the steps on the road to independence is a process in which mother and child engage jointly . . . Issues that arise in a child's development regarding dependence and independence have no arbitrary resolutions within fixed time frames. It is unquestionably useful for a mother to have guidelines about when and how children generally accomplish certain developmental milestones."

Sidney Cornelia Callahan, in *Parenting: Principles and Politics of Parenthood* (Garden City, NY: Doubleday, 1973), writes, "Specific programs and detailed rules for parenting are inadequate because what is appropriate at one time, in one place, and with one set of unique persons, may be thoroughly inadequate at another time . . .

"Parents who willingly take the time to give sustained attention to their children open the way to mutual warmth and enjoyment . . . Parental response makes a responsive child . . . As the first human partners in playing all games, learning all skills, and meeting all problems, good parents initiate and sustain an ongoing dialogue . . .

."One of the essential goals of parenthood is to make children glad they were born and eager for life . . .

"The growth of intelligence progresses as inner capacities and experience grow; and much of this important childhood experience arises because parents have intervened or prepared the environment . . . (Some parents will be better adjusting to certain stages than others.)"

Parents Can Teach Responsibility

In *For the Love of Children* (Garden City, NY: Anchor Press/Doubleday, 1977), Edward E. Ford and Steven Englund write, "A child who has learned, by the time he reaches school age, to be patient and take care of himself for limited periods of time is going to be a stronger child than one who has not. This lesson won't be learned by pampering an infant throughout the first five years . . .

"A teacher, even a good one, can't easily derail a child from the track of dependency that his parents may have unwittingly put him on in the first five years of life . . .

"No child can be expected to learn responsibility entirely on his own, or simply because he is lucky enough to have loving parents . . . The crucial initial advantage that a loving relationship with your child gives you is access to him even when the going is rough."

Pediatrician T. Berry Brazelton writes in *On Becoming a Family: The Growth of Attachment* (New York: Delacorte Press, 1981) that "The most difficult thing about having a second baby is the necessary 'desertion' of the first one . . . Certainly it is a universal fear that the older child will suffer and be damaged by the rivalry he will feel for the new baby. The truth is that most children profit enormously by having to share, by having to learn to adjust to a sibling."

Parenting Skills Are Learned over Time

In *Ourselves and Our Children: A Book By and For Parents* (New York: Random House, 1978), members of The Boston Women's Health Book Collective write, "Parenting is not automatic or instinctive; rather it is knowledge, experience, and skill which are *learned* over time. Much of that learning takes place as a natural part of being parents, in talking with friends, with a spouse, in interactions with our children. But in these times, when the shapes of families and the roles of men and women are changing, we may need help in thinking and experimenting to find the ways of being parents that feel right to us."

Some Facts About the Family Constellation

In *Parents' Handbook: Systematic Training for Effective Parenting* (Circle Pines, MN: American Guidance Service, 1976), Don Dinkmeyer and Gary D. McKay write that "The place of children in the family can generally be described by these characteristics: the firstborn is, for a while, an only child who receives considerable attention, but when the second child arrives, is suddenly dethroned . . .

"The second-born is confronted with someone who is always ahead. This child may feel inadequate because of inability to keep up with the older sibling . . .

"If a third child enters the family the second child becomes a middle child. The middle child frequently feels squeezed out, deprived of the rights and privileges of the oldest and of the baby . . .

"The youngest child is inclined to take advantage of the position of being cute and pleasant . . . or by becoming a clown, or openly rebelling.

"The *only* child lives the formative years among persons who are bigger and more capable. [Some] only children may feel they are special and entitled to have their own way."

The Importance of Fathers

In *Responsible Parenthood* (New York: Holt, Rinehart & Winston, 1980), Gilbert W. Kliman, M.D., and Albert Roseneld write, "There have been numerous studies of children whose fathers have been absent for years at a time . . . and in every such study the children . . . have a higher incidence of emotional problems than children who have both parents . . . Sometimes the father is so completely absorbed in his work . . . or has so little interest in his children, that he might almost as well not be there . . .

"Girls, too, are affected negatively by the lack of a father. In some cases, they may be chronically suspicious of men or anxious in their presence; in others, they may form a highly idealized . . . picture of what men are like.

"On the whole, it seems safe to say that scientific observation confirms what common sense already tells us—that a child of either sex is better off with two caregivers than one."

Open Communication Benefits All Family Members

Jane B. Brooks writes in *The Process of Parenting* (Palo Alto: Mayfield Publishing Co., 1981) that "Parents must consider their own needs as well as those of their children. When parents examine their relationships with their children, they often discover that they are clear about their children's needs, wishes, and feelings, but vague about their own . . .

"Children are open and reveal their feelings in everything they do and say; in gestures, tone of voice, posture, and the content of what they say. When parents pay attention, they find the clues to understanding the child's feelings. When parents communicate feelings, use effective forms of praise, eliminate sarcasm, bribes, threats, and promises, they are treating the child with respect, and when children are respected, they are more likely to want to follow the rules of the house."

Some Parenting Problems

In *The Parent Test: How to Measure and Develop Your Talent for Parenthood* (New York: G. P. Putnam's Sons, 1978), Ellen Peck and Dr. William Granzig write, ". . . parenthood is a very tough job, one that even the experts haven't figured out. Some individuals have a greater aptitude for parenthood than others. You may have an aptitude for dealing sensitively and patiently with one child, but not with more. You may be able to handle parenthood in an urban setting with convenient da care, but not in a small town as a 24-hour-a-day parent. Yo may be impatient with infants, but superb at stimulating th thinking of a preschooler (or wonderful with infants, but impa tient with a preschooler's chatter) . . .

"Expectations about parenthood should be realistic . . Many expect too much of parenthood . . .

"It seems helpful if parents can be flexible in their approac to teaching their children, and in their approach to discipline.

In *What We Really Know About Child-Rearing* (New York Basic Books, 1976), Seymour Fisher and Rhoda L. Fishe corroborate this view. They write, "Many of the difficultie mothers and fathers get into evolve from going too far in on direction or the other. The scientific literature contains man illustrations of how parents who move too far from a middl ground force their children into untenable positions. Childre do not fare well if their parents usually inflict punishment c great severity or unrealistic lightness. Also, extremes in be havior about achievement do not work. If parents push to hard to make their children come out on top, or if they set thei expectations far too low, the result is that the children adopt distorted and usually troubled approach to achievement de mands."

Four Major Parenting Courses

There are four major courses available in the United States While each program is different in its approach and emphasis each one tries to help parents remain on an even keel as the meet the daily emotional ups and downs of child-rearing.

- *Parent Effectiveness Training* (P.E.T.), devised in 1962 b Thomas Gordon, a clinical psychologist, is the largest. I advocates the need for parents and children to communi cate their feelings, and offers methods for resolving parent child conflicts. Devotees attribute its record of success to the fact that "it works!" Dr. Gordon's methods are fully describe in his book, *P.E.T.—Parent Effectiveness Training* (Nev York: Wyden, 1973).
- *The Parent Involvement Program* (*P.I.P.*) is an adaptation o William Glasser's Reality Therapy. Its premise is that ther can be no behavioral change in a child unless an affection ate and honest relationship is established between the chil

and his parents. The program emphasizes praise for success rather than punishment for failure in the modification of unacceptable behavior patterns.

- *The Responsive Parent Training Program* at the University of Kansas, with Marilyn Clark and Vance Hall as mentors, teaches parents standard behavior-modification techniques in a small-group lecture format. The philosophy behind this course appears to be "Whatever works, use it," although the emphasis is on positive reinforcement (usually in the form of praise) and sometimes mild punishment.

- The fourth parent education group is under the aegis of the Alfred Adler Institute in Chicago, which offers parents various programs. One course is based on *Children: The Challenge* (New York: Hawthorn, 1964), a book written by Rudolf Dreikurs, M.D. Dr. Dreikurs opposes the concept of rewards and punishments, and favors instead encouragement and discipline (the latter seems to dominate his philosophy). Although the ultimate aim of this program is similar to the ones mentioned previously, some child-rearing professionals think that it is overly manipulative and parent-dominated.

The American Red Cross has excellent courses throughout the United States on parenting from birth to five. Adult education centers and colleges also offer such courses. You might wish to check their availability in your area.

Ask yourself the following questions before you enroll in any parent education program (or buy a parenting book or magazine):

- Is it informative, thought-provoking, and well documented?
- Is it relevant to me and my family?
- Does it encourage self-discovery and learning?
- Is its approach caring and compassionate, and not guilt producing?

SAFETY

Young children are curious, active, and fearless explorers whose fingers and feet get them into places you would never think of. The industrial slogan SAFETY IS NO ACCIDENT applies equally well inside and outside the home. Accident prevention means home fire drills, auto safety (including seat belts and

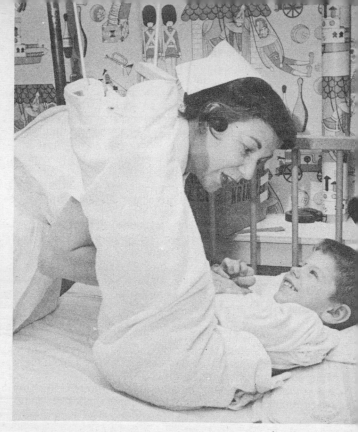

good parental driving habits), swimming pool fences, lawn mower maintenance, correct home canning procedures, and so on. Newspapers are full of tragedies that could have been averted by timely attention to basic safety principles or operating precautions. The hard facts are that more than one-third of all childhood deaths are caused by accidents; three out of four accidents involving children under four take place in the home, and fully 90 percent of these are preventable.

Make Your Child's World Safe for Exploration

- Inspect all electric cords and discard any that are not in perfect condition (frayed, split, etc.). Cover unused wall outlets with plugs made for that purpose (available in hardware stores). All metal objects small enough to go into such outlets must be kept away from children (pins, bobby pins, paper clips, nails, bits of wire). There are plug locks that can be installed to keep wall outlets from being pulled, and wall outlets in which the openings close automatically when a plug is pulled out. Remember not to leave lamps plugged in without bulbs in them. All electric appliances should be kept away from the bathtub or other places where the child is bathed.

- Use gates in front of steps and stairs, and guards on windows to prevent falls. (See, however, the discussion of accordion gates on p. 467.)
- Keep needles (including knitting needles and crochet hooks, knives, broken glass, opened cans, razor blades, scissors, and all other sharp, pointed objects) where a small child cannot get at them.
- Plastic bags should never be accessible to young children.
- If you have venetian blinds, cut open the loop at the end of the cords with which you raise and lower the blinds. This will eliminate the danger of the child getting his head caught in the cord.
- Sharp plastic toys with cracks and metal toys with sharp edges should be discarded.
- Keep matches out of reach.
- Never have firearms (loaded or unloaded) or ammunition where a child can get at them.
- All power and hand tools need to be stored out of reach. In addition, small children need to be kept away from all power equipment when in use.
- Always turn the handles of pots and pans away from the front of the stove during cooking. Hot items need to be placed in the center of the table, not near the edge. Never leave a pail or kettle of hot water on the floor. Make sure the electric coffee pot and other electrical cookers cannot be upset by pulling the cord—and cannot be reached by young explorers.
- It is important to be especially cautious with water wells, tanks, and cisterns. They should be securely covered at all times. *Never* leave a small child in water unattended—either in the house or outside. Even shallow pools (for example, inflated plastic play pools) can be dangerous. When at the beach or lake, or around a swimming pool, a child should

wear a life jacket until he can swim at leat 100 feet. Swimming pools must be unavailable to children unless chaperoned. Life jackets should always be worn when in boats.

- Never leave a young child alone where there is a lighted stove, burning fireplace, grill, hibachi, lighted candle, or a lamp using oil or kerosene.
- Learn to identify plants and other vegetation that are poisonous, and keep young children away from them.
- A low table and chair are safer than high ones for a small child.
- Discarded refrigerators, and upright freezers, and stoves must have their doors removed.
- Use special precautions when you take a small child on outings. A carriage or stroller should have a harness for a child who is at the climbing stage.
- Use a safe car seat and its safety belt for your child, even on short trips in the car. Many serious accidents are caused by letting young children sit or stand on the seats of cars without this protection.
- *Never* leave a young child alone in a house, in a parked carriage or stroller, or in a parked car.
- To avoid a potentially frightening or even dangerous incident, keep young children away from strange animals.

Parents of young children should keep on hand, where they can always be found immediately, a properly stocked first-aid kit and a first-aid manual. You should also paste on the inside of your medicine chest a chart listing poisons and antidotes, and procedures to follow if a child swallows one of the poisons. Your doctor or librarian can recommend a good first-aid manual.

To save time when accidents occur, familiarize yourself beforehand with the immediate steps to take—and not to take—in an emergency. Keep near your telephone the numbers of your doctor, the fire department, poison control center nearest you, ambulance, and hospital.

For a free copy of the National Safety Council's *Pocket Guide to Emergency Action* write to the Public Information Department, National Safety Council, 425 N. Michigan Avenue, Chicago, IL 60611.

Traditional Accordion Gates Can Entrap Young Child's Head*

Sometimes toddlers need to be protected against their urge to explore, but the wooden accordion gates and corrals most parents rely on to keep them out of danger may not be safe barriers after all. The United States Consumer Product Safety Commission has received enough reports of strangulations and injuries involving the familiar folding gates and playpens to have manufacturers hire engineers to redesign their products.

In the meantime, owners of the ten million accordion gates currently in use should be aware that children who stick their heads between the slats could choke themselves to death. The accordion corrals used in 158,000 homes are shaky and apt to close up when a child agitates the slats.

There is another type of baby-fence on the market, a solid gate consisting of a sliding plastic mesh panel framed in a rectangle of wood. Although somewhat more costly than the traditional accordion gate, presumably it is considerably safer.

Of course, no playpen, gate, or fence will always keep adventuresome crawlers, beginning walkers, and toddlers from exercising their power of locomotion and simultaneously trying to satisfy their boundless curiosity.

Dr. Vincent J. Fontana writes in *A Parents' Guide to Child Safety* (New York: Crowell, 1973), "One must practice eternal vigilance, not only by sight but also in the mind's eye. If a child can think of it, you'd better believe that sooner or later he may try it!"

In childhood, the major threats to life are principally accidents and poisonings. Very young children will touch and taste everything within easy reach.

Poisons in the Home

The most common causes of poisoning in preschool children are, respectively, drugs and medicines of all kinds, poisonous plants, personal care products, and household cleaners.

Parents should keep ipecac (available without a prescrip-

*Parts of this page adapted from *Today's Child News Magazine,* Vol. 30, No. 9, June 1982.

tion) on hand to induce vomiting in cases of poisoning. (Ipecac's shelf life is five years.) It should be used only if you are directed to do so by a poison control center or by your physician.

POTENTIALLY HARMFUL HOUSEHOLD SUBSTANCES
ammonia
antifreeze
aspirin
auto polish
benzene
bleach
borax
car polishes
cement and glue
cleaning fluids and powders
contraceptive pills
cosmetics
cough syrups
deodorants
depilatories
detergents
fabric softeners
floor waxes and wax removers
furniture polish
gasoline
hairsprays, hair tonics, hair dyes
headache remedies
heart medicines
ink
insecticides
iodine
kerosene and petroleum distillates
laundry products
laxatives
lighter fluid
lye
metal polish
mothballs
oil of wintergreen
paint
perfumes and colognes
permanent-wave solutions

pesticides
plant sprays
reducing pills and diuretics
rodent poisons
room deodorizers
rubbing alcohol
rug and floor cleaners
shampoos
shoe polish
sleeping pills
stove and oven cleaners
toilet bowl and drain cleaners
tranquilizers
turpentine
varnish
vitamins
washing soda
weed killers

To avoid accidents, be careful in your disposal of the containers of all potentially dangerous substances.

Poisonous Plants, Shrubs, and Trees

Poison control centers throughout the United States report that parts of certain plants, wild flowers, shrubs, and trees top the list of products that are accidentally ingested by children under five. Your knowledge of the toxicity of plants, flowers, berries, and so on will help you plan a safe garden, get rid of poisonous wild flowers and other shrubs near your house, and avoid harboring potentially dangerous plants in your home.

To make your home safe, put the plants that you purchase on high shelves beyond the reach of your own or visiting young children. Aside from the possibility of touching or chewing the poisonous part of a plant, there is the danger of your child's pulling a potted plant off a table or knocking one over that was positioned on the floor. Never put any plant in your young child's bedroom.

In case—despite your best efforts—there should be an incidence of accidental plant poisoning *immediately* telephone your doctor, the poison control center nearest you, or your local hospital emergency room. Do *not* induce vomiting without express professional instructions to do so. The degree of poisoning will depend upon the size of your child, the season of the year, and the amount and part of the plant that has been eaten.

Although toxic plants rarely cause death, the reaction to contact with the poisonous part of a plant can vary from a rash or itching to violent illness that may require hospitalization.

Below is a list of plants, shrubs, trees, and fungi and their poisonous parts:

Amaryllis—bulb
Atropa—all parts
Autumn crocus—all parts
Azaleas—all parts
Baneberry—roots, foliage, berries
Belladonna—all parts
Bittersweet—all parts
Black locust—all parts
Bleeding heart—foliage, roots
Boxwood—leaves, twigs
Buckeye—sprouts
Caladium—all parts
Castor bean—seeds
Chinaberry tree—berries
Chokecherry—leaves, pits
Christmas rose—all parts
Daffodil—bulb
Daphne—leaves, bark, berries
Delphinium—young plants, seeds
Dieffenbachia—all parts
Dumb cane—stems, leaves
Elderberry tree—roots, stems
Elephant's ear—all parts
English holly—berries
English ivy—leaves, berries
Foxglove—all parts
Golden chain tree—seeds, pods, flowers
Horsechestnut tree—nuts
Hyacinth—bulb
Iris—rhizome, leaves
Jack-in-the-pulpit—all parts
Jerusalem cherry—berries, leaves, flowers
Jessamine—flowers, leaves
Jimsonweed—all parts

Laburnum—seeds, pods, flowers
Lantana—unripe berries
Larkspur—seeds, young plants
Laurels—all parts
Lily-of-the-valley—all parts
Mayapple—all parts
Mistletoe—berries
Narcissus—bulb
Nicotiana—leaves
Nightshades—all parts
Oak trees—all parts
Oleanders—all parts
Opium poppy—unripe seed parts
Philodendrons (some)—all parts
Poinsettia—leaves, flowers
Poison hemlock—roots, foliage, seeds
Pokeweed—roots, berries, foliage
Privet—berries, leaves
Rhododendron—all parts
Skunk cabbage—all parts
Toadstools—all parts
Wild black cherry tree—leaves, pits
Wisteria—seeds, pods
Yew—seeds, needles, bark

In addition, some care must be taken regarding the common potato and rhubarb. All the green parts (vines and sprouts) and spoiled parts of potatoes should *not* be consumed. Death has occurred from eating *large* amounts of the green parts of potatoes. Spoiled white or sweet tubers should always be discarded.

If the leaf blades of rhubarb, whether raw or cooked, are consumed, abdominal pain, vomiting, and convulsions will follow in a matter of a few hours after ingestion. Without immediate professional treatment, permanent kidney damage or even death may occur.

Poison Ivy, Poison Oak, and Poison Sumac

Learn to recognize these common irritants and teach your children to recognize them also—and avoid them! The danger of poisoning is greatest in spring and summer and least in late fall and winter. Poisoning from poison ivy, poison oak, and poison sumac is caused most often by contact with some part of the bruised plant; actual contact with the poison is necessary to produce skin irritation. Even a very small amount of the toxic substance can produce severe inflammation of the skin in susceptible people and, unfortunately, most of us are.

Dogs and cats often contact these plants and then transmit the toxins to children and adults. Smoke from burning poison ivy, poison oak, and poison sumac can carry the poisons and can cause severe cases of poisoning. Washing with brown laundry soap within a few minutes after contact may get rid of the poison on the skin. Mild poisoning usually subsides within a few days. However, if the inflammation is severe or extensive, consult your doctor.

A Note About Clothing

All young children's sleepwear must now be labeled to ensure its conformity with government standards regarding noninflammability—and so must fabrics that might be used for this purpose by the home sewer.

According to the Consumer Product Safety Commission, 20 percent of all children's sleepwear on the market contains Tris, a flame retardant that is a cancer-causing agent. The consumer group has asked that the sale of children's garments containing Tris be prohibited. The chemical can be absorbed through the wearer's skin, as well as through the mouth when the clothing is sucked by babies.

Fire and Fire Protection

Buy a good fire extinguisher (Type ABC), put it where it can be reached easily, and have it checked once a year to make sure it is in good condition. Read the instructions for its use carefully. Also explore the use of room smoke detectors. There are many different models on the market.

Conduct regular fire drills with your family to make sure everyone knows exactly what to do in the event of a fire. Should a fire occur, get everyone out of the house as quickly as possible. Use an outside phone to summon help, or call the telephone operator (dial 0) to report the fire, giving your name and address. Once the whole family is outside, never let anyone return for *any reason*. Locate the nearest fire alarm box, turn it on, and stay at the box until the fire department arrives.

Do not overload the electricity; replace worn electrical cords; have your heating, gas, and electrical units checked periodically, as well as the flue in the chimney.

Clean out the attic regularly; wash or discard oil-stained rags; clean up any oil slick in your garage. Do not store old magazines or newspapers where they may cause a fire.

Of course, keep matches and all inflammable fluids out of the reach of young children.

Toy Safety

Poorly designed or misused toys can be dangerous playthings. Falls on or against toys are a frequent type of accident. Children also have been seriously injured when they swallowed or choked on small parts, placed tiny toys in their noses or ears, or cut themselves on sharp edges and points.

The United States Consumer Product Safety Commission has set safety regulations for certain toys and other children's articles. Manufacturers must design and manufacture their products to meet these regulations, and products that violate CPSC toy standards are subject to recall. Some of the current toy regulations include the following stipulations:

1) No sharp points or edges in toys and other articles intended for children under eight years of age.
2) No small parts in toys intended for use by children under three years of age.
3) Elimination of pacifiers and baby rattles small enough to lodge in a baby's throat.
4) Banning of aluminized polyester film kites that can become entangled in power lines and cause electric shocks.
5) Limiting to less than 0.06 percent in the amount of lead in paint used on toys and other children's articles. (*We believe there should be absolutely no lead in all children's toys and other children's articles.*)
6) No use of poisonous or otherwise harmful chemicals in toys and other articles intended for use by children. (Chemistry sets and other products designed for older children may be sold if accompanied by instructions and warning labels.)

Not all toy-related injuries can be prevented by regulations.

Parents need to teach their children safe play habits. The Commission has the following suggestions for toy safety:

1) A toy should suit the abilities and interests of the individual child—one that is safe for an eight-year-old may be hazardous for a younger child.
2) Read labels and instructions carefully before buying a toy.
3) Use your own judgment in deciding whether a toy is suitable or too difficult for a specific child.
4) Toys that shoot objects may injure the eyes.
5) Check toys used by children under three for any small parts or broken pieces that they could put in their mouths and choke on.
6) Demonstrate to your children how to use toys safely.
7) Encourage your children to put their toys away after use so that no one will trip over or slip on them and they are not broken.
8) Examine toys periodically. Check for sharp edges and points. Sand down splintered wooden surfaces. Repair broken toys and discard any that cannot be fixed.

The Commission estimates that each year over 12,000 children suffer from tricycle injuries serious enough to require hospital emergency room treatment. The major causes of such accidents include:

1) Instability that causes a tricycle to tip over (often when the rider makes a sharp turn or speeds up).
2) Striking obstacles and colliding with other tricycles.
3) Inability to stop the tricycle.
4) Getting caught in the tricycle's moving parts.
5) Collisions with cars when riders lose control or ride into the street.
6) Poor construction or design.

When you buy a tricycle or supervise your child on one, the Commission suggests:

1) Match the size of your child to the size of the tricycle. If a child is too large for the tricycle, the tricycle will be unstable. If the child is too small, he or she may have trouble controlling the tricycle properly.

2) Low-slung tricycles with seats close to the ground offer more stability, but may make the rider less visible if he or she goes into the street.
3) For extra stability, look for wheels that are widely spaced.
4) Look for pedals and handgrips with rough surfaces or treads that would prevent the child's hands and feet from slipping.
5) Never let your child ride in or into the street, or in busy parking lots.
6) Caution your child against riding with a friend on the back of the tricycle, which increases instability.
7) Try to teach your child that riding down hills is dangerous.
8) Teach your child to avoid sharp turns, and to keep hands and feet away from moving spokes.
9) Check regularly for missing or damaged pedals and handgrips, loose handlebars and seat, broken parts, and other defects.
10) Don't leave tricycles outdoors overnight—moisture can cause rust and weaken metal parts.

Safe Car Use

According to the Department of Public Safety of the State of Minnesota, *automobile accidents are the number one killer of young children in the United States,* and the vast majority of those fatalities could easily have been prevented with the regular and proper use of dynamically-tested and approved child-restraint systems. In addition, each year thousands of children are permanently disabled (either physically or mentally) from injuries suffered in automobile accidents when car restraints are not in use. Parents should buckle up to set a good example, and for their own and their children's protection. Occupants who are not restrained could injure others who are belted in should a crash occur.

Today's car seats are designed to prevent serious injuries should a car be involved in a crash. The U.S. Department of Transportation has upgraded standards so that all devices made after January 1, 1981, must withstand actual crash tests. For full information on car safety restraints, and crash-tested devices on the market, write to Physicians for Automotive Safety, 50 Union Avenue, Irvington, NJ 07111, and request a copy of their brochure, *Don't Risk Your Child's Life.*

You can also write for more information on auto safety seats to Project Childsafe, 145 Hamm Building, St. Paul, MN 55102, and to the National Highway Traffic Safety Administration, 400 Seventh Street, S.W., Washington, DC 20590.

Aside from the vital need for *all* car occupants (driver and passengers) to use proper care safety devices, parents should know that the back seat is the safest place in the event of a car accident. Actually the middle of the back seat is even safer. The most dangerous position is the passenger seat next to the driver.

All the doors of a car should be locked before moving to reduce the possibility of their opening in the event of a crash. It is important to get locks on car doors that cannot be opened by passengers, only by the driver.

Preschool children are unpredictable pedestrians, and too many are killed or disabled from darting in front of moving cars. In most cases, drivers are not to blame for accidents involving darting children.*

Verbal instructions, car safety jingles, and warnings do *not* deter preschoolers. Child specialists stress that in order to understand the undependable behavior of young children around cars, it is necessary to remember that (1) Their visual development is not complete. It takes them longer to focus, and their vision may be blurred. (2) Their thinking is concrete rather than abstract (danger and safety are abstract concepts). (3) Their attention span is short and they are easily distracted. Their emotional reactions are translated into actions rather than words. (4) They cannot see the roadway over shrubs, snowdrifts, or the hoods of parked cars.

Young children need repeated lessons on how to cross a street. They must be given countless opportunities to indicate their growing awareness of safety requirements. Awareness is of the utmost importance: Many preschoolers are run over by cars backing out of driveways and parking spaces because they have not been taught to recognize the signals that show a car is about to move.

Teach your children to listen for the sounds of an engine starting, to watch for the tail-pipe exhaust, to look for the white back-up lights, and to get out of the way promptly when these signals appear. Explain how traffic lights and WALK signs work.

---

*Adapted from an article, "Preschoolers Dart to a Different Drummer" in the June–September 1978 edition of *Today's Child News Magazine*.

Make your child aware of the sounds of traffic: horns, police whistles, the whirr of an approaching car, the screech of brakes, etc.

Young children need to be trained that it is necessary to wait at all times until a road is completely devoid of traffic before attempting to move to the other side of any street. Young children should not cross the street without holding the hand of an adult or older, responsible child.

SEPARATION AND DIVORCE

Increased mobility, recognition of the rights of women, liberalized divorce laws, and changing religious and moral values have all contributed to an increase in the frequency of divorce, which now terminates one out of every three marriages. Second divorces are also becoming more numerous.

Divorce is easier today than it has ever been, and while this may herald a new freedom for one or both of the parents involved, the needs and feelings of children are often disregarded or overlooked in the mounting tensions that precede this action.

In addition to liberalized grounds for divorce, alternate life-styles and single-parent families have contributed to some modification of the belief that children must simultaneously have one parent of each sex in order to mature properly. Despite the burden of guilt that this has lifted from the shoulders of single parents, it is still broadly recognized as desirable for a child to have two parents close at hand in the course of growing up. The drastic steps leading to separation and divorce should not be undertaken without sober and thorough consideration of the rights and needs of *every* family member.

Of course, there are those whose religious persuasion precludes release from an unsatisfactory marriage by means of a divorce. For those and others, separation arrangements or annulment of the marriage offer relief and rights.

Some Problems of Divorce

In most states, the only legal way to terminate a marriage is for one of the partners to prove the other guilty of an offense that is considered grounds for divorce. Because so many marriages are ending in divorce, divorce proceedings have become lucrative business for lawyers. Legal costs of an uncontested divorce with support agreements can range from $500 to $5,000 or more.

For a woman with children and no money or career of her own, divorce can be an overwhelming problem. Before she takes final action, she should consult friends who divorced their husbands, as well as women's organizations, to explore other ways out of marital difficulties.

Many problems continue to beset each parent after all the papers have been signed—the economics of daily living, medical care, psychological effects on the children. Even with sufficient money for alimony and child support, the adjustment to a new way of life does not come easily. For children, the divorce of their parents tends to be a heavy blow, and may distort their own later attitudes toward marriage and parenthood.

Marriage and Family Counseling

If you fear that your marriage is disintegrating, seek professional help promptly. Counseling fees are scaled according to available income and may even be provided free of charge in qualified cases.

Start with your doctor, a member of the clergy, or a rabbi, who are trained to deal with personal problems. They should be able to refer you to an individual or agency counseling service. If you live within driving distance of a community medical center, inquire whether it has a mental health program. If so, you will find marriage and family counselors and counseling programs to help you. Otherwise you can look in your telephone Yellow Pages under "Marriage and Family Counselors." The National Institute of Mental Health (5600 Fishers Lane, Rockville, MD 20852) will send you a free listing of marriage counselors in your area upon request.

Filing for Divorce

To file for divorce, papers must be drawn up and filed in probate court in the county in which both partners had their most recent residence together. This is normally handled by attorneys. A marriage license is needed as evidence. In most states, a husband or wife must be living apart at least thirty days before filing a petition for divorce. Actually, the length of time of separate residency of husband and wife varies from state to state (anywhere from one to about two years).

Grounds for Divorce

While the classical legal framework of a divorce action involves the concept of "fault," namely, that one of the marital partners has been guilty of a serious breach of the marriage contract, there now appears to be a trend toward "no-fault" divorce laws. Some states are already recognizing divorces based on incompatibility, legal separation for a fixed period of time, and other consensual grounds.

Given the wide variety of divorce laws from state to state, a wife and husband contemplating divorce would be wise to consult a qualified attorney, or an agent of the state in order to best determine the rights and options of each.

Divorce is normally a manifestation of irreconcilable differences between the adult partners in a marriage. Some states recognize as grounds for divorce the injustice of parental friction on children, as well as some other deleterious conditions. For example, although drunkenness or the use of drugs is not often used as grounds for divorce, if either condition affects the children adversely and continues up to the date of filing, they could be reasons for the granting of a divorce decree.

Temporary Support and Custody Arrangements

When a couple has filed for divorce and action is pending, one partner can get a temporary restraining order to keep the other out of the house. If either parent can prove that the other is negatively affecting the physical and/or mental health of a minor child, a stronger decree can be secured (with extensive fines and jailing), ordering the offending parent out of the house. In many states, one partner—man or woman—can get a temporary custody order while the case is before the courts, as well as a temporary support decree. Such orders must be part of the first filing petition.

Child Support and Alimony

In all divorce actions, the judge has enormous discretionary powers even if the final papers are mutually agreed to by both partners. The judge can change any and all agreements with respect to the division of marital property, support, alimony, child custody, etc.

Alimony and/or child support are paid weekly or monthly (in some cases where the husband is a bad financial risk, it could be decreed that a lump sum be provided). In a few states, men can sue for alimony.

Alimony payments are usually tax deductible from the provider's income; the recipient has to pay the tax (if the tax laws apply to either sex). Child support, however, is not the wife's tax burden; the husband pays the tax on this. If you are a mother and can prove that your contribution to child support is larger than your husband's (more than $1,200 per child per year), you can claim the child as your dependent on your income tax returns.

When there is a failure to pay alimony due, or child support payments, a court order can force the husband (or the wife) to pay. It can also take account of new financial circumstances.

Child Custody

Custody of the children is usually awarded to the mother unless the court finds her to be unfit. However, nowadays fathers can also find themselves responsible for raising children alone. In most divorce proceedings, fathers are allowed to see their children once a week.

The Separation Agreement

A separation agreement between an estranged husband and wife is a *private contract* that does not involve a court order. It is a private document for settling spousal affairs prior to a divorce. Parties already separated or who separate immediately upon completion of a separation agreement have not *legally* dissolved their marriage. This can be done only in court through the instrument of a divorce action. A separation agreement states, in part, that a husband and wife are living apart for various justifiable reasons.

The main purpose of a separation agreement is to fix the property rights of the wife and husband, including alimony, division of assets and obligations, child support/custody, and mutual promises not to make claims against the other's estate. A separation agreement may also make provision for the custody of children and visitation rights, as well as for the use or disposition of the marital home. The terms of a separation agreement may be incorporated in a divorce decree should the separation end in divorce. All of the above are matters that require the expertise of competent attorneys.

Psychological Implications of Divorce

Most psychiatrists are adamant about the suffering a child goes through in a divorce. Many say flatly that divorce is un-desirable but, like any blanket statement, this would not be true in all instances. Some divorces may be the only tolerable course to take where parents are forever battling or are in frozen animosity. In such negative situations children usually get the feeling that "marriage is a relationship of hate rather than love and understanding," according to psychoanalyst Hiag Akmakjian in *The Natural Way to Raise a Healthy Child* (New York: Praeger, 1975).

A child will sustain the *least* damage if the parents can act as mature adults and do nothing to destroy the loyalty a child has for *both* parents. Make it clear to your child that although the departing parent may not have been a satisfactory mate, he or she is still a caring parent. It is important to preserve the integrity of each parent. If this is impossible, silence would be better than criticism, since the latter places the child in the position of being Mommy's or Daddy's protector—an emotional burden too heavy for any child. Both parents must be careful to explain that the child was in no way responsible for the divorce. Children tend to feel that they are the cause of divorce, or that they can bring the parents together again.

Be careful not to say, "Daddy (or Mommy) left us." In this approach the child is apt to feel personally deserted. It is better to say that "Mommy and Daddy decided to separate, but still love you very much and always will."

Sensitive parents do not involve their children in their own feelings of hatred or revenge, which are often aroused by divorce. They do not use their children to spy on spouses, or talk about lateness of alimony payments, or try to prevent the scheduled visits of the absent parent.

While the adults are the principal participants in any divorce proceeding, the children usually are the victims. Denied understanding and hope as avenues of acceptance, their collapsing world can result in personal, social, and educational upheaval. To be certain that your child's school performance is not judged unfairly during the period of marital dissolution, advise the teacher or school supervisor of your home situation without going into unnecessary detail.

Changes in Family Structure Affect Children of Divorce

When one parent leaves, changes in the family's makeup and in the parents' behavior immediately add to the problems that must be faced by all children of divorce. They need to learn to adapt to a different relationship with each parent, and to cope with confusing alterations in accustomed parental rules, routines, and expectations. Mealtimes, bedtime, and school arrival times are inconsistent in households rallying from divorce. Communication between parents and children inevitably suffers, and parental control in dealing with the children's behavior is usually weak. The upheaval in parent-child relationships seems to crest at the end of the first year after divorce.

Disruption of stable parental function tends to be less drastic and of shorter duration when divorced parents are able to retain a cooperative, working relationship regarding their children's needs. However, according to Dr. Akmakjian, one of the difficulties is "that many people who get divorced were not mature enough for marriage and are, therefore, not mature enough for the problems created by divorce. They simply act out their problems to the detriment of their children."

A longitudinal study of forty-eight divorced families by E. Mavis Hetherington, Martha Cox, and Roger Cox used such techniques as interviews with parents, observations of the parents and children in the laboratory and at home, and a behavior checklist administered at two months, one year, and two years after the divorce.

The study concluded that "Mothers and fathers encountered marked stresses in practical problems of living, self-concept and emotional adjustment, and interpersonal relations following divorce. Low self-esteem, loneliness, depression, and feelings of helplessness were characteristic of the divorced couple."

According to this study, which was reported as "The Aftermath of Divorce" in *Mother/Child, Father/Child Relationships,* published in 1978 by the National Association for the Education of Young Children, Washington, DC, divorced parents appeared to have poor control over their children's behavior. It was found that the children were less obedient and more disruptive than the children in the forty-eight intact families that were also included in this study.

Co-Parenting

An alternative to the more traditional forms of child custody arrangements is known by several labels: *co-parenting, joint parenting, co-custody, shared custody,* or *joint custody.*

Co-parenting makes it possible for both parents—each functioning in a separate household—to apportion their time equally and divide responsibility for the welfare of their children. The mother and father create a warm, nurturing association with their children.

In *Co-Parenting: Sharing Your Child Equally* (Philadelphia: Running Press, 1978), Miriam Galper writes, "When parents share equally in caring for a child, even though they are separated or divorced, that child experiences his parents' love for him." The cooperation encompasses all the physical, emotional, learning, social, and financial needs of the child.

"Many co-parents share financial responsibility on a prorated basis according to their individual incomes . . . Today more ex-spouses are choosing to stay in touch with each other and define their relationship as society dictates . . .

"Transition times are difficult for all children who spend time with one parent and then another. Mothers in traditional custody situations often report that when their children return from a weekend or a day with Daddy, they are very difficult to live with. Similarly, in co-parenting, parents report difficulties at the time of switching from one house to another . . .

"One of the effects on children living in a co-parenting situation is that they become extremely close to both parents."

SINGLE-PARENT FAMILIES

Bringing up a child without a partner is difficult for both the parent and the child, but it is somewhat easier now than it has been in the past. Once ostracized for placing personal happiness above the needs of their offspring, single parents of both sexes (whether divorced or unmarried) are now finding a degree of social acceptance and understanding. About twelve million children under the age of eighteen live in single-parent families, with 90 percent headed by women.

The single parent who has never married is still fairly uncommon, but with the relaxation of social pressures that formerly made unmarried mothers the object of pity or derision, more women are electing to raise their children by themselves. Current adoption laws are permitting single women—and single men—to adopt children if they are otherwise qualified.

A family that has suffered the loss of one parent (whether by death, desertion, separation, divorce, or long-term hospitalization) experiences a period of transition during which the children and the remaining parent undergo painful and difficult readjustments to a different way of life. The remaining mother or father becomes of greater emotional importance to the children precisely at a time when the parent can least afford the extra demands.

During this time, most young children regress in their development and behavior. Some withdraw and express only a rigid desire to please. Others exhibit various patterns of rebellion and negativism. This period of adjustment is inevitable for all involved families. However, just how hard and long-lasting it is depends upon the makeup of each family member.

According to the late Dr. Margaret Mead, world-famous anthropologist, single parenthood by choice rather than as the result of death or desertion is definitely on the rise in U.S. society—a drastic change in family structure that needs to be rethought in terms of children's needs. Dr. Mead believed that the single-parent household is an unsatisfactory arrangement for raising growing children.

Most single-parent mothers must manage with less money. In cases where the mother has always been a homemaker, the lowered income may be especially troublesome. (One advantage of the single-parent father may be his higher financial status.) The lack of sufficient time to get everything done is punishing to all single parents. Single-parent mothers are continually challenged to balance their own needs with the requirements of their children and the household. The single-parent father must also learn to juggle working, parenting, attending to the home, and dating. Once a workable balance is achieved, the problems of daily living will not go away, however, though often they will be a little less difficult to resolve.

Parents Without Partners

More than just a social club, although social events are scheduled regularly, Parents Without Partners provides support for women and men who are in a process of transition. Members' ages range from the twenties to the sixties. The only requirement for membership is that the parent is single and has a child or children; who has custody is not a factor.

There are over seven hundred chapters in all fifty states, as well as Canada. For the address of the chapter nearest you, consult your telephone directory or write to Parents Without Partners, 7910 Woodmont Avenue, Suite 1000, Washington, DC 20014.

Parents Without Partners publishes a journal, *The Single Parent,* ten times a year, with articles by professionals in the human relations, legal, economic, and other fields; book reviews; human-interest stories; and updates on chapter activities across the country. Write to the above address for current subscription costs.

Books for Single Parents

To guide newly single parents through the difficult areas of economic, emotional, and social readjustment, we recommend *The World of the Formerly Married* by Morton Hunt (New York: McGraw-Hill, 1966). *Family in Transition* by Arlene S. Skolnick (Boston: Little, Brown, 1971) is also helpful.

For those not only not formerly married, but not intending to get married, there is *The Single Parent Experience* by Carole Klein (New York: Avon Books, 1973). This is a level-headed appraisal of the rapidly expanding social phenomenon in the U.S.—the single-parent family.

For women experiencing or contemplating a separation, *Separation: Journal of a Marriage* by Eve Bagudor (New York: Simon & Schuster, 1972) will speak to the condition of most women who find themselves without a husband, and often are at a loss as to how to take up the reins of daily living by themselves.

Widow by Lynn Caine (New York: William Morrow, 1974) offers comfort and guidelines to others facing this crisis situation. *Teaching Your Child to Cope with Crisis* by Suzanne Ramos (New York: David McKay, 1975) has a good chapter on how to help children deal with death.

A small but useful booklet, *The One-Parent Family* by Anna W. M. Wolf and Lucille Stein (both authors were on the staff of the Child Study Association of America for many years), Public Affairs Pamphlet No. 287, can be obtained by sending your request and 75¢ to the Public Affairs Committee, 381 Park Avenue South, New York, NY 10016.

New Child-Rearing Lifestyles

The single parent comes in a variety of forms and styles. In most instances, *today's single parent*—male or female, young or middle-aged, white, black, or Hispanic, heterosexual or homosexual, out-of-wedlock mother, biological or adoptive mother or father—*has chosen this role.* However, most psychiatrists and child-care authorities hasten to advise that early on the single parent should try to bring people of the opposite sex into their child's life.

According to Carole Klein, author of *The Single Parent Experience* (mentioned above), "Some people will probably go on to reject the idea of family entirely, choosing to live in total independence. Other people will live in groups. Homosexuals will live together without apology as homosexuals. Some marriages will encompass outside sexual relationships; other marriages will choose monogamy. Some marriages will last a lifetime; others will be for particular stages of life. Social theorists say that if marriage is to survive at all, it must be open to this kind of free-wheeling interpretation of its possibilities. In a world that has such a variety of value systems, it is absurd to think we can continue to declare only one pattern of living legitimate, particularly when so much evidence exists that the pattern is so far from perfect."

"Being a single parent is never going to be easy," writes

Joan Bel Geddes in her book, *How to Parent Alone: A Guide for Single Parents* (New York: Seabury Press, 1974). "In addition to the many problems which concern all parents, the parent operating on his or her own carries a double load. No one else is there to share daily tasks and worries. No one is consistently on hand to consult on important decisions, to back one up when firmness is needed, or to counteract it when firmness has gone too far, or to give special comfort and support in times of emergency or hardship. No one is there to provide a salutary balance that will compensate for personal limitations in regard to temperament, judgment, knowledge, aptitudes, and attitudes . . .

"But if you don't let that scare you too much, you will find that doing the best you can . . . brings huge rewards, immeasurably greater than any of your problems."

On the other hand, even today there is a respected group of child-rearing authorities, especially psychoanalysts Hiag Akmakjian, Anna Freud, and Erik Erikson, who question the idea of single parents leaving their offspring in the care of others at a very early age because of the emotional stresses that may ensue, possibly creating psychological problems in their adult lives.

Single Fatherhood

In *Non-Sexist Childraising* (Boston: Beacon Press, 1977), Carrie Carmichael writes, "Choosing single parenthood in some cases, having it thrust upon them in others, single fathers have to be father and mother to their children. When a terrified and insecure little boy needs holding and stroking and reassurance in the middle of a long night, there is no space for a loving father to ask, 'Is this manly?'"

Michael McFadden, a divorced freelance writer who is rearing his three young children, writes in *Bachelor Fatherhood: How to Raise and Enjoy Your Children as a Single Parent* (New York: Walker & Co., 1974), "With moral, legal, and economic sanctions against divorce rapidly disappearing, the reason many people still endure an unhappy or uncomfortable marriage is simply for the children . . .

"There are not any real statistics available, but the number of men who are willing to take their children is increasing rapidly, and perhaps more important, so is the number of women who are willing to give them up . . .

"Bachelor fatherhood is only one alternative, and for many it is just a transitional stage, but as we evolve new institutions, we also begin to break away from our old ideas of masculine and feminine roles, and in doing that perhaps we are building a better society."

STEPPARENTHOOD

Stepfamilies (also referred to as "blended" families or "reconstituted" families) continue to grow in number and complexity with each passing year. In the United States just a few years ago one out of every three marriages was a remarriage, and in one-third of these remarriages, both spouses had children from a prior union. Today the projection is that at least one child in every four will be a stepchild.

In *How to Discipline with Love,* renowned psychologist Fitzhugh Dodson presents six reasons for his belief that stepparenting is more difficult than "regular" parenting: 1) in families of biological parents and children, parental deficiencies are smoothed over by long-standing emotional bonds; 2) blended families are more complicated than biological families and often encompass more individuals; 3) members of blended families may experience deep feelings of ambivalence and jealousy; 4) the blended family will always be haunted by ghosts from the biological family. If the absent biological parent is dead, children may create an idealized image of this parent that no real person can measure up to; 5) former spouses (mothers more frequently than fathers) may use the children to attack the biological parent and the stepparent; 6) there are no clear guidelines for being a stepparent. Each stepparent must create the role, depending upon his or her temperament, the ages and sexes of the children, and their living arrangements.

It is encouraging that Dr. Dodson thinks that "This does not mean that stepchildren in a blended family are bound to be more unhappy or maladjusted than children in a biological family." He goes on to say, "In fact, I know of children in blended families who are happier and better adjusted than many other children. But it takes knowledge and skill to achieve this."

"Although there are many sociological and psychological studies of marriage, the family, children, and divorce, there are few studies of remarriage and almost none of stepchild or stepsibling relationships," writes Lucile Duberman, Ph.D., in her book on the subject, *The Reconstituted Family: A Study of Remarried Couples and Their Children* (Chicago: Nelson-Hall, 1975).

The object of Dr. Duberman's study was to explore the sociological factors that affect step-relationships; and to explain the dynamics of the reconstituted family, its possible effects on society, and societal influences upon it.

Reconstituted families experience most of the problems of biological families, in addition to problems specific to step-families. Among the most obvious are the self-consciousness of the adults and the children; the awkwardness of maintaining a relationship with the living biological parent who is of the same sex as the stepparent; the matter of adoption; rivalry between stepparent and stepchild; competition between step-brothers and stepsisters and between biological parents and stepparents; and money as a source of irritability. In short, the most deleterious elements in a stepparent-stepchild-stepsibling relationship are the hostility, jealousy, and competition generated by feelings of insecurity and role uncertainty on each one's part.

Dr. Duberman's study brought these conclusions to light:

- The degree of stepfamily integration was higher for younger couples than for older ones.
- A difference in religion did not seem to have any effect, nor did educational background.
- Integration was greater in those stepfamilies where there was a child (or children) from the present marriage.
- When both parents worked, family integration was higher when there was no difference in their occupational status. (Integration was highest when the wife was not working outside the home.)
- The stepfather generally had a better relationship with his stepchildren than the stepmother had with her stepchildren. This was because the stepmother was more involved with the stepchildren than the stepfather, leaving her more open to their animosity.

In Dr. Duberman's study of eighty-eight reconstituted families residing in the Cleveland area, all were Caucasian couples who had remarried during the years 1965–1968, were under forty-five years of age, and had children under eighteen at the time of the remarriage. She concluded that the majority of these families seemed to be making sincere efforts to form healthy new families. Dr. Duberman felt that the "chances of the reconstituted family becoming like the ideal type are great because the reconstituted families considered the ideal type a value they were striving to attain."

According to Emily B. Visher, Ph.D., and John S. Visher, M.D., joint authors of *Stepfamilies: A Guide to Working with Stepparents and Stepchildren* (New York: Brunner/Mazel, 1979), widespread divorce, single parenting, and remarriage are a relatively new development in American society, and there are few traditions or models to follow. Nonetheless, they believe that there are positive values and strengths in remarriage and that many stepfamilies do achieve family unity.

Sociological research on stepfamilies is just beginning in earnest, but to wait until the data are available for the use of family counselors and therapists would deprive many people of needed help. Write the Vishers, "Stepparents do not know what to expect of themselves; other family members do not know what to expect of stepparents; and society has no idea what to expect . . . Some stepparents have a clear idea of the role they wish to play in their new family, and when this choice meets the needs of the other family members, no particular conflict results."

The Adjustment of Stepsiblings

"Many children do not perceive the back-and-forth trek from one household to another in a positive light. They feel helpless and out of control . . . and unless the children have some help in recognizing that there are many different acceptable patterns of living, they may constantly battle at least one pattern. Many times the children's upset at going back and forth between two homes is a result of the children's recognition that one parent is threatened if they enjoy the other environment."

Some studies indicate that when both sets of children reside in the same house, their interrelationships are apt to be more agreeable than when they live in different homes.

Fredrick P. Capaldi II and Barbara McRae, in their book *Stepfamilies: A Cooperative Responsibility* (New York: New

Viewpoints/Vision Books, 1979), present the following guidelines for stepparents:

- *"Be yourself."* Your own natural actions are your best tools.
- *"Be a spouse first; a stepparent second."* Your first responsibility is to yourself, then to your marriage, then to your role as a stepparent.
- *"Be honest."* Your marriage depends upon the bond between you and your spouse. The children's sanction of the marriage is not necessary. However, you must recognize your stepchildren's rightful place in the new family.
- *"Assert yourself."* Be open with your spouse about your need for complete support in your stepparenting role. Work with your spouse in exchanging ideas on how you can jointly best nurture the children in your care.
- *"Be open to compromise."* Children need space and the freedom to act like children. They should not be made to feel unwelcome in your home.
- *"Be realistic about the past."* Accept the reality of your spouse's past without jealousy. Remember that if his or her ex-spouse or previous family really comes first, he or she would still be living with the ex-spouse! Do not make the former family constellation a taboo topic.

The Child in the Stepfamily

Stepchildren face many problems, not the least of which is the loyalty conflict. Many stepchildren are trapped by their feelings of love and identification with the absent biological parent and their growing respect for the stepparent. The absentee parent may make this distressing dichotomy of feelings worse by encouraging the children to express negative feelings about the stepparent. Absentee parents may also express feelings of rejection if their children verbalize good feelings for the stepparent, again throwing the children into a situation of conflicting loyalties.

Many children harbor resentment against their biological parent for leaving them or for not visiting them frequently enough. Therefore, they will hang their hostility on their stepparent. The defense mechanism of withdrawal is used by some stepchildren as they joust with their stepparents.

Psychosomatic illness is another defense mechanism stepchildren may employ. Although their headaches, stomachaches, flu-like aches and pains, etc., are real enough, these stepchildren may be trying to handle their tensions by escaping into sickness.

Stepchildren need reassurance that they are wanted. They want to know that they will indeed be an important part of the new family constellation. All children need at least one consistent and dependable parenting figure. Usually this is the biological parent with custody, but sometimes this may be the stepparent.

Stepfathers as Parents

A study of stepfathers as parents, conducted by Paul Bohannan, Professor of Anthropology at the University of California, Santa Barbara, and reported by Herbert Yahraes in a National Institute of Mental Health Science Monograph, indicates that children living with stepfathers do just as well or just as poorly on all the behavioral characteristics studied as do children living with their biological fathers. They generally are just as happy or just as unhappy. They do as well in school and in their social relationships. In short, they appear to get along with their stepfathers as well as other children do with their biological fathers.

Children with stepfathers have lost a biological father either by divorce or death, and usually they have lived in a one-parent household for a span of time. Then a new man may enter their lives—a stepfather. In the study, these children seemed to be more mature than children living with both biological parents, partly because of the troubles the family members had experienced and their greater need to pull together; and partly because they often had to assume more responsibility.

Dr. Bohannan found that on the whole stepfathers pay more attention to being "fathers." They worry about their role and also work harder at it. It's a very conscious, demanding step they have taken, one not all biological fathers take seriously.

Published in 1979 in *Families Today, Volume 1,* the study noted further that "Better than 40% of the new stepfamilies lived in the mother's house; not quite 40% moved to a different place; 18% moved to the stepfather's house. The investigators have the impression that it's best for the children to stay on in the mother's home, but there are some advantages to moving to a different place . . . Other common problems were styles of discipline, division of labor and, of all things, food—because the stepfather's tastes were frequently far different from his predecessor's."

There are students of this subject who think a stepparent actually fluctuates between being a parent, a stepparent, and a nonparent. One must know what role one is in, and when it may be necessary to switch parts. The trick is to be able to do so without resentment or self-pity. If one resides with stepchildren, one is a parent in terms of discipline, planning family activities, setting limits on children's behavior, etc.; one is a stepparent when certain visits, events, and planning have to be shared with the absent biological parent; and one is a nonparent when, for whatever reason, one withdraws and lets the spouse take care of those aspects of family relations in which one is not or does not wish to be a part.

"One's ability to function as a stepparent is very much dependent upon how one feels one is doing in the eyes of one's spouse and the stepchildren. The growth of confidence in one's new role as stepparent is highly influenced by the feedback from the family."*

Discipline is a major issue in stepparenting (as it is in biological parenting). Research indicates that stepparents are accepted better when the children are very young or are young adults. Adolescents are least able to accept a new parent because they are often battling with their biological parents while trying to come to grips with any authority.

Experts suggest that stepparents wait until they are accepted by their stepchildren before they initiate a reasonable standard of acceptable behavior.

Often stepparents make a beneficial contribution to children's growth because they can sometimes be more objective about stepchildren than the biological parents.

One of the major tensions in many stepfamilies is due to the fact that the parents have unreal expectations for themselves and their association with the children. Inasmuch as the partners love each other, they suppose that they will love the children, and that automatically the love will be reciprocated. Their presumptions are often coupled with a tendency to ro-

*Adapted from *The Joys and Sorrows of Parenthood* by The Group for the Advancement of Psychiatry (New York: Charles Scribner's Sons, 1973).

manticize what transpires in biological families. When this happens, comparisons invariably reflect badly on the step-family and create difficulties. Of course, in biological families there is a background of caring between parents and children. Yet countless biological parents feel that their children neither appreciate their efforts nor value them.

Mrs. Brenda Maddox, author of *The Half-Parent: Living With Other People's Children,* is a stepparent herself. She believes that possible rewards of stepparenting can accrue only when stepparents realize that they cannot replace the biological parents—nor should they want to—and when their ambivalent feelings for their stepchildren are discussed rather than buried.

Her candid book treats many of the complicated aspects of stepparenting, especially from the angle of stepmothers. Mrs. Maddox's thesis is that stepparenting can be a growth-enhancing experience for everyone in the new family unit, even though stepparents and stepchildren have to create their relationship as they go along.

Most stepparents are well-intentioned. They want to help restore the psychological balance of their often troubled step-children. Unfortunately, stepparents usually face insurmountable obstacles because children who have experienced a great loss are not immediately able to respond to overtures of affection and caring, especially from a stepparent.

Researchers have presented generalizations regarding differences in the adjustment of a stepchild to a stepparent when a biological parent dies or leaves the original family as the result of divorce. Writes Mrs. Maddox, "For my part, I think the distinction between death and divorce explains very little. There are a great many natural parents, divorced and alive, who might as well be dead for all their children ever see or hear of them. And there are a great many parents who die whose marriages would have ended in divorce if they lived long enough."

Rights and Duties of Stepparents

Mrs. Maddox warns stepparents that they have none of the rights of biological parents, that parental rights are protected in law, and that stepparents would be wise to become acquainted with these rights. The prime right held by both biological parents is custody of their offspring. In a custody battle, the stepparent is usually in a less favored position.

Stepparents have no legal obligation to support their stepchildren. Nonetheless, stepfathers cannot always evade paying the stepchildren's bills (particularly if the biological father refuses to support them, or is deceased).

Adoption of Stepchildren*

Very little has been written on the subject of adoption by stepparents. Research is yet to be conducted on the advantages and disadvantages of such a procedure.

Mrs. Maddox believes that there are legal and psychological advantages in adopting stepchildren. Adoption affords the stepchild equal rights with any other child of the union. For many stepfamilies adoption provides a sense of emotional security.

Stepgrandparenthood

When stepchildren enter a family constellation, grandparents also face the difficult task of sorting out their conflicting feelings.

Stepchildren bring their own grandparents with them into the extended family that is the outcome of a remarriage. When children have more than two sets of grandparents, it is easy for all of them to ignore the grandchildren. At the same time, when grandparents find the number of their grandchildren increased by the addition of several stepgrandchildren, it is hard for them to refrain from giving emotional preference to those who are biologically related.

Of course, stepgrandparents vary in their feelings for the stepchildren their adult children suddenly are raising. Like stepparents, stepgrandparents can be capricious. They may harbor unrealistic expectations, and may too quickly withhold their affection and interest when they feel aggrieved, are busy, or are presented with biological grandchildren. Just as it takes sufficient time for stepchildren and stepparents to become well acquainted, the adjustment is slow for stepgrandchildren and stepgrandparents.

*Adapted from *The Half-Parent: Living With Other People's Children* by Brenda Maddox (New York: M. Evans & Co., 1975).

"There wouldn't be so many books on the market about stepparenting if it were easy to be a stepparent," writes Suzy Kalter in *Instant Parent: A Guide for Stepparents, Part-time Parents and Grandparents* (New York: A & W Publications, 1979). She suggests that "If your problems with the ex-spouse are working against you and the marriage, maybe it's time for professional help."

TESTING: INFANTS, TODDLERS, KINDERGARTNERS

John A. Glover, author of *A Parent's Guide to Intelligence Testing: How to Help Your Children's Intellectual Development* (Chicago: Nelson-Hall, 1979), believes that "there are some loosely set limits placed on an individual by his genetic endowment, but that within these bounds, experience makes the difference between a person of average intelligence and a person of above-average intelligence." He includes in a definition of intelligence those traits that generate problem-solving abilities in verbal, concrete, and abstract situations. Furthermore, these skills may be enhanced or discouraged by an individual's total environment of people, places, and experiences.

Most parents want to know the intelligence, competence, and talents of their offspring. However, testing at too early an age can provide misleading information. For example, a toddler may not be verbal at eighteen to twenty-four months and both the parents and pediatrician may begin to worry when, suddenly at thirty months, an avalanche of words spurts forth. After the age of two-and-a-half years, it is better to be calmly concerned than to completely ignore verbal slowness because emotional and learning problems lay down their roots during this period and can be corrected. In later years, any correction would be remedial, difficult, and costly.

Intelligence Quotient Tests

During the early 1900s in France, Alfred Binet created an intelligence test for identifying mentally deficient children. In 1905, the original Binet-Simon test appeared. This particular IQ test and subsequent revisions by Terman (1937) and Merrill (1960) have used a general definition of intelligence as the standard for evaluating test results. There are test items at twenty different levels of ability that range from those that are geared to the average two-year-old through those that are mastered only by superior adults.

The Stanford-Binet (a derivative of Binet and Simon's original tests) is the best known. It provides a single mental age score that is used to compute an IQ (intelligence quotient). Given to children five years and up, it is an individual test administered to one child at a time by the tester.

The components of the Stanford-Binet test cover abilities in language, memory, conceptual thinking, reasoning, numerical reasoning, visual-motor skill, and social intelligence. The test measures language skills in four ways: (1) parts of the test relate the vocabulary of the child to standard preschool levels of vocabulary in order to determine the extent of the child's vocabulary; (2) the number of words the child can define is measured and compared to the age level of other children; (3) the quality of vocabulary (which is inferred from responses to the abstract words test, rhymes, word identification and definition) is assessed; (4) the understanding of verbal relations is measured.

Measuring Memory

The ability of children to remember things is measured in three forms: auditory memory, idea memory, and attention span. Memory is one of the basic mental processes that seems to be a mandatory skill in order to function successfully in life.

Memory is measured on the Stanford-Binet by the examiner reading a story to the child and then asking questions about it; showing the child a series of geometrical designs and later having the child attempt to identify them; noting the apparent length of the child's attention span; showing the child pictures and asking questions about them after they have been put away.

The figure 100 on the Stanford-Binet indicates an average IQ; above 100, above average; and below 100, below average.

The Stanford-Binet Intelligence Scale, which is predominantly verbal, has been criticized because it draws on learned or acquired knowledge. It is clearly unsuitable for deprived or linguistically dysfunctional children.

Developmental Tests

Many child psychologists and researchers still use the Gesell Developmental Scales (developed in the 1930s and 1940s) which examine a child's motor, language, adaptive, and personal-social levels. Three-dimensional materials are used to evoke response. The Gesell tests have served as a model for other child psychologists and researchers, who have improved upon them. The Merrill-Palmer Test provides very young children with manipulative materials and sensory stimulation. It can be scored for verbal and nonverbal items.

A standardized infancy test is the Bayley Infant Scales of Mental Development, widely used as a basis for measuring the beginnings of intelligence of babies and toddlers up to the age of two and one-half years. The items below, taken from the scale, illustrate the kinds of behavior that the test measures. (Numbers in parentheses indicate the age in months and days at which 50 percent of the children tested passed the item.)

- Imitates words (12.5)
- Builds tower of 2 cubes (13.8)
- Says 2 words (14.2)
- Uses gestures to make wants known (14.6)
- Attains toy with stick (17.0)
- Imitates a stroke (17.8)
- Places 2 round and 2 square blocks in a formboard (19.3)
- Follows directions in pointing to parts of a doll (19.5)
- Points to 3 pictures (21.9)
- Builds tower of 6 cubes (22.6)
- Names 2 objects (23.0)
- Mends broken doll (23.6)
- Names 3 pictures (24.0)
- Names 3 objects (24.9)
- Names 5 pictures (25.5)

Most of the items on this test, like those on other scales, tap sensorimotor skills. Many of them also involve simple understanding and use of language.

Parents, please note that most researchers believe that the scores obtained on infancy scales are *not* predictive of later intelligence. However, such tests may indicate whether a baby has had a disease or injury to the brain.

The Peabody Picture Vocabulary Test, the Goodenough-Harris Draw-a-Man Test, and the Slosson Intelligence Test for Children are also indexes of intelligence. They are commonly used in screening and evaluation because they are easy to administer. While the Goodenough is indicative of cognitive development, it could easily be contaminated by emotional factors, such as a very negative self-image. The Slosson is an abbreviated, individual test that provides fairly good indications of intelligence levels.

The *Wechsler Intelligence Scale for Children* (WISC-R, revised) is another important individual test for intelligence that is in use for children from seven to fifteen years of age. It is considered by many educators to be a reliable intelligence test. It is divided into two sections: verbal and performance (nonverbal), which are divided further into subtests that measure different aspects of intelligence—some of which are sensitive to perceptual or sensory dysfunction. It is favored over the Stanford-Binet by some examiners for elementary school-age children.

For children from four to six-and-a-half years of age, the Wechsler Preschool Primary Scale (WPPSI) is used.

The Denver Developmental Screening Scale, created by Drs. William K. Frankenburg and Josiah B. Dodds, is based on long-term testing in Denver of a large cross-section of children from birth to six years of age. It measures the growth of intelligence, and helps doctors to identify children who may score in the retarded range on further testing. The Denver Scale gives four different age levels for each test item showing when 25, 50, 75, and 90 percent of children develop each skill. Parents need not be concerned if their children fail to perform one or two of the test items at the age when 90 percent of children can. However, if their children consistently fall into the lowest 10 percent, a physician would probably decide to make more diagnostic tests to evaluate their mental abilities.

Developmental Damage and Lag

The main reason for testing children under two-and-a-half is to ascertain whether there is any neurological (brain) damage that might cause learning or emotional difficulties. If you suspect any problem, you should first discuss it with your doctor or a pediatric nurse in a maternal-child clinic for referral to a competent professional in the field. You can also contact your state health department for referral to community agencies concerned with developmental lags.

The Denver Developmental Screening Scale and the Cattell Infant Intelligence Scale, both popular tests, have been criticized as less reliable than the Gesell Developmental Scales and the Bayley Infant Scales of Mental Development.

Inasmuch as norms vary widely throughout the country regarding the results of various achievement tests, parents need to be extremely careful in accepting normative data on any such test.

Intelligence Testing of Preschool and Older Children

Standardized intelligence tests for preschool and older children yield a score, the IQ, that is commonly considered an index of intellectual capability and potential cognitive achievement. It is estimated that in North American schools alone over 250 million IQ tests are administered yearly.

A child's intellectual growth is neither static nor necessarily predetermined. It varies throughout life, depending upon the interaction between one's inherited characteristics and one's environment. Many factors may affect cognitive growth: the emotional climate at home, whether a child is encouraged or discouraged, whether or not the child's drive is strong, whether there are adequate and appropriate opportunities for experience and learning that are geared to the child's capacities, etc.

Limitations and Criticisms of the IQ Test

The concept of the stable IQ score appears outmoded. Many factors affect scores on intelligence tests, most of which are capable of manipulation. For example, in their book *Blueprint for a Brighter Child* (New York: McGraw-Hill, 1973), Brandon Sparkman and Ann Carmichael report that the scores culturally deprived youngsters make on IQ tests can be substantially improved through concentrated efforts on language development, especially from the ages of eighteen to twenty-eight months. They reveal that an increase of 15 to 20 IQ points in one year is not uncommon. They also stress the fact that "IQ does not measure the innate capacity of a child to learn; it merely indicates the degree to which he is able to learn at that moment."

Other studies indicate that children have the ability to alter their IQ scores markedly. Drs. Mussen, Conger, and Kagan report that "many children undergo significant changes in IQ between early childhood and later ages. In fact, there are marked changes, sometimes as much as 20 points, between the nursery school period and later childhood." They suggest that extremely favorable or unfavorable changes in environment may produce such shifts in intellectual performance.

Other research on personality and IQ change showed that such qualities as high achievement, competitive striving, and curiosity about nature were correlated with gains in IQ score because these qualities may facilitate the acquisition of the skills that are measured by intelligence tests.

A high IQ score alone does not indicate superiority in every area of living. On the whole, the IQ may help in predicting successful academic performance in school. However, a child may have an average IQ, but excel in social behavior, motor skills, creativity, etc., or have a high IQ and be immature for his age in his general behavior.

While intelligence tests measure the potential capacity of a student to learn, they do not measure achievement. Moreover, it is possible for a child to have a very high intelligence quotient but still show only average or below-average results on achievement tests. When children show disparity between their IQ scores and their achievement test scores, it is up to the parents to look into the matter because it has been found that parents can do more to upgrade the level of their children's progress than anyone else.

Another important consideration concerning all tests is that errors due to less than perfect presentation and scoring, through a child's not performing at optimum capacity, and through poor testing conditions (discomforts, noise, etc.) are likely to have negative effects on any test performance.

John A. Glover, mentioned earlier, believes that "Although studies have not led, as yet, to any consistent or accurate criteria that allow us to identify creative people directly, eleven characteristics (though not all are truly personality traits) can be listed as occurring frequently among people who have been identified as creative: a strong sense of curiosity, highly developed problem-solving skills, an ability for self-amusement, a strong level of self-determination, a strong fantasy life, stick-to-it-iveness, a strong tolerance for ambiguity, a strong sense of humor, an ability to see complex relationships, an ability to redefine and elaborate on problems, and high inventiveness."

Parents' expectations can be a help or a hindrance in the development of their children. Too much emphasis on achievement can be as damaging as too little concern. Parents can avoid undue pressure by being aware of the chronological and developmental ages of their children. Intelligence is not a fixed, objective trait to be identified and somehow converted into an IQ score—once and for all. Therefore, ask questions about the tests administered to your child, and continue asking questions until you are satisfied with the interpretations you are given.

In *The Stranglehold of the IQ* (Garden City, NY: Doubleday, 1975), Benjamin Fine writes that IQ tests do not measure native intelligence and a child's capacity for learning and achievement, but what a child has already learned through home or school experience. He believes that IQ tests are biased in favor of highly verbal, middle-class children and that they do not assess problem-solving ability or creativity—factors basic to succeeding and contributing in the real world.

Intelligence, Creativity, and the IQ

There are many educators, psychologists, and so on who believe that standardized mental tests are unfair to the bright but unorthodox person, to the culturally disadvantaged, and to those who simply do not do well under the pressure of any standardized test.

For too long, society in general and our schools in particular have viewed the IQ test as the only measure of an individual's capabilities and potentials. The IQ test measures convergent thinking (memory, recognition, ability to analyze and to reason). It does *not* measure divergent thinking (the ability to be creative, exploratory, venturesome, flexible, and inventive). Clearly, then, the IQ test provides only a limited index of personal capacity.

At the University of Minnesota, elementary school children

were tested for both intelligence and creativity. Seventy percent of the most creative children did not distinguish themselves on the IQ test, a situation very reminiscent of the young Thomas Edison, and numerous other highly inventive persons. In another study, Donald F. MacKinnon, a psychologist, tested a group of successful young architects chosen as most creative by experts in the field. Their IQ scores ranged from very high to very low, with a mean of 113.5 (a very average score).

The traditional academic curricula of our schools and colleges are becoming increasingly dependent upon verbal communication, verbal memory, and the same kind of abstract reasoning that is measured by mental tests. Our schools are trapped by the tyranny of the test. As society leans more and more heavily upon the test score to categorize people, schools provide curricula that tend to promote success on the tests, but not necessarily in living.

An informative pamphlet is available from The Psychological Corporation entitled "Some Things Parents Should Know About Testing." This pamphlet presents in a clear, concise manner the terminology used in testing, together with related questions and answers. For a free copy write to The Psychological Corporation, 757 Third Avenue, New York, NY 10017.

TWINS

In the past, prospective parents were in the dark up to the very last moment about the sex and number of babies to expect. Doctors used different signs of carrying during pregnancy as indicators of sex: high or low, wide or all over. Often a double heartbeat and/or the knowledge that twins ran in the family of one of the parents-to-be alerted them to the probability of a multiple birth. Modern medical technology enables obstetricians to predict the number of embryos with a greater degree of certainty. Hence, today's parents-to-be have a few precious months in which to adjust to the stunning idea of twin birth, to shop for equipment, and prepare their home.

The statistics concerning multiple births indicate that they are on the rise, due perhaps to the fertility pills that have been used successfully by couples having problems conceiving. Twins are more common than triplets and quadruplets, and the chance of having twins is 1 in 90. The incidence of triplets is 1 in 9,000 births. Multiple births beyond three continue to be a medical wonder every time they occur.

Rearing Twins Is Especially Hard

During their infancy, most mothers of twins are overwhelmed by the work load they face day after day, and by their utter exhaustion trying to keep pace. Every mother of an infant, and most especially one with twins, needs to utilize any time- and step-saving idea or device that can make her life easier. Housecleaning, for example, need not be done as meticulously as perhaps it once was, nor as often. After all, there will always be dust, but infants have a way of growing up very quickly. A rested mother is always to be preferred over a freshly scrubbed bathroom.

Taking care of twins requires more than doubling up of the effort and equipment needed for rearing a single child. In every detail of feeding, bathing, clothing, sleeping, equipment, toilet learning, in their adjustment to each other and to other children, as well as in their effect upon their parents' lives, twins present extra responsibilities and concerns.

The following books offer valuable insights to parents of twins:

- *Having Twins* by Elizabeth Nobel (Boston: Houghton Mifflin Co., 1980).
- *Parallels: A Look at Twins* by Ted Wolner (New York: E. P. Dutton, 1978).
- *The Curious World of Twins* by Margaret and Vincent Gaddis (New York: Warner Books, 1973).
- *Twins: Twice the Trouble, Twice the Fun* by Betsey H. Gehman (Philadelphia: J. B. Lippincott, 1965).
- *Twins and Supertwins* by Amram Scheinfeld (Baltimore: Penguin, 1973).

Differences Within the Twin Population

Fraternal (nonidentical) twins come from two fertilized eggs, and may or may not be of the same sex. While the tendency is to treat identical twins (who come from one fertilized egg) as much alike as two individuals can be treated, greater distinctions are made between fraternal twins because of their dissimilarities in sex, looks, and abilities.

Twinship Should Not Be Emphasized

Twins are usually regarded as a unit, and are expected to have a very tight association. Identical twins tend to develop this naturally. Indeed, very young identical twins frequently form a sort of closed corporation. Fraternal twins also close their ranks early. Nevertheless, twins are individuals who need to develop their own personalities from the very beginning of their lives. Their parents, grandparents, and other close relatives and friends should not stress their twinship, since it is essential that each twin is given ample opportunity to develop positive feelings of independence, uniqueness, and self-esteem.

Emphasis on each child's singularity is one of the most important aspects of healthy twin development. Child-rearing authorities do not recommend the use of rhyming names, identical clothes and toys, or shared classrooms. Each twin will have different mannerisms, abilities, preferences, and friends, and parents must respect and support this.

Many parents of twins feel that when their twins are ready for nursery school, or when they begin to take an interest in choosing their own clothes, they should not be dressed alike. Most parents of twins (and most grown-up twins themselves) think that dressing alike should certainly stop when twins enter grade school. Not only does not being dressed alike help stress the individuality and separateness of each twin, it also enables teachers and classmates to identify each more easily.

The Language Acquisition of Twins

Twins usually talk later than single-birth children because they develop their own private means of communication with each other, using gestures, sounds, and a special jargon only they understand. Inasmuch as they mirror each other, stammering and stuttering are exacerbated unless parents intervene to help their twins acquire language. (As with all children, parents should never imitate nor ridicule the imperfect speech of their twins, nor foster their baby talk. What may be quaint at twenty-five months will sound odd at sixty months!)

Parents and older siblings can further the word learning and simple sentence formation of twins by speaking clearly at all times. (See Chapters 1 and 2, which include discussions of beginning language acquisition.)

Above all, twins need to be talked to as separate and distinct individuals so that each child will learn to function and talk as an independent entity.

The IQ of Twins

The IQ of identical twins varies only by about 5 points; the scores of fraternal twins may vary by less than 10 points. It has been found that the IQ scores of other siblings in the same family will span as much as a 10- or 15-point difference.

Feelings of Rivalry Among Twins

More feelings of rivalry exist between fraternal than identical twins because the former are more unlike and tend to compete with each other in stressing their individuality. Although twins learn to share and wait their turns at an earlier age than non-twins, their feelings of rivalry and jealousy can be stronger than are those of siblings of different ages. However, as twins mature and attain feelings of self-identity and self-confidence, their competitive feelings usually decrease.

Many twins are able to function happily in the same schoolroom without developing competition and/or dependency problems. In many instances, they are less insecure and anxious when they attend school together. In any event, it is advisable not to separate twins before they are ready.

The special status of being a twin also causes some problems in their relationships with their other siblings, who sometimes feel left out due to the unusually close companionship between twins.

The Social Development of Twins

It is difficult for parents of twins to learn how long to let their twins enjoy the security and pleasure they derive from their exclusive, satisfying relationship without permitting them to grow so dependent upon it that one twin feels lost without the other. Often twins become socialized later than singletons, and with more difficulty on the part of their parents. It is not easy to discipline twins who take off in different directions!

After twins become mobile, inadequate language due to their private babbling style can interfere with attempts to reach out to other children and adults. At the same time, playing with other children seems extraneous to young twins who often give the appearance of being sufficient unto themselves.

Experienced mothers of twins agree that help in the form of willing grandparents, relatives, or a hired homemaker is essential. Of course, the single most important helper is a loving, cooperative, resourceful father who can be a tremendous energy- and time-saver to his wife—and an interacting father with his twins.

Although there are instances in which older twins have told their parents that they really did not relish their twinship, most twins appreciate their unique relationship and remain close throughout their lives.

WORKING MOTHER/DAY CARE

Opinions about working mothers and the effects upon them and their families have come from sociologists, White House conferences, psychologists and psychiatrists, husbands, teachers, and so on. However, as of this writing, there is no conclusive data about all the positive and negative effects upon the toddlers and preschoolers of mothers who are in the work force.

One important consideration is how sensitive and responsive the working mothers themselves are, not how many hours a day they spend or do not spend with their very young children. Some researchers are finding that even children under three do not necessarily suffer emotionally, mentally, or socially when they are nurtured by familiar, competent caregivers while their mothers are away at work. Some studies have found that well-organized, well-conducted toddler daycare centers may promote well-being in both the children and their working mothers.

In an article that appeared in a 1979 issue of *Families Today, Volume 1,* a Science Monograph of the National Institute of Mental Health, Mary C. Blehar writes, "It is intriguing to speculate why maternal employment apparently plays such a small part in wives' attitudes toward themselves and their lives. Outside work for the average woman emerges neither as a personal panacea, an automatic source of self-esteem and personal contentment, nor as a great strain on personal resources.

"However, working wives do report themselves as less satisfied with the quantity and quality of time they spend with their children. This finding seems incongruent with the popularly espoused notion that it is *quality* of time alone which will influence the nature of the mother-child relationship. Working mothers also felt that they had less control over their children and less opportunity to instill in them the values they consider important.

"One wonders whether the working mothers may not be reflecting guilt relayed to them through the media and other sources which insinuate that outside work dilutes the mothering role."

Problems of the Working Mother

A big problem that faces the working mother is that she comes home tired (though full-time mothers have the same complaint). They are overscheduled, and do not have a moment to themselves when they can be alone, think, read, or relax. Nonetheless, most working mothers are happy with their jobs and will not trade places with their stay-at-home counterparts. They claim that fathers are more helpful and understanding, and feel that they have the best of both worlds. They love the new variety in their lives and the money because both give them a feeling of being valued and needed, and a great sense of independence.

Kay Kuzma is a working mother with a doctorate in child development. She is an Associate Professor of Health Services at Loma Linda University, and resides in California with her husband and their three children. In her book, *Prime-Time Parenting* (New York: Rawson, Wade, 1980), Dr. Kuzma writes, "As more mothers join the work force, more fathers are becoming actively involved in child-rearing. It is possible to combine a paying job—even a demanding career—with the job of parenting, and raise healthy, competent children. *But it isn't easy.* It doesn't come naturally, and there are no magic formulas that produce immediate success."

Dr. Kuzma suggests that careful planning is a basic requirement of successful parenting, and recommends that parents remember to frequently and sincerely relay to their children their feelings of affection, respect, caring, and encouragement.

"The combination of working and parenting is not problem-free. In addition to inadequate child care, three major problems beset working parents: *not enough time, too much guilt, illness,* and *fatigue.*

"Nonworking mothers have as many problems with their children as working mothers . . . If you continue to feel guilty about working, carefully consider the reasons. If work is not an economic necessity, consider part-time employment or a less demanding job when the children are young and need you most."

Day-Care Alternatives

There are three main types of day care available in the United States: in-home care (simply put, this is a day-care arrangement that takes place in the child's own home); family day care (an arrangement wherein the mother takes her child to someone else's home, usually a woman with young children of her own); and public or private day-care centers (where several adults take care of a group of children).

Private, nonprofit child-care centers include parent cooperatives, industry-sponsored centers (set up for very young children of employees), church-operated centers, university or college-run centers, and centers conducted by such service organizations as the YWCA. Private, profit-making day-care centers are established and operated by individuals or as franchises to generate good financial returns.

Public day-care centers are funded by a state, county, or school district. Most of these receive some federal and state financial support. They are the most strictly regulated of all day-care centers.

Co-operative Playgroups

For mothers who need half a day to work, or to pursue an outside interest, there is the co-operative morning or afternoon playgroup under the direction of a qualified early childhood teacher who is paid by the participating parents splitting the cost of salary, toys, and equipment. Parents make their homes available for such activities, a different home each week. These mothers usually become friends, while their very young children gain a sense of ease with exposure to various kinds of children and adults.

Paid Child Care in Your Home*

If your child is very young, you may decide to employ a paid child-care worker in your home. You can locate caregivers by contacting your local child-care information service or by placing an ad in neighborhood newspapers. You should also ask your friends, and call a local church, college, or perhaps a low-cost housing facility that may have some capable older tenants. Inasmuch as the cost of in-home child care varies, you will have to ask other parents what the current rate of pay is.

In-home child care enables you to set your own schedule; it also permits your child to stay in her own setting, with one consistent caregiver to relate to. A live-in parents' helper is well-suited to families in which both parents work full-time outside the home or to single-parent families.

Of course, you need to investigate thoroughly any person you decide to hire as a caregiver. Get references and be sure to call them. Then arrange for an interview. In addition to reviewing hours, responsibilities, and salary, try to discern whether the person will function well with your particular child.

If your child will be cared for in the caregiver's home, arrange an interview there. You need to determine whether the house looks like a place where a child would be welcome, safe, and happy; and whether there are enough play activities for a young child to enjoy. Note how the person relates to her own child if she too is a mother. Talk about customary routines, discipline, toileting, and play activities. Try to find out whether the person really likes to be with young children.

After you have selected a caregiver, have her take care of your child on a trial basis. Do not take anything for granted. Be on the alert for warning signals; i.e., is your child tense, unhappy? Although very young children commonly cry when their parents leave (and when they return!), if your child appears distressed most of the time you will know you must talk with the caregiver or find a replacement.

---

*Adapted from *Ourselves and Our Children* by The Boston Women's Health Book Collective (New York: Random House, 1978).

Family Day Care

In *The Day Care Book: A Guide for Working Parents* (New York: Fawcett-Columbine Books, 1979), Grace Mitchell writes, "There are three types of family day care. The first is licensed . . . Most states require that when a woman cares for four or more children in her home, she must be licensed. This is difficult to enforce . . . Usually [the caregivers] are not intentionally breaking the law; they feel that what they are doing is not the government's business . . .

"Registered family day care does not require inspection. The caregiver merely places on file with the appropriate agency data that outline her facility and qualifications . . .

"In supervised family day care . . . a family day-care agency employs the family day-care mother. A staff member inspects her home for health and safety factors, and the availability of outdoor play space. Several interviews are held to learn about her theories on early education and discipline. If she passes this initial test, she is brought into the center for training."

The Working Parents' Guide to Child Care

An up-to-date, comprehensive book on child care is *The Working Parents' Guide to Child Care* by Bryna Siegel-Gorelick (Boston: Little, Brown, 1983). Dr. Siegel-Gorelick discusses all aspects of the alternatives available in in-home or live-in care, family day care, and the day-care center. She reviews research and practical considerations that may influence your child-care decisions; for example, what it is like to spend part or all of the day in the different care environments; what hourly costs are in different regions of the country; what type of care may be best for your child and feasible for you; and so on. The author also examines the adjustments that must be made by both parent and child.

Experts agree that a good day-care center will supplement family life. It has more indoor and outdoor space than the average home can provide for child-related activities. Most families cannot afford or do not choose to make a short-term investment in the equipment that is part of a well-run day-care center.

Competent adult caregivers can contribute to the social and cognitive development of the children in their care. When very young children first participate in a group, their personalities have many rough edges; they are completely egocentric. However, as they learn to function in a group and to respect the needs of others, some of their selfish characteristics are slowly sandpapered away.

Judging the Quality of Day Care

It should come as no surprise that child-care services and personnel can range from acceptable to awful, and "the consumer in the age range one month to six years will not write letters to the management regarding the quality of service (nor is he in a position to withdraw his patronage)," writes Selma Fraiberg, author of *Every Child's Birthright: In Defense of Mothering* (New York: Basic Books, 1977).

"When substitute mother care is considered for a child of any age, the questions which need to be asked are: (1) What are the needs of my child at *this stage* of development? (2) Who can serve as a mother substitute for my child, given these needs? . . .

"With luck and perseverance some mothers have found day-care centers in which the principles of child care are derived from the psychological needs of small children, programs in which exceptionally qualified teachers or aides provide mother substitute care individualized for each child." Mrs. Fraiberg states, "I myself know of only a handful of day-care centers in this country which operate on these principles."

These criteria for judging any day-care center should be kept in mind:

- Does the person in charge really care about each child as an individual?
- Is there at least one trained professional to care for each four to five children?
- Is the environment bright, airy, clean, and free of safety hazards?
- Are there enough clean toilet facilities?
- Is there sufficient appropriate indoor and outdoor play equipment and play space?

- Are parents' suggestions for the care of their children welcome and listened to?
- Are snacks and meals nutritious and free of additives and junk foods?
- Do the caregivers and children appear to be enjoying themselves?
- Is TV used constructively rather than as an electronic babysitter?
- Are parents welcome to visit at any time, with or without advance notice?
- Have the staff members had recent medical exams that indicate they are free of any communicable disease—and healthy and strong enough to care for active children?
- Is there a telephone so that parents can be reached in an emergency?

Day Care versus Nursery School*

Most preschool arrangements are center-based rather than home-based. The major difference in preschool programs is between *day care* and *nursery school*.

A day-care center provides for children so that both parents can hold down jobs. Many open their doors at 7:30 A.M., serve breakfast and lunch, and keep the children until they are called for by the parents at about 6 P.M.

Nursery schools have much shorter hours (generally, three hours in the morning), and some meet only a few days a week. Full-time mothers usually choose a nursery school for their children. A nursery school program gives a full-time mother some needed time off.

As you look for the right center for your child, cost will be an important factor, but it should not make you settle for a place you think will not be completely right for your child. Any child-care center or nursery school with unloving, rigid, or unenthusiastic caregivers can be destructive to your child's happiness.

---

*Adapted from *The Father's Almanac* by S. Adams Sullivan (Garden City, NY: Doubleday, 1980).

Effects of Day Care on Young Children

Recently Jerome Kagan, an outstanding child researcher and Harvard professor, reported the findings of a research project conducted at Harvard which indicates that the ties between the mother or consistent caregiver and the two-year-old are not strained because the toddler attends a part- or full-time day-care center or nursery school. This study appears to show that often a woman can be a better mother because she also has a career outside the home. Generally, working mothers do not "live through their children" as do most nonworking mothers. In addition, most working mothers usually give priority to their children and their husbands.

In fact, in many studies, it was discovered that high-quality infant day care has positive effects in all areas of child development. One study clearly demonstrates that infants cared for in a good day-care center and those reared at home follow similar paths in their social, personality, and intellectual growth. Dr. Kagan, however, believes that the home environment is still the single most important factor in the behavior of children.

Additional research studies report that young children whose mothers work outside the home are not deprived intellectually when they are placed in the hands of responsive and competent caregivers, in a stimulating and attractive environment.

Other considerations relate to whether the mother works part-time or full-time; whether she enjoys her outside work; whether her child is healthy and happy; whether the mother is able to cope comfortably and efficiently with her job, child, and home responsibilities; and whether her family is supportive of her.

Increasing numbers of infants and toddlers are experiencing some kind of out-of-the-home day care and, according to Dr. Edward Zigler, Professor of Psychology at Yale University, "Nobody knows the effect of the kind of care most infants are in."

Only 17 percent of U.S. children attend day-care centers or licensed family day-care homes; the rest appear to be in unlicensed family day-care homes. No one seems to know what the quality is of the informal family day-care arrangements, or how most available day-care programs affect the development of their very young charges.

While researchers agree that the quality of day care is important, it is apparent that few parents in the United States can afford quality day care for their young children. Caught in an economic stranglehold, most working parents find themselves accepting whatever care they can find—and afford.

LOOKING BACK AND LOOKING AHEAD

We have tried to familiarize you with the milestones that normal children reach and pass through in their physical, intellectual, social, and psychological development in the belief that when parents recognize and understand the ages and stages of early childhood, with all their ramifications, they are better able to tolerate and cope with their children's demands, trying behavior, interminable questions, health and other requirements, and general ups and downs.

Childhood researchers Arnold Gesell, Frances Ilg, Jean Piaget, Benjamin S. Bloom, Jerome Kagan, and many others, have presented data that corroborate the fact that the attainment of self-confidence, independence of spirit, competence, joy of living, and the ability to meet life "head on" is predicated on the establishment of a firm foundation laid down during the first five to eight years of a child's life.

If during the past five years you will have made it possible for your child to flourish in every regard—to become a healthy, alert, loving, caring, sensitive, thoughtful human being—then you will have readied him or her for the challenges, accomplishments, and rewards of the school years and adulthood, as well as for the uncertainties, the disappointments, and the wonders of life itself.

Above all, we sincerely hope your parenting is affording you deep satisfactions that mitigate your times of self-denial, impatience, hard work, worry, and feelings of self-doubt and even of guilt.

BIBLIOGRAPHY

Akmakjian, Hiag. *The Natural Way to Raise a Healthy Child.* (New York: Praeger Publishers, 1975)

Ames, Louise Bates, and Frances L. Ilg. *Your Four-Year Old.* (New York: Delacorte Press, 1976)

——. *Your Three-Year-Old: Friend or Enemy.* (New York: Delacorte Press, 1976)

——. *Your Two-Year-Old: Terrible or Tender.* (New York: Delacorte Press, 1976)

Bloom, Benjamin S. *All Our Children Learning.* (New York: McGraw-Hill, 1981)

Boston Women's Health Book Collective. *Ourselves and Our Children: A Book by and for Parents.* (New York: Random House, 1978)

Brazelton, T. Berry, M.D. *On Becoming a Family: The Growth of Attachment.* (New York: Delacorte Press, 1981)

Brooks, Jane B. *The Process of Parenting.* (Palo Alto: Mayfield Publishing Co., 1981)

Callahan, Sidney Cornelia. *Parenting: Principles and Politics of Parenthood.* (Garden City, NY: Doubleday, 1973)

Caplan, Frank, editor, The Princeton Center for Infancy. *The Parenting Advisor.* (Garden City, NY: Anchor Press/Doubleday, 1977)

Carmichael, Carrie. *Non-Sexist Childraising.* (Boston: Beacon Press, 1977)

Chess, Stella, Alexander Thomas, and Herbert G. Birch. *Your Child Is a Person: A Psychological Approach to Parenting Without Guilt.* (New York: Penguin Books, 1977)

Chukovsky, Kornei. *From Two to Five.* (Berkeley and Los Angeles: University of California Press, 1965)

Church, Joseph. *Understanding Your Child from Birth to Three: A Guide to Your Child's Psychological Development.* (New York: Random House, 1973)

Cohen, Dorothy H. *The Learning Child: Guidelines for Parents and Teachers.* (New York: Pantheon Books, 1972)

Cratty, Bryant J., Ed.D. *Perceptual and Motor Development in Infants and Children.* (New York: Macmillan Co., 1970, 2nd edition 1979)

Dodson, Fitzhugh, Ph.D. *How to Parent.* (New York: New American Library, 1973)

Duberman, Lucile, Ph.D. *The Reconstituted Family: A Study of Remarried Couples and Their Children.* (Chicago: Nelson-Hall Publishers, 1975)

Fisher, Seymour, and Rhoda L. Fisher. *What We Really Know About Child Rearing: Science in Support of Effective Parenting.* (New York: Basic Books, 1976)

Fraiberg, Selma. *Every Child's Birthright: In Defense of Mothering.* (New York: Basic Books, 1977)

Freud, Anna, and Dorothy Burlingham. *Infants Without Families: The Case for and against Residential Nurseries.* (New York: International Universities Press, 1944, 5th printing 1970)

Galinsky, Ellen. *Between Generations: The Six Stages of Parenthood.* (New York: Times Books, 1981)

Galper, Miriam. *Co-Parenting: Sharing Your Child Equally.* (Philadelphia: Running Press, 1978)

Gesell, Arnold, Frances Ilg, and Louise Bates Ames. *Infant and Child in the Culture of Today.* (New York: Harper & Row, revised edition 1974)

Granger, Richard H., M.D. *Your Child from One to Six.* (Washington, DC: HEW, Children's Bureau Publication, 1974 edition)

Green, Martin I. *A Sigh of Relief: The First-Aid Handbook for Childhood Emergencies.* (New York: Bantam Books, 1977)

Hall, Eleanor G., and Nancy Skinner. *Somewhere to Turn: Strategies for Parents of the Gifted and Talented.* (New York: Teachers College, Columbia University, 1980)

Heffner, Elaine. *Mothering: The Emotional Experience of Motherhood After Freud and Feminism.* (Garden City, NY: Doubleday, 1978)

Hymes, James L., Jr. *Teaching the Child Under Six.* (Columbus, OH: Charles E. Merrill Publishing Co., 1968, second edition 1974)

Jenkins, Gladys Gardner, and Helen S. Shacter. *These Are Your Children.* (Glenview, IL: Scott, Foresman, 1975)

Kaplan, Louise J., Ph.D. *Oneness and Separateness: From Infant to Individual.* (New York: Simon & Schuster, 1978)

Kellerman, Jonathan, Ph.D. *Helping the Fearful Child: A Guide to Everyday and Problem Anxieties.* (New York: W. W. Norton, 1981)

Killinger, John. *The Loneliness of Children.* (New York: Vanguard Press, 1980)

Kliman, Gilbert W., M.D., and Albert Rosenfeld. *Responsible Parenthood.* (New York: Holt, Rinehart & Winston, 1980)

Kuzma, Kay, Ed.D. *Prime-Time Parenting.* (New York: Rawson, Wade Publishers, 1980)

Leach, Penelope, Ph.D. *Babyhood.* (New York: Alfred A. Knopf, 1976)

———. *Your Baby and Child: From Birth to Age Five.* (New York: Alfred A. Knopf, 1980)

Maddox, Brenda. *The Half-Parent: Living with Other People's Children.* (New York: M. Evans & Co., 1975)

McCall, Robert B. *Infants.* (Cambridge, MA: Harvard University Press, 1979)

McFadden, Michael. *Bachelor Fatherhood: How to Raise and Enjoy Your Children as a Single Parent.* (New York: Walker & Co., 1974)

Mitchell, Grace, Ph.D. *The Day Care Book: A Guide for Working Parents.* (New York: Fawcett-Columbine Books, 1979)

Montagu, Ashley, Ph.D. *Touching: The Human Significance of the Skin.* (New York: Columbia University Press, 1971)

Moore, Raymond S., and Dorothy N. Moore. *Better Late Than Early.* (New York: Reader's Digest Press, 1977)

Moore, Raymond S., Dorothy N. Moore, et al. *School Can Wait.* (Provo, UT: Brigham Young University Press, 1979)

Newson, John and Elizabeth. *Toys and Playthings: A Practical Guide for Parents and Teachers.* (New York: Pantheon Books, 1979)

Peck, Ellen, and Dr. William Granzig. *The Parent Test: How to Measure and Develop Your Talent for Parenthood.* (New York: G. P. Putnam's Sons, 1978)

Pulaski, Mary Ann S., Ph.D. *Your Baby's Mind and How It*

Grows: Piaget's Theory for Parents. (New York: Harper & Row, 1978)

Ridenour, Nina, and Isabel Johnson. *Some Special Problems of Children Aged Two to Five Years.* (Child Study Association of America, 1966, 1969)

Rubin, Zick. *Children's Friendships.* (Cambridge, MA: Harvard University Press, 1980)

Samuels, Shirley C. *Enhancing Self-Concept in Early Childhood.* (New York: Human Sciences Press, 1977)

Selzer, Joae Graham, M.D. *When Children Ask About Sex: A Guide for Parents.* (Boston: Beacon Press, 1974)

Sharp, Evelyn. *Thinking Is Child's Play.* (New York: Avon Books, 2nd printing 1971)

Singer, Dorothy G., and Jerome L. Singer. *Partners In Play.* (New York: Harper & Row, 1977)

Smart, Mollie S., and Russell C. Smart. *Preschool Children: Development and Relationships.* (New York: Macmillan, 1978)

Sparkman, Brandon, and Ann Carmichael. *Blueprint for a Brighter Child.* (New York: McGraw-Hill, 1973)

Stewart, Mark A., M.D., and Sally Wendkos Olds. *Raising a Hyperactive Child.* (New York: Harper & Row, 1973)

Sullivan, S. Adams. *The Father's Almanac.* (Garden City, NY: Dolphin/Doubleday, 1980)

Talbot, Nathan B., M.D., editor. *Raising Children in Modern America: Problems and Prospective Solutions.* (Boston: Little, Brown, 1974, 1976)

Tomlinson-Keasey, Carol, Ph.D. *Child's Eye View.* (New York: St. Martin's Press, 1980)

Trimmer, Eric, in association with Elinor Goldschmied. *The First Seven Years.* (New York: St. Martin's Press, 1978)

Visher, Emily B., Ph.D., and John S. Visher, M.D. *Stepfamilies: A Guide to Working With Stepparents and Stepchildren.* (New York: Brunner/Mazel, 1979)

Warner, Silas L., M.D., and Edward B. Rosenberg. *Your Child Learns Naturally.* (Garden City, NY: Doubleday, 1976)

Winick, Myron, M.D. *Growing Up Healthy: A Parent's Guide to Good Nutrition.* (New York: William Morrow, 1982)

Yates, Alayne, M.D. *Sex Without Shame.* (New York: William Morrow, 1978)

INDEX

A

Abusive parents, 101, 427–32

Accidents, 100–1
  of forty-three-month-olds,
    306–8
  of twenty-five-month-olds, 108
  See also Safety

Accordion gates, dangers of,
  467

Active play of twenty-five-month-
  olds, 165

Adaptive behavior
  adjustment to stepsiblings,
    491–91
  defined, 2
  of forty-three-month-olds to
    nursery schools, 299–300
  of twenty-five-month-olds,
    110–12, 153

Adoption, 399, 421–27, 495

Adoption Resource Exchange of
  North America (ARENA),
  424

Adult participation in forty-three-
  month-olds' play, 302–3

Aggressive behavior
  of forty-three-month-olds, 297
  influenced by television, 414
  of twenty-five-month-olds,
    154–55

Akmakjian, I Iiag, 177, 205, 210,
  481, 482, 487

Alimony, 480, 482

Allergies, food, 94

Alternative child care, *see* Day
  care; Nursery schools;
  Playgroups

American Association for Gifted
  Children, 442

Ames, Louise Bates, 124–25,
  156, 203

Animals
  dealing with fear of, 67
  play, for forty-three-month-
    olds, 296
  thirty-one-month-olds' fear of,
    208

Anxiety
  play inhibited by, 350
  separation, 67
  in thirty-one-month-olds,
    207–10
  See also Fears

Aristotle, 17

Arithmetic, *see* Science and
  math

Arts and crafts, 91–92
  for forty-three-month-olds,
    275, 303–4
  for sixty-one-month-olds, 369,
    382, 405–6, 408–9

ABOUT THE AUTHORS

FRANK and THERESA CAPLAN are directors and editors of The Princeton Center for Infancy and Early Childhood, a self-supporting parent education group that writes books and prepares growth charts and card files for parents and professionals. They are coauthors of *The Power of Play* and *The Second Twelve Months of Life.* Frank Caplan has been general editor of other parenting books, including the best-selling *The First Twelve Months of Life, The Parenting Advisor,* and *Growing-Up Years.*

In 1944 the Caplans founded Creative Playthings, the world-renowned innovative educational toy manufacturing company. Frank Caplan served as president of the CBS Learning Center in Princeton, and subsequently founded the Princeton Center for Infancy and Early Childhood. For over thirty-five years he and his wife have been pioneers in the field of early childhood education and playthings for the home and school. They introduced play sculpture to American playgrounds, initiated lab learning in mathematics and science, and simulation game play in social studies and geography for the early elementary school years.

They are avid collectors of world-wide folk toys and folk art, and hope their fascinating collection will soon find a public home as The Museum of Fantasy and Play.

Theresa and Frank Caplan have two grown children and find their seven grandchildren exhilarating.